Trade, Aid and Development

Published volumes in the series
"The Atlantic Policy Studies"

HENRY A. KISSINGER
The Troubled Partnership:
A Reappraisal of the Atlantic Alliance

ZBIGNIEW BRZEZINSKI
Alternative to Partition:
For a Broader Conception of America's Role in Europe

JOHN O. COPPOCK
Atlantic Agricultural Unity:
Is It Possible?

HAROLD VAN B. CLEVELAND
The Atlantic Idea and Its European Rivals

MIRIAM CAMPS
European Unification in the Sixties:
From the Veto to the Crisis

THEODORE GEIGER
The Conflicted Relationship:
The West and the Transformation of Asia, Africa and Latin America

JOHN PINCUS
Trade, Aid and Development:
The Rich and Poor Nations

Trade, Aid and Development

The Rich and Poor Nations

JOHN PINCUS

A Volume in the Series,
"The Atlantic Policy Studies"

Published for the Council on Foreign Relations by

McGRAW-HILL BOOK COMPANY

New York Toronto London Sydney

The Council on Foreign Relations is a non-profit institution devoted to the study of political, economic and strategic problems as related to American foreign policy. It takes no stand, expressed or implied, on American policy.
The authors of books published under the auspices of the Council are responsible for their statements of fact and expressions of opinion. The Council is responsible only for determining that they should be presented to the public.

TRADE, AID AND DEVELOPMENT

Library of Congress Catalog Card Number: 67-10626
First Edition
50011

To the memory of B. M. P.

The Atlantic Policy Studies

The Atlantic Policy Studies, a series of major works on the future of the Atlantic Community, was undertaken in 1963 by the Council on Foreign Relations with a grant from the Ford Foundation. John Pincus's study of the trade and aid policies of the Atlantic Community countries as they bear on the development of the underdeveloped countries is the seventh of these studies to be published.

Undertaken out of a conviction that a re-examination of United States relations with and policies toward Western Europe was urgently needed, the Atlantic Policy Studies are an attempt to come to grips with basic questions about the future of America's Atlantic relations.

The studies are policy-oriented, seeking not only to describe and forecast but also to prescribe. Each of the ten studies is the responsibility of its author, but each considers its special problems in the light of the general aims of the program as a whole. The program has been under the guidance of a Steering Committee, with Charles M. Spofford as chairman.

The Atlantic Policy Studies are divided into four broad categories, dealing with economic relations among the Atlantic countries and between them and the less-developed countries; with the external environment of the West; with the broad strategic problems of the Atlantic Alliance; and with Atlantic political relations.

Mr. Pincus's book is the second of four studies of economic relations. The first, by John O. Coppock, entitled *Atlantic Agricultural Unity: Is It Possible?* was undertaken in cooperation with the Food Research Institute of Stanford University, of which Mr. Coppock was a member. It was published in May 1966 by McGraw-Hill, which is also publishing all of the other volumes in the Atlantic Policy series. Trade arrangements and economic integration within the Atlantic Community and among the industrial countries are the subject of a third economic study, by Bela Balassa of the International Bank for Reconstruction and Development, in collaboration with a group of economists from the United States, Europe, Canada and Japan. Richard N. Cooper, Associate Professor of Economics at Yale University, will examine international financial arrangements and monetary institutions among the Atlantic nations and prescribe policies for the future in this area.

Of the two studies of the external environment of the Western countries, the first, *Alternative to Partition,* by Zbigniew K. Brzezinski, Director of the Research Institute on Communist Affairs of Columbia University when the book was written and now on leave as a member of the Policy Planning Council of the Department of State, was published in May 1965. The second is Theodore Geiger's study of the nature of the great transition now going on in Asia, Africa and Latin America and its implications for the future of relations with the Western world. It is appearing in January, 1967.

Atlantic military problems are considered in their political context by Henry A. Kissinger, Professor of Government at Harvard University, in *The Troubled Partnership: A Re-Appraisal of the Atlantic Alliance,* published in April 1965.

Political relations among the Atlantic nations are the subject of three studies. The future shape of these relations is examined in my book, *The Atlantic Idea and Its European Rivals,* published in November 1966. Also published in November was *European Unification in the Sixties: From the Veto to the Crisis* by Miriam Camps, Research Fellow at Chatham House and the Council on Foreign Relations. Stanley Hoffmann, Professor of Government at Harvard University, gave a series of lectures at the Council in the spring of 1965, which reviewed the principal constraints, particularly the domestic constraints, on United States action in Atlantic affairs. His lectures have been revised for publication as a volume in the Atlantic Policy series.

Harold van B. Cleveland
Director, Atlantic Policy Studies
Council on Foreign Relations

Preface

In the preface to my *Economic Aid and International Cost Sharing,* I said that I hoped to return to some of the topics treated therein, particularly as they affect the relations among trade, aid, and the economic growth of underdeveloped countries. This book fulfills that threat and deals with some of the same themes as the first volume. But in this one I have tried to bring together the various elements of international economic policy as they bear on the economic development of underdeveloped countries. The setting is broad, the tone discursive, the aims political.

The Council on Foreign Relations, through its program of Atlantic Policy Studies, sponsored the research and writing of this book. I am particularly indebted to Harold van B. Cleveland, who served as director of the Atlantic Policy Studies during the time I was writing this volume. The members of the Council's study group on the Atlantic Community and the Underdeveloped Countries provided a constructive forum for discussions of a number of the policy questions. The chairman of the study group, Professor Isaiah Frank, of The Johns Hopkins University, not only devoted a great deal of time to the work of the group, but also stimulated, criticized, and encouraged my work on this book over a period of nearly two years.

A number of people have read the manuscript, and have offered suggestions. The most comprehensive and useful comments were by Professor W. Arthur Lewis of Princeton University. As a result of his suggestions, this book is better than it would otherwise have been. Professor Lewis of course bears no responsibility for the final product.

The staff of The RAND Corporation has contributed to this work. The management of the Corporation granted me leave of absence to write the volume, and allowed me to use its research facilities during that time. Two members of RAND's Economics Department, Charles Wolf, Jr., and Hans Heymann, Jr., read the manuscript and made valuable suggestions for revisions. Robert Butler assisted me with a number of the computations. Helen Turin copyedited the manuscript ably, under the pressure of a demanding publication schedule. Dolores Pope, Jean Scully, Diane Lovel, Doris Corbin, and Jan Turner have typed various versions of the manuscript. The index is the work of Ellen Seacat. To all of them, and to the many whose help I have not specifically acknowledged here, my sincere appreciation.

Because all aspects of development are related, it is not possible to cover the subject thoroughly in a single volume, and I have not attempted the impossible. Even in the more restricted sphere of economic policy, this book devotes little space to two of the major elements: international monetary arrangements and the effects of the domestic economic policies of poor countries on their trade, capital flows, and growth. The first of these topics is ably discussed elsewhere —notably in a forthcoming volume in the Atlantic Policy Studies series by Professor Richard Cooper of Yale University—and is also reviewed in a recent study of U.S. economic policies toward underdeveloped countries by Professor Harry Johnson of The London School of Economics, published by The Brookings Institution. I felt that I had nothing significant to add to the existing treatments.

I regard the second omission as more important. It reflects necessary limitations of space and time. Rather than attempting to summarize the domestic aspects of development policy in a single chapter, necessarily inadequate in detail, I chose to restrict this study to the international elements and to reserve the others for later.

John Pincus
Washington, D.C.
October 1966

Contents

PART TWO: A Review of Trade and Development Theory

PART THREE: The Policy Issues

TABLES

PART ONE

The Political and Economic Settings

CHAPTER ONE

The "Atlantic Community" and the Developing Countries: The Political Base

Contemporary folklore assumes that the virtues of enriching poor countries are beyond question, somehow transcendent. Everyone will benefit from the rapid growth of income in underdeveloped countries. For poor countries this view is, unsurprisingly, an article of faith; and for the rich, international development has become a major element of foreign economic policy.

Although this book will discuss economic issues primarily, I will begin by questioning this political article of faith: Why should the "Atlantic Community" be interested in the underdeveloped countries? [1] Chapter 1 analyzes both the self-interested and the charitable motives for their concern. To what extent do Atlantic countries have common interests in underdeveloped countries, to what extent do their interests diverge, and what does this blend of common and divergent interest imply for the rich countries' policy toward the less-developed countries (LDC's)?

Chapter 2 deals specifically with the economic factors in North-South relations. It asks how great an economic stake the two regions have in each other and reviews recent economic trends and their implications. In light of differences in outlook and performance, it is clear why rich and poor countries seek different results from eco-

[1] Africa, except South Africa; Asia, except Japan; and Latin America are referred to in the text as "poor countries," "underdeveloped countries," "less-developed countries," "LDC's," "the South."

Canada, the United States, Western Europe, Japan, Australia, New Zealand, South Africa are referred to in the text as "rich countries," "the Atlantic Community," "the industrial countries," "the North," or in contrast to the Soviet Bloc, "the West." The area is neither Atlantic nor a cohesive community, but the title is sometimes convenient.

nomic policy. The United Nations Conference on Trade and Development provides a focus for reviewing the major issues in the North-South confrontation.

Chapters 3, 4, and 5 are excursions into the theory of economic development and are prefaces to the succeeding discussion of current economic policy issues. Chapter 3 first reviews the leading classical theories of economic development, stressing in particular those that link growth and trade. Chapters 4 and 5 then go on to discuss contemporary theories and to develop an eclectic view of the trade-aid-growth relationship.

Chapters 6–8 take up the major current issues in North-South economic relations—commercial policy toward manufactured products, commodity policy, and capital flows. The principal issues for manufactured products are tariffs (particularly the question of tariff preferences), quantitative restrictions, and other non-tariff barriers to trade. For agricultural products and raw materials, there is also the issue of price policy in respect to both price levels and fluctuations. The discussion of capital flows reviews the level and terms of economic aid, the merit of various forms of income transfer—grants, loans, international compensation for declines (or slow growth) in export earnings, public subsidy of interest rates for international lending, and the role of private investment. The analysis includes estimates of probable effects of these proposals, if adopted, on income in poor countries and their probable costs to the Atlantic Community.

Chapter 9 suggests the elements of a proposed Atlantic Community policy aimed at promoting trade and development and analyzes both the potentials and limitations of the North's role in promoting economic growth elsewhere through the tools of international economic policy. Finally, the chapter discusses the role of international institutions, including the Organization for Economic Cooperation and Development (OECD), the General Agreement on Tariffs and Trade (GATT) and the United Nations Conference on Trade and Development (UNCTAD).

The study is clearly wide-ranging; yet in another sense narrow. It gives only a faint reflection of a larger screen where we might project a more complete image of economic and social metamorphosis. The field is ample, and the degree of uncertainty in the conclusions great. In a more learned work, much of the text would have to be taken up with disclaimers and qualifications of the argument; in a less scholarly one, much of the ensuing underbrush would be swept away. For all of the theses advanced here reflect the limitations of what we know about the effects of economic policy as an agent of economic transformation. Therefore the conclusions of this study sound more certain than the expert knowledge might allow, and yet less sure than the reader might wish, for simplicity's sake.

THE INDUSTRIAL COUNTRIES' INTEREST

The idea of an Atlantic Community arose from several sources; the establishment of such "Atlantic" institutions as NATO (1949) and the Organization for European Economic Cooperation (1948), supplanted by the Organization for Economic Cooperation and Development (1961); an underlying community of political interest, as brought forth by Soviet pressures on Western Europe during the years after World War II; common economic interests reflecting both the political situation and a substantial interdependence in economic structure; and finally a broad similarity of cultural patterns and social systems.

The Atlantic Community could be defined in a number of ways. Some, of course, have questioned the value of defining it at all. Those who wish to recognize or encourage its existence face a choice among definitions.

It could be limited to the 15 members of NATO, or the 22 members of the Organization for Economic Cooperation, or expanded to include all the 25 non-Communist industrial countries—Western Europe, the United States, Canada, Australia, New Zealand, Japan, and South Africa. It is this last definition that we will use here, at the risk of depriving the word "community" of its usual meaning. Even though it violates geographical and cultural boundaries, it comes closest to marking simultaneously the economic lines between industrial and underdeveloped countries, and the political lines that delineate the West. South Africa is clearly an exception and is included only because of its economic ties to the Atlantic countries.

Obviously, no such demarcation is perfect. Australia, Denmark, and New Zealand are industrialized only in the sense of having a relatively small proportion of their labor forces in agriculture; they still rely heavily, although decreasingly, on agriculture and raw materials as sources of income and export earnings. Portugal, Turkey, and

Greece would more properly be classed as underdeveloped countries in terms of income and occupational structure; but, as members of the various Atlantic institutions, we sometimes include them in the North. By the same token, we exclude the Communist countries from both the developed and underdeveloped categories, and despite their political and economic importance, this study deals very little with them. They play a very small—though growing—part in North-South economic relations. To examine that role most effectively, we would have to investigate East-West trade problems.

This definition, although based on community of interests, reflects only part of the story; the rest is composed of differences of interest. Indeed, much of the recent political history of the West could be written in terms of the shifting balance between unifying and separatist influences. Thus NATO, once relatively united in face of Soviet presence, today appears to be unraveling. Similarly, OEEC, an effective element in the post-war reconstruction and integration of Europe, has so far failed to play a similar role in its new translation as an economic directorate for the West. We are, for the time at least, in an era when the institutional symbols of Western unity seem to be flagging, when even the fate of such particular subgroupings as the Common Market and EFTA is in doubt. It is probably too early to say whether these trends are irreversible. Renewed Soviet hostility against the West, major unifying political evolution in Western Europe, or a strong threat from China could lead to renewed unity. But for the moment at least, the strongest political ties that bind the West are not reflected in alliances or other institutions but in common political and economic interests that in time of crisis generally outweigh the differences, and will probably continue to do so for some time.

Like most modern communities, therefore, the community we are discussing is a creation both tenuous and enduring, marked by constant convergences and divergences of interests. Under the spur of crisis or simply with the passage of time, coinciding and conflicting interests shift in nature and importance.

The Political and Security Bases

Why should rich countries, as a matter of self-interest, care about what happens in the poor nations of the world? To some, the answers may seem obvious. To others, the issue is remote from the trade and financial matters that this study deals with. I believe that the answers are less obvious and more complicated than it may seem, and that we cannot say anything very useful about economic policy unless we have a clear view of our interests.

In one sense, the answer seems simple. Nations want or need friends in the political arena. Each country has a viewpoint to advance, a position to defend in international negotiations. If a rich country shows no interest in the welfare of poor nations, it will be harder to enlist support when it may be useful: votes in the United Nations, trade concessions, use of bases or communications facilities, transit rights, and the myriad large and small aspects of international political and economic dealings. In short, political cooperation and economic aid are instruments of foreign policy.

But this rationale, satisfactory though it may be for some purposes, does not go deep enough. The underlying questions are about the goals of foreign policy. Nations do not make major long-run political and financial commitments simply to facilitate routine diplomatic negotiations. Furthermore, there is abundant evidence that the great powers have often harvested nettles in return for the concessions they have offered to underdeveloped countries. We must, therefore, go beyond description to discuss the enduring motives for Northern interest in the South. The rest of this section analyzes those motives: military security, maintenance or extension of power and prestige (and its corollary, a latent fear of change), economic advantage, charity, and a sense of community.

The first two elements, military and political, are closely linked. Military security has been the primary public justification for U.S. foreign aid since the Marshall Plan was first proposed in 1947. It seems obvious, however, that the military security of the Atlantic countries, in the sense of security from enemy attack or conquest, depends only to a minor extent on what happens in underdeveloped countries. It rests primarily on U.S. nuclear deterrence, although East-West warfare in underdeveloped countries is evidently not so deterred. Underdeveloped countries have two roles in nuclear strategy: as bases for weapons and as sources of intelligence and communications facilities. With the development of intercontinental and sea-based missiles, this role will be of declining importance. A Cuban missile crisis in 1975 would evoke an even smaller local military reaction than did that of 1962. (It goes without saying that major international political crises have military implications. When I refer to declining military content of crises, I mean that the *local* military aspects are secondary.) It is also likely that technology will allow intelligence and communications facilities, if necessary, to be provided more and more readily from bases in the Atlantic Community, on the oceans, or in space. Such changes in defense policy might well bring with them increased defense costs, but against such costs must be weighed the obvious advantages of dispensing with reliance on foreign bases and the concomitant political hostages to fortune.

If nuclear deterrence and the growth of technology combine to reduce the military importance of underdeveloped countries, does it follow that the Atlantic Community has wasted the billions of dollars it has spent toward ostensibly military objectives since 1950? The reply is that in the past, the Atlantic Community's military security may often have depended on foreign bases more than it does now, and more today than it will later. It is clear that past aid to Korea and Taiwan, for example, did accomplish a military purpose. However, some of the most significant long-run effects of this aid were economic or political. Military assistance itself has political significance, so that pure military effects or pure political effects can generally not be distinguished.

One might argue that military action in Korea or military support in Taiwan was undesirable on other grounds. But there are normally conflicts among means and among goals, and the business of politics is to settle on actions that represent some kind of consensus on the weights to be given to conflicting objectives. In any event, the military element in Northern relations with underdeveloped countries will not suddenly disappear. To the limited extent that it does continue to play a role in the defense of the Atlantic countries, it constitutes a part of the basis for Atlantic Community interest.

The reply, therefore, is not particularly informative, and obviously leads to a further question: Does national security have a broader meaning than military security?

This is where issues of power and prestige arise. The Atlantic Community could as a matter of military technology survive surrounded exclusively by hostile states, but it might not want to live that way, for various reasons. It might believe that its political and cultural values could not survive in such an atmosphere, even if it were safe from military attack. An Atlantic Community dominated by a garrison state mentality might feel itself forced to adopt the very values it sought to combat. It might fear that its own resistance would fail, and that it would in effect surrender to its enemies by a subtle attrition.

It is such considerations as these that often lead Atlantic Community nations to their stated views about the importance of developing countries to Western security. The "falling dominoes" argument so frequently heard in the United States stems fundamentally from these issues of ideology and power, and *not* primarily from issues of military security. The dominoes argument states that the West must aid each country threatened by Communism, because the fall of that country would make it easier for Communism to triumph somewhere else, and each country would be more costly for the West to defend. This is undoubtedly true, but as often presented, the argument is used to draw unwarranted inferences about military security when people are really talking about power and ideology. If the communizing of a half-dozen countries is of little importance to Western military defense, then the military security arguments for opposing the fall of dominoes are unlikely to be impressive. On the other hand, the political arguments for bracing the dominoes may be persuasive and ultimately dominant.

With the passage of time, the national security argument tends to turn more and more on political issues, not military ones. In the past, the West's political interest in underdeveloped countries was expressed largely through establishment of overseas empires. Presumably the colonies, providing men, treasure, and geographical domination, helped enhance the metropolitan powers' prosperity, their readiness for war, and their sense of national prestige. Since the end of World War II, direct colonial territorial claims have virtually disappeared. What, then, do we care about power and ideology so long as the West prospers and maintains its defenses? I said above that the answer involves both our views about the kind of world we would like to foresee and shape and our concern that a passive Western garrison state policy would lead to an undermining of its reigning democratic, liberal ideology. Will public law and standards conform to contemporary Western views, or to what we think of as anti-democratic views?

In politics, of course, ideology is simply another face of the drive for power. Therefore, intertwined with the apparent "ultimacy" of ideology, is another reality—force. The operative function of ideology is to provide an acceptable rationale for the use of power or energy. The West tends to view the underdeveloped countries ideologically as an arena where the forces of freedom and Communist absolutism battle for control. The Soviet Bloc looks on it as the center of the struggle of the impoverished masses to overthrow imperialist control. The great powers really want the same thing: for the world to be organized in their own images, or at least in ways that are not hostile to their images. They fear the spread of hostile ideology, because it is the symbol of hostile power aiming at their destruction.

This is the basis of the great powers' political interest in underdeveloped countries. It is clearly the obverse of a drive for conquest, and it is the essence of such latter-day shibboleths as "encirclement," "containment," and "falling dominoes." From the viewpoint of underdeveloped countries, this cultural lag, reflecting an ancient and long-valid view of power, has its advantages. It leads East and West to woo them competitively with the devices of economic and military aid, political support, and, increasingly, by favorable commercial policies. If the great powers were to adopt a more realistic political view —namely, that the fate of the underdeveloped countries has only the remotest direct connection with the survival of great powers—then a large part of the political basis for an interest in underdeveloped countries would decline.

But ideologies die hard, and this is all far away. In today's perspective, each great power inevitably tries to thrust its views on the weak. Furthermore, it is probably true that the "loss" of many underdeveloped countries would lead the West either to defeatism or to increasing rigidity, suspicion, and insistence on doctrinal orthodoxy. Since neither prospect pleases, the underdeveloped countries can look forward to continued solicitousness, aid, and political interference on the part of East and West.

A realistic view leads us to somewhat paradoxical conclusions. It says first that East and West have very little motive in coldly considered self-interest to concern themselves with what happens to underdeveloped countries, because there is almost nothing that those countries can do politically to harm or help the great powers. Yet the same realism must observe that the great powers are still wedded to the tradition that geographical domination and territorial political control are the keys to survival. Therefore, it is operationally true to state that political motives are an important aspect of their concern for developing countries. Such consideration may be largely irrelevant to an objective view of national security, at least for the major powers of the world and their allies. But they are decidedly relevant to most of the world's present views of what constitutes national security.

These views are an important part of the realities of power—one might nearly say they *are* the realities of power—and cannot be ignored. Believers in voodoo when skewered in tiny effigy obligingly fade away, apparently defying physical laws. In like manner, East and West both seem to believe that surrounded by hostile states they would be sapped of their strength and, bewitched, expire. This prophecy is probably not too far from the mark; the changing forms of magic do not after all obscure its apparently eternal sway.

Much of the great powers' foreign aid has been devoted to military action and its aftermath in formerly colonial areas: France and the United States in Indochina; Great Britain in Malaya; United States, Russia, and China in Korea, and so on. If these countries want to fight colonial wars, support revolution and counter-revolution, or simply test each other's strength in remote areas of the world, in the present state of world affairs, that is their privilege. Such behavior clearly stems from the power drives discussed above. But it has almost nothing to do with their military security.

These are obviously oversimplified considerations, largely because I have been discussing long-term tendencies. Underdeveloped countries do play some part in the defense of the West, and are therefore pawns in the traditional political framework. Furthermore, as we shall see in discussing the economic aspects, if underdeveloped countries are hostile to the West, certain financial costs may arise. There are also other costs—tourism and cultural exchange may be inhibited, the world may become less accessible to its inhabitants, and citizens of the Atlantic Community may not want to be the object of worldwide hostility, even if its expression is largely verbal.

This speculation is about a world that we cannot well envision. A Western policy of indifference to the underdeveloped countries might have any of a spectrum of political results, ranging from slight shifts in the *status quo ante* to a loose federation of Communist countries united only by hostility to the Atlantic nations. Doubts about our ability to deal with a radically different world political system provide a legitimate although inconclusive argument for trying to maintain the existing system.

Economic and Ethical Interests

The above issues are usually considered paramount, whether or not they should be. But economic and humanitarian elements are also often considered to be important aspects of North-South relations. It is sufficient to say here that (1) the Atlantic countries have a modest short-run economic stake in the underdeveloped world; (2) under the most likely hypotheses, they have no important short-run economic motive for adopting policies aimed at benefiting underdeveloped countries; (3) the underdeveloped countries have a substantial interest in their economic relations with the developed countries; (4) the Atlantic Community has a substantial interest in the long-term development of the South, for economic motives, but this is a minor element in today's perspective. The long run is still far off, and the relation between Northern concessions and development is unclear.

Assuming for the moment that these statements are true, they tend to reinforce the implication that the Atlantic Community has rather little basis in self-interest for helping the developing countries. In what way is this conclusion affected by introducing "disinterested" motives?

Underdeveloped countries are poor; the Atlantic Community is rich. The tradition of the North is for the rich to help the poor, both through voluntary local charity and through governmental measures of income redistribution, such as welfare grants, Social Security payments, and the like.

The North generally points to the concern for human welfare as an underlying motive for aid and preferential trade policies. In the case of smaller donors, such motives, intermingled with a desire to avoid either conflict with one's allies or the appearance of stinginess, must be dominant. The political stake of the Scandinavian countries, for example, is negligible. Among larger donors, it has been pointed out, humanitarian claims involve a certain paradox. Such countries as France and the United States lay some public stress on the welfare aspects of aid, but the appropriation of funds is usually based on advantages to be gained for defense, or on political and economic ties or commitments. Thus the larger aid donors give their bilateral aid almost entirely to countries that are either friendly or neutral politically, and not to avowedly hostile states. Yet, if humanitarian motives were paramount, the claims of starvation in China should be no less than those of famine in India. And it is a peculiar, one might say inquisitional, view of humanitarianism that refuses aid to the Chinese people on the grounds—almost surely false—that the spur of present suffering will lead them to ultimate redemption via the collapse of the existing autocracy. In effect, the humanitarian sentiment that does prevail among large donors has much in common with aspects of private philanthropy—it is a judicious mixture of altruism and self-serving. If a *rentier* gives large sums to the Community Chest he gains the simultaneous advantages of self-esteem, prestige, and tax savings. Why then should he give large anonymous donations to non-tax-exempt causes, particularly if the latter, no matter how deserving, are hostile to *rentiers* as a class? He would probably claim that with limited funds, his first obligation is to those with whom his ties are closest.

Nations behave in much the same way. The amount of surplus food is limited, it benefits India no less than it would China, and besides we believe in rewarding friends, not enemies. If a critic were to observe that this is a calculating form of humanitarianism, the obvious reply is that motives for action are normally mixed. An element of political calculation is not incompatible with an element of concern for the welfare of the individual. For example, domestic welfare programs are proposed and voted with an eye both to their political effects and their welfare effects. One might say that the motives are basically charitable or basically political. The results may be the same.

We cannot expect humanitarian motives to be the sole factor. As Mason has said in discussing U.S. aid: [2]

> An administration unable to show that taxes levied in support for foreign aid have some fairly direct relation to the economic interests of important political groups or to the safety of the state will have difficulty in continuing their programs and, probably, continuing in power. Presumably this is the reason why the President [Kennedy] who in his inaugural address used fine words to the effect that we favor foreign aid because it is the "right thing to do," as Congressional hearings on the aid bill approached, appointed an advisory group with the rather pretentious title of Committee to Strengthen the Security of the Free World.

There is also in some countries a psychological preference, in the name of realism, for attributing self-interested motives to one's own disinterested acts. In the United States it is easier to obtain funds for the Alliance for Progress on the grounds of anti-Communist efforts than on grounds of concern for Latin American poverty; and after all, anti-Communism *is* a motive.

The quest for a valid rationale for aid or concessions is ultimately

[2] E. S. Mason, *Foreign Aid and Foreign Policy,* New York, Harper and Row, 1964, pp. 27–28.

insoluble when we limit our analysis to "objective" considerations, and forgo any resort to questions of values. Because this is so, the North is uneasy about aid. It seeks so-called objective criteria for determining aid levels. These criteria are essentially devices for avoiding ethical judgments. Yet ethical considerations, uncomfortable though they may be in a power-centered world, are underlying elements of North-South economic relations. If there were no ethical issues involved, then the present situation would be quite satisfactory from the North's viewpoint; aid could even be reduced.

But these issues do exist. They are as real as any other factor in world politics, although more erratic in their influence on events. We cannot and should not rewrite economic analysis as a theory of social justice. But views of justice permeate and shape economic and political systems. Once the analysis is done, stubborn issues of equity remain.

As I see it, therefore, the case for aid must ultimately rest in part on grounds of income redistribution. The Atlantic Community is wealthy, and much of its potential production is untouched. Most of its members believe in domestic income redistribution policies through progressive taxation, welfare programs to promote the growth of depressed areas, and the like. In the international sphere, there is some acceptance of this principle. Contributions to international agencies, such as the United Nations, are mildly progressive, in the sense that countries with higher per capita incomes generally pay a percentage of these organizations' budgets that is greater than the rich countries' share of world income.

With the passage of time, it has become increasingly clear that the *Realpolitik* elements of the official aid rationale are not valid. The North has given aid to Indonesia, Cambodia, Ghana, Burma, and Iraq without winning their political allegiance or suffering markedly from their hostility. From the viewpoint of self-interest, it was largely money down the drain. Appeals to self-interest are therefore becoming increasingly implausible as a basis for aid. In the United States, at least, such appeals, the inevitable stuff of official statements, are likely to meet an increasingly unreceptive audience.

We seem therefore to be heading toward a kind of dilemma. The old appeals are losing the color of realism, while the redistributive argument for large-scale aid lacks momentum. For those who believe that the North should continue and expand the large-scale transfer of resources, the prospects are bleak for the time. The developments that are most likely to promote such a trend are the shock caused by important new Communist expansion, the possible effects of reductions in defense spending, or espousal by Atlantic Community leaders of large-scale aid as a deliberate and relatively disinterested Northern policy. This would be something of a break with tradition, at least for the major donors.[3]

Failing this, it seems fair to say that the North will continue to have only a modest immediate interest in underdeveloped countries. Therefore, we should not expect the Atlantic Community to depart greatly from its present policies. Inertia and the desire to create a favorable image will tend to maintain the present flow of economic aid, as well as the limited commercial policy concessions that the North now offers. Further aid and concessions will come about only as a result of the kind of developments discussed above, or through persistent and skillfully applied pressure from the poor countries themselves.

The case that I have stated here will not be congenial to everyone. Some people may feel that it ignores political dynamics. The Atlantic countries, they would claim, cannot sit idly by while avowed enemies establish anti-Western regimes throughout the underdeveloped nations. But this criticism is misconceived. It is not a question of giving China and the Soviet Union a free hand in the South.[4] But we have seen that the motives for Northern intervention have little to do with the security of the West, because national self-protection is usually not at issue. Therefore, it is important to probe for the genuine springs of action.

Political changes in underdeveloped countries, whatever their complexion, pose little threat to Western security and offer little advantage to the East. There are some exceptions to this generalization.

For some nations, although not for Russia or most of the Atlantic countries, military security may be seriously affected by what happens in underdeveloped countries. Israel is one case in point. South Africa may be another. And conversely, for developing nations themselves,

[3] I say "relatively" disinterested; one could hardly expect them to help avowed enemies, or countries that used the aid entirely as a substitute for domestic taxation. Ultimately there are always strings.

[4] For that matter it is far from certain that the Eastern powers have benefited very much from their political triumphs in the South. Is the USSR today content with the results of the Chinese revolution, or China with the Cuban revolution, or either of them with the strife in Vietnam? Why has Soviet economic aid to the South declined in recent years? Obviously there are no simple answers. That is why the questions recur.

the support of rich countries is often vital to military security, but that is not a reason for the North to offer support.

The real issue for the major Northern countries is much simpler and goes much deeper. There is a certain vision of the world that each wants to create or preserve. To fulfill such desires, they try to promote congenial political conditions in the South. This effort is not justified today by the traditional concerns of world politics—the security and power of the national state.

The long-run Northern interest in underdeveloped countries today can be justified legitimately only on very different grounds: some ideal of a world community that goes beyond conceptions of immediate interest. Now this is clearly deep water. Ambitious men, and the institutions they create, always manage to define their utopias so as to be quite consistent with their own personal goals.

But whether or not ethical views are self-serving is almost beside the point. They exist, they move men to action, and they influence decisions about Northern concessions to the South. To say that the North seeks a world congenial to free institutions is to say something very important. But it has little to do with Northern safety. It is either a way of disguising power drives with fancy language, or of expressing an ethical judgment, or both.

In dealing with important issues, nations and their citizens should be clear about motives. Otherwise they are likely to make serious errors, through confusing the words they use with the things they want. When the two diverge, it is asking too much to expect luck to bridge them. If the North seeks more power in the world, it should know it, and aim at it, as the Soviet Union and China clearly do. If it seeks a fairer distribution of the world's goods, without much regard for effects on national power, it should follow policies aimed at that goal. If, as is most likely, it seeks both, then it should recognize that it is likely to achieve neither to its satisfaction. The two goals are generally not consistent, and the means of achieving one goal are almost sure to be inadequate for meeting both.

Some Other Interpretations of Rich Nations' Interest

This section is an extended coda to the discussion. Because some people might disagree with my views, it seems fair to set forth other opinions here. This section selects two of the more impressive contemporary rationales for aid. The first looks upon Northern concessions as a form of insurance. The second considers concessions as a solvent for international discord.

Aid as a Cheap Form of Insurance. The first argument starts out by rejecting the traditional motives. Military objectives, the argument runs, probably do not justify a sum that even approaches the $6–7 billion nominal annual flow of public funds from the North to the South. Economic motives justify trade, but it is hard to show that aid on concessional terms benefits the Atlantic Community as much as expenditure of the same sums at home. In short, once base rentals are accounted for, and excluding welfare motives, the primary reasons for helping underdeveloped countries are: (1) we are committed to it; (2) the real cost is much less than the nominal cost so that aid is a relatively cheap hedge against uncertainty;[5] (3) we desire to promote the growth of non-Communist states as a matter of ideological preference, or to promote prosperous ones as a lightning rod against world political unrest.

The first of the three motives listed above—commitment—is dominant in the short run. Great powers are expected to honor their commitments; the rules of the game do not allow the Atlantic Community suddenly to eliminate or sharply reduce foreign aid, no matter how little its interests are served by continuing it. The sums involved just aren't that important to the donors. However, a gradual reduction of aid and preferential trade is entirely feasible.

Because the existence of prior commitments is dominant in the short run, it tends also to monopolize the discussion. It takes concrete form when Western governments decide whether to offer aid to governments threatened by Communist insurrection, even if the prospects for victory of the insurrection are favorable. There is no general answer. The "realistic" statement is that there is no use backing horses whose chances of losing are greater than the odds they carry; that's just a way of transferring money to those who back the winners.

But of course we can't always know the chances of winning in advance. And politics is different from betting on horses. Politics often

[5] Because donors frequently have unemployment and excess capacity in industry and agriculture so that resources used for aid are not diverted from domestic production; because the practice of tying aid, as in Public Law 480, the U.S. food disposal program, results in considerable overstatement of the value of aid; and finally, because most Northern aid is in the form of loans, which are presumably repaid with interest.

forces the bettor to keep investing in a loser (although he may hedge); the bettor's behavior in one race affects the outcome of the next; and finally, in some political races everybody loses, while in others everybody wins.

The second and third motives in the list turn out to be closely related. If aid does not cost much and if it promotes both our ideological preferences and a more harmonious world, then we should be glad to offer it as a matter of self-interest. Furthermore, as Northern incomes rise, the sacrifice involved in making economic concessions declines steadily.

However, as has often been pointed out, the fact that apparent costs are low does not mean that benefits come cheaply. Assuming that aid actually does promote development, it is clear that development often tends to create tensions in the short run. It thus may lead to instability rather than encourage the political stability that the North has traditionally tried to promote in the South. The North has accepted this risk in the interests of longer-run goals, but it is nonetheless a cost, according to the rules of the game as now played.

In short, there is no guarantee that aid will promote the development of stable, non-Communist societies, despite a presumption that *in the long run* growth is a necessary condition of democracy. It is becoming increasingly clear to people in the North that the official political and economic rationales for aid are at best only partly valid, and that its accomplishment has fallen short of the exaggerated claims so often made. In recent years this has led to reductions in U.S. aid appropriations; to the rise of *Cartierisme* in France, based on the proposition that foreign aid should be diverted to the backward areas of France; and even to a decline in the ever-lagging German aid effort. The official reaction to such discontent has generally been to point out that development is a slow process, requiring patience and effort on all sides. Thus President Kennedy said in 1961, of foreign aid:

> I know there are those who are tired of carrying what they regard as a burden, and it is a burden, but if they say that, then they mean they are tired of the struggle.
>
> . . . I therefore urge those who want to do something for the United States, for this cause, to channel their energies behind the new foreign-aid program to help prevent the social injustice and economic chaos upon which subversion and revolt feed. . . .[6]

[6] *The New York Times,* June 17, 1961.

I have tried to show above that this case is simply not persuasive in the nuclear age. The road to London, Paris, and Washington no longer passes via Peking and Calcutta. As Feis has said: "The struggle against Communism has been the most energizing cause of American liberality." [7] In the future, this is less likely to be true. The probable course of Chinese expansion in Asia will alienate many who have believed in aid as a counterweight to Communism while it demonstrates that Communist expansion does not have major effects on the Atlantic Community's ability to defend itself.[8]

Aid as a Solvent for World Tensions. Cheapness and the quest for a stable and ideologically sympathetic world have been combined into another argument for aid. The world is a community, both in hope and in fear. Aid should be increased steadily. Wealthy societies can pay for it easily from growth of income. They *should* pay because it is important that men's creative energies be harnessed to build a world community with a sense of mutual obligation. They *must* pay because the alternative—a world composed of satisfied rich states and discontented poor ones—is likely to mean constant friction and danger, particularly in the nuclear era. A number of semi-industrial poor countries, such as India, Pakistan, and Egypt, could easily become nuclear forces, and with the power they gain thereby, and as discontented have-nots, promote a dangerous and unstable world. If the North helps them with the constructive effort of enriching themselves, the argument runs, their energies would be harnessed in the mutual interests of all countries.

This picture of a world community created by its solidarity in material aspirations is tempting, but, as I believe, unconvincing. It is not simply because the link between aid and the establishment of a peaceful, "progressive" world is tenuous. The proponents of the idea of community recognize that aid is no panacea. The weakness of their case, to my mind, lies in their belief that rapid economic growth is a solvent for international discord. It is undoubtedly a solvent for domestic tensions related to income distribution, and, as I have said above, probably a necessary long-run condition of democratic institutions. But the effects in the international sphere are uncertain. To the

[7] Herbert Feis, *Foreign Aid and Foreign Policy,* London, Macmillan and Co., 1964, p. 64.

[8] This effect may of course be offset by reactions of fear, leading to greatly increased aid in the name of anti-Communism. Much depends on the form of Chinese expansion.

argument that slow growth will produce a South peopled by resentful and militaristic states, one can oppose the contention that more rapid growth will simply make it easier to finance militarism. I find neither argument convincing; any outcome is possible. All arguments for aid based on appeals to national self-interest reduce ultimately to the unverified statement that the risks of inaction are greater than those of action, while the costs are small. Aid is cheap, both as hush money and as a sort of insurance.

This statement is unlikely to appeal to those who seek an unqualified rationale for aid. We are therefore driven back to the same ethical issues. If these are not persuasive, then aid and trade concessions will be forthcoming only on the basis of mutual advantage. This is the theme of Chapters 6, 7, and 8.

Aid as an Attribute of the System of Power. Of course, it is possible to eliminate all such involuted discussions of motives as we have conducted here by viewing the matter in terms of observed behavior. In that way, we avoid the quest for a rationale in favor of an operational approach. At the beginning of this chapter, I pointed out that rich countries give aid because they want to influence others. Some such hypothesis could be tested by designing an index of international participation. The index would presumably consist of some weighted combination of national income, international political participation as measured by treaty commitments and extent of recent military involvements, and international economic participation as measured by trade and investment. The greater the concentration of power and international interests, so defined, the greater the tendency for worldwide involvement, and the greater the relative size of concessions to the South.

Thus, a country like the United States with a large population and income, major military forces, and substantial international investment is very active throughout the world, and defining its activity as self-interest, spends money in support of that interest. The Soviet Union, with substantial income and military power, also sees itself as having world-wide interests, and distributes somewhat smaller sums abroad from analogous motives. China, with a large population, small income, and a significant military force, pursues a somewhat smaller range of interests worldwide and spends less in pursuit of them.

Under this approach, "Why foreign aid?" cannot be answered in terms of motives. The major relevant questions become instead,

"What are the country's population, income, military forces, foreign investments?" "Has it previously had colonies?" and, possibly, "Is it a nuclear power?"

The North's interest in the South is thereby reduced in effect to a question of statistical testing. The explicit issue of motives is hidden in the computations. For those who prefer their value judgments to be implicit, this device may have its advantages. But as we have seen already, it does not take us far enough to satisfy most people. If it did, there would be no need for political rationales based on self-interest that the major donors inevitably seek.

DIFFERENCE OF INTEREST AMONG THE RICH NATIONS

These views of self-interest vary widely among the Atlantic countries. The reasons are obvious: (1) some countries, such as the United States, France, or Great Britain, consider that they have worldwide responsibilities or special responsibilities as former colonial powers, while others feel that they have little or none; (2) some countries (Japan, Great Britain, the United States) have substantial trade or investment interests, while others do not; (3) some of those with no material interest want to make a contribution from charitable motives or in order to do—and to seem in others' eyes to do—their part in a common effort. The discussion of the aid programs of each major Northern country allows us to identify differing motives, and to stress some of the more specific political considerations that were set aside in the preceding analysis of long-term Northern interests.

United States

The United States has been extending foreign aid since the Lend-Lease and UNRRA programs during World War II, and large-scale aid to developing countries since 1950; yet it has never evolved a satisfactory rationale for aid. The preceding section indicates the difficulty of developing any conclusive political or economic case that would justify special attention by developed countries. In the United States these uncertainties have been accompanied by almost incessant official discussion of the issues. Since 1950, for example, U.S. Presidents have appointed no less than eight official advisory committees composed of distinguished citizens, all instructed to make recommendations about the goals and magnitude of foreign aid. Furthermore, there is an annual confrontation between the Administration and Congress about the current foreign aid appropriation. Finally, there has been a steady output of books and articles on the subject in the United States.[9] This body of official and private discussion naturally includes a variety of opinions, but certain points seem quite clear.

The U.S. interest in the South, as expressed in foreign aid, is based primarily on military-political considerations. Humanitarianism and commercial elements clearly enter into the picture, but nominally at least they are not decisive in establishing the level or destination of aid.[10]

The official case is generally stated in the form of an implied syllogism: (a) economic development of LDC's is necessary to counter Communism and to help build a world of peaceful independent states; (b) these results favor U.S. interests; (c) economic aid is a catalyst for economic development; (d) therefore, the U.S. should give economic aid to LDC's. The syllogism has often been attacked,[11] but the outcome is inconclusive; aid continues to be justified on grounds that are insufficient to still doubts. Yet those who introduce a different rationale have never succeeded in convincing the majority. The U.S. foreign aid agency itself has clearly been uncertain as to the appropriate blend between "political" and "efficiency" conditions in aid allocation. In recent years, at least, the verbal emphasis has been on helping those who help themselves, but the reality may well be more complicated.

Despite valiant efforts to establish a "rational" allocation of aid,[12] the stubborn facts remain. There are a variety of motives for aid, and encouragement of high investment rates is only one among them. For example, one "best" way to allocate aid in the interests of

[9] See, for example, Mason, *Foreign Aid and Foreign Policy;* R. A. Goldwin (ed.), *Why Foreign Aid,* Chicago, Rand McNally, 1963; Hans Morgenthau, "A Political Theory of Foreign Aid," *American Political Science Review,* Vol. 56 (June 1962), pp. 301–309.

[10] Mason, *Foreign Aid and Foreign Policy,* p. 30.

[11] For example, Hans Morgenthau, "A Political Theory of Foreign Aid"; Milton Friedman, "Foreign Economic Aid: Means and Objectives," *Yale Review* (Summer, 1958), pp. 500–516.

[12] See, for example, Department of Defense and Agency for International Development, *Proposed Mutual Defense and Development Programs, FY 1965,* Washington, D.C., Government Printing Office, 1964.

efficiency is to give foreign exchange to countries who can earn the highest rate of return on aid-financed investment. But this rule will typically lead to investment in such countries as Mexico, Israel, and Yugoslavia which are already able to make effective use of resources and are therefore likely to be at relatively high income levels now. The conflict between efficiency and equity goals, or between either of these and political objectives, is inherent so long as foreign aid resources are limited. This conflict is, as will become evident, a recurrent theme in aid policy.

In the U.S. debate on aid allocation, there have been efforts to assume this problem away by defining "absorptive capacity"—a limit to the amount of foreign aid that the recipient country can use effectively. If annual absorptive capacity is equal to or less than the annual aid flow, then there might be some case for allocating aid on efficiency grounds; "why throw the aid away?" In fact, of course, this line of argument is no solution. Absorptive capacity is not a fixed amount for any country at any time; more can always be invested at lower rates of return, or possibly in apparent defiance of static economic theory, at increasing rates. Or aid-financed consumption subsidies may be considered as one method of calling forth more incentives for production and investment.

United States foreign aid doctrine has evolved toward a "nonpolitical" brand of realism. Starting in 1949 with what now seems to have been a naïve faith in the powers of technical assistance, it then emphasized the importance of large-scale development aid, presumably reflecting the success, although under dissimilar conditions, of Marshall Plan capital investment programs. Under the impact of the Korean war, building up LDC defenses became the prime focus of foreign aid. This became associated in the mid-1950's with a policy of helping friends and not helping neutrals. This policy made sense only if the primary purpose of aid was to build up military defenses against Soviet attacks on allies of the United States. By the late 1950's, there was a tendency to recognize that this was not an adequate criterion for aid, and that friendship for the United States was not an essential qualification.

This return to an earlier (pre-1950) doctrine, modified by some continued emphasis on the importance of military elements, has remained relatively constant in recent years. Nonetheless, most United States aid goes to countries that are close to Soviet or Chinese borders; that is, Turkey, Iran, Pakistan, India, Korea, Vietnam. The post-1961 stress on efficient aid allocation and helping those that help themselves should be viewed as yet another effort to come to terms ideologically with aid.[13]

Latin America has taken on particular importance over the years, with the Cuban revolution playing a catalytic role. An increasing proportion of U.S. aid has been channeled to South America since 1960; and the Kennedy Administration attempted to endow the aid with an aura of its own, à la Marshall Plan, by entitling it "The Alliance for Progress" and establishing international institutions to allocate the aid, reminiscent of the Marshall Plan's Organization for European Economic Cooperation.

United States difficulties in stemming Communist-led and Communist-supported advances in Southeast Asia (Vietnam, Indonesia, Laos) have starkly raised the basic issues of the nature and extent of U.S. interest. The answers are likely to emerge from operational decisions, and those who seek general policies of isolation or of commitment for the United States are likely to be perpetually disappointed.

Total amounts of U.S. economic aid seem to remain relatively stable at a level of about $4 billion annually; the endless controversy seems to mask a good deal of stability in Congress' estimate of LDC needs and of the public temper toward aid.

The latest version of U.S. aid policy has put great stress on three elements aimed at helping the South toward self-sufficiency: (a) support of education programs; (b) assistance to population control efforts; (c) support of measures aimed at increasing agricultural productivity, nominally financed by the proceeds of surplus food sales. From the perspective that we have reviewed here, this is a new variant of the effort to allocate aid resources efficiently. It may well possess durable advantages compared with earlier efforts because it focuses on elements that are both dramatic and significant for economic development. But the results of this latest approach cannot be felt quickly. Each of its elements takes many years to be translated into higher living standards. It seems safe to predict therefore that these initiatives will not still the public debate over aid.

Basically the United States has never decided what it wants to

[13] This history can be traced in the Presidential foreign aid reports from 1950 to 1963. See particularly, *Report to the President on Foreign Economic Policies*, Washington, D.C., 1950 (Gray Report); Commission on Foreign Economic Policy, *Report to the President*, Washington, D.C., 1954 (Randall Report); *Composite Report of the President's Committee*, Washington, D.C., 1959 (Draper Report).

gain from its aid to underdeveloped countries. Thus its pronouncements swing from emphasis on development to stress on military factors, back to pump priming for those who help themselves, then to a policy of rewarding friends, and so on. Many of these policies are carried on simultaneously. The record of U.S. aid is the best testimony for the thesis I advanced earlier in this chapter. If governments do not know what they want, they are unlikely to be content with the results of policies that perpetually redefine issues verbally without clarifying the goals they seek. The real difficulty lies with the underlying syllogism that relates the interests of the United States to the welfare of developing countries. That syllogism defeats all attempts at redefinition. It always re-emerges because it is the only enduring rationale that domestic politics will permit, under the current rules of the game. But, as we have seen, it does not hold today; hence the perpetual discussion.

While U.S. officialdom and academia have wrestled unendingly with an aid rationale, the American public has apparently found the problem less difficult. All public opinion polls taken in the past decade show a majority in favor of foreign aid.

Of course, it is hard to know how to interpret public attitudes toward such questions as these. Thus the Gallup poll asked in 1958, 1963, and 1966: "In general, how do you feel about foreign aid—are you for it, or against it?" In 1958, about 60 per cent of those expressing an opinion favored aid; in 1963, the proportion rose to about 65 per cent. In 1966, it was shown to be 60 per cent again. But this support is expressed for the "principle" of aid, not for financing it by taxes. If the question were rephrased along different lines, such as "Would you rather have foreign aid continued at the same level next year, or have it cut down and your taxes reduced?" then the response might be different. Despite the ambiguous meaning of opinion poll responses,[14] they do evidence a reservoir of general good will toward foreign aid, although its priority is probably low compared with major domestic programs.

Great Britain

Great Britain, like other colonial powers, had in effect provided technical assistance and incentives to private investment in its overseas territories for many years. Direct grants-in-aid or public loans were

[14] Eva Muller, "Public Attitudes Toward Fiscal Programs," *Quarterly Journal of Economics,* Vol. LXXVII (May 1963), pp. 210–235.

exceptional before the era of decolonization; but the colonial tradition provided the psychological bridge for foreign aid.

Nevertheless, with the continued increase of British foreign aid both to colonies and to independent countries of the Commonwealth after the mid-1950's the Government considered it necessary by 1963 to issue a White Paper,[15] on aid. The report looked upon foreign aid as a natural responsibility of rich countries.

The purpose of aid was "to help buttress stability in the developing countries." Development in LDC's would also benefit donors in the long run. The White Paper said that LDC's would need aid for a long time, and that donors should be prepared to keep giving for many years.

British aid, the report pointed out, was largely destined for British colonies and for newly independent members of the Commonwealth. As of 1962, more than half of the $200 million aid total went to colonies, and two-thirds of the rest to independent Commonwealth nations.

> The developing countries of the world must necessarily depend largely on their own exertions; but the developed nations recognize a responsibility to help them, both by giving financial aid and by providing advice and training facilities. . . .
>
> The promotion of development by means of overseas aid should help to buttress stability in the developing countries, and this is in the interest of the whole world. Moreover, the economic progress of the countries now receiving aid should eventually be to the benefit of the donor countries as well as of themselves, as it will contribute to an expansion of world trade. Ultimately it is on growing outlets for their trade that the developing nations must depend for their continuing advance.
>
> . . . although the era of aid, viewed in the perspective of history, may be a transitory one it does not follow that it will be short, still less that its end is in sight. . . .
>
> The task of helping the developing nations is, then, a continuing one.[16]

Several points in the passage are worth stressing: (1) developed countries have a responsibility to give aid; (2) its purpose is to buttress stability in developing countries (this is reminiscent of the United

[15] *Aid to Developing Countries,* London, HMSO, September 1963.
[16] *Ibid.,* p. 5.

States' "official" rationale), (3) aid benefits the donors, (4) LDC's development will ultimately depend on the growth of their trade, (5) aid is a long-term enterprise for the donors.

The White Paper goes on to describe British aid. Its composition has been shaped by the history of empire. More than half of the bilateral aid has gone to the colonies. The aid total doubled in the decade from 1955 to 1964, reaching a level of £175 million in 1964, and £190 million in 1965. Much of the increase was directed to those Commonwealth countries that became independent after 1945. In 1964, for the first time, the independent Commonwealth countries received slightly more British aid than the ever-dwindling list of colonies.

The report emphasizes that British ability to give increasing amounts of aid is dependent on the nation's balance of payments. This leads to a case for tying British aid to purchases in the United Kingdom; but the report says "we are prepared to take part in any genuine international move towards the untying of aid." This may not unfairly be viewed as a relatively safe gesture in view of strong domestic pressures in the other major donor countries to continue tied aid. The report specifically supports the use of surplus farm product deliveries to LDC's.

British aid was more concentrated in high-interest loans than that of other countries. The 1963 report proposed lengthening amortization periods to 30 years and waiving interest and principal payments for the first seven years. This would have the effect of making British aid terms roughly comparable to the traditionally generous U.S. lending conditions. This initiative was further extended by the Labour government in 1965.

British aid evolved from a tradition of colonial assistance, so that there has been in that country relatively little strenuous domestic unease of the sort associated with American aid. Even today, less than 10 per cent of British bilateral aid is offered to countries that never belonged to the Empire, and even that modest portion goes largely to countries that have close historical ties with the United Kingdom such as Jordan, Sudan, and Nepal. However, the 1963 White Paper implies that aid to what it terms "foreign countries" will increase. The Labour government has not noticeably stressed the point.

The expansion of British aid took place under Conservative governments. During that period (1955–64) the Labour Party's criticisms of aid policy were based on the alleged inadequacy and disorganization of government aid. In debate, party spokesmen said that a Labour government would increase the aid level to 1 per cent of GNP annually, compared with a then current level of about 0.5 to 0.6 per cent; and would also establish a Ministry of Overseas Development to administer the program, which, under the Conservative government, was the responsibility of several existing agencies. Upon assuming office in 1964, Labour honored its pledge to establish a new ministry. The planned expansion of aid, however, was held back by the balance-of-payments crisis of that year.

In a White Paper of August 1965, the Labour government stated its policy, emphasizing that actual aid levels would depend on the balance-of-payments situation.[17]

The objective of British aid, the report states, is to help developing countries in their efforts to raise living standards.

> The basis of the aid programme is therefore a moral one. . . . It can at the same time be defined in political terms. . . . (But) aid is a means of promoting long term economic development . . . not a means of insuring the friendship of individual countries. . . . The process of development must sometimes increase strains, for a time at least, and we should not expect aid to be an insurance against political tensions. Nevertheless, we must recognize that poverty in a world of growing wealth causes discontent and unrest to which economic and social development is the only possible answer.[18]

The report goes on to emphasize in its introductory sections the importance of international coordination of aid efforts, and to cite the potential long-run economic and political gains from aid. Many of its themes, notably the stress on the tenuousness of the relations between aid and short-run goals, are similar to those brought out earlier in this chapter.

The report makes its economic case for more aid on the basis of slow growth rate of LDC income, shortages of foreign exchange and of skilled manpower, and increasing population pressure. It states that the present aid flow is not adequate to help the LDC's meet their development goals. Therefore there must be increases in both aid and technical assistance. Great Britain, however, is not in a position to practice what it preaches. The report links any increase in current aid levels to balance-of-payments considerations.

The Labour report marks an advance in one respect from the

[17] Ministry of Overseas Development, *Overseas Development: The Work of the New Ministry*, London, HMSO, August 1965 (Cmnd. 2736).

[18] *Ibid.*, p. 6.

1963 White Paper. It announces a policy of interest-free loans in appropriate cases, designed to reduce debt service costs to developing countries whose economic position is precarious.

If Labour does eventually decide to redeem its earlier pledge to raise the level of aid further, it can be expected that aid will become much more of a subject for public debate, as in France and the United States. There is today surely less public and parliamentary opposition to aid in the United Kingdom than in any other major donor country. An era of unease is in prospect, and would probably be the more likely to prevail if much of the increased aid went to non-Commonwealth countries.

France

France is by far the largest aid donor relative to GNP, and second only to the United States in absolute annual flow of aid. By the OECD definition of aid, France provides from \$750 to \$950 million annually, while the United States supplies \$3.5–\$4 billion. But 90 per cent of French aid is in grant form, so that the difference between the two countries is somewhat smaller than it seems. Relative to GNP, France gives more than twice as much aid as the United States. Ninety-five per cent of French bilateral aid goes to countries of the franc zone. The French government sees its interest in aid as political, maintaining and expanding French influence among LDC's.

The Jeanneney Report, submitted to the French government in 1963 by a special study commission, states the position clearly.[19] The objectives of France are: (1) to recognize solidarity among peoples; (2) to spread French culture and civilization; (3) in the long run, to gain political advantages for France and for like-minded Western countries without making aid into an instrument of cold war. Passages of the report merit quoting, because they assert explicit judgments on some of the issues discussed earlier in this chapter.

> The concept of a policy of aid to developing countries is difficult because of the breadth, complexity, and novelty of the problems it poses. Such cooperation links economics, strategy and politics; it affects each nation's own vision of its solidarity with the rest of humanity. Therefore, a review of the possible motives for giving aid must be done prudently, in an

[19] Ministère d'Etat Chargé de la Réforme Administrative, *La Politique de Coopération avec les Pays en Voie de Developpement,* Paris, July 1963.

attempt to analyze dispassionately, sifting out the false motives and stressing the essential. It is useful for this purpose to distinguish carefully between the interests of the French nation or of the host country and those of some particular part of the population or some special sector of the economy. When these special interests are legitimate and deserve to be maintained for themselves independently of national interests, they then should be supported as such, by a deliberate choice.[20]

The report minimizes the importance to France of special interests in the franc zone, stating that France's economic interest lies in the much longer-range gains from trade that will arise from the progressive development of LDC's. The immediate economic importance of LDC's is small in the eyes of the rich countries. "At the risk of suicide on their part, the underdeveloped countries must export in order to import; the only complementary market that is both wide open and solvent is that of the advanced industrial countries, principally in Europe." [21]

The real reasons for French aid, therefore, do not lie in some conception of short-run interest. They stem from "the duty of human solidarity," and from the need to spread the vision of France. This need to shine forth ("rayonnement") is essential to France: "it must be the accomplishment of men who are ready to become expatriates and of a culture whose goal is the universal. . . . France wishes, more than any other country, to broadcast far and wide its language and its culture."

Finally, there are long-range motives of self-interest. These include advantages for France itself: (1) the growth of political cooperation with the emerging countries, which can help France in international forums; (2) possibly strategic advantages ("although strategy is constantly renewed by science, it is possible that France, in organizing its defense, could still gain from the good will of the countries of the third world; not, as in the past, by the supply of their fighting men, but by obtaining intercontinental bases for observation, telecommunication and transport, which will strengthen France both within the concert of the West and in the face of potential adversaries"); [22] (3) possible economic advantages from spreading a knowledge of and demand for French products, particularly those incorporating advanced technology, among peoples who will one day become good customers.

[20] *Ibid.*, p. 35.
[21] *Ibid.*, p. 42.
[22] *Ibid.*, p. 45.

There are also long-run gains that will accrue to France as a member of the Western community of nations. One such gain is economic:

If the aid supplied by France contributes in the long run, to delivering people from misery and to accelerate their development, then these people will become partners whose new-found prosperity will reinforce and sustain the long-established prosperity of the West. The process of mutual development which now plays its beneficial role primarily within the Atlantic economy, will expand and intensify by spreading out over other continents.[23]

Another long-run Atlantic Community gain is political, affecting the future conditions and choice of sovereignties; and thus, in a sense, going beyond immediate cold war perspectives. According to the Jeanneney Report:

If aid is provided properly, if its aims are appropriate to the real needs and feelings of the country, it will maintain and reinforce the spontaneous desire that most countries of the third world feel for preserving their political sovereignty. The aid-receiving countries must be brought to the status of true nations, developing themselves by themselves and for themselves, with a growing consciousness of their own personalities. We must recognize and even proclaim their eternal right to free political choice; we must do whatever is in our power to assure that this choice is that of the nation itself; we must respect that choice and provide our disinterested support for its realization. Of course there can be no guarantee that this method will always avoid adherence to coalitions built up against us, but it has every chance of being fruitful. In the long run, it is the only way that ever could be.[24]

While the Jeanneney Report sounded a chord based on humanitarianism and enlightened self-interest (not dissimilar from the British White Paper of 1965), there were also other notes being rung both in private and official circles.

First, there is obviously a large body of opinion in France that looks upon aid as a method of maintaining close political and economic links with the African countries of the franc zone. As Ambassador Chauvel has said:

France makes a great effort for some sixty million people, but devotes very little by comparison to the rest of humanity. It is also clear that among the powers that established and then decolonized empires, France

[23] *Ibid.*, p. 46.
[24] *Ibid.*, p. 47.

alone exerts itself so greatly on behalf of the people she has led to independence.[25]

Ambassador Chauvel goes on to say that this is a legitimate exercise of special responsibility which should be followed by other donors in other areas. However, many voices in and out of France have viewed the concentration of national efforts in North and West Africa as an attempt at neocolonial control, willingly acceded to by the local ruling classes, particularly in tropical Africa. The analogy has been drawn with the U.S. Alliance for Progress as a similar imperialist device. French aid is often considered to be a more direct device of control, however, because it concentrates more money among fewer people in poorer countries, and reinforces the financial aid with massive technical assistance, as well as the pervasive leaven of French culture and education.

As in the case of the United Kingdom, aid to former colonies is considered a natural outcome of empire. However, there is a strong undercurrent of opposition to the volume of aid, to certain aspects of administration and forms of aid, and to some of the political implications. Much of this opposition has been focused in the name of *cartierisme,* in tribute to M. Raymond Cartier, the publisher of *Paris-Match*. Cartier's attacks on French aid date back to the mid-1950's; he now concentrates largely on aid to Africa,[26] emphasizing two issues: (1) At great expense France is supporting African governments that are incompetent or uninterested in furthering economic development. The long-run results of such aid must be to waste French resources without gaining popular allegiance or higher living standards in Africa. (2) France could effectively use the same funds at home for modernizing its productive plant, raising living standards and improving its education and public health.

The Cartier position apparently reflects widely held public attitudes. A poll conducted for the government by the French Institute of Public Opinion in 1962 showed that the public was about evenly divided in answering the question "Should France help French-speaking African countries?" On the other hand, there was a strong "yes" vote when the same question was introduced into a broader inquiry concerning Franco-African cooperation. The Institute concluded that

[25] *Ibid.* (Annex), pp. 43–44.
[26] See for example, *Paris-Match,* February 29, 1964; March 14, 1964.

there was no clear public image of the meaning of foreign aid, and said in its report, "the majority of Frenchmen retain an attitude towards African countries that is very marked by colonialism." In detailed questions concerning the motives for aid, 40 per cent of the respondents agreed inferentially with Cartier: aid should be limited or stopped because the needs of France's own underdeveloped regions should have priority. Yet, many of the responses endorsed the existing French aid system. Large majorities favored bilateral aid over multilateral aid, technical and cultural assistance (which are important elements of French aid) to financial aid, and aid to former colonies over worldwide aid distribution.

The French public shows a somewhat confused and reluctant support of large-scale aid, with racial views strongly affecting the respondents' endorsement. Not surprisingly, the government's statements also reflect a certain confusion of motives. The chief elements in public statements are: [27] (1) aid is a logical form of continued cooperation in the post-colonial era; (2) it supports French national interest and material advantages; (3) it spreads French language and culture, hence the stress on bilateral aid.[28]

The Jeanneney Report recommended that in the future more aid be devoted to countries outside the French community. A parliamentary critic has suggested that French capital assistance should be entirely through multilateral channels.[29] President de Gaulle, while clearly in no temper to offer substantial increases in French contributions to United Nations agencies, has made several gestures in the direction of more bilateral aid to Asia, the Middle East, and Latin America—this obviously in the interests of a French political *rayonnement* that the Jeanneney Report inferentially deplored.

France, as so often before, finds itself in a unique position among the Western nations. Among all aid donors, France makes the largest sacrifices on behalf of poor countries; it professes, from the LDC viewpoint, the most liberal motives; almost alone among donors, it is willing and eager to grant, in addition to direct aid, the commercial policy concessions that the poor nations have sought vainly from other powers. Yet, it is widely believed by rich and poor countries alike that France, perhaps more than any other donor, uses aid as an

[27] Ministère de la Cooperation, *1959–1964: Cinq Ans de Fonds d'Aide et de Coopération,* Paris, 1964.

[28] Statement by Prime Minister to National Assembly, June 10, 1964.

[29] Bonnefous, *Les Milliards Qui s'envolent,* Paris, Fayard, 1963.

instrument of neocolonialist domination.[30] And within France, attitudes toward aid are strikingly ambivalent, even considering the perennial involutions of the foreign aid rationale. Finally, the French government is clearly moving away from a system of bilateral aid that was exclusively aimed at former colonies toward a far wider interest in LDC's. Yet it has evolved no convincing rationale for such an interest, and, in its commercial policy proposals, it remains firmly wedded to a system that would perpetuate strong and unique political and economic ties between France and its EEC partners on the one hand and the states of the French Community on the other. As in the case of the United States, the most likely short-run outcome is a continuation of aid at substantial levels. This does not exclude some declines, reflecting pressure of other demands created by the current quest for *la gloire*. French aid fell from $977 million in 1962 to $865 million in 1963 and $841 million in 1964.

Germany

Germany has been reproached by other donors for its relatively small foreign aid contributions (see Table 1). It is true that Germany gives less than its "fair share" of OECD members' aid by flat rate or progressive tax criteria applied to donor countries' per capita income.[31] But, as the table shows, a number of countries, including Canada, Italy, Japan, and the United Kingdom, pay a smaller share of aid than they would under those standards of public finance.

The flow of official funds from Germany to underdeveloped countries is not strikingly low compared with aid from other donors. Furthermore, if we consider that Germany has no colonial heritage to provide a pattern and a rationale for interest in LDC's, the German performance is in some ways more impressive. Other wealthy countries with no colonial tradition (Canada, Sweden, New Zealand) give far less relative to national income.

The motives for German interest in underdeveloped countries seem relatively clear and are reflected both in the forms of official aid

[30] Thus when Guinea refused to join the French community, it lost French aid. Similarly in 1965 and 1966 aid to Algeria declined from the high levels of the early 1960's.

[31] See my *Economic Aid and International Cost Sharing,* Baltimore, Johns Hopkins Press, 1965, Chapter 5; and I. Kravis and M. Davenport, "The Political Arithmetic of International Burden Sharing," *Journal of Political Economy,* Vol. 71 (August 1963), pp. 309–330.

TABLE 1. Net Flow of Official Resources from OECD Donor Countries to LDC's in 1963

Country	*Total Aid (\$ millions)*	*Aid as Per Cent of OECD Donor Aid*	*GNP as Per Cent of OECD Donors' Total GNP (1962 prices)*
Belgium	90	1.5	1.4
Canada	98	1.6	3.8
Denmark	10	0.2	0.8
France	843	13.9	7.5
Germany	422	7.0	9.1
Italy	64	1.1	4.1
Japan	172	2.8	5.8
Netherlands	38	0.6	1.4
Norway	21	0.4	0.5
Portugal	47	0.8	0.3
United Kingdom	414	6.8	8.2
United States	3,842	63.4	56.8
Total	6,063 [a]	100.0	100.0

Source: OECD, *Development Assistance Efforts and Policies, 1965 Review,* OECD, Paris, 1965; GNP from Table 4 below.

Note: Columns may not add to totals shown because of rounding.

[a] Includes \$4.3 million from Austria.

and in the public discussions. First, the public discussion emphasizes the moral and humanitarian motives for German interest. Security motives are negligible.

Second, there is obviously a strong commercial interest in LDC's. Discussions of aid constantly emphasize the importance of private investment; and in fact often refer to investment as a form of aid, even to the point of describing it as the most desirable form of aid. Furthermore, commercial motives clearly underlie the extensive system of government suppliers' credits and of official lending, even though the latter is nominally not dependent on procurement in Germany.

Third, there is, as with all donors, a political motive. Germany's is virtually unique; it does not involve colonial ties, long-range military or security goals, nor even a very marked desire to spread German culture and long-term influence. It seems to focus largely on two objectives: (1) to create the image among allies and LDC's alike of Germany as a good citizen of the world community and a loyal member of the Atlantic alliance (hence large-scale aid to India and Pakistan, the perennial favorites of U.S. and British largesse); (2) to accomplish certain such short-term political goals as giving aid to countries that might otherwise recognize the East German regime, or, as a counterweight, to those that resent the substantial German reparations payments to Israel.

As in the case of the United States, German emphasis on private investment has not been effective in raising the flow of private capital to LDC's. Net German private capital investment declined substantially between 1959 and 1964; in the latter year it amounted to $107 million, or about one-fourth as much as the net flow of official capital. The commercial emphasis, however, shows up in the official aid flow. Almost all German aid, with the evident exception of reparations payments, takes the form of loans. Furthermore, loans tend to be of shorter duration than those of other major donors, and, until recently, were at relatively high interest rates. German official aid doctrine stresses that loans are preferable to grants because they instill the necessary financial discipline. For somewhat similar reasons, German aid goes to specific projects rather than to general balance-of-payments purposes.

Although Germany has few historical ties with LDC's, bilateral aid has still been by far the most important element of German foreign assistance. In the words of the Minister for Economic Cooperation, "multilateral as much as necessary, bilateral as much as possible."

Not only is German aid primarily bilateral, but it is also largely concentrated in a small number of countries. In recent years, at least half of German aid has gone to the Middle East and Asia, mostly to Israel, India, and Pakistan. The concentration of aid is deliberate. Apparently it is based on the belief that the aid will be more effective if it is large enough to make a substantial effect on investment totals or patterns—something that could not be accomplished by broadcasting the funds uniformly among most or all LDC's within the present aid ceiling of about $400 million annually.

Finally, German public opinion seems to support the principle of aid, as well as its practice, at existing levels. The official doctrine of both government and opposition stresses that if need be additional funds should be appropriated to awaken the public to the merits of foreign aid rather than retrench under the presence of possibly unfavorable public opinion. However, the lagging pace of U.S. aid after 1962 has obviously had its effect on German willingness to increase its aid.

Japan

Japan's worldwide interest in LDC's is largely commercial, although political motives, notably promotion of Asian regional "solidarity" and stability, obviously play a major role also. Japan's view of its job in Asia is to build up trust in her motives, particularly in her willingness to promote the peaceful and independent growth of other nations, without appearing to dominate their political or economic life; and also to act as a bridge or link between Asia (perhaps ultimately including China) and the West. This task is not easy, despite some surface appearance of success in recent years. Naturally, in countries that Japan conquered during or before World War II, resentments run deep. Thus, "normalization" of Japanese-Korean relations is presumably a secular task. Nor will close political ties with Burma, Indonesia, the Philippines, and Vietnam develop easily. At the same time, because Japanese reparations and aid are willingly accepted, economic links are being forged that are likely to have long-term political effects.

During the period 1960–63, more than 80 per cent of Japanese aid went to Asia; the rest went largely to Latin America, in quest of expanded commercial ties. Between 30 and 40 per cent of Japanese aid is classified as grants, but almost all of these grants are reparations payments to Southeast Asia. The bulk of aid is in the form of loans at relatively high interest rates (about 6 per cent average) and relatively short maturities (less than 15 years average). Most of the lending is tied to purchase of Japanese goods by the borrower. In view of Japan's rather low per capita income, the total outflow of aid and reparations (about $175 million annually) is far from negligible. Interest rates, although higher than those of other donors, are lower than the average of domestic long-term rates in Japan. Aid is closely tied to provision of services by Japanese contractors and suppliers, perhaps to a greater extent than in other countries.[32]

There was little evidence of significant public opposition to foreign aid in Japan until the early 1960's, probably because it was then

[32] John White, *Japanese Aid,* London, Overseas Development Institute, 1964.

that aid levels began to increase. Consequently, there was notably less discussion of aid policy than there is in the major donor countries. Because Japanese economic policy toward LDC's was largely aimed at export promotion and at making honorable amends for the conquests of World War II, it is not surprising that there was small opposition to the program initially. However, a 1963 proposal by the Ministry of Trade and Industry to expand the program was received without great enthusiasm and took three years to implement, as aid became for the first time a matter of controversy. Paramount among the factors that led to the uncertainty was Japan's own indecision about its future political role in Asia. Recent setbacks in Japan's phenomenal postwar growth may also have fortified the case for retrenchment. However, by 1966, the proponents of more aid had apparently won their case for the time. Japan's Finance Minister announced in April 1966 that Japan would raise its annual foreign aid budget to one per cent of national income. If this pledge is carried out, Japan would be the second largest aid donor by the end of the 1960's. Its political stake and commitment in Asia would grow, and the region's political power balance would consequently shift.

Other Countries

The smaller industrial countries (Italy, Canada, the Netherlands, Belgium, Norway, Portugal, Sweden, Denmark) fall into two categories. Italy, Belgium, Portugal, and, until very recently, the Netherlands, have focused their interest on former colonies. Unlike the large donors, their security interests in LDC's are usually negligible. Portugal falls into a somewhat anachronistic category because, in a sense, all of its aid is given largely for security motives, to maintain African colonies under Portuguese rule.

This first group of countries disburses almost all of its aid either for maintaining the budgetary costs of its client governments or for technical assistance (salaries of foreign teachers and civil servants). Very little of it goes to finance development projects or programs, *per se*.

Scandinavia, Canada, Switzerland, New Zealand, and Israel have virtually no colonial interest. These countries generally give foreign aid in very small amounts relative to their per capita national incomes. The motives are varied: a sense of obligation to LDC's and to the Western alliance, export promotion, and a blend of public relations and diplomacy. They often give much of their aid through multilateral agencies and place considerable stress on bilateral and multilateral technical assistance. To the extent that they give capital assistance, it is done largely through formal or informal multilateral institutions: the International Development Association, the Colombo Plan, the various World Bank and OECD consortia that have been formed to channel funds to India, Pakistan, Turkey, and other major aid recipients. Israel has apparently been particularly successful in using bilateral aid as an instrument for winning both political and economic gains in Africa; but Israel's situation obviously puts a premium on winning support abroad. Hence bilateralism is essential.

The attitude of these non-colonial countries toward aid casts a certain light on the perennial question of fair shares of aid costs. Obviously, if ability to pay is the criterion, this group of countries is underpaying markedly. Their aid is in the neighborhood of 0.2 per cent of GNP annually, by the OECD aid definition, while the major donors contribute from 0.5 to 1.5 of their annual product to LDC's. But, as Chapter 8 will indicate, ability to pay is only one consideration. The most important one in practice is the nature and extent of the donor's interest, and these countries' interest is normally limited.

CONCLUSIONS

We have seen that each country that offers aid or other concessions does so in the expectation of receiving benefits. How does this square with the general propositions we made earlier? (1) short-run economic and political benefits are normally modest; (2) long-run material gains may be important, but they are also uncertain.

The answer lies in the initial distinction that I made between operational factors that "explain" the levels of aid and the formulation of a motivated rationale for providing it. Clearly, donor nations do have day-to-day commercial and political interests. It is one aim of foreign policy to promote them. Foreign aid as a tool of policy may contribute to these ends.

It is only when we go behind apparent motives to inquire into their relation to concepts of national security, variously defined, that we see that operational explanations do not offer an acceptable rationale. The widespread doubts and continuing controversies about the merits of aid in the major donor countries is the clearest testimony in this respect.

In our quest for a more convincing rationale, we have followed certain paths, which at first sight may seem dated. Thus, it appears odd to lay stress on the relation of the South to problems of nuclear strategy. After all, there have been a number of wars since 1945, none of them fought with nuclear weapons. Yet if the issues are survival and prosperity, it is for the rich countries ultimately a question of the nuclear threat. The reason that world power struggles since 1945 have taken their peculiar form is because that threat does exist. North America and Western Europe must therefore look far beyond the traditional justifications for aid to find a rationale that will still their citizens' doubts. Today the security and the prosperity of the West do not depend in any significant way on the fate of the underdeveloped countries. The North often asserts that these issues are related, but the widespread dissatisfaction with aid rationales indicates that the North does not fully believe its own protestations. Fifty years from now, of course, that situation may well be changed. Today's underdeveloped countries may then play a major role in Northern security. But the policies of nations are not normally built upon secular prospects; nor for that matter, upon ethical judgments except when spurred on by the coincidence of morality with perceived self-interest.

But the argument for a "disinterested" element in the approach to aid is not a quest for ethical purity. There is not much basis for ascribing moral superiority to welfare motives. Such motives are rarely devoid of some vision of the society that the donor would like to see prevail. If one element of "no-strings" aid is an ambition to mold the world closer to the heart's desire, can we in practice dissociate philanthropy from the drive for power?

CHAPTER TWO

"Atlantic Community" Interest: The Economic Base

THE BALANCE OF ECONOMIC INTERESTS

Aid and Trade

What do the rich countries and the poor ones gain from their trade and investment relationships? In light of the Northern and Southern economic and political interests what should be the relative roles of aid and trade in the development process? We have so far discussed the matter in terms of the political basis for aid. Now we turn to trade and investment. But aid and trade are not watertight components. They substitute for each other to a limited extent. They may also act to reinforce or offset each other's effects.

In theory, trade should be based on comparative advantage. In my view aid should be based, in part, on absolute advantage. If I can do everything better than you, we still gain from trade with each other, but I should also give you economic aid. The reasons are simple, at least in the essentials. Trade increases the value of world output, thereby making all parties to it better off than before trade. Aid is capital transfer that may or may not be more productive abroad than at home. When people are better off, they have more capital. If they want to help poor countries, they can give or lend the resources more easily than if they had less capital. Thus trade, by enriching both parties, simultaneously makes it easier for the rich to give aid and less necessary for the poor to obtain it as a condition of growth. For the world as a whole, aid may increase output, decrease it, or leave it unchanged; but in any event, the donor is better off if he keeps his capital instead of giving it away. Therefore if the donor country seeks to help an LDC develop at a given rate and at minimum real cost, it will look upon aid, which involves real costs, as a supplement to trade, which is costless. From the recipient's viewpoint, the situation is not symmetrical. Aid (at least the concessional element of it) costs the recipient nothing. Trade, according to comparative advantage, costs less than any other use of resources. Thus the recipient gains on the grounds of both income transfer and comparative advantage. In this simplified world I have described (given that rich countries want to help poor ones but are reluctant to raise aid levels), the rich should seek to promote trade, and the poor to promote both aid and trade. But then the qualifications start to crowd in and may end up transforming the situation.

Southern Motives. From the LDC viewpoint it should be recognized that there are forces acting both to offset and to support the attractiveness of trade. Let us first examine those that may discourage trade in LDC eyes. Aid and trade may be alternatives, not complements. If a country's exports rise steadily, improving its balance-of-payments situation, donors are likely to reduce aid. The aid is a transfer that adds to total resources, whereas the exports use resources that could be devoted to Southern domestic production. The recipient faced with such an implicit choice is theoretically better off with a given increase in aid than with an equivalent increase in exports.

Other factors may make trade unattractive in theory, whether or not aid is offered. World demand for a particular export product may be inelastic, so that with or without aid, the exporters of some commodities would be better off behaving like monopolists and restricting output. But given the inability of commodity exporters to agree in restricting output, the failure of the individuals to expand production may be more irrational than the expansion would be. From the viewpoint of the government, it would be better to buy up stocks and export only enough to maximize profits. However, the same considerations apply to governments as to individuals. The typical commodity-producing nation faces a rather elastic world demand for its output, as it supplies only a small fraction of the world market. Thus, individual or national interest may conflict with those of exporters as a group.

Production for the home market is often more attractive than production for export. Even if comparative advantage, with full regard for demand elasticities, favors production for export, the home market is more certain, with respect to protection both from competition via the tariff and against world market fluctuations caused by declining external demand. In addition to being uncertain, the foreign market may be unknown, particularly if the product has not previously been exported. This may be particularly relevant if the importer is sensitive to quality, and if style changes and product variations are considered relevant. Most important of all is the close historical relation between import substitution and industrialization. LDC preference for import substitution, even at high short-run cost in terms of export opportunities forgone, may be facilitated by aid.

Without aid, the only way to maintain import substitution might be through the difficult step of devaluation. But even devaluation is not a substitute for aid in terms of industrialization goals, because it encourages exports at the expense of import substitutes. Therefore the various motivations that encourage import substitution create strong forces tending to make aid at least a partial substitute for trade.

There are also forces at work that encourage trade in Southern eyes. Some of these incentives are created and complemented by aid; some, on the other hand, arise from Southern dissatisfaction with aid. First, there are performance criteria. Donors may give more to those whose trade flourishes. Or even if there is a negative correlation between export growth and aid levels, resources used to produce exports may be immobile. Exporting will then pay so long as marginal revenue from trade exceeds the decline in aid.

Aid is a transfer of resources, including capital and technical assistance. If aid succeeds in increasing output and productivity, it will probably also increase the ability to export over time.

Two forces based on opposition to aid may increase trade: resentment of aid, and uncertainty about its future. Aid always has strings attached, even if they are as impalpable as a sense of dependence on largesse. Anything that increases output or foreign exchange receipts, at a given level of aid, may help to reduce the dependence. This includes the whole range of political considerations that have been discussed elsewhere: reluctance to be aligned with colonial powers, or with potential losers in world power struggles; reluctance to pay a price for aid in terms of changing domestic policies, or even reducing freedom of maneuver; suspicion of donor's motives, or the fear that even if his motives are not inimical, the results of aid-induced changes may be uncongenial.[1]

Finally, there may be a preference for incomes received through the market. This reflects a number of considerations: (1) ethical views about the connection between work and income; (2) a preference for the *status quo:* (3) doubts about the reliability of "permanent" subsidy as a major source of personal income or government revenue; and (4) perhaps most important, a preference for resource transfers that disguise the nature of the transaction, and give it simultaneously the status of an impersonal market force and of earned income. This is probably a major motivation of the UNCTAD trade proposals, although the tacit assumption that this form of concession will reduce either the sense of dependence or the North's ability to influence Southern policies is probably not warranted.

Recipients will therefore not always seek simultaneous expansion of trade and aid. There will often be motives discouraging one or the other, despite the apparent advantages for LDC's inherent in the pursuit of both.[2]

Northern Motives. The donor's viewpoint must also be considered. His presumptive preference for trade over aid may also be greatly modified by special considerations that lead him to give aid rather than to make trade concessions.[3] There is a widespread belief that aid does provide political advantages, or more broadly, that it allows a greater exercise of influence. In theory at least, it can clearly be a more flexible instrument of policy objectives than trade concessions, although the distinctions may blur somewhat in practice. This is consistent with and arises from the political, economic, and security motivations discussed in Chapter 1. Furthermore, if trade concessions are simply a disguised resource transfer, as in the case of commodity agreements, there is no *a priori* reason to consider it a cheaper way than aid of promoting political or developmental goals.

[1] Chapter 1 above; Pincus, *Economic Aid,* Chapter 3.

[2] This treatment of forces that encourage or discourage trade is almost completely divorced from that taken in other treatments of the subject; for example, Gerald Meier, *International Trade and Development,* New York, Harper and Row, 1963. There is no inherent disagreement; we are just dealing with different concerns.

[3] The word donor is ambiguous in respect to trade concessions. A movement to free trade is in principle no gift. Preferential treatment does involve some resource transfer, if the preferential price is above the world price; but for manufactured products, the transfer element is negligible. Price fixing commodity arrangements do involve a considerable transfer. (Cf. Chs. 6, 7.)

If Northern protectionist forces are strong, the political costs of opening up markets to the South are likely to outweigh any consequent savings in aid. Furthermore, it is not clear either on theoretical grounds or from observation that LDC trade expansion necessarily reduces the need for aid. Therefore, the North's reluctance to offer access may be all the stronger. Why fight protectionism when the marginal gains from trade are small, the political difficulties great, and the aid requirement unaffected or perhaps even increased? Furthermore, in this situation, if Northern governments want to promote aid, trade concessions conflict with the goal. They may, in the public's view, undermine the case for aid.

If the donor is concerned about balance-of-payments problems, or wants to promote the long-term market for his exports, aid may be preferable to trade. It is easier to tie aid than trade, although no method is completely foolproof.

The donor may simply want to transfer more resources. The clearest example is food and supplies for disaster relief. At another level, it arises from the desire to accelerate development. This motive in turn is allied to the political or other considerations discussed above.

Acting in the opposite direction, to reinforce the donor's preference for trade concessions over aid, there are several considerations, all of them partly tactical. Aid is a nuisance to administer. Claimants' demands have to be reconciled. Aid creates problems of administration for both donor and recipient. Political considerations and elementary prudence require that the expenditure of aid be supervised by the donor or at least in some way justified to him by the recipient. Nations are reluctant to justify their behavior to others, and this is likely to offset some or all of the political advantages gained by the original offer of aid.

Second, there is one aspect of the question of absorptive capacity. Many LDC governments are not particularly efficient economic agents. The private sector's ability to absorb private investment profitably, or to make effective use of export revenues, may be far greater than that of the public sector. In that case, government-to-government aid may be not only economically unproductive, but actually counter-productive. It may build up a strong, inefficient economic force that can hamper the growth of the private sector. Another way of looking at it is to say that trade and investment promote a market discipline that stimulates growth, while aid may not.

Third, the government that seeks to aid LDC's may be more concerned about domestic enemies of aid than about opponents of trade concessions. In that case, moves to open Northern markets or even to embody transfers in trade transactions may be desirable for tactical reasons. This is one of the arguments used to support commodity price-fixing internationally. It should be noted that this is in part a question of the forms of aid, and not of the merits of trade and aid.

Fourth, there may be an ideological preference for trade as an agent of growth.[4] As implied in the discussion of the disadvantages of government-to-government aid, this preference may be based on fact. On the other hand, it may be beside the point, if the world fails to conform to the theory.

Conclusions on Aid and Trade. The forces that pull donors and recipients to favor aid or trade may result in almost any attitude on either side. Some recipients renounce aid, and some donors express preferences for aid increases (direct or disguised) over trade liberalization. Yet the basic assumption remains that donors prefer to minimize real costs of aid, while recipients seek increases in both trade and aid. But in choosing among concessions of equal monetary value, recipients normally prefer aid to trade.

Aid (including the aid aspects of the UNCTAD trade proposals) and trade are aimed at different goals. Aid transfers the location of the world's stock of resources from motives that we have discussed above. Trade improves the efficiency with which those resources are used and takes place primarily from motives of economic gain. The two may interact because the transfer may facilitate trade or inhibit it. In one way it obviously facilitates trade because it finances it. The inhibition arises in other ways, such as in encouraging import substitutes, or in offering alternatives to devaluations.

The purpose of development or aid is not to increase trade. Nor is it the object of trade growth to decrease aid. They may of course interact and substitute for each other to some extent, but each has a role to play.[5] Aid is economically important so long as we are dissat-

[4] Harry Johnson, *Economic Policies Toward Less Developed Countries*, Washington, D.C., The Brookings Institution, 1966, Chapter 2, gives an admirable summary of the economic case for trade as an agent of growth, and of the objections to it.

[5] For example, aid can be used as a method of altering trade policies or unsatisfactory economic policies; if the encouragement is successful, the need for aid in the future may be reduced.

isfied with the present world distribution of income and the incidence of its growth, given the present organization of international economic policy; or, for that matter, if we are satisfied with it, so long as we think that less satisfactory results might emerge from reducing aid.

More liberal trade is economically important so long as we think that it pays us to increase world output from a given resource stock, or if we think it will have favorable dynamic effects on growth, or (even if Northern gains do not outweigh the politico-economic losses arising from readjustment) if the benefits to the South seem to merit a move to liberal trade.[6] There may also be a role for disguised aid in the form of trade concessions linked to transfers. These should be supported if we think that the South should get more aid than it does now, and that aid appropriations are not forthcoming; or if we think that aid should be distributed via the market and not via subsidy; or finally, even when we oppose such devices, if we think that the concessions will favor growth enough to overcome the many disadvantages to be discussed in Chapters 6 and 7.

Finally, sticking to economic considerations, each of these approaches to increasing LDC real income must be judged in light of its effects in different countries. Mexico or India can probably benefit substantially from trade preferences for simple manufactures. But they cannot benefit much from a commodity agreement fixing the price of cocoa, or as exporters, from free trade in jet airplanes.

Nor do aid or trade concessions do much good economically if they subsidize policies that have proven to be unworkable. Of course a country is better off if it receives aid than if it doesn't, other things being equal. But the transfer of wealth can act not only to underwrite desirable policies but also to support undesirable ones, in view of development objectives. It is in each case a nice question what the effect of giving or withholding aid will be. In purely economic terms, it could be said that aid should be given or withheld according to whether it promotes self-sustaining economic growth. But one might willingly support aid in some cases whether or not it promoted this goal. Other goals might seem more important than growth. And, for similar reasons, one might withdraw aid that was being used effectively.

There can be no clear-cut generalizations about the absolute

[6] The latter view involves an estimate that protection is better than free trade for the North; free trade (or at least market access) is better than protection for the South; and the balance of interests should favor the South.

merits of aid and trade. The viewpoint of each party and the conditions under which aid and trade are conducted will determine the preferences of each.

Trade Interests

There are two aspects to the gains from trade: those deriving from specialization according to comparative advantage, and those deriving from and contributing to the process of economic development over time. Today, economists discussing development emphasize the latter set. They are not necessarily inconsistent with the former, and modern versions of neoclassical economic theory emphasize the view that specialization according to comparative advantage will be likely to promote rapid growth.[7]

The principle of comparative advantage states in effect that to maximize world output at any point in time, each country should export those goods it produces relatively cheaply and import those it produces relatively dearly. The total world output from a fixed quantity of resources is thereby increased compared with production without trade. Sweden could, with hothouses, produce coffee; but it exports lumber and imports coffee. Switzerland could, without artificial climate, produce both watches and autos; but it exports the first and imports the second, and consequently has a higher real income than if it produced both and imported neither. This is true even if Switzerland's production costs for both watches and autos are lower than those of its trading partners, providing that the Swiss ratio of watch production costs to auto production costs is lower than its trading partners' ratios.

The static gains from trade are presumably greater as the differences between trading partners' resource endowments and production and demand conditions are greater. It is difficult to measure the actual value of these gains, however; in the absence of data on prices and costs, we must resort to gross measures. The combined national products of the Atlantic Community are about $1,165 billion U.S. dollars at official exchange rates (1964 estimates). Their total exports in 1964 were about $118 billion, of which one-fifth went to underdeveloped countries. In other words, exports to underdeveloped

[7] See for example, G. M. Meier, *International Trade and Development,* Ch. 7; Gottfried Haberler, *International Trade and Economic Development,* Cairo National Bank of Egypt, 1959. Chapter 4 below discusses these issues in some detail.

countries are equivalent to only 2 per cent of Atlantic Community production. Therefore, gains from trade with the South are less than vital to Northern prosperity. For the South, trade with Atlantic countries accounts for at least one-tenth of total output. Small wonder, therefore, that the future of North-South trade is a perpetual concern of developing countries, while the North tends to look upon such issues as somewhat secondary. Table 2 shows the relevant trade and income estimates for 1964.

Table 2 probably gives a slightly misleading impression of the North's trade stake in the South. Although North-North trade is much larger, the gains per dollar of trade are probably greater in North-South trade. Gains from trade are presumably greater when countries differ widely in resource endowments and demand patterns. For example, Norway and Brazil have approximately the same annual export levels at exchange rate equivalents, about $1.5 billion. If, for some reason, the United States wishes to produce the kinds and quantities of goods that the two countries export, its costs would be more than $1.5 billion in either case, but much greater for Brazil's export basket. The United States is higher on the comparative advantage ranking in producing the temperate forestry, fishery, and agricultural products and light manufactures that Norway exports; and lower ranked in comparative productive efficiency for the tropical crops that Brazil exports. Furthermore, United States and Brazilian demand for goods probably differs more than United States and Norwegian demand, because of differences in income and tastes. Unless demand and cost differences are offsetting, this tends to enhance the gains from trade.

This conclusion that the North has a relatively minor interest in trade with the South applies *a fortiori* to some of the dynamic aspects of gains from trade. The transmission of technology and skills through trade and investment is predominantly from North to South. The economic reorganization and market expansion the South seeks will utilize the experience, products, and markets of industrial countries. In general, the industrial countries' dynamic gains from trade —those that result in expanding markets and in lowering costs by increasing scale of output or introducing new techniques, thereby raising productivity—stem primarily from trade with each other. However, their dynamic gains are probably relatively smaller per unit value of trade anyway, because the state of the arts varies less among them than between them and LDC's. New technique (more specifi-

TABLE 2. Free World Exports and Product, 1964

A. TOTAL TRADE, 1964 [a]

Region	1964 Combined GNP	1964 Exports (f.o.b.)	1964 Imports (c.i.f.)	Exports as Per Cent of GNP
	($ billions)			
Industrial Countries	1,165	118	125	10
Underdeveloped Countries	240	35	35	15 [b]
Total	1,405	153	160	11

Notes: [a] Includes Free World imports from and exports to Communist countries; excludes trade between Communist countries.

[b] The United Nations has estimated LDC exports as amounting to 18 per cent of combined domestic product in 1961. (*The Growth of World Industry 1938–1961: International Analyses and Tables,* New York, 1965, p. 33.) The estimate in the table may therefore be too low.

B. NORTH-SOUTH TRADE, 1964

Exports	*$ Billions*	*Per Cent of 1964 GNP*
From Industrial Countries to Industrial Countries	85	7
From Industrial Countries to Underdeveloped Countries	25	2
From Underdeveloped Countries to Industrial Countries	25	10
From Underdeveloped Countries to Underdeveloped Countries	7	3

Source: United Nations, *Monthly Bulletin of Statistics,* March 1966.

cally, embedding technological progress and productivity growth in the economy) is probably a central element in the dynamic gains from trade, although it is evidently linked in practice to cost reductions stemming from economies of scale.

Investment Interests

Turning from trade to investment, the relative stakes change somewhat. Atlantic Community annual net private investment, including portfolio investment, in underdeveloped countries averaged about $2.5 billion during the decade ending in 1964, and showed no particular trend. LDC investment in industrial countries is small, although much of it is presumably unrecorded and no reliable figures exist. Thus, if, as an extreme example, the South were to confiscate Northern investments, the one-time loss to the North would be large. The value of U.S. private capital invested in LDC's was estimated at about $13 billion in 1964. Of course, Northern and Southern stakes in private foreign investment are not adequately measured by the value of sunk capital. In the long run the dominant issue is the potential returns on investment, both to private individuals and to society as a whole.

Confiscation is therefore not only an extreme example, but an oversimplified one. Usually the issue is not whether to confiscate, but what kinds of restrictions or encouragements to apply to foreign capital. However, it is worthwhile to couch the issues initially in terms of confiscation, because it brings out many of the underlying points.

It is commonly stated that private investment benefits the host country by providing capital, transferring technology, increasing the productivity of labor and thereby allowing increases in domestic savings and investment, further stimulating growth. Thus, confiscation, by cutting out the flow of capital and technique, is presumably unwise from the viewpoint of the host country. However, much depends on the circumstances of the case. Confiscation allows a country to save on scarce foreign exchange by eliminating repatriation of profits and interest; and also thereby allows the government to increase its savings without increase in domestic taxation. The decision as to whether to confiscate depends therefore on a variety of factors: views as to the validity of contracts; the prospects for retaliation (this need not be retaliation in kind—if India confiscates U.S. investments, the retaliation probably takes the form of cessation of foreign aid); the prospects for private domestic and foreign investment in the absence of confiscation (countries with an active private sector whose natural resources, long exploited by foreign investors, offer no important new foreign investment appeal are in a better position to confiscate); the domestic political and ideological appeal of confiscation; and the urgency of foreign exchange or savings constraints.

Confiscation of foreign investment has a long and almost honorable tradition in the form of defaults on bonds. In recent years it has been applied to both debt and equity, as in Eastern Europe, Cuba, Indonesia. No *a priori* judgment is possible as to whether the Atlantic

Community or the LDC's have a greater economic stake in protecting existing investments and promoting new ones. It requires in each case a balancing of net gains and losses. Such countries as Puerto Rico and Israel clearly gain economically from avoiding confiscation, despite the high level of foreign investment, because potential losses of markets and capital inflows are more important than the gains of confiscation. So do such countries as India and Pakistan, because they now receive large inflows of official capital that might be cut off. On the other hand, such countries as Iran, Saudi Arabia, and Chile could profit substantially from confiscation if they could assure themselves of marketing channels in the vertically integrated industries they serve. Countries that have severe foreign exchange problems, Brazil for example, would face a dilemma. Confiscation allows foreign exchange economies and also permits increased domestic savings, but the amounts so gained may not compensate for possible retaliation in trade and aid.

In practice, the operative question is restriction of foreign private investment, rather than the extreme example of confiscation. It is rather difficult to speak in quantitative terms of Northern or Southern stakes in liberalizing or restricting investment, because each country is *sui generis*. Thus, the great economic advances achieved in Hong Kong or Puerto Rico can be cited as examples of the cost that restriction of foreign private investment imposes on those LDC's that fail to encourage foreign investment. But there are many countries that offer favorable terms to private investors without attracting their capital; not every country that restricts foreign investment is a Puerto Rico *manqué*. From the economic viewpoint, restriction doesn't make much sense for a capital-poor country unless there is concern either about the balance-of-payments effect of repatriated profits or about other bottlenecks (such as skilled labor) that the new investment might aggravate.

The issue, as in the case of confiscation, is primarily not economic but political. At the bargaining level, the larger the foreign capital investment, the greater the leverage that a host government can potentially command. For example, British governments do not take economic sanctions against South Africa because British investment there is so great; and those against Rhodesia, where British trade interests are much smaller, were taken only under the pressure of international political imperatives. The hostile actions that the French government has passively accepted in Algeria, or the United

States and Netherlands in Indonesia, can be interpreted partly in these terms, although partly also in terms of broad political goals. If a capital-poor country restricts investment, it may act from a justified fear of foreign political and economic domination. But if the fear *is* justified, then the government must consider itself weak, indecisive, or unable to control corruption. More likely, restriction proceeds from fears of domestic political consequences such as the opprobrium that often attaches to cooperating with imperialism, or to an ideological preference for socialism.[8] The economic loss of new investment arising from restrictions is largely the host country's because the investing country's capital can go elsewhere. For existing investment, restriction generally takes the form of control over repatriation of capital and profits, and of requirements for domestic participation. The new effect on capital availability depends on whether discouragement of new investment exceeds gains resulting from controls.

Obviously, the decision to invest or not is ultimately a question of profit. From the viewpoint of the foreign investor, his return (including discounts for unusual risks arising from investment in LDC's) is the primary criterion. In that light, restriction is simply one aspect. It affects the degree of risk or the expected profit. Profitable foreign investment in the South has been largely limited to mining and refining, although in recent years there has been some investment in manufacturing.

Outside of extractive industries, the record of returns to Northern investment in the South is not spectacular compared with returns to domestic investment in the North or foreign investment in other industrial countries. The level of investment has remained relatively stable since the mid-1950's. There seem to be no grounds for believing that the current annual level of investment will increase substantially without major changes in Northern and Southern investment policies. The nature of the problem and of policy alternatives is discussed briefly in Chapter 8.

In any event, looking at both trade and investment from the static viewpoint, the industrial countries taken together have a rather modest interest—although there are significant exceptions, such as Japan, which does half of its export trade with LDC's and could not readily shift these exports to markets in the North. The specter of a North

[8] See, for example, Elliott J. Berg, "Socialism and Economic Development in Tropical Africa," *Quarterly Journal of Economics,* LXXVIII (November 1964), pp. 547–573.

deprived of vital raw materials by a hostile South owes more to imagination than to analysis. At most, if raw materials exporters insisted for political motives on denying themselves export earnings —an unlikely event—there would be an increase in raw material costs. This in turn would presumably be offset, at least in part, by induced technological changes in industrial countries. For example, if the Atlantic countries were deprived of Middle Eastern oil, they would proceed to develop their oil shale and tar sand reserves more rapidly.

Similar conclusions apply to the process of economic growth over time. Some economic theories of trade and development tend to support the view that trade is an agent of economic growth. Historically there is no doubt that it has operated to promote the interests of both advanced and underdeveloped countries. Trade was a major element not only in the growth of the United Kingdom and the white dominions but also in that of many long-settled primary-producing countries (for example, Nigeria, Gold Coast, Brazil). To the extent that trade now operates as an agent of growth for the Atlantic countries, however, the developing countries play a minor role in the process. Only one-fifth of Northern trade is with LDC's, and the proportion to total trade has been falling in the post-World War II period. It is the intra-Northern trade that has grown most rapidly among the market economies, particularly intra-European trade. Again, as in the case of static gains, there are exceptions. The remarkably rapid post-war growth of Japan must reflect in part the increased specialization and economies of scale made possible by the expansion of its exports to the South, and by the development of new raw material sources in underdeveloped countries.

Although the North's interest is less vital than the South's, it is far from negligible. Furthermore, the process of growth in North and South alike may intensify the Northern interest. Northern growth will increase the demand for imported raw materials, including some in which it is now largely self-sufficient. Southern growth will increase its demand for Northern products. The South's population, even excluding China, is more than 1.5 billion, two and one-half times that of the North, so that the increase in demand could be substantial. At the same time, cost conditions in the two areas will change, and each may export goods it now imports. Each can benefit from trade under situations where comparative costs change. But this is far ahead, because the South's demand is now sharply constrained by the interacting effects of low income levels and foreign exchange restrictions. However, as the next section points out, taking a long view, we can foresee vast increases in LDC trade and income by the end of this century. In the past 150 years the United States has risen from an insignificant role in world trade to a major one. Over the generations to come, the underdeveloped regions may also play an increasingly important part.

CURRENT TRENDS IN INCOME AND TRADE

Aggregate Growth

It is generally believed that economic growth in the underdeveloped countries has been slower than that in developed countries in recent years. If we define growth as a percentage of increase in national product, this belief is not so—the two areas' incomes grew at an average compound rate of about 4.5 per cent annually from 1950 to 1962 with the LDC rate if anything slightly higher than that of the Atlantic countries.[9] Growth of per capita income has been faster in the Atlantic countries, the amount of the spread from year to year being influenced not only by faster population growth in LDC's, but also by changes in U.S. income growth, because the United States accounts for more than half of Atlantic income. In the period 1950–55, when the U.S. economy was growing rapidly, the per capita growth of rich countries averaged 3.4 per cent annually, as against 2.5 per cent in poor countries. During the years 1956–60, U.S. income grew more slowly, and Northern per capita income grew at 2.0 per cent average rate, compared with 1.8 per cent in the South. Since 1961, U.S. income has been growing faster, and the gap in per capita income growth rates is wider again. Thus during the period 1957–58

[9] These data are taken from *United Nations World Economic Survey,* 1962, and from the Agency for International Development. All such aggregate income statistics are inaccurate, particularly for LDC's, and errors do not necessarily cancel out. For example, I have computed Northern growth rates for the period 1950–52 to 1961–64 at 3.9 per cent (2.6 per cent per capita), compared with Southern growth of 4.4 per cent (2.2 per cent per capita). The 1965 U.N. study of world industry shows both Northern and Southern output growing at a 3.9 per cent rate from 1950–60. What does emerge from all the various estimates is: (1) Per capita income is growing faster in the North; (2) Total income in both North and South is growing at about the same rate, somewhere in the vicinity of 4 per cent a year.

to 1963–64, per capita income growth was 3.1 per cent in the North and 2.4 per cent in the South, according to AID.

Finally, in addition to the percentage growth of total and per capita national product, one could compare the absolute increases in total or per capita income. It is a foregone conclusion that such an aggregate comparison will for decades show only increasing North-South disparities. The combined domestic products of the Atlantic Community countries in 1964 amounted to about $1.165 billion U.S. dollars at official exchange rates, nearly five times that of the LDC's; per capita incomes were more than twelve times as great. For the size of the total gap to narrow, LDC income would initially have to grow five times faster than that of rich countries; for the size of the per capita gap to narrow, LDC's would initially have to grow twelve times as fast, unless relative rates of population growth changed. Use of official exchange rates overstates the discrepancy in real incomes; but the real per capita income difference is at least of the order of 8:1.

If it were not for rapid population growth in the South, economic growth rates in the two regions would be about the same (other things being equal). With annual growth in per capita incomes of 3 per cent then entirely feasible, incomes per head would double every 23 years; [10] by 1985 this would bring Western Europe roughly to U.S. 1960 per capita income levels; and by 1990: (1) Latin America would be at 1960 Western European levels; (2) Africa at 1960 Latin American levels; (3) the Far East at 1960 Japanese levels; and (4) Japan at 1960 United Kingdom levels (about 20 per cent above 1960 Western European averages).[11] This may not be a vision of perfect felicity, but it is relatively encouraging and it could be accomplished by reducing birth rates, or by raising income growth rates from the current 4.5 per cent annually to a level of 5.5 per cent,

[10] These illustrations are based on official exchange rates. These rates overstate the real income gap. No one could live at an income level of $80 per head in U.S. prices, yet about one-fourth of the world lives at this income level according to the statistics. Restating income levels in terms of purchasing power might shorten the time spans indicated above, but not by much. Part of the catching up process is a sort of statistical phenomenon. The economy shifts from a subsistence to a money basis. At the same time cost and demand patterns come to resemble those of advanced countries, so that by the time the poorer country catches up with the richer one, the degree of bias involved in use of exchange rates to compare income levels is greatly reduced. Thus, the Swedish crown or Canadian dollar offer, at exchange rate equivalent, reasonably good measures for economic welfare comparisons with the United States, while the Indian rupee or Greek drachma do not.

[11] At the growth rates prevailing over the period 1950–64, per capita Japanese GNP would reach 1960 U.K. levels by the end of the 1970's.

or by a combination of the two. If LDC population and income continue to grow at current rates, then per capita income will double only every 35 years, and the results projected above for 1990 will not take place until about the year 2015. If population grows faster than now, the South might not reach a relative standard of comfort until perhaps the middle of the next century, at present rates of income growth.

The South is legitimately concerned with what may seem to be rather small percentage differences in annual growth of output; this concern is reinforced by the general belief that there is not much that can be done easily in the short run to reduce the rate of population growth. Nor, for that matter, is it necessarily to the long-run economic interest of the relatively thinly settled areas of Latin America and Africa to slow down their population growth, particularly if people are not allowed to migrate freely between countries in search of work, nor manufactured goods in search of markets.[12]

It is largely on the basis of this concern for small differences in growth rates and on the alleged limitations of growth caused by lack of foreign exchange that underdeveloped countries in economic rationality can justify their preoccupation with trade and aid concessions from the North. It is possible to argue one or both of two cases to support the need for faster export growth as a condition of faster output growth: (1) foreign exchange limitations create a barrier to output growth; (2) domestic savings or domestic markets for goods cannot be increased readily, so that increased imports are the only way to increase investment; or increased exports the only way to find markets (because domestic demand is small, or domestic productive factors are immobile as among industries).[13] Both arguments are made by underdeveloped countries.

Industrial countries, on the other hand, generally do not argue so strongly for trade expansion on these grounds. Their case for more trade is to a greater degree on the comparative cost arguments and, in the case of smaller countries, the desire to benefit from economies of scale.

In any event, there is clearly no unique relation between trade

[12] Because labor immobility and restrictions on trade in manufactures mean that domestic prosperity can be achieved only by building up large domestic markets. In most LDC's, this means either international economic integration or bigger home markets. (I abstract here from the market possibilities offered by devaluation of currency).

[13] See Chs. 3–5 for exposition.

and economic development. The percentage growth of Atlantic Community exports was nearly twice as great as its income growth during the past decade; underdeveloped countries' exports rose a little slower than income. Yet income in the two areas grew at nearly the same rate. Table 3 compares industrial and underdeveloped countries' trade growth from 1950 through 1965.

These data underline the error inherent in equating income growth and trade growth uniquely for all countries. The industrial countries' prosperity has been marked by rapid increases in trade, probably reflecting: (1) dismantling of the trade restrictions created

TABLE 3. Growth and Shares of Exports, 1950–1965

	Average Export Growth Rates (per cent per year)		*Shares of Total Exports* [a] *(per cent)*		
	1950–1960	*1960–1965*	*1950*	*1960*	*1965*
Industrial Countries	8.6	8.4	66	76	78
Underdeveloped Countries	3.6	5.8	34	24	22

Source: UNCTAD, *Handbook of International Trade Statistics,* Doc. E/Conf. 46/12/Add. 1, February 28, 1964; United Nations, *Monthly Bulletin of Statistics,* May 1966.

Note: [a] Excludes trade between Communist countries; includes Free World exports to Communist countries.

during the Depression of the 1930's, and maintained until after World War II—in effect a sort of catching up to normal trade patterns after a long period of restriction; (2) increasing specialization in production of manufactures, made possible by increases in demand, and encouraged by preferences for widely advertised products; (3) the internationalization of tastes made possible by modern communications, and encouraged by the growth of international corporations, which are also often their own customers in world trade; (4) the marked and continuing decline in transportation costs in this century.[14]

[14] For statistical confirmation, see R. Cooper, *National Economic Policy in an Integrated World Economy,* New York, McGraw-Hill, forthcoming, Ch. II.

Growth of the underdeveloped countries has taken place under a variety of trade conditions. They have benefited, either as exporters or importers, from the factors listed above, but the results for trade have been generally modest. The situation varies greatly among countries. The basic points accounting for the difference seem to be: (1) the buoyancy of world demand for manufactures has allowed all Northern countries to share, albeit unevenly, in the rapid growth of trade; (2) often lacking that opportunity, some Southern countries, usually the larger ones, were able to expand rapidly by maintaining the traditional but slow-growing exports, substituting domestic industrial production for exports, and using the foreign exchange savings for importing capital goods; while others grew either by outpacing the average LDC export performance or else failed to grow. The data of Table 3 offer some evidence of changes in this pattern since 1960. Southern exports have increased faster than in the preceding decade, and their exports of manufactured products have continued to rise at a faster rate than all exports combined (see Chapter 6). It is still too early to say whether this trend marks a shift in the forces that propel Southern economic growth, or portends a rise in aggregate growth rates. It could be largely the reflection of short-run fluctuations in commodity price levels.

Trends in the Industrial Countries [15]

The salient factors in Northern economic development since 1950 have been: (1) rapid increases in Western European output, particularly in Germany and Italy; (2) slow growth in the United States (up to 1962) and the United Kingdom; (3) a phenomenal development in Japan before 1965. This growth was marked by the expansion of trade among industrial countries, as shown in Table 3 above.

Table 4 compares 1950 and 1963 per capita incomes for the 24 Northern countries at constant prices. Table 5 compares their rates of income growth during the same period. Table 6 shows how Northern trade grew from 1950, by country. Beginning in 1964, there was some slowdown in the income growth of Western Europe and Japan;

[15] This section is a very brief summary. For full treatment of industrial countries' post-war growth and trade, see Angus Maddison, *Economic Growth in the West*, New York, Twentieth Century Fund, 1964; and the volumes in the Atlantic Policy series by Bela Balassa and Richard Cooper.

and an increase in the United States, Canada, Australia and New Zealand.[16]

The following summary for the period 1953–63, which confirms the data of Table 3,[17] also shows how much the North's trade fed on itself. Intra-Northern trade grew nearly twice as fast as North-South trade.

Direction of Trade	*Growth of Trade 1953–63 (per cent per year)*
A.C. Exports to A.C.	8.8
A.C. Exports to L.D.C	4.7
A.C. Exports to World	7.8

Table 6 gives the detail by country and region, with trade growth rates corrected for terms of trade changes, to reflect the international purchasing power of each country's exports. The fastest growth in trade was achieved by the countries with the fastest income growth. In fact, there is considerable support for the contention that trade growth has been an important factor in relative GNP growth in the North.[18]

[16] The rankings of Table 4 are only approximate indicators of real income levels, because they are based on conversion of GNP to U.S. dollar equivalents at official exchange rates. It has been shown that this procedure tends to understate low-income countries' real incomes compared with the United States; it also appears that the lower the nominal income, the greater the relative understatement involved in the process. Thus according to Table 4, Italian per capita output was 27 per cent of U.S. levels. But when both Italian and U.S. output are measured at U.S. prices, the ratio rises to 48 per cent. The comparable figures for Germany are 54 and 73 per cent. See M. Gilbert and Associates, *Comparative National Products and Price Levels,* OEEC, Paris, 1957; M. Gilbert and Irving Kravis, *An International Comparison of National Products and the Purchasing Power of Currencies,* OEEC, Paris, 1954; Wilfred Beckerman, "International Comparison of Real Per Capita Consumption Levels," *Development Centre Studies No. 4,* OECD, Paris, 1965 (mimeo).

[17] For more detail on world commodity trade patterns, see Chapters 6 and 7. Also R. Cooper, *National Economic Policy;* GATT, *International Trade 1963,* Geneva, 1964.

[18] Using rank correlation methods, the coefficient of correlation between trade growth and GNP growth for the period 1950–64 is 0.43, significant at the .05 level. Using the more restrictive product-moment correlation, the coefficient is 0.65, significant at the .01 level. In other words, there is less than one chance in a hundred by correlation criteria that there was no significant association between Northern trade growth and GNP growth during the period. However, the association may well not be causal. For example, the fact that Germany had access to a plentiful labor supply from East Germany and Italy may be the primary factor accounting for both trade growth and GNP growth.

TABLE 4. Industrial Countries' GNP, 1950 and 1963

(1962 prices; countries listed in descending order of 1963 per capita GNP)

Country	Gross National Product ($ billions, U.S. equivalent) 1950	1963	GNP Per Capita ($ U.S. equivalent) 1950	1963
1. United States	371.9	577.0	2,442	3,048
2. Canada	23.6	39.2	1,725	2,076
3. Sweden	6.3	15.0	902	1,977
4. Switzerland	5.7	11.2	1,213	1,924
5. New Zealand	3.1	4.4	1,628	1,720
6. Australia	13.7	18.1	1,659	1,679
7. West Germany	36.1	91.5	753	1,652
8. Denmark	4.8	7.6	1,116	1,620
9. France	41.6	76.6	996	1,601
10. United Kingdom	54.5	82.9	1,077	1,552
11. Norway	3.4	5.6	1,030	1,516
12. Belgium-Luxembourg	9.2	14.0	1,033	1,453
13. Iceland	.16	.27	1,096	1,416
14. Finland	3.1	5.4	768	1,195
15. Netherlands	7.7	13.9	762	1,159
16. Austria	3.9	7.5	561	1,041
17. Italy	19.5	41.9	417	830
18. Ireland	1.7	2.2	562	784
19. Japan	18.2	59.2	220	617
20. South Africa	5.0	9.3	398	545
21. Greece	1.8	4.3	241	507
22. Spain	6.4	15.1	229	487
23. Portugal	1.6	2.9	190	322
24. Turkey	3.5	7.2	166	238
All Industrial Countries	646.5	1,110.60	1,122 [a]	1,640 [a]

Source: United Nations, *Yearbook of National Accounts Statistics,* various years.

Note: [a] Average per capita GNP.

TABLE 5. Growth by Region of GNP in Industrial Countries, 1950/52 to 1961/63

(per cent per year in constant 1962 prices; countries listed by region in descending order of national per capita growth)

	GNP Growth					
	1950/52 to 1955/57		*1955/57 to 1961/63*		*1950/52 to 1961/63*	
Country and region	*Total*	*Per Capita*	*Total*	*Per Capita*	*Total*	*Per Capita*
United States	3.4	1.7	2.7	1.1	3.1	1.4
Canada	4.2	1.5	3.1	0.8	3.6	1.1
North America, total	3.5	1.7	2.8	1.0	3.1	1.3
Germany	8.2	7.2	6.5	5.3	7.3	6.2
Greece	7.1	6.1	6.2	5.3	6.6	5.7
Italy	5.5	5.0	6.2	5.6	5.9	5.3
Spain	7.1	6.3	5.0	4.2	5.9	5.1
Austria	6.1	5.9	4.6	4.3	5.3	5.0
Portugal	4.3	3.9	5.3	4.7	4.9	4.3
Switzerland	4.6	3.4	5.8	3.9	5.3	3.7
France	4.6	3.7	4.7	3.6	4.6	3.6
Netherlands	5.7	4.5	4.1	2.7	4.8	3.5
Finland	3.9	2.8	4.8	3.9	4.4	3.4
Sweden	3.7	3.0	3.9	3.4	3.8	3.2
Denmark	2.5	1.8	5.0	4.3	3.9	3.2
Norway	3.8	2.8	3.7	2.9	3.8	2.9
Ireland	1.6	2.0	2.5	2.9	2.1	2.5
Belgium-Luxembourg	3.3	2.6	2.8	2.2	3.0	2.4
United Kingdom	2.7	2.4	2.7	2.2	2.7	2.3
Turkey	5.0	2.2	4.8	1.9	4.9	2.1
Iceland	4.9	2.8	2.4	0.3	3.5	1.4
Western Europe, total	4.9	4.0	4.7	3.7	4.8	3.8
Japan	7.1	5.8	10.2	9.3	8.8	7.7
South Africa	5.3	3.0	4.5	2.0	4.9	2.4
Australia	1.7	(−0.5)	4.0	1.9	3.0	0.8
New Zealand	2.2	(−0.4)	3.6	1.5	3.0	0.8
Australia, South Africa, New Zealand, total	2.8	0.4	4.1	1.7	3.5	1.1
Industrial Countries, total	4.1	2.8	3.8	2.5	3.9	2.6

Source: Computed from United Nations, *Yearbook of National Accounts Statistics* and *Demographic Yearbook*, various years.

TABLE 6. Trade Levels and Trade Growth by Region, Industrial Countries, 1950/52 to 1961/64

(countries listed in descending order of export growth)

Country and region	*Export Value ($ billions)* 1950	1964	*"Real" Export Growth*[a] *1950/52 to 1961/64 (per cent per year)*
United States	10.3	26.6	5.0
Canada	3.1	8.1	3.9
North America, total	13.4	34.7	4.7
Germany	2.0	16.2	14.7
Italy	1.2	6.0	12.6
Austria	0.3	1.4	9.3
Netherlands	1.4	5.8	9.3
Iceland	0.03	0.11	8.3
Switzerland	0.9	2.6	8.1
Denmark	0.7	2.1	8.0
Belgium-Luxembourg	1.7	5.6	6.8
Norway	0.4	1.3	6.3
Spain	0.4	1.0	6.2[b]
Sweden	1.1	3.7	6.1
France	3.0	9.0	4.8
United Kingdom	6.4	12.3	4.4
Portugal	0.2	0.5	3.6
Turkey	0.3	0.4	3.6
Greece	0.1	0.3	3.5
Finland	0.4	1.3	3.1
Western Europe, total	20.5	69.6	7.8
Japan	0.8	6.7	15.6
South Africa	0.6	1.5	5.3
New Zealand	0.5	1.1	2.4
Australia	1.7	3.0	2.3
Australia, New Zealand, South Africa, total	2.8	5.6	3.0
Industrial Countries, total	37.5	116.6	

Source: Computed from United Nations, *Yearbook of International Trade Statistics,* various years.

Notes: [a] Export values divided by import price index (1962=100).

[b] 10.1 per cent for the period 1955/57 to 1961/64; 1.0 per cent, 1950/52 to 1955/57.

The same results are evident from inspection of Tables 5 and 6; it can be seen there that all of the countries that experienced rapid income growth also experienced rapid trade growth. Correlation is no proof of causation, and it may be that the income growth was the cause of the trade growth, or that both caused each other, or that both were caused by other factors. But there is evidence that trade competitiveness was a major factor in accounting for differences in European growth rates. The dominant element in the growth of that trade has been intra-Northern exchanges of manufactured products. Atlantic Community exports of manufactures rose from $33 billion in 1953 (62 per cent of total exports) to $70 billion in 1963 (68 per cent of total).

Another striking development has been the rapid growth of EEC trade. From 1955 to 1964, members' exports grew at the rate of 9.9 per cent a year, half again as fast as Northern trade in the aggregate; and EEC countries' trade with each other, as would be expected, rose even more rapidly—at the rate of 12.5 per cent. EEC countries' income growth also exceeds the Northern average.

Exports to LDC's played a small and declining role in Northern trade, accounting for only 22 per cent of Northern exports in 1963, as compared with 27 per cent a decade before. This combination of slow growth of North-South trade and rapid growth in North-North trade, mainly in manufactures, naturally implied an increasing role for manufactured goods in world trade. Exports of manufactures rose from 45 per cent of world trade in 1953 to 55 per cent in 1963. This development (or what it stands for in Southern eyes) is significant in explaining LDC demands for a greater export role in world trade in industrial products.

Not only was the North increasingly its own best customer, but it also appeared in Southern eyes to be consciously moving ever more in that direction. The work of GATT and OECD in removing trade barriers has primarily benefited the North, both as a producer and as a consumer. This follows naturally from the larger role played in the North by manufacturing production and consumption, relative to total output and demand. Liberalization measures have primarily affected trade in industrial products, where the South offers both little competition as a producer (because it is underdeveloped) and a small market as a consumer (thanks to low incomes, protectionism, and foreign exchange restrictions). Viewed in this light, the Kennedy Round of tariff negotiations offers little psychological appeal to the South, whatever the actual effects on its trade of a general tariff reduction for manufactures may prove to be.

Finally, of the differences in economic structure among industrial countries, the most important for our subject are those that affect North-South trade. For a variety of reasons—partly geographical or historical, reflecting the course of empire; partly structural, reflecting a comparative disadvantage in commodity production; and partly political—there is a great variation among Northern countries' trade interests in LDC's. Northern exports by area for 1963 are shown in Table 7.

Relative to its total trade, LDC's are particularly important to Japan. Among other major Northern areas, North America has the next largest proportion of trade with the South (26 per cent of the North American total) and the largest absolute value, $15.5 billion of exports and imports combined in 1963. A significant portion of the exports is financed by U.S. foreign aid, including surplus food disposal.

Latin America is the most important Southern region in North American trade, accounting for about half of the region's total trade with the South. Southern exports to North America have increased more slowly than to other regions; North America accounted for 27 per cent of LDC exports in 1953 and only 21 per cent a decade later.

For EEC and EFTA, the South plays a relatively small trade role. One-fifth of EFTA exports and one-sixth of EEC's go to underdeveloped countries. For both groups, Africa is the best customer among LDC regions. Asia is also a major buyer of EFTA exports. In both cases, the trade pattern seems to follow the colonial heritage. Despite the increasing role of intra-Community trade, EEC has been second only to Japan in the growth of its imports from the South and has in recent years imported more from there than has any other Northern region. EFTA's record in this respect is somewhat less impressive, reflecting slower growth of output and demand, particularly in the United Kingdom.

The growing importance of Western Europe and Japan as buyers from LDC's is a natural consequence of the economic structure of these industrial areas, based on imports of food and raw materials and interchange of specialized manufactures. For any given increase in GNP, they tend to increase their imports from the South more than countries that are also major commodity exporters such as the United States, Australia and Canada. To this extent, Europe and Japan have a stronger common trade interest with LDC's than the mere recital of statistics would imply.

This is particularly true for Japan. The interest stems not only from economic complementarity, as represented by the high levels of Japanese-LDC trade, but also from potential competitiveness. Japan relies on exports of a number of manufactured goods—notably textiles, plastics, and a range of light manufactures—that many LDC's also hope to develop for export. Should any of the preferential schemes discussed in Chapter 6 be adopted, Japan might well suffer substantial export loss unless she could readjust her pattern of production and trade.

For most of the North, however, the opening generalizations of this chapter apply to a greater or lesser degree. Their present economic stake in the LDC's is rather small. Trade with other industrial countries is dominant, and for that reason, also dominates the attention of policymakers, as discussed in Chapters 6 and 7. The result, as might be expected, is that trade benefits to the South are considered in fact, if not always in speeches, as incidental to the main purposes of Northern commercial policy.

Trends in the Underdeveloped Countries

Despite the great variety in economic structure, growth, and trade interest among the Atlantic Community countries, they are relatively homogeneous, compared with the 100 underdeveloped countries of Asia, Africa, and Latin America. The LDC's considered here range in population from less than a half million to more than 450 million; and in per capita income, at exchange rate equivalents, from $40 to nearly $500.[19] Table 8 ranks underdeveloped countries by per capita income and region for the year 1963.

Several points are worth noting from the table. First, many of the countries are small. Of the 90 countries listed, 72 have less than 15 million population; and 51 have less than 5 million. Therefore, trade is of great importance to most of them. They are too small to produce a full line of products, particularly of machinery and equipment.

Statistical testing of hypotheses about LDC's is a perilous procedure, because the basic data are poor. However, using rank correlation

[19] A few countries listed in the table—Kuwait, Israel, Cyprus, Venezuela, Puerto Rico, Trinidad, Argentina—exceed the $500 per capita income level. They interest us here primarily as success stories or as special cases in other ways.

TABLE 7. Industrial Countries' Trade with LDC's, by Area, 1963
(*$ billions*)

A. INDUSTRIAL COUNTRIES' EXPORTS

Exports from ↓ *Exports to* →	*Africa*	*Latin America*	*Middle East*	*Asia (excl. Japan)*	*All LDC's* [a]
North America	1,060	3,350	860	2,640	7,770
EEC	2,960	1,500	1,250	1,130	6,330
EFTA	1,890	800	970	1,380	4,520
Australia, New Zealand, South Africa	204	30	50	295	720
Japan	470	720	240	1,610	2,550
Total	6,720	6,130	3,490	7,110	22,260

B. LDC EXPORTS

Exports from ↓ *Exports to* →	*North America*	*EEC*	*EFTA*	*Japan*	*Australia, New Zealand, South Africa*	*All Industrial Countries* [a]
Africa	750	3,240	1,670	215	125	6,180
Latin America	3,710	2,030	1,050	420	37	7,490
Middle East	500	1,930	1,110	550	120	4,630
Asia (excl. Japan)	1,430	885	1,160	1,015	150	4,970
Total [a]	6,740	7,660	4,810	2,100	810	22,930

Source: United Nations, *Monthly Bulletin of Statistics,* March 1965.
Note: [a] Total includes some exporting and importing countries not included in subtotals.

methods, it can be shown that small countries, developed or not, are generally more dependent on trade than large ones.[20]

The general point seems clear: the smaller the national population, the greater the dependence on trade, providing the market economy plays any significant role. Thus the South, with a preponderance of small countries, places great stress in UNCTAD and elsewhere, on measures aimed at expanding trade.

A second point emerges from the table. Regional differences are very great. By African and Asian standards, Latin American countries (except Haiti, Bolivia and Paraguay) are prosperous. Of the 30 African LDC's listed, only four—Libya, Algeria, Ghana, and Southern Rhodesia—approach the Latin American average. In the Near East and Asia, only Malaysia and Lebanon (and Kuwait where 400,000 people have the highest per capita income of any country) attain Latin American averages.

Third, population size seems to be unrelated to per capita income levels, both between and within regions. For 62 countries, I have tested the hypothesis that there is no relation between population and per capita GNP. Neither for developed countries, nor for undeveloped ones, by region or in total, is there any significant correlation;[21] and it is therefore impossible to refute the hypothesis on the basis of this statistical test.

This finding has an interesting corollary. On *a priori* grounds, we would be inclined to believe that if there were no trade, population would be correlated with per capita income. As population increases, economies of scale become possible in more industries, other things being equal. As real unit costs fall, per capita income increases. This is a partial analysis of course, because other things, including resource endowments, may not be equal. Chapters 3 and 4 discuss some of the theoretical possibilities. Unless national population is negatively correlated with resource endowments, skills, or other wealth-creating factors, however, then the lack of correlation between

[20] For all 24 developed countries, there was a negative correlation of —0.73 between population and exports plus imports as per cent of GNP (1961–64 data). This was statistically significant at the .01 level. For 21 Latin American countries, the correlation was also negative (—0.58), significant at the .01 level. For 8 Far Eastern countries, the correlation was —.59, significant only at the 0.1 level. It was not possible to collect enough data for a valid test of Africa and the Middle East. Combining the data for the two regions gave a sample of sixteen countries, producing a correlation of —.62 between population and the trade-GNP ratio, significant at the .02 level.

[21] The same conclusions apply for both product-moment and rank correlation.

TABLE 8. Estimates of Gross National Product in Underdeveloped Countries, by Region, 1963

($ equivalent at current prices and exchange rates; countries listed in decreasing order of per capita GNP by region)

Country and region	GNP (*$ millions*)	GNP *per capita ($)*	*Population, 1963 (millions)*
A. AFRICA			
Libya	450	359	1.3
Ghana	1,640	226	7.2
Rhodesia (Southern)	878	219	4.0
Senegal	674	200	3.4
Gabon	90	200	0.5
Ivory Coast	720	196	3.7
Algeria	2,000	185	10.8
Tunisia	833	185	4.5
Morocco	2,200	173	12.7
Liberia	176	170	1.0
Zambia	535	153	3.5
Congo (Brazzaville)	144	150	1.0
Mauritania	105	135	0.8
Sierra Leone	219	100	2.2
Sudan	1,285	110	12.8
Nigeria	3,870	93	41.8
Cameroon	400	92	4.4
Central African Republic	116	90	1.3
Malagasy Republic	530	90	5.9
Kenya	787	89	8.8
Congo (Leopoldville)	1,216	80	15.1
Other Africa (13 countries and colonies)	5,563	65	85.2
Total Africa	24,431	105 [b]	231.9
B. MIDDLE EAST			
Kuwait	1,122	3,000	0.4
Israel	2,640	1,111	2.4
Cyprus	365	620	0.6
Lebanon	750	383	2.0
Iraq	1,566	228	6.9
Other Middle East	471	223	2.1
Iran	4,790	216	22.2
Jordan	360	199	1.8
Saudi Arabia	1,120	175	6.4

TABLE 8. (*Continued*)

Country and region	*GNP (\$ millions)*	*GNP per capita (\$)*	*Population, 1963 (millions)*
B. MIDDLE EAST			
Syria	800	148	5.4
U.A.R.	3,900	139	28.0
Yemen	360	90	4.0
Total Middle East	18,244	222 [b]	82.1
C. ASIA			
Hong Kong	1,320	367	3.6
Malaysia	3,180	295	10.7
Taiwan	2,041	169	12.1
Ceylon	1,512	142	10.6
Cambodia	750	127	5.9
South Vietnam	1,740	114	15.3
South Korea	3,070	114	26.9
Thailand	3,130	106	29.6
Laos	210	87	2.4
India	40,000	86	467.0
Pakistan	8,828	81	109.4
Afghanistan	1,100	80	13.8
Indonesia	8,065	80	100.8
Burma	1,715	72	23.7
Nepal	573	59	9.7
Total Asia	77,214	92 [b]	841.5
D. LATIN AMERICA			
Puerto Rico	2,900	952	2.5
Venezuela	5,987	728	8.2
Trinidad	585	630	0.9
Argentina	12,873	614	21.0
Chile	3,930	483	8.1
Uruguay	1,420	478	3.0
Panama	525	448	1.2
Jamaica	750	429	1.7
Mexico	15,375	402	38.3
Colombia	4,700	292	16.1
Central America— (Costa Rica, El Salvador, Guatemala, Honduras, Nicaragua)	3,275	281	11.6

TABLE 8. (*Continued*)

Country and region D. LATIN AMERICA	*GNP ($ millions)*	*GNP per capita ($)*	*Population, 1963 (millions)*
Dominican Republic	900	269	3.3
Peru	2,845	262	10.8
Ecuador	940	199	4.7
Brazil	15,160	196	77.3
Paraguay	358	193	1.9
Bolivia	625	154	4.1
Haiti	355	80	4.4
Other Latin America	930	358	2.6
Total Latin America	74,433	333 [b]	221.8
Total LDC's [a]	194,322	141 [b]	1,377.3

Source: Agency for International Development, unpublished data.
Notes: [a] Excludes Mainland China, North Vietnam, Mongolia, Cuba, North Korea.
[b] Average.

population and per capita income implies that trade is likely to be more important to the development of countries with small populations. The negative correlation between population and trade as a percentage of GNP accounts in effect for the fact that size of country doesn't influence income levels. The world market is a substitute for import-substitution, which is one reason for the importance of trade in economic development.

There is a final point worth noting from Table 8. Differences in income among LDC's are very great. Therefore, the differences in their economic structures are also substantial, and it is not to be expected that adoption of any given economic policy will benefit all developing countries. The rather wide range of measures recommended at UNCTAD should be viewed therefore not simply as a grab-bag of Southern demands, but as an effort to meet the needs of countries as disparate as Argentina, Ghana, India and Lebanon. One of the most persistent errors in discussions of trade and aid policies toward the South is the tendency to reject proposals because they would benefit only a few LDC's, not the South as a whole. There is no trade policy that can benefit all LDC's equally. The differences among them are too great. These structural differences underlie the South's demand for many forms of concessions, rather than one or a few.

Differences in economic structure are discussed in more detail in Chapters 6 and 7. The following review is limited to the general trends in economic growth and in trade. Variations in growth rates in developing countries are substantial, as Table 9 shows.[22] Latin America and Africa lag behind the Near East and Far East in per capita income growth. Population increases, while rapid in all LDC's, are particularly striking in Latin America and the Far East—they are now more than twice the rate of Northern population increase.

TABLE 9. GNP Growth Rates, 1957/58 to 1963/64

(per cent)

	Rate of GNP Growth	*Rate of GNP Growth Per Capita*	*Rate of Population Growth*
All LDC's	4.5	2.1	2.4
Latin America	4.1	1.3	2.8
Near East	5.5	3.2	2.3
South Asia	4.4	2.1	2.3
Far East	5.6	2.8	2.8
Africa	3.4	1.1	2.3
All Industrial Countries	4.4	3.1	1.3
Europe	4.8	3.8	1.0
United States	3.7	2.1	1.6

Source: Estimates prepared by Agency for International Development, 1965; reproduced in OECD, *Development Assistance Efforts and Policies, 1965 Review,* OECD, Paris, 1965, p. 22.

The variation among individual LDC's is naturally greater than that among regions. Some countries have had virtually no improvement in per capita living standards in recent years. In certain cases (such as Argentina, Morocco, Indonesia, Malawi, Algeria, Paraguay, Costa Rica), the population may on the average be worse off economically than a decade ago.

Meanwhile, other countries have maintained rapid rates of economic growth per capita, despite population trends. The outstanding

[22] These figures (particularly those for Africa) are rough approximations. They also exclude Communist countries as well as Algeria, Indonesia and Congo for which no data are available.

examples, for which there are reasonably good data, are Israel, Jordan, Taiwan, Thailand, Peru, Trinidad. Among the larger countries, income in Brazil, Mexico, and Pakistan increased faster than others. Table 10 gives a ranking for the period 1957–58 to 1963–64.

When we attempt to isolate the sources of growth in those LDC's that have grown fast, no single pattern emerges. Some countries have received an important stimulus from foreign aid. They include Israel, Jordan, and Taiwan. Israel, where income has grown at the rate of 10 per cent annually from 1950–52 to 1961–63, has benefited from a variety of factors: a skilled and trained labor force, large inflows of foreign aid and reparations, playing a dual role of financing imports and investment. Exports increased tenfold during the period, and domestic capital formation grew by nearly 11 per cent a year.

For Jordan, foreign aid has been a major factor in growth. Others include growth of agricultural production, aided by favorable weather in recent years; steady income from tourism; and the development of some import-substituting domestic industry. Taiwan's economy has also evolved very rapidly, at the rate of 7 per cent annually since 1950. The economy was then primarily agricultural. Less than 10 per cent of GNP in 1950 came from industry, which now rivals agriculture in importance. Foreign aid and the post-1950 influx from the mainland were the initial stimuli.

In other cases, such as Peru, Trinidad, Mexico, Thailand, and Iraq, foreign aid was not a propulsive force. Peruvian growth (5.1 per cent annually from 1950–52) was compounded of export expansion for fishmeal, sugar, cotton, and copper, and growth of import-substituting industry. Trinidad's growth (7.6 per cent annually since 1955–57) reflects tourism and petroleum exports. Mexico maintained a 5.6 per cent growth rate during the decade ending 1961–63. The principal factors have been rapid industrialization, growth of a varied line of exports, and a profitable tourist trade. Thailand, increasing its exports of rice, corn, and tin to compensate for declining rubber exports, has also been able to develop domestic manufacturing; but there seems to have been a steady growth in all sectors, with no one element dominating. Iraq, representative of several small Middle Eastern countries, owes its progress to oil exports.

If anything emerges from such a mixed record, it is the inability of any single formula to explain economic growth, or its absence, in the South. It seems reasonably clear that sustained and violent domestic political and social turmoil is not compatible with continued economic growth. But such growth can stem from a number of different elements, including import-substituting industry, development of traditional exports or new ones (including tourist expenditures), foreign aid, and improvements in agriculture. Each country, despite important elements in common, is to some extent unique.

The UNCTAD resolutions and the report of its Secretary-General

TABLE 10. GNP Growth and Trade Growth, Fast-Growing LDC's, 1950/52 to 1961/64

(annual increases; countries listed in decreasing order of GNP growth)

Country	*GNP Growth Rate (per cent)*	*Trade Growth* [b] *(per cent)* *Imports*	*Exports*
Populations under 10 million			
Israel	10.0	6.0	17.0
Jordan	9.8 [a]	10.5	13.1
Iraq	8.4	9.7	11.7
Trinidad	7.6 [a]	9.2	9.6
Jamaica	7.0	9.4	12.3
Venezuela	6.7	1.4	4.2
Puerto Rico	5.6	9.1	10.0
Nicaragua	5.3	8.1	7.2
Ghana	5.3	7.6	3.0
Populations over 20 million			
Mexico	5.6	4.7	3.7
Brazil	5.6	1.6	−2.1
Thailand	5.4	12.6	4.9
Philippines	5.4	3.8	3.7
Burma	5.2	−1.1	3.5
Turkey	4.9	2.9	3.6

Source: Computed from UN data.

Notes: [a] 1955/57 to 1961/64.

[b] Corrected for terms of trade changes, 1962 = 100.

stressed inadequate command over imports as the major factor in slow growth. While there is evidence to support this claim, an examination of all the facts supports a somewhat more complex interpretation.

First, sustained economic growth is almost always associated with at least some growth of imports, often financed in part by foreign capital. There have been a few exceptions in modern times, necessarily associated with major efforts at import substitution. But to cite the exceptions, such as Brazil, the Soviet Union, and possibly Australia in recent years, only stresses the special conditions required—a large domestic market and a varied natural resource base.

Second, the smaller the country, the greater the need for trade growth as a condition of income growth. Small countries (less than 10 million population) that grow fast *always* have a rapid growth of imports. Table 10 shows the relationship for countries with average annual income growth of more than 5 per cent where data are available for the period 1950–52 to 1961–63.

In most cases, import growth is somewhat faster than income growth for small countries. The principal exceptions are Venezuela, where changes in oil company imports of capital equipment have been an important source of variation; and Israel, faced with serious trade deficits and aided by capital inflows and a rapidly growing home market for import-substituting industry and agriculture.

Third, rapid import growth is not a necessary condition for rapid income growth, where the market is large enough to allow domestic industrialization, or substitution of domestic for imported commodities. Thus, as shown in Table 10, Mexico's income grew at the rate of 5.6 per cent, while imports increased at the rate of 4.7 per cent. For the Philippines the comparable figures are 5.4 per cent and 3.8 per cent. In Brazil and Burma, imports actually declined over the period.

In sum, rapid peacetime growth of imports has been a sufficient condition for the growth of income in the South, but not a necessary one. The reasons for the association are clear. Steady growth of imports is financed either by an equivalent export growth or a capital transfer. In the latter case, the recipient benefits from increased investment without the immediate need for corresponding savings. The continuation of such a transfer normally means that private or public investors in the North are confident of the capital importer's economic potential.[23] If the import increase is largely export-financed, as is the case for most of the small countries of Table 10, then it implies that the country is able to compete effectively in world markets, and is presumably in a favorable growth situation.

If, on the other hand, a developing country finds itself unable or

[23] Of course, the motive for the transfer may be political. In extreme cases (Vietnam, Korea), long-term potential is virtually irrelevant. Cf. Chapter 1 above.

unwilling to finance steady import increases by exports or borrowing, the record shows that rapid growth may still be possible *if* the domestic market is large enough and the resources and organization are present to permit large-scale import substituting investment. In such cases, the close relationship between trade and growth recently observed in the North no longer holds, and import substitution becomes the leading sector in growth.

Some economic writing insists that the trade-development relationship is essential to growth (see Chapters 3 and 4). In fact, the world allows a variety of sources of growth; a high and fast growing level of trade is perhaps indispensable only for small nations or those with a particularly uneven distribution of resources. The combined populations of 70 developing nations with less than ten million inhabitants each do not equal half the population of India, but they exercise together a disproportionate political weight in international forums. This fact has shaped the nature of the UNCTAD recommendations, particularly its insistence on the international element in growth.

UNCTAD AND THE BALANCE OF INTERESTS

With Northern per capita incomes already a dozen times as large as those of the South, and with the disparity still increasing thanks to rapid population increases in the South, the developing countries as a group see little cause for rejoicing, despite their own acknowledged gains, in the great expansion of world income and trade that has marked the years since the end of World War II. The United Nations Conference on Trade and Development, convened in Geneva from March to June 1964, provided the South with a forum to codify its objections to the existing system. The measure of Southern dissatisfaction is found not only in the program proposed in its Final Act, but also in the establishment of the Conference as a permanent United Nations organization. The principal existing institutions dealing with trade, the General Agreement on Tariffs and Trade (GATT) and the Organization for Economic Cooperation and Development (OECD), were considered to represent the trade interests of industrial countries rather than those of the South.

The pattern of commercial policy established by the North after the post-war reconstruction consisted of:

1. Reduction of tariffs on manufactured products on a most-favored-nation basis (no discrimination among trading partners) through bargaining in the framework of GATT.

2. Maintenance of controls over trade in agricultural products, to protect domestic farm prices and incomes.

3. Creation of customs unions and free trade areas which served partly to increase trade among members of these blocs, and also, by increasing their incomes and demand, to increase their extra-bloc trade.

4. Opposition to systems, other than customs unions and free trade areas, designed to increase some countries' trade at the expense of others. The beliefs underlying the system essentially reflect a liberal trade bias in the North, modified by the political pressures evoked by high-cost agriculture and by certain weak or declining industries.

The UNCTAD rejected both the underlying rationale and the policies themselves. The theoretical critique of the existing system was provided by the Secretary-General of the Conference, Raul Prebisch, in his report, *Towards a New Trade Policy for Development*. His argument can be summarized as follows:

1. Underdeveloped countries cannot grow at a satisfactory rate (5 per cent annually) unless they can dispose of more foreign exchange.

2. Free trade cannot do the job because the North's imports of Southern primary commodities increase too slowly as the North's incomes grow. Nor is domestic industrialization a remedy. LDC domestic markets are too small, and most of the easy forms of import substitution have been adopted already.

3. Removal of agricultural protection in the North would be helpful, but not decisive, because world demand for commodities is increasing too slowly. There is a long-term tendency for the terms of trade to turn against Southern agriculture, thanks to the influence of monopoly elements in Northern labor and industry.[24]

4. The solution to this "trade gap" problem lies in four kinds of measures (in addition to the traditional method of granting increased access to Northern markets by lowering trade barriers that must affect the South):

a. Granting of temporary tariff preferences in Northern markets to Southern manufactured products. This subsidy will help the South compensate for its small markets and initial high cost. There is an

[24] See Chapter 4 below for exposition of this theory.

analogy to infant industry protection for newly established industries, except that the protection in this case involves a transfer of income internationally rather than domestically, and still requires the beneficiaries to compete with domestic producers in preference-granting countries.

b. Establishing customs unions and free trade areas among underdeveloped countries. This will enlarge the market and contribute to greater specialization and economies of scale.

c. Organizing commodity markets to assure higher prices for Southern staple exports. This is designed to help compensate for the alleged deterioration of LDC terms of trade, and is to some extent the counterpart of domestic farm-price fixing in the North, except that once more the transfer is international.

d. Establishment of a fund to compensate LDC's for long-term declines in export earnings when they fall below some agreed level. This will enable them to plan and carry out development programs with the assurance that foreign exchange will be available.

Prebisch specifically rejects currency devaluation as a method of increasing exports, decreasing imports and narrowing the trade gap, because it means that the cost of export subsidy would have to be borne by LDC's rather than by the North which is better able to afford it.

The Secretary General's report was endorsed by all the developing countries. Much of its substance found its way into the Final Act of the Conference, thanks to the majority bloc of 77 votes that the South was able to summon for virtually all resolutions presented.

The North was much less enthusiastic, viewing the Prebisch proposals both as an attempt to break up a trading system that had served Northern interests well; and as a demand for additional North-South income transfers. Some industrial countries, notably France, backed the demands for organization of commodity markets and tariff preferences, while others voted for the measures, or abstained, confident that United States opposition would prevent any of the resolutions from taking effect. The United States, intentionally or unwittingly, put itself in the position of leading the opposition to virtually all the LDC-sponsored resolutions, in some cases standing forth as the sole opponent.

The Final Act in effect rejects the non-interventionist, non-discriminating principles of GATT, and proposes a positive, or—more accurately—interventionist role for trade policy:

. . . it is essential that the flows of world trade should help to eliminate the wide economic disparities among nations. The international community must combine its efforts to ensure that all countries—regardless of size, of wealth, or economic and social system—enjoy the benefits of international trade for their economic development and social progress.[25]

The rejection of the existing system, with its stated aim of offering no special privileges, is categorical:

. . . it is essential that action be taken by both the developing and the developed countries . . . to raise the level and accelerate the rate of growth of earnings of the developing countries from trade, as a means of helping them to overcome their persistent external imbalance.

(UNCTAD) was convened in order to provide . . . solutions to the problems of world trade in the interest of all peoples and particularly to the urgent trade and development problems of the developing countries.[26]

The preamble of the report goes on to discuss trade and development in much the same terms as the Secretary-General's report. The developing countries have failed to participate in the post-war expansion of trade; volume of trade has increased slowly and terms of trade have been unfavorable. They have therefore been unable to import the capital goods they need for development, and growth has been held back. Stable commodity prices and increased exports of manufactured goods are needed to assure an appropriate change in the present structure of international trade; the root of the existing problem is excessive dependence on primary commodities. The appropriate remedy is to adopt a set of measures, which are, in effect, the Prebisch proposals cited above.

The body of the Final Act, as voted item-by-item at Geneva, consists of seven sections: I. General and Special Principles; II. International Commodity Problems; III. Trade in Manufactures and Semi-Manufactures; IV. Financing for Expansion of International Trade; V. Institutional Arrangements; VI. Special Problems; VII. Program of Work.[27] As noted above, this text represents the views of a voting bloc of 77 LDC's, modified in some instances by the desire to reach a

[25] Preamble to the Final Act of the United Nations Conference on Trade and Development, reprinted in United Nations, *Proceedings of the United Nations Conference on Trade and Development,* New York, 1964, Vol. 1.

[26] *Ibid.,* p. 4.

[27] Text is reprinted in UNCTAD, *Proceedings,* Vol. I, pp. 3–16.

workable compromise with the North whose cooperation would be essential for the success of the resolutions.[28]

The General Principles are a series of fifteen generally unexceptionable statements, stressing the importance of supporting economic development in the South and of using trade and aid as devices toward this goal. The United States, for reasons that are not always clear, abstained or voted against eleven of them.

The eleven Special Principles endorsed (in face of lonely U.S. opposition or abstention on nine) a series of policies including:

1. Establishment of North-South trade targets;

2. Infant industry protection in the South;

3. Recommendations aimed at maintaining markets for LDC commodities in the North in face of agricultural protection, competition from synthetics, and surplus commodity dumping;

4. Establishment of a fund to compensate LDC's for terms of trade declines;

5. Increases in multilateral economic aid, and easing of terms of bilateral aid, with provision for repayment in local currency or merchandise;

6. Endorsement of measures to improve LDC balance of payments on service account (shipping, insurance, tourism, and so on).

The last five sections of the Final Act reflect the work of the Conference's main committees, on commodities, manufactures, financial aspects, institutions, and principles for international trade. Section II endorses the principle of international commodity agreements, aimed at raising low prices, stabilizing those that fluctuate, increasing Northern imports, and adjusting world production and consumption. Measures to be taken include removal of obstacles to commodity trade (tariffs, quantitative restrictions, and agricultural protections in general). There are also a series of recommendations on promotional measures for commodity trade; encouragement of South-South commodity trade; promotion of world food aid; research and policies aimed at meeting competition from synthetics; studies of the organization of world commodity trade. An analysis of these issues is reserved for Chapter 7 of this study.

Section III, on manufactures, proposes establishing a new United Nations agency for industrial development; measures to promote ex-

[28] The Soviet bloc played a minor role, voting with the South when its own economic interests were not at stake, and abstaining or voting against when it was asked to make significant aid or trade concessions.

port industries in the South; endorsement of tariff reductions and removals of other trade obstacles to LDC manufactured exports; further study of trade preferences for LDC's; cooperation among LDC's in promoting South-South trade in manufactures. Chapter 6 below discusses these topics.

Section IV, on financial arrangements and invisible items in the balance of payments, endorsed a series of guidelines for foreign aid, which generally supported planning, multilateral institutions, flexible aid conditions, and continuity in aid; several resolutions aimed at increasing the flow of aid and reducing debt service burdens, including establishment of a U.N. Capital Development Fund and consideration of an interest subsidy scheme for multilateral loans to LDC's; promotion of Northern private investment in the South; study of a system of compensatory finance for LDC's whose export proceeds fall below reasonable expectations; resolutions aimed at improving LDC's earnings from shipping, insurance, tourism, and the conditions of access to new technology. Chapter 8, below, examines some of these proposals.

Section V provides for establishment of UNCTAD as a permanent organ of the General Assembly, meeting at three-year intervals. There shall also be a permanent Trade and Development Board of 55 members (22 from Asia, Africa and the Middle East, 18 from the Atlantic Community, 9 from Latin America, 6 from Eastern Europe) providing for an LDC majority on the Board. The voting machinery, as actually established, also calls for a conciliation procedure to make sure that proposals voted by the Board take adequate account of minority interests. Finally, the new institution will have its own secretariat, which will carry out the program of studies voted by the conference. Mr. Prebisch was appointed as first Secretary-General of the UNCTAD in 1965.

Section VI provides for miscellaneous matters, including a proposed convention for land-locked countries' transit trade; an organization to support the interests of countries exporting depleting resources, such as minerals; encouragement of long-term North-South trade agreements; and for a program of studies on trade and development and related subjects. Section VII, the program of work, is a list of studies and other actions voted in the preceding sections.

The strongest impression that emerged from the conference was the breadth and depth of the gulf that separated Northern and Southern views of aid and trade policy. There was a certain agreement about objectives, but at a level of generality so broad as to be virtually devoid of practical significance. There is no difficulty in agreeing that it is desirable to promote the growth of Southern income and trade through international action; the difficulty lies in agreeing on means. To the South, this meant a reorientation of world trade policy away from the GATT principle of non-discrimination, and toward a policy of using trade as a device for increasing the amount of North-South income transfers. In Southern eyes, non-discriminatory trade is largely a method of perpetuating the economic dominance of the North and the poverty of the South.

Northern views were less than unanimous, except on one issue; neither the Atlantic countries nor the Soviet bloc was willing to commit itself to increasing its aid to poor countries, except in expressions of good will that implied no necessary commitment. In respect to the major specific issues raised at the conference—higher commodity prices, preferences, compensatory finance, removal of tariff and non-tariff barriers to LDC exports—a number of developed countries, generally trailed by a reluctant and often obdurate United States, were willing to accept the principles. This willingness may have been more apparent than real. France, for example, presented its own ambitious program for income transfers, including a large scale surplus food grant, high prices for tropical crops, preferences for manufactures (selective as to product and country), and regional economic unions for LDC's.[29] However, the French government was presumably aware that U.S. and British opposition would prevent any action being taken to implement those measures that would be most costly to the North. In fact, the French proposal was widely regarded by North and South alike at UNCTAD as being primarily a propaganda document.

Similarly, several nations, including Japan, stated that they would be willing to participate in a system of tariff preferences toward the South if other industrial nations also cooperated. In view of the well-advertised U.S. reluctance to endorse preferences, such good will gestures were harmless. This was particularly welcome to Japan, which is perhaps the only Northern country that might face significant loss of markets from a preferential system favoring LDC's.

From the Southern viewpoint, the principal accomplishments of

[29] "Memorandum Concerning Certain Items on the Agenda of the United Nations Conference on Trade and Development," reprinted UNCTAD, *Proceedings,* Vol. VI, pp. 18–27.

UNCTAD were the opportunities to make a formal presentation of a new approach to world trade and aid policies; to obtain a permanent forum where they could campaign for acceptance of their program; and to work together as a unified group to bring pressure on the North. In Northern eyes, the accomplishments were less clear, because their goals were largely defensive: politically, to appear sympathetic with developmental aims; economically, to avoid making concessions that would cost money, hurt producer interests, or change the existing multilateral trading system. In the political sphere, the success was dubious. Economically, the North was more successful, at least for the time; it made no significant material concessions but only promised to study issues. Whether these studies combined with LDC pressure will lead to actual policy changes remains to be seen.

UNCTAD gave clear expression to three different conceptions of the international economy, in addition to the Soviet view. Two of them are advanced by countries that are reasonably content with their present level and share of the world's income. First there were the multilateral, liberal-trade advocates, led by the United States, Britain, and Japan. The second view was that of the regional free trade bloc system of the EEC, led by France, seeking to use trade concessions as a method of creating and maintaining political ties. The third viewpoint is that of the South, expressed in the Final Act. Profoundly dissatisfied with the present distribution of world income, it seeks to transform the world trading system into an agent of its efforts to obtain parity of income. There is an obvious analogy to the efforts of the farmers in the North, who also use public policy as an agent of their income parity goals.

It does not seem likely that the South will succeed with Northern governments in the way that Northern farmers have. In economic policy, governments still maintain too much of a mercantilist heritage to adopt such policies willingly; while politically, such concessions to the South find very little support from Northern interest groups and, on the other hand, face considerable opposition from those producers who would be hurt. However, there are also forces in the North that favor concessions to the South for political and social reasons, and the long-run outcome is not predictable.

There is no objective answer as to which of these ways of molding the world economy is the best one. First, we would have to answer the question, "Best for whom?" Once that is decided, the answer is still elusive; economic theory tells us a good deal about efficient use of resources but offers no definitive theory of the relationship among trade policy, economic growth, and different versions of equity.

The U.S. delegation has been sharply criticized both for its inability to offer constructive alternatives and for the consistent record of negative votes on General and Special Principles. There is a good deal to these criticisms, but they have been overdrawn. There is a natural consequence of the fact that many of the resolutions were worked out by negotiation. Negative votes stand out clearly in the record, while positive accomplishments fail to stand out from the façade of unanimity.

The negative appearance of the U.S. voting record resulted from several factors. First, even the most innocuous-sounding principle ("Economic relations between countries, including trade relations, shall be based on the principle of sovereign equality of States, self-determination of peoples, and non-interference in the internal affairs of other countries") could conflict with actual U.S. policies, for example, toward China and Cuba. To have accepted the wording, as many countries did, would have been a contradiction. Second, the delegation was instructed not to abstain when it actually disagreed. These evidences of rigorous "honesty" may well be criticized. The spectacle of France, Indonesia, Ghana, and the Soviet Union voting for a policy of non-interference in the internal affairs of others should have spurred on lagging American hearts. If that incentive were inadequate, the United States might well have turned to its own past votes in the United Nations. A careful scrutiny might have revealed some precedents for imperfect integrity.

Third, the unanimous support for a number of UNCTAD resolutions, such as that on guidelines for international financial cooperation (loans, grants, technical assistance, private investments, etc.) owes a great deal to U.S. success in sponsoring the measures. However, it was usually judged most politic to avoid the tag of "U.S. resolutions." Thus, the negative impression created by the voting on principles was not offset by the results of constructive work behind the scenes.

Fourth, this constructive effort was to some extent dampened by the unwillingness of some UNCTAD officials and delegations to compromise. This was a natural enough consequence of the determination to create a "third force" in economic policy as well as of some delegates' desire to maintain a suitably militant posture for home consumption. However, it was often inconsistent with even the appearance of North-South agreement.

The more legitimate grounds for criticizing U.S. policy lies in its failure to come to UNCTAD with a program of action. The underlying reason was political. The grand design of U.S. economic policy was founded on welding together an Atlantic bloc. The Kennedy Round was a symbol of that policy, and intra-governmental efforts to ask for Presidential or Congressional approval of competing policies were fruitless. But by the spring of 1964, it was already clear that the French government would successfully resist any moves toward Atlantic integration. Therefore the subordination of other goals in the interests of the Kennedy Round and of Atlantic cooperation was probably ill-advised, a collective Gatsbyian pursuit of vanishing illusions.

However, this does not mean that U.S. objections to such devices as preferences, price-fixing, and increases in aid were illegitimate on all scores, as will become apparent in light of the difficult questions examined in Chapters 6–8.

To espouse without reservation policies as complex as trade preferences, compensatory financing, or commodity price-fixing in the free-wheeling confusion of a 120-nation conference implies a certain irresponsibility. Although the United States is free of guilt on this score, it remains indictable both for an excessively rigorous verbal devotion to liberal trade principles that it violates daily and for failing to propose positive measures beyond those expected from the long-oversold GATT negotiations.

PART TWO

A Review of Trade and Development Theory

CHAPTER THREE

Trade and Development Theories: A Historical Survey

Rich and poor countries have diverse and sometimes incompatible interests in aid, trade, and investment. This chapter and the two that follow summarize what economic theories say about the trade-development relationship. These chapters are digressions from our main theme: today's economic policy choices. Chapter 6 resumes the discussion of economic policies. Professional economists will find little novelty in these three chapters. Both they and the reader who is primarily interested in policy issues can turn directly to Chapter 6 with little loss of continuity.

The underlying assumption of UNCTAD and of the forces it represents is that trade is a necessary catalyst of development. Economists and policy makers have not always agreed with this view. The prevalence of protectionism is testimony to the political power of autarchic policies. In reviewing these theories, therefore, we are not simply cataloguing dead issues. The history of economic thought is, among other things, a persistent intellectual struggle, normally couched in a prose that is both long-winded and obscure, between supporters of economic nationalism and internationalism, protectionism and free trade, economic intervention and liberty. None of these issues has found a permanent political solution. Each generation and each place has its own perspective. By reviewing briefly what classical and modern economists have said about these subjects, starting with the successful attacks of Smith and Ricardo against protectionism, we can perhaps gain a perspective on contemporary issues. It does not follow that today's decisions will therefore be wiser, but some sense of continuity should promote better understanding of the issues and, at the very least, broader perspective for error. The reader is warned that these chapters cover in relatively few pages the subject matter that would ordinarily take up a lengthy book. If the argument seems compressed or too unqualified, the reader is referred for enlightenment to standard works on the subject.[1]

These chapters should cast some light on what can and cannot be expected from trade as an agent of growth, and thus on the merits of the UNCTAD view. But there are some difficulties in the way. "Pure" economic theories, unless they are mainly descriptive—as for example, theories that mark off economic development as a series of historical stages—are efforts to spin out deductions into tautologies that illuminate the subject.[2] Whether these forms of tautology are useful for policy will obviously depend on whether the particular illumination seems relevant to economic issues of the day. Keynes' general theory presented a novel approach to the theory of national income determination; it won its renown, not on the basis of elegance or rigor, but because it seemed relevant to the economic conditions of the time.

But theories of development are another matter. All the classical economic theories and some of the modern ones deal with time stretching out over generations. Although the strength of economic theory lies in simplification, explaining economic processes by singling out strategic variables from the myriad, it cannot carry the burden of forecasting the centuries. During that time, the values of the strategic variables shift unpredictably, and unforeseen new ones arise. Economics is much more modest than it once was in its claims to foretell development, although some would claim it is still too arrogant. The economic determinism of Ricardo and Marx has ceded by and large to partial explanations, usually dwelling more on internal structural logic of economic variables or on modest verifiable hypotheses than on the course of society's evolution. Economists today generally believe that the theory of development is too large a subject for economists to handle; they dwell instead on its economic aspects,

[1] Of which Joseph Schumpeter's *History of Economic Analysis,* New York, Oxford University Press, 1954, is perhaps the most rewarding, though hardly the easiest to read.

[2] They may also be hypotheses about behavior, subject to empirical tests. In that case, they may be far more fruitful scientifically than the purely deductive analyses, but it is asking too much to expect them to offer statistically verifiable explanations of economic development.

leaving such essential elements as social and political change and technical progress to others.

The modern trend, however faint-hearted compared with the classics, is all to the good in the interests of realism. It makes explicit the essential weakness of economic development theory: other things are not equal. Economic growth is an irreversible process that has profound social causes and effects. Thus an industrial economy, devastated by war, can move from near starvation to comfort in a decade; while, in favorable circumstances, an underdeveloped country *might* make the journey in fifty years—and among major countries only Japan and Russia have done so in this century.

Therefore, we must regard theoretical insights into the trade-development relationship as being useful for policy purposes within the limits set by the relevance of their assumptions and results and as of no great value at other times or under other skies.[3] Malthus and Marx may be of interest today to poor countries because these countries in some relevant ways are closer to 19th- than to 20th-century Europe; but they have much less to offer to development planners in Europe today. And even theories that are written for today's conditions must admit that there is no safe way to infer the actual course of growth from the limited number of variables we are able to incorporate into models of development. Therefore, in examining the relation between trade and development, we should look primarily for insights, not for answers. Those few answers that we do find to be reasonably sure will often turn out to be more tautological than illuminating. For example, it is incontrovertible but not useful to state that, with fixed techniques, the best way to minimize the real cost to the world of producing a given income is for each country to export the things it produces relatively cheaply and import those it produces relatively expensively. The statement is necessarily true under the usual assumptions.[4] But it tells us nothing about development policy, particularly for the legendary country that, in the face of logic, has a comparative disadvantage in producing everything; or, in the face of justice, finds its compara-

[3] They are therefore different in essential degree from the theory of static economic equilibrium, which can legitimately assume away the impact of changes in the social matrix and thereby emerge with a generally valid explanation of the simultaneous determination of the prices and quantities of goods and productive agents. It is formally possible to dynamize such static systems, but then they are likely to be caught by the increasing irrelevance of one or more assumptions as time passes.

[4] This also assumes that decisions are made in the absence of a risk.

tive advantage in products with negative income elasticity of demand, and price elasticities that are low downward and high upward.

THE CLASSICAL THEORIES

The great classical economists—Smith, Ricardo, Malthus, Marx—were generally pessimistic about economic progress in the long run. They believed that industrial countries would reach a point of stagnation (or, as Marx believed, collapse) at low levels of per capita income. However, they were reasonably optimistic about the growth prospects for underdeveloped countries, as a stage on the route to ultimate stagnation or revolution.[5] Among their successors before the Second World War, such theorists as Schumpeter, Keynes, and Hansen were also on the whole pessimistic about the probable long run growth of per capita income in developed market economies, although they apparently saw no necessary impediment to the development of LDC's.[6]

Singer has termed this view D-pessimism/U-optimism. Both groups are doomed, but underdeveloped countries (U) have a longer course to run than developed ones. He believes that the post-1945 period saw this view replaced by D-optimism/U-pessimism. The difficulties of introducing a self-sustaining growth process in underdeveloped countries are stressed by such writers as Nurkse, Myrdal, and Prebisch. The 19th-century pessimism about developed countries has been largely dispelled by the steady growth of the North over the past two decades, and the apparent disappearance there of the issues that concerned Marx, Malthus, Ricardo, and Keynes.

In fact, as we shall see, the division between pessimistic and optimistic is not quite so neat, but the generalization is interesting. The science that once made gloomy forecasts of the rich countries' prospects now often seems to be the dismal science of the poor nations. Let us trace the evolution of development theory to the present day to see how this has come about. As noted, we will focus on the trade-development relationship. However, it cannot be usefully examined in

[5] H. W. Singer, *International Development: Growth and Change,* New York, McGraw-Hill, 1964, pp. 3–6.

[6] For a different estimate of Hansen's views, see B. Higgins, *Economic Development,* New York, W. W. Norton, 1959, pp. 167–198.

a vacuum, and our review will also dwell on the nature of the development process, in which trade may be subordinate.

Adam Smith

Smith's views on development are difficult to summarize, because they are not presented systematically.[7] He stressed the specialization and division of labor as the basic elements in productivity growth and pointed out the role of capital formation as a necessary element in economic development. His dictum that the division of labor (and hence increasing productivity) is limited by the extent of the market is a recognition of the role of demand in economic growth. He appears, in a general way, to see growth as a self-sustaining process based on increasing division of labor, rising savings and technological improvements. However, the development process has its limits, and each nation eventually moves toward a "stationary state" in which: (1) a country meets its full development potential; (2) investment possibilities and capital accumulation decline and ultimately cease; (3) wages therefore fall (because Smith, like the other classical economists, looked on capital stock as a wages fund); (4) finally, profits fall to a near-zero, wages are low, rents are high, and the economy is in some sort of long-run equilibrium.

Smith laid particular stress on trade as an agent of growth.[8] Three elements have been defined in the classical view of trade and development.[9]

1. *Comparative costs:* The static gains from trade are a source of profits and hence permit capital accumulation and growth. This element becomes predominant in Ricardo and the neo-classical writers; and is sometimes incorrectly described as the only element of classical trade theory.

2. *The vent for surplus:* Foreign demand provides a market for surplus productive capacity, which might otherwise have no alternative employment—for example, in the production of tropical crops or minerals in underdeveloped countries. There is a large surplus of productive capacity over domestic requirements for these products

[7] Adam Smith, *An Inquiry into the Nature and Courses of the Wealth of Nations,* New York, The Modern Library, 1937.

[8] *Ibid.,* p. 416.

[9] See H. Myint, "The 'Classical Theory' of International Trade and the Underdeveloped Countries," *Economic Journal,* Vol. LXVIII (June 1958), pp. 317–337.

(Brazilian coffee and Chilean copper are cases in point). Yet in the absence of foreign demand, domestic resources could not readily be transferred to production of other goods. This is partly because some natural resources (copper mines, coffee land) are of value primarily for a specific purpose, and partly because human and capital resources are relatively immobile for a variety of reasons (of which the principal economic ones are lack of education, techniques, management skills, infrastructure, demand for goods at a level that will permit scale economies in production, and so on).

Vent for surplus can be viewed as an aspect of comparative costs, in which a poor country has a very great advantage in producing certain goods.[10] However, this is not a useful way to look at it because the crucial elements for underdeveloped countries are the opening up of new markets for products with negligible domestic demand, and the opening up of remunerative occupations for factors that would otherwise be idle or would be producing very little.[11]

3. *Increases in productivity:* The proposition that trade stimulates productivity and therefore economic growth is stressed by Smith as an aspect of widening the market. By widening the extent of the market, trade permits greater division of labor and a higher level of domestic productivity. In Smith's words:

> By means of [foreign trade], the narrowness of the home market does not hinder the division of labour on any particular branch of art of manufacture from being carried to the highest perfection. By opening a more extensive market for whatever part of the produce of their labour may exceed the home consumption, it encourages them to improve its productive powers, and to augment its annual produce to the utmost, and thereby to increase the real revenue and wealth of society.[12]

These three elements of gains from trade—comparative costs, vent for surplus, and productivity increase—combine in *The Wealth of Nations* to establish trade as an essential element in the growth of underdeveloped countries. However uncertain the long-run prospects for economic growth, Smith sees no inherent obstacles to the trade-led growth of backward countries. Neither he nor the other classical economists envisioned any potential conflict between growth and the

[10] It is so discussed by G. Haberler, *International Trade and Economic Development,* p. 9.

[11] Myint, "The 'Classical Theory' of International Trade and the Underdeveloped Countries," pp. 321–322.

[12] Smith, *Wealth of Nations,* p. 413.

specialization implied by comparative cost principles—a subject much discussed in protectionist writings and in recent discussions of trade and development. One important reason for this apparent oversight is that classical economists were usually in controversy with mercantilist writers who opposed free trade. To indulge in unverifiable speculation about possible long-run conflicts would simply have given support to the opposition.

David Ricardo and Thomas Malthus

Ricardo's theory of economic development,[13] unmistakably D-pessimistic/U-optimistic, requires no detailed exposition here. It can be expressed as a formal dynamic system [14] that tends toward a stationary state where wages are at subsistence level, profits are near zero, and landlords absorb as rent most of the society's net revenue above subsistence and capital replacement costs. Ricardo's system reaches these gloomy results because he assumes that there are diminishing returns to increased factor use in agriculture, constant returns in industry, no substitution possible between labor and capital in response to price changes, and a rate of population increase that maintains wages at or near subsistence levels. Furthermore, technological improvements are not enough in the long run to compensate for the rise in wages and fall in profits occasioned by diminishing returns. As the Ricardian system operates, increases in demand for food (occasioned by population growth) under conditions of diminishing returns raise the money wage rate and lower the profit rate, thereby diminishing the incentive to invest. Capital accumulation declines and then halts, ushering in the stationary state.

Ricardo's theory is primarily concerned with the distribution of output rather than economic growth. His interest in the trade-development relationship therefore does not emphasize the increases in productivity and external economies that flow from trade. He stresses the merits of free trade in two connections: static gains from trade arising from differences in comparative costs; and advantages for an industrial country of importing food, thereby keeping down the level of money wages and maintaining profits. Trade thus allows developed countries to delay the advent of the stationary state.

[13] *Principles of Political Economy and Taxation,* London, 1817 (reprinted by Everyman's Library, London, 1911).

[14] See Benjamin Higgins, *Economic Development,* pp. 87–99.

Malthus, Ricardo's contemporary, is principally known today for his views on population. But his *Principles of Political Economy,*[15] while restating the classical doctrines on many issues, introduces some significant novelties, with particular stress on the role of demand in economic growth. He states that economic growth requires increases in effective demand. Thus the growth of population is not in itself a source of economic development because it does not necessarily lead to greater demand. Nor does savings automatically create its own investment demand. This denial of the proposition that supply creates its own demand was later used by Keynes as a basic element of his general theory. According to Malthus the path of economic development requires that both savings and effective demand increase. If either is relatively overemphasized, then growth will be slowed. Savings allow increases in productive capacity, and greater consumption is needed to create the demand for the new capacity. This is the original under-consumption theory, to be restated later in different form by Marx and Hobson.

The trade-growth relation enters Malthus' work in three ways: first, as with all classical economists, in the form of the terms of trade between agriculture and industry, and in the international sphere, in the contribution of trade in offsetting diminishing returns in agriculture. Second, he views trade as providing an incentive to increased domestic output. People who are offered the chance to buy imported goods will show at any wage rate a greater preference for work over leisure than they would if imported goods were not available.[16] Malthus saw this phenomenon as having favorable effects on development through increasing the supply of labor (and presumably, in the example he cites, of capital). Some modern economists have looked at it differently, in ways reminiscent of the orthodox classical school. They state that the availability of foreign goods and knowledge of higher living standards elsewhere may impede the growth of poor countries, because they bring aspirations for higher living standards, and thus tend to reduce savings (the "abstinence" of Ricardo and Malthus).[17]

The third role of trade in development, according to Malthus, involves yet another concept adopted by modern writers, balanced

[15] Thomas R. Malthus, *Principles of Political Economy,* second edition, London, 1836 (reprinted by A. Kelley, New York, 1951).

[16] *Ibid.,* p. 354.

[17] *Ibid.,* pp. 341–343.

growth. In an underdeveloped country, agriculture and industry may fail to expand because the market for the output of each is too small.[18] There is no incentive to increase output or hire additional labor; and with population pressing against food supply, unemployment will be persistent and poverty widespread.

This can happen even if the country is well endowed with land and other resources. Say's Law, which states that supply creates its own demand, is, as Nurkse has said,[19] not applicable to the product of a single industry. The expansion of agriculture does not mean that farm workers and landlords will necessarily consume the increased output. Agriculture fails to expand, remains poor, and the market for industry remains small. Thus, in Malthus' view, trade, acting as a vent for surplus in LDC's, creates the markets for agriculture and, by increasing farm income, promotes demand for manufactures. Trade is an engine of economic growth, not because of comparative costs, but because it helps to create domestic mass markets for agriculture and industry. Without trade, the nation may simply stagnate at low levels of income.

> Without sufficient foreign commerce to give value to the raw produce of the land; and before the general introduction of manufactures had opened the channels for domestic industry, the demands of the great proprietors for labor would be very soon supplied; and beyond this, the laboring classes would have nothing to give them for the use of their lands.[20]

The stagnation may be particularly marked if incomes are unequally distributed. If most people earn only a minority of national income, then the growth of demand is inhibited, and the growth of both population and average income will be held back.

The contrast between Malthus' emphasis on the role of markets and other classical writers' insistence on supply factors has persisted among development theorists. The debate concerning relative importance of supply and demand in price and income determination under conditions of full employment has been resolved, at the theoretical level, by the development toward the end of the last century of static general equilibrium theory, which shows that in the economic system

[18] See R. Nurkse, *Problems of Capital Formation for Underdeveloped Countries,* London, Basil Blackwell, 1953; and W. F. Stolper, "A Note on the Multiplier, Flexible Exchanges and the Dollar Shortage," *Economia Internazionale,* Vol. III (August 1950), pp. 772–773.

[19] *Problems of Capital Formation,* Chap. 1.

[20] Malthus, *Principles of Political Economy,* p. 342.

all prices, quantities traded, and incomes are mutually determined by the interaction of demand and supply. However, the general equilibrium system does not resolve the relative roles of supply and demand as catalysts of development; and the old arguments continue to flourish in such modern forms as, "Is inflation a stimulus or deterrent to growth"; "Is the expansion of LDC trade limited by overvalued exchange rates or by inadequate growth of external demand?" The Ricardo-Malthus controversy remains an essential and unresolved issue of economic development policy today.

John Stuart Mill

Mill's role in economic thought is often mistakenly seen as one of elaborating Ricardian doctrine. It is not our task here to examine the body of his work.[21] In the sphere that interests us, Mill's work is superior to Ricardo's because he specifically dealt with the growth of national income as a matter of prime interest, as well as with some dynamic elements in the trade-development relationship. Furthermore, Mill's views of economic analysis reflect the great breadth of his interests and knowledge. While this tends to make his writing diffuse compared with Ricardo, it also infuses it with a realism that is reminiscent of Smith. Mill recognized the similarity of approach. In the preface to the first edition of *Principles of Political Economy* (1848) he said:

> The design of the book is different from that of any treatise on Political Economy which has been produced in England since the work of Adam Smith.
>
> . . . Except on matters of mere detail there are perhaps no practical questions even among those which approach nearest to the character of purely economical questions, which admit of being decided on economical premises alone . . . Adam Smith never loses sight of this truth . . .[22]

Mill restated and refined the Ricardian comparative cost argument. He pointed out that trade allows a more efficient use of world resources. This in his view was the direct (or static) gain from trade.

[21] For discussion of Mill's contribution, see J. Schumpeter, *History of Economic Analysis,* Part III; and the introduction to Mill's *Principles of Political Economy* in the W. J. Ashley edition (reprinted by A. Kelley, New York, 1961).

[22] John Stuart Mill, *Principles of Political Economy,* pp. xxvii–xxviii.

He rejects Smith's view of trade as a vent for surplus,[23] because he assumes that the factors of production are mobile among occupations, and by implication that the techniques required to produce import-substituting goods are available. In underdeveloped countries, as Smith and Malthus perceived but failed to express clearly, these assumptions are often invalid. Largely on Mill's authority, Smith's vent for surplus argument was generally considered invalid by 19th-century writers, except Marx and Hobson; and has been rehabilitated slowly in recent decades,[24] frequently with reservations that may reflect the neo-classical predisposition to assume that factors of production are mobile within each country.

It is in his discussion of the "indirect effects" or dynamic aspects of trade that Mill presents a clear advance over the Ricardian system. His views incorporate elements of both Smith and Malthus but are expressed more comprehensively and with more lucidity:

> Such, then, is the direct economical advantage of foreign trade. But there are indirect effects which must be counted as benefits of a high order. One is, the tendency of every extension of the market to improve the processes of production. A country which produces for a larger market than its own, can introduce a more extended division of labour, can make greater use of machinery, and is more likely to make inventions and improvements in the processes of production. Whatever causes a greater quantity of anything to be produced in the same place, tends to the general increase of the productive powers of the world.[25]

This restatement of Smith stresses technological change and economies of scale, those elements that Myint has characterized as the "productivity" theory of trade. The remainder of this passage incorporates ideas developed by Malthus and Ricardo:

> There is another consideration, principally applicable to an early stage of industrial advancement. A people may be in a quiescent, indolent, uncultivated state, with all their tastes either fully satisfied or entirely undeveloped and they may fail to put forth the whole of their productive energies for want of any sufficient object of desire. The opening of foreign trade, by making them acquainted with new objects or tempting them by the easier acquisition of things which they had not previously

[23] *Ibid.*, pp. 579–580.

[24] Myint, "The 'Classical Theory' of International Trade and the Underdeveloped Countries"; J. H. Williams, "The Theory of International Trade Reconsidered," *Economic Journal*, Vol. XXXIX (June 1929), pp. 195–209.

[25] Mill, *Principles of Political Economy*, p. 581.

thought attainable, sometimes works a sort of industrial revolution in a country whose resources were previously undeveloped for want of energy and ambition in the people: inducing those who were satisfied with scanty comforts and little work, to work harder for the gratification of their new tastes, and even to save, and accumulate capital, for the still more complete satisfaction of their tastes at a future time.[26]

This section illustrates once more the persistent split in economic thought between those who view increases in the desire to consume, stemming in this case from trade, as a catalyst for economic growth, and those who believe that the increased propensity to consume will mean less savings and slower economic growth. Mill, like Malthus, believes that this so-called "international demonstration effect" will make people work harder, and be more willing to adopt new techniques. In his eyes, the emulation of rich countries' consumption standards is a cause of industrial revolution in poor countries and will even encourage increases in total savings. For those who, like Ricardo and Nurkse, look on peasants' longing for transistors as the enemy of economic growth, the gains from trade tend, in some not very rigorous way, to be offset by the losses from the international demonstration effect. In other words, it is good to sell coffee, but it is bad to import *nouvelle vague* movies with the proceeds.

Whatever its psychological basis, this difference of emphasis (between those who look upon the desire for increased consumption as the enemy of growth and those who consider it a positive catalyst) also involves some economic factors.[27] First, if we assume that resources are immobile among economic activities, then by the previous argument there is probably no ready alternative to trade as a source of additional savings, and the growth "loss" from new consumption demand is more than compensated for by the additional savings made possible by trade. Furthermore, if there is no alternative, there is nothing to argue about. On the other hand, if factors move freely between occupations, and if there are no new imports needed for growth, then the demonstration effects of trade, if harmful to growth, might be avoided by a policy of domestic industrialization, without much static loss (depending on the comparative cost structure).

[26] *Ibid.*, p. 581.

[27] We postpone here a discussion of the possible conflict between more consumption and more development that could result from foreign exchange scarcity. We follow the classical assumption that savings or demand will be the operative constraints on growth.

Second, and more important, does development require a stimulus to effort in the specific form of new *imported* consumer goods? The answer depends both on psychological assumptions and, once more, on the nature of alternative production possibilities. Some countries that trade rather little have grown faster than those that trade a lot. If a country is very backward, then trade is probably a necessary stimulus to growth, unless the government is prepared to use force as a substitute for consumption incentives.

Finally, there is an important distinction between static and dynamic issues, implicit in the foregoing discussion. Capital formation requires that some current income not be spent for current consumption. But new capacity created by investment means that demand must increase over time (otherwise investment will not be profitable). If population is growing slower than output per capita, demand must grow at a rate sufficient to take up the new capacity in each investment period.[28] Demand, ultimately consumption demand, must increase. This does not mean that full use of new capacity requires a general increase in the propensity to consume. However, if investors are dubious about current demand prospects, such an increase may well stimulate investment, domestic and foreign. In an underdeveloped country, these increases in demand will most probably stem initially from trade, which is the principal source for learning about the possibilities for new mass consumption goods. Naturally, if consumption plans and investment plans increase simultaneously, there will probably be inflationary pressures, particularly if foreign capital is not available to supplement domestic goods. The effects of inflation on development cannot be predicted in general. They depend on the degree of inflation and its influence on wages and profits, and may either spur or retard real growth rates. As Malthus and Mill in effect pointed out, the international demonstration effect may make people more willing over time to enter the labor market, thus possibly acting to offset inflation.

On another plane, Mill endorses trade as an agent of development for reasons that go beyond economic effects:

But the economic advantages of commerce are surpassed in importance by those of its effects which are intellectual and moral. It is hardly possible to overrate the value, in the present low state of human improve-

[28] Evsey Domar, "Expansion and Employment," *American Economic Review*, Vol. XXXVIII (March 1947), pp. 34 ff.

ment, of placing human beings in contact with persons dissimilar to themselves, and with modes of thought and action unlike those with which they are familiar. Commerce is now what war once was, the principal source of this contact.[29]

The optimistic attitude that Mill shows toward trade and development extends also to general economic progress. While he, like the other classical writers, foresaw a stationary state, he did not share the gloomy visions of Ricardo and Malthus, nor their preoccupation with the consequences of diminishing returns to land and of unregulated human fertility. Mill's stationary state is a reasonably prosperous and placid condition. He thus departs notably from Singer's generalization about U-pessimism/D-optimism. But, like all the classicists, he believes U prospects are more favorable than D prospects.

Karl Marx

Marx held cataclysmic views about the long-run course of D-development as it precedes the revolution. We are concerned here not with his theory of capitalistic development leading via working class poverty, the growth of imperialism, and world conflict to socialist revolution, but primarily with the special function of trade between rich and poor countries in the Marxist system.[30] Marx is, from the capitalist viewpoint, both D-pessimistic and U-pessimistic, but in his system, imperialism acting as a link between rich and poor countries catalyzes the ultimate overthrow of capitalism. Much of the contemporary debate over the growth-trade relationship is, in effect, a reflection of differences concerning the validity of Marxist doctrine.

Imperialism emerges as the last stage of monopoly capitalism. In Marx's view, capitalism, motivated by the search for profit, attempts to maximize the rate of exploitation, which is defined as the ratio of surplus value to variable capital. Surplus value is the difference between value of product and the labor, materials, and equipment costs of its production. Variable capital is the value of labor inputs into production. With a fixed labor force, the higher the ratio, the greater the capitalists' profit.

[29] Mill, *Principles of Political Economy,* p. 581.

[30] The Marxist system is set forth in Marx's *Capital* (three vols.) which cannot be classed as light reading even by professional standards; the general reader is advised to refer to secondary sources such as J. Schumpeter, *Capitalism, Socialism and Democracy,* New York, Harper and Brothers, 1947; or Paul M. Sweezy, *The Theory of Capitalist Development,* New York, Oxford University Press, 1946.

According to Marx there is an inherent tendency for profit rates to fall, as industry adopts ever-more capital-intensive methods. Capitalists, anxious to maintain and raise profits, turn increasingly to colonial trade. Colonialism, one of the early instruments of capitalist development, becomes transformed to imperalism, world conflict, and the final stages of capitalist destruction.

The doctrine of colonialism and imperialism, as discussed by Marx, Lenin, and Hobson, merits considerable reflection, because it provides the basis of an ideology that is ruling in many underdeveloped countries, and powerful in all of them. Like other ideologies, it serves as a focus for goals and resentments far removed from its ostensible thesis. The sociology of discontent in the underdeveloped countries is beyond our task here, but the economic vessel that gives it form is our concern; and we will concentrate on that.

The Marxist theory of imperialism is attractively simple. Accumulation leads to declining profits. The search for profit leads capitalists to seek new sources of cheap labor (a higher rate of exploitation). The need to protect the investment in LDC's, both from local hostility and from the competition of other capitalist countries, leads to colonization—that is, to political control by the rich countries. This colonization process, as chronicled by Lenin and Hobson, reached a peak in the latter part of the 19th century. However, as Marx points out, colonial profits can also form the basis for accumulation in the early stages of capitalist development as, for example, the Dutch and British gains from colonial trade during the 17th and 18th centuries.

As capitalism develops, trade with poor countries plays a number of roles simultaneously. First, it provides a vent for surplus for manufactured products of the capitalist countries, which in a mature stage become chronically afflicted by the problems of surplus capacity. Second, it provides cheap primary products for the benefit of the rich countries. Third, to the extent that the terms of trade can be rigged by protectionism and monopoly, imperialist countries can accumulate capital even more rapidly. Therefore, there is, under pressure of worldwide competition and falling profits, a strong incentive for each capitalist country to carve out protected colonial markets and sources of supply secure from outside competition. Naturally, the capitalists stand to benefit most from both trade and investment if they are monopoly suppliers and buyers. This leads to preferential trade in colonial markets, in association with the rise of monopoly capitalism, a late stage of capitalist development. Meanwhile, protection in the home market prevents unwelcome competition by other capitalist countries. Such devices as "Empire free trade" are simply methods of combining protection and imperialism in palatable form.[31] But the downward pressures on profits are continuous so that competition among imperialists for investment outlets becomes even more intense. This stage is accompanied by use of force in two directions: to keep the LDC's in subjection, and to contest the colonial claims of other imperial powers. Ultimately, of course, these measures are all unavailing. Imperialist wars and domestic social unrest work together to undermine the imperialist powers, and capitalism is overthrown. In Lenin's words:

> Imperialism is capitalism in that stage of development in which the dominance of monopolies and finance capital has established itself; in which the division of the world among the international trusts has begun; in which the division of all territories of the globe among the great capitalist powers has been completed.[32]

The Marxist formulation is appealingly simple, combining economic, social, and political forces into a single system of capitalist development. It has particularly strong appeal in many underdeveloped countries because it offers a ready scapegoat for the apparently insoluble problems that beset them. Furthermore, the theory can readily be buttressed by factual examples.[33] By avoiding examples that do not fit the theory, a strong case can be built for it. Without accepting those aspects of Marxism that are obviously erroneous, such as the increasing misery of the working classes, or the necessity for a declining profit rate, it seems clear that the theory of imperialism provides a reasonably good explanation of some of the forces at work in 19th century colonial expansion. That is, there was a great increase in productive capacity; a drive for protection; an effort to carve out colonial markets; a development of large-scale manufacturing production facilities, often combined into trusts;[34] and increasing rivalry for colonial annexation among the developed countries. It would be naïve to validate the Marxist view on the basis of such

[31] J. A. Hobson, *Imperialism,* London, George Allen and Unwin, 1938, pp. 104–109.

[32] Lenin, *Imperialism,* New York, International Publishers, 1939, p. 89.

[33] See Hobson, *Imperialism;* and Lenin, *Imperialism,* Ch. VI.

[34] For the Marxist writers, imperialism and monopoly capitalism were virtually synonymous. Cf. Lenin, Ch. VII. The rise of monopoly and the need for markets and for more exploitation were considered inseparable.

trends alone but no less unreasonable to reject its explanatory force during the era of modern colonialism. By the same token, it is obvious, for a variety of reasons, that the doctrine of imperialism, whatever its political appeal today, is invalid as a general explanation of trade and political relations between rich and poor countries.

First of all, as pointed out in Chapter 2, the rich countries' economic stake is relatively modest: they are more interested in trade with each other. Serious conflict about colonial markets is not worthwhile. Naturally, there is still an incentive to maintain existing privileges (the franc zone, the vestiges of British Imperial preference), but not at the price of jeopardizing more important politico-economic relations.

Second, the poor countries are relatively independent politically, and while it might be maintained that their political leaders share the class economic interests of the leaders of the capitalist states, the argument cannot be carried very far. Surely, it is difficult to see what political or economic interests of their own the leaders of Burma, Ghana, or Egypt would serve today by deliberately subjecting their people to exploitation and rigged markets.

Third, to the extent that markets *are* rigged against LDC's through such devices as agricultural protection and restrictions on low-wage imports, the economic costs fall on rigger and rigged alike. It would be hard to maintain for example, that, even indirectly, poor countries pay the lion's share of farm subsidies in the United States or the Common Market.

Furthermore, as capitalism has become more powerful, or at least more wealthy, its political strength has declined both internationally and domestically. A relatively bland and homogeneous social democracy tends to be the ruling economic ideology in the Atlantic Community; and "monopoly" capital is long since resigned, as Lenin foresaw, to sharing its profit increases with "monopoly" labor. On the international scene, force applied for economic motives has become a social sin; statesmen would rather be considered appeasers than run the risk of being known as imperialist aggressors, at least for patently economic motives.

Of course, in Lenin's eyes, this development of a bourgeois society, fattening itself through imperialist exploitation of the working classes in poor countries, was entirely consistent with Marxism. The working class in rich countries acquires to some extent the same interests in international exploitation as the capitalist class, and their compact is signed with the unholy bond of protectionism. In Lenin's words, "Imperialism has the tendency to create privileged sections even among the workers, and to detach them from the main proletarian mass." [35] This view, like much of Marxist theory, makes at least a temporary appeal to our sense of realism. It is well known that labor and capital in rich countries cooperate politically to exclude low-wage imports and economically to prevent declining prices.[36]

The only trouble with this approach is that, like other conspiracy theories of history, it is wrong. In order to reject the systematic economics of Marxism-Leninism, it is not necessary to affirm the nobility of the social systems of the West—virtue has rarely been in oversupply anywhere. It is sufficient to point out that both the volume of, and profits from, North-South trade and investment are of secondary importance in the economic system of the North. This is not to deny that profits from investment in LDC's may be high; it would be imprudent of a foreigner to invest in a backward country unless he expected a premium over potential earnings at home. Furthermore, the theory advanced by Prebisch and others, that trade is *de facto* normally rigged in favor of rich countries, could also be true, although it is far from the status of received economic doctrine north of the Rio Grande. This argument, although advanced from different motives, could be grasped by neo-Marxists. Accepting these contentions, what do we have? The answer, as we saw in Chapter 2, was that the combined annual product of the North is valued at about $1200 billion in 1964, while its trade with the South was valued at about $22 billion. It seems somewhat easier to credit the Protocols of the Elders of Zion than the contention that capitalist prosperity is fueled today by the impoverished masses of Asia.

Finally, Marxism may fail to construct a logically credible picture of how the trade-development relation works, but this does not mean that we can therefore dismiss it. There is some argument for many of the Marxist and neo-Marxist tenets of imperialism. Even if the net gains to the North from imperialist policies are relatively small, they loom large in the eyes of the poor countries. No one wants to be exploited. Furthermore, what is a modest amount in the Northern balance may be a large one in the Southern scale. For example, if all tropical commodity prices could be fixed by agreement at prices as

[35] Lenin, *Imperialism,* p. 106.

[36] As we shall see, these phenomena have provided the basis of modern non-Marxist argument for protection in LDC's.

much above equilibrium levels as oil prices probably are, the South would probably gain many billions of dollars annually in trade revenues. Unfortunately for the South, such rigging is impossible for any but a few products;[37] yet the secret conviction lingers. It is in this connection that Marxist theory finds its primary strength—offering a potential solvent for the injustices of the world.

THE NEO-CLASSICAL CONTRIBUTION

The Great Tradition

After 1870, economic development generally lost its central place as a subject of economic theories, except among the Marxist writers. Neo-classical economics, in retrospect dominated by the figures of Marshall, Walras, and Pareto, was concerned in its formal structure with general and partial equilibrium analysis of prices and incomes, both domestically and through international trade. Only two significant works dealt in an essential way with economic development, and neither of them with trade.[38] Those who dealt with trade tended to overlook its importance for development. Thus, the neo-classical view of trade and development was largely implicit in their writings on other subjects.

It is not entirely clear why neo-classical economists more or less abandoned the subject. The standard explanation is not convincing. By 1870, the explanation runs, it had become clear that the possibilities for economic progress were greater than had been previously believed. The fears of a stationary state were thereby expunged. At the same time, it was recognized that the interrelations among population, income, capital, and technique were quite complex and by no means fully determined by economic factors.

All of these explanations carry weight, but it is still puzzling that the retreat from dynamics was so complete. It has been claimed that it was not total, that there was a neo-classical theory of develop-

[37] Pincus, *Economic Aid and International Cost Sharing,* Chapter 6; also Chapter 7 of this volume.

[38] J. A. Schumpeter, *The Theory of Economic Development,* Cambridge, Harvard University Press, 1934, translated from the German edition of 1907; and Allyn Young, "Increasing Returns and Economic Progress," *Economic Journal,* Vol. XXXVIII (December 1928), pp. 527–542.

ment.[39] To the extent that there was a capital theory, there was certainly an element of a theory of economic development. But a cursory review of the principal neo-classical capital theorists—Marshall, Bohm-Bawerk, Wicksell, Cassel, Fisher—reveals the inadequacy of neo-classical capital theory *as a theory of development*. The capital theory, like the trade and value theories, was focused on questions of allocative efficiency. In effect, it dealt with one major aspect of resource use under *ceteris paribus* assumptions, without considering directly that the form of the growth path might substantially influence the developmental outcome. To the extent that this obvious point was recognized, it was not explicitly introduced into the analysis.

In the neo-classical view, economic development results from capital accumulation and technological progress. If the marginal productivity of capital decreases slowly as accumulation proceeds, and if technological changes continue, the stationary state can be postponed indefinitely. In the Ricardian tradition, the theory emphasizes the vital role of thrift, without which capital accumulation cannot proceed. Abstinence is an offset both to diminishing returns and to its handmaiden, population growth.

This is all very well, and with the standard assumptions of full employment, competitive markets, steady (though unexplained) technical progress, given factor supply conditions, and resource mobility, it is unexceptionable. It just doesn't say very much about how economic growth happens. Implicitly, Marshall recognizes this; his most interesting discussion of growth lies outside the formal body of his analyses. Thus, in the preface to his *Principles of Economics,* he decribes his view of economic development:

> Economic evolution is gradual. . . . And though an inventor, or an organizer, or financier of genius may seem to have modified the economic structure of a people almost at a stroke; yet that part of his influence, which has not been merely superficial and transitory, is found on inquiry to have done little more than bring to a head a broad constructive movement which had long been in preparation.[40]

It is, of course, this broad constructive movement, if it exists, that we are interested in. Marshall's discussion of this movement, however, is not analytical, but historical.

[39] Meier and Baldwin, *Economic Development,* New York, John Wiley, 1957, pp. 64–78; Meier, *International Trade and Development.*

[40] *Principles* (8th edition), New York, Macmillan, 1930, p. xiii.

It has been suggested that Marshall's practice of discussing economic development without presenting any formal dynamic theory was quite deliberate.[41] He was obviously concerned with development issues, and despite his optimism about the smooth and harmonious nature of growth, he saw economic progress in part as a struggle between increasing and diminishing returns. However, he probably believed that economic analysis was incapable of handling such issues effectively through the device of formal dynamic systems.

This reluctance, however well founded in realism it may be, had some unfortunate consequences for the course of economic theory. First, by concentrating on "short period" equilibrium situations, it focused economists' attention on a series of issues that are essential to an understanding of how economic systems work, but tell us rather little about how they grow. Second, when their analytical discussions incorporate growth, it is through the mechanism of capital theory. This has tended to result in a mechanical treatment of growth, as a process of capital accumulation. Although it is true that accumulation and growth are inseparable, there is much more to the story than that. As we shall see, development economics today is all too often a partial prisoner of neo-classical preoccupations with equilibirium and with raising rates of capital formation.

Neo-classical writers improved considerably on the basic Ricardian theory of international trade, both with respect to the theory of comparative costs and the theory of balance of payments adjustment. As in their discussions of general and partial equilibrium: (1) the emphasis is on relatively short-run processes; (2) the economies are assumed to be relatively developed (productive factors are mobile, market economy predominates).

We will disregard here the technical advances of neo-classical trade theory except insofar as they bear on our subject.[42] First, their stress on the gains from trade leads to the general inference that free trade and international specialization will promote economic development. Because trade raises national incomes of all participants, it allows a higher level of savings, capital formation, and income growth than would be possible without trade. This emphasis on com-

[41] Bruce Glassburner, "Alfred Marshall on Economic History and Historical Development," *Quarterly Journal of Economics,* Vol. LXIX (November 1955), pp. 577–595.

[42] For detailed analyses, see Richard Caves, *Trade and Economic Structure,* Cambridge, Massachusetts, Harvard University Press, 1959.

parative costs is synonymous with an emphasis on productive efficiency in a relatively short run setting.

Second, they recognize that free trade is not necessarily the best medicine for every country and industry. (1) One country can rig terms of trade in its favor by imposing a tariff. (2) Infant industry protection may be justified for a limited time as a method of industrial development. (3) Earnings of labor, capital, or some other factor may decline as a result of free trade.

Third, the analysis usually assumes that labor and capital don't move between countries. Thus the economic implications of large-scale international economic aid, which today finances a large part of LDC trade and investment, are not discussed. There is, however, some discussion in the writings of Marshall and others about the developmental effects of investment in new countries in opening up the country for trade and industrialization.

It remained for later writers to point out that comparative cost was a tautological principle that said nothing *per se* about optimum development policy. Although Young and Schumpeter did not explicitly discuss trade theory, they are the first of the neo-classical school to stress that discussions of economic efficiency may be beside the point. Unfortunately, the discussion of efficiency versus growth has at times taken on the dimensions of an ideological controversy. But, as we shall see below, the fruitful issues lie along another road.

Schumpeter

Much of Schumpeter's theory, for all its originality, lies outside of our main interests here. Almost alone among the non-Marxists, Schumpeter, in his *Theory of Economic Development,* denies the smooth and harmonious nature of growth. For him, as for some of today's theorists, economic development is a disequilibrium system. He was also unique in his time in making the development process the heart of his formal analysis.

Economic development depends on the creative role of the entrepreneur. In contrast to neo-classical capital theory, in which investment and growth are viewed as parts of a continuous process of capital accumulation, Schumpeter's system emphasizes that investment is a risky business, requiring imagination and daring. The entrepreneur steps into a stationary economic system and operating with borrowed money introduces innovations (new goods, new techniques, new markets, new materials sources) into the economy. Innovators are followed by imitators and investment increases. This leads to the business cycles superimposed on the growth path, because the innovation-imitation sequence is not smooth, but comes in swarms of activity followed by depression.

The implications for LDC's are of some interest. First, capitalist economic development is *not* primarily a matter of capital accumulation, but of creative action in which a certain productive vision is brought to fruition in the face of uncertainty. Capital availability is not a sufficient condition for economic growth. The neo-classical writers, Schumpeter believed, missed the heart of the matter.

Second, the trade-development relationship is treated explicitly as part of the formal system. New markets or new sources of supply offer the basis for entrepreneurial action. Thus, the strong trade orientation of most overseas investment in LDC's, and even of a good deal of home investment, is easily understandable by Schumpeter's system. The investment is linked to innovation. If LDC domestic markets are small and the entrepreneurial tradition virtually unknown, then possibilities for innovation may be, in effect, non-existent. Paradoxically, this may be true no matter how high the theoretical rate of return on new domestic investment. The new products (for example, tropical crops) and the new sources of supply (for example, oil discovery) may be entirely tied to foreign outlets. New markets may arise in the LDC's following the increase in output resulting from trade-oriented investment; but even then foreign demand may often be the primary source of new markets that innovators create. Thus, if the field for innovation reflects foreign demand, and if the innovators themselves are mostly foreigners, investment will be shaped accordingly. Other things being equal, investment and growth patterns in Japan or the United States, where domestic entrepreneurship and markets were already present, were likely to lead to creation of a sequence of domestic supplying and consuming industries; import substitution could advance quickly. There could be greater awareness of domestic market and supply opportunities, and therefore of more innovations that take advantage of them. It follows, although without explicit statement from Schumpeter, that the path of development, including its dependence on trade, depends not only on resource endowments and demand patterns, but on the pattern of innovations actually undertaken.

As has often been pointed out in the discussions of Schumpeter's system, it leads to no clear policy conclusions for economic development. The system places great stress on entrepreneurship, which in turn implies support for private enterprise, for restricted access to markets and factors, and for a good deal of social mobility as well as any other economic or social conditions that might encourage innovation. These are methods of assuring a flow of entrepreneurial talent. Schumpeter would presumably have believed that the ideological hostility to capitalism so often found in LDC's would act as a drag on growth by discouraging entrepreneurship. He would also have doubted that government entrepreneurial activity could substitute for individual creativity. While a reminder of the ultimate importance of individual initiatives in economic change is always useful, it is not in itself a development policy for LDC's. Furthermore, the core of Schumpeter's thesis in *Capitalism, Socialism, and Democracy*—that government cannot fill the entrepreneurial role for a developing economy—is not necessarily true. While government entrepreneurship has been unsuccessful as a catalyst in many LDC's, there are others (Yugoslavia, Pakistan, Israel, Puerto Rico, Jamaica) where the government has been the innovator, whether or not it actually managed the means of production. Schumpeter's intellectual vision illuminates significant elements in economic growth, but in such a special framework that it offers only a fragmentary guide to policy.

Allyn Young

In September 1928, Allyn Young delivered the presidential address to the Economic Science section of the British Association for the Advancement of Science on the subject of increasing returns and economic progress. His lecture marks a return of analytical interest in economic growth. His lecture is about economic development, and does not refer specifically to trade. Yet much of the current trade-development controversy is best understood if we can first see his view of the development process.

He starts out by explaining that he is not dealing with static equilibrium concepts:

> The apparatus which economists have built up for the analysis of supply and demand in their relations to prices does not seem to be particularly helpful for the purposes of an inquiry into these broader aspects of increasing returns . . . reliance upon it may divert attention to incidental or partial aspects of a process which ought to be seen as a whole.[43]

[43] Allyn Young, "Increasing Returns and Economic Progress," p. 533.

Young points out that the conventional neo-classical distinction between internal economies (those reductions in unit costs of production stemming from expansion of scale of a firm) and external economies (those reductions stemming from sources external to the firm) is only partially useful in studying growth. One firm's internal economies are external economies to another firm. There is much more to increasing returns, however, as Young points out, than a summation of all firms' internal economies.

New products are appearing, firms are assuming new tasks, and new industries are coming into being. In short, change in this external field is qualitative as well as quantitative. No analysis of the forces making for economic equilibrium will serve to illumine this field, *for movements away from equilibrium, departures from previous trends are characteristic of it.*[44]

Here is a note reminiscent of both Schumpeter and Marx. Like Schumpeter, he believes that this movement is irregular. "Progress is not and cannot be continuous." But Schumpeter's creative destruction is transformed into a vision of the economic process in which the developmental flux reflects the operations of an entire system of forces; Schumpeter's entrepreneurship is seen to be a shorthand expression for a far more complex world.

Young points out that this conception of economic development derives from the older economists, notably Smith's dictum that the division of labor depends on the extent of the market. But:

. . . just what constitutes a large market? Not area or population alone, but buying power, the capacity to absorb a large annual output of goods. . . . In an inclusive view, considering the market not as an outlet for the products of a particular industry, and therefore external to that industry, but as the outlet for the goods in general, the size of the market is determined and defined by the volume of production . . .

Modified, then, in the light of this broader conception of the markets, Adam Smith's dictum amounts to the theorem that the division of labor depends in large part on the division of labor.[45]

It is this inclusive view of the market that provides the basis for the modern proponents of "balanced growth" policies.

In order to develop, a country must expand the market in view of both productivity and demand effects. This requires the simultaneous expansion of a number of industries as suppliers and customers. But

[44] *Ibid.*, p. 528. Italics supplied.
[45] *Ibid.*, p. 533.

this is no easy task for an underdeveloped country, and the implications are not cheerful.

Young takes a more unhurried view than the modern balanced growth theorists.

An industrial dictator with foresight and knowledge could hasten the pace somewhat, but he could not achieve an Aladdin-like transformation so as to reap the fruits of a half-century's ordinary progress in a few years.[46]

There are two kinds of obstacles to forced draft growth: first, "the human material" resists change; second, the necessary accumulation of capital takes time.

After explaining the dual functions of the market in increasing returns, Young turns to some realistic qualifications. First, acting to *impede* increasing returns:

(1) The demand for some products is inelastic, with respect to price. However, producers of such commodities benefit, through cost reduction, from expansion of scale in supplying and purchasing industries.[47]

(2) Bottlenecks may exist on the supply side for some products; they make it more difficult to realize the benefits of economies in other fields.

(3) Finally, "progress is not and cannot be continuous. The next important step forward is often costly and cannot be taken until a certain quantum of prospective advantages has accumulated."

Second, acting to *reinforce* increasing returns:

(4) Resource discoveries and the growth of scientific knowledge are the most important. He points out that the causal connections run both ways.

(5) Population growth *may* have such an effect, but need not.

(6) The search for markets must be assigned the central historical role. "The search for markets is not a matter of disposing of a 'surplus product,' in the Marxian sense, but of finding an outlet for a potential product. Nor is it wholly a matter of multiplying profits by multiplying sales; it is partly a matter of augmenting profits by reducing costs."

These points may seem simple, even obvious. It is only in review-

[46] *Ibid.*, p. 534.

[47] Young might also have distinguished here between price and income effects on demand; if income effects are substituted, his qualification tends to vanish.

ing the earlier literature that Young's statement of the issues comes into proper relief. First, he points out that static partial and general equilibrium analysis often obscures the major theme, the causes of the wealth of nations.[48] Second, he argues that the interaction of supply and demand must be viewed not only as determining prices and quantities, but also as a propulsive force in the broader conception of a market adapting itself over time. The interrelation of economic activities is thus seen as a constant, though uneven, process of creative destruction in which old firms pass away and new kinds of firms, producing new kinds of products, replace them. "With the extension of the division of labour among industries, the representative firm, like the industry of which it is a part, loses its identity."

Third, his point about the effect of bottlenecks in a particular sector, as reflected throughout the economy, is important for our subject. Indeed, if we consider, for example, an inelastic domestic supply schedule for capital goods as such a bottleneck, we can then see that he has in effect restated an aspect of the trade-development problem.

Fourth, progress is uneven. This is an abrupt departure from the neo-classical school, and one that is of course applicable to both balanced growth and unbalanced growth arguments.

Fifth, the search for markets is elevated to the role of a major determinant of economic progress. His attempt to distinguish between this view and the Marxist one is not wholly successful. He does not explain why surplus capacity might not be an equally valid cause of the quest. But this does not lessen the significance of what he says. The application to LDC's is clear. The prospective market is limited by demand and supply restrictions. Hence follows the familiar modern balanced growth case for simultaneous expansion of many sectors. But Young's point also leads us along another line, reminiscent of the vent for surplus approach to Smith and Mill. If, in fact, the search for domestic markets in LDC's is unrewarding in respect to demand or supply of required productive factors, then whatever trade potential exists must be exploited. If there are factors uniquely adapted for export production (for example, coffee land plus surplus farm labor), then the sequence described by Smith and elaborated by Myint [49] can follow. Now it is clear that the increasing returns se-

[48] Other neo-classical writers were well aware of the issue, but their treatments of it lack clarity. There is generally an uneasy effort to reconcile it with equilibrium analysis. Alfred Marshall, *Industry and Trade,* 2nd ed., New York, Macmillan, 1919.

[49] "The 'Classical Theory' of International Trade and the Underdeveloped Countries."

quence described by Young *can* follow from such beginnings. Whether or not it will is primarily a question of the linkages created or forced by the process of establishing the export industry. Thus, the whole unbalanced growth sequence may also emerge from this quest for markets.

Young's own final summation of his views is difficult to improve on:

First, the mechanism of increasing returns is not to be discerned adequately by observing the effects of variations in the size of an individual firm or of a particular industry, for the progressive division and specialization of industries is an essential part of the process by which increasing returns are realized. What is required is that industrial operations be seen as an interrelated whole. Second, the securing of increasing returns depends upon the progressive division of labour, and the principal economies of the division of labour, in its modern forms, are the economies which are to be had by using labour in roundabout or indirect ways.[50] Third, the division of labour depends on the extent of the market, but the extent of the market also depends upon the division of labour. In this circumstance lies the possibility of economic progress, apart from the progress which comes as a result of the new knowledge which men are able to gain, whether in the pursuit of their economic or non-economic interests.[51]

Young's lecture has nothing to recommend directly about development policy. What he offers is a view of the process. The sometimes contradictory recommendations that have since stemmed from his work reflect the fact that the development process has many facets; each beholder can concentrate on one that attracts him. The operational question, of course, is whether he selects the significant one for the particular situation. The next chapter examines modern development theories with this question in mind.

[50] This statement should imply not only higher capital-labor ratios in a given industry but also the establishment of new firms and industries. (J.P.)

[51] Young, "Increasing Returns and Economic Progress," pp. 539–540.

CHAPTER FOUR

Trade and Development: A Survey of Contemporary Theory

INTRODUCTION

Economic development returned to the forefront of economic theorists' discussions after World War II. The causes of the resurgence after a century of quiescence are almost surely political. Since 1945, sixty new nations have been established, virtually all of them in early stages of economic development. In the preceding century, the North considered the problem of underdevelopment abroad as the primary concern of private investors and of Colonial Offices moving in mysterious, though not necessarily separate, ways. The foreign ministries had no need to concern themselves with LDC economic growth. To the extent that development entered international relations, it was as a problem of protecting the foreign investments of rich countries' citizens; or of the competition for raw materials and markets.

Today development is important to LDC's partly as an end in itself; it is also of interest to the rich countries as an instrument of foreign policy, to influence LDC behavior. Hence, the perpetuation of foreign aid as discussed in Chapter 1 and the interminable public and official discussion of the subject.

On the academic front the subject has apparently become equally absorbing. No issue of an economic journal is complete without at least one article on the theory of development. Every month, several new professional books on economic development are published. No country, however remote, seems to be able to avoid an international conference or colloquy convened in order to illuminate the world's understanding of the subject.

This proliferation is so great and our perspective so close that we cannot safely distinguish what is enduring. If we limit ourselves primarily to economists who discuss the trade-development relationship, the job is somewhat easier, if only because the field is smaller. Much of the current controversy stems directly from the 19th century and we will have occasion to draw the analogies. Even in this more restricted field, there are hundreds of books and articles and dozens of competent writers at work adding to the list steadily. I make no attempt here to cover the entire range of modern theory on the subject. Instead I will select several of the outstanding views, representing a spectrum of contemporary thought, and analyze them as being fairly representative of what economic theory now tells us about trade and development.

Although underdeveloped countries vary greatly in respect to level of development and rate of economic and social change, they nearly all have some common economic characteristics. In addition to our per capita income cutoff point, these include relatively low rates of income growth per capita because of high rates of population growth,[1] a relatively small per cent of gross domestic product devoted to investment, high proportions of the work force engaged in agriculture (generally more than 50 per cent), low literacy levels, shortages of technical and managerial skills, and generally low levels of per capita investment in public works and services.

If, under these conditions, a country is poor and wants to become rich, it needs time and resources—capital goods, a skilled work force, a modern technology, and so on. The economic requirements for growth can be bought with these inputs. The issues we will discuss in the rest of this chapter revolve around the choice of policies aimed at the sometimes conflicting goals of minimizing the time span and the human and material capital needed to achieve some target rate of growth or level of development. We do not discuss the political, social, and institutional barriers to growth. It is beyond my task here to treat these matters comprehensively, and useless to dismiss them with a perfunctory statement.

I have not asked heretofore whether it is sensible for the govern-
merits of that goal from the viewpoint of the government.
ment of an underdeveloped country to try to accelerate its growth. I want to conclude this introductory section with a digression about the

The advantages of faster growth are evident; it allows people to raise their consumption levels faster than they otherwise could, and

[1] Some LDC's—Taiwan, Puerto Rico, Thailand—have had rapid rates of per capita income growth in recent years; see Chapter 2.

governments to dispose of resources that might otherwise not be available. Most people want to be better off, and most governments seek more power. Therefore development presumably coincides with the political interests of both citizens and government. It allows the government to increase its tax base for spending on defense or other purposes not directly or primarily related to consumption standards. It offers, in short, the possibilities of prosperity and power. Thus we normally think that rising living standards will promote the self-interest of all parties.

But it may also involve costs to the government. As noted in Chapter 1, an abrupt acceleration of economic growth reflects and induces social changes that may create as many problems for the government as they solve.[2] If a government wants to command more of the national resources in order to invest more in public works, government-owned industry, military spending, and so on, there may be easier ways to do it than by a major effort at economic transformation. Confiscation of foreign assets is likely to be more effective in the short run, and also more popular politically, than efforts to increase taxes or to devalue.[3]

Furthermore, the government may either overestimate the importance of economic development as a condition of holding effective power, or else it may underestimate the problems created by the attempt to transform the economy. People who are active politically or are active in the modern sector of the economy may have a strong interest in promoting development. Clearly, there is nothing to lose politically by proposing to make the economy more prosperous. But: (1) if confiscation is ruled out; (2) foreign aid is not increasing; and (3) the short-run benefits of technical assistance are already largely realized, some other method will be needed in order to expand the market. Almost any such method will have political costs because it will normally require higher savings and less current consumption in

[2] Cf. Mancur Olson, Jr., "Rapid Growth as a Destabilizing Force," *Journal of Economic History,* Vol. 23 (December 1963), pp. 529–552.

[3] Confiscation may mean losing foreign aid or at least the aid given by governments whose nationals lose property. But this is a politico-economic calculation that each government must make for itself. The political gain from rejecting aid, under the circumstances of a dramatic confiscation, may outweigh the loss. If there are few foreign assets, for example, there will be nothing much to confiscate, but this may simply make confiscation economically painless for all parties. For a discussion of the economic advantages, see Martin Bronfenbrenner, "The Appeal of Confiscation in Economic Development," *Economic Development and Cultural Change,* Vol. III (April 1955), pp. 201–218.

the short run than would be possible if the savings rate were lower.[4] The government must judge whether it is worthwhile to pay the costs in the interests of development. Sometimes, naturally, it will try to achieve the growth targets without paying the price. This attempt is usually associated with domestic inflation, and ordinarily tends to postpone the political reckoning. Whether the delay is advantageous or not depends on the case. The experiences in Turkey (1950–61) and Brazil (1950–63) suggest certain political dangers. In those cases, governments that followed "easy" wage and price policies were ultimately overthrown by force. But in neither case did the proximate cause of the overthrow arise directly from the effects of economic policy. It might be maintained, however, that in both cases the government's futile effort to control the political opposition was itself a desperate measure resulting largely from economic impasse. On the other hand, governments have also been overthrown for trying to introduce financial "discipline" and tax reforms, or simply for refusing to abandon the *status quo,* or for almost any other reason conceivable.

In this study I assume simply that LDC governments do in fact want faster growth, or at least, higher incomes, whether or not it makes sense politically. In this way, we avoid a discussion of some of the most difficult issues, namely the balance between national growth objectives and other goals of policy on the part of government, pressure groups, political parties, and individuals. But there is no shortage of complications in what remains.

FOUR STRANDS OF CONTROVERSY

The contemporary theoretical discussion of trade and development initially concentrated on four issues, all more or less directly linked: free trade and protection, balanced and unbalanced growth, price stability and inflation, and investment criteria for economic develop-

[4] Although, in practice, countries with rapid income growth also have steady increases in consumption, unless the government priorities are devoted to war or defense. The problem cited above arises when the government tries to institute measures leading to new and higher savings. If they are successfully instituted and prove productive, the conflict between savings and consumption loses its explosiveness for that level of savings.

ment. This chapter discusses the first two issues in some detail, and the latter two more briefly. This is not a measure of the relative importance of the subjects, but only a method of exposition. In fact, the least important issue of the four is balanced versus unbalanced growth, which is largely a semantic argument. However, the controversies about balanced growth and protectionism reveal rather fully the persistent and complex issues that bar the way to a general economic theory of economic development for poor countries. As we will see, they are all, from a certain viewpoint, simply aspects of a single topic, different parts of the same puzzle.

Recently, economists have come to see this most clearly by applying an operational research approach to development theory. If a nation, or its economic planning agency, sets itself a certain growth target in light of a given set of resources of labor and capital, known production relationships, known world prices for internationally traded products, and known rates of transformation of importable into exportable goods, then its production potential can be tested in light of the targets. It may turn out that the targets are not consistent, and are unbalanced in the sense that they cannot be achieved without external assistance, or in the sense that they can be achieved only through an implicit set of relationships among factor and product prices, or foreign exchange rates that society would reject. Furthermore if the targets exceed the economy's capacity to produce, or set up a very high implicit price for foreign exchange, it is safe to assume that inflationary pressures will soon assert themselves. Therefore, a general equilibrium approach to planning indicates that balance, inflation, comparative advantage, and investment criteria are all aspects of a more general framework. To make the discussion manageable here, I take these issues separately. Furthermore, for expository reasons, this chapter treats these controversies in polarized terms, although in fact they are not "either/or" issues.

Free Trade and Protection

This was a staple topic of economic debate in the last century. In the years since 1950 it has returned, with a few new twists. The argument for free trade as a policy for promoting economic development rests on the theory of comparative advantage as developed by Ricardo and Mill.

The protectionist view stems from such 19th century writers as List and Carey and this century from Manoilesco.[5] The case rests on a variety of arguments: economies of scale, external economies, static gains from tariff imposition, effects on domestic income distribution, differences in productivity between industry and agriculture in LDC's, operation of an international demonstration effect, greater security of the domestic market, and a tendency for LDC terms of trade to deteriorate. Singer, Myrdal, and Prebisch have been among the chief contemporary advocates.

The Free Traders. The theory of comparative costs developed by Ricardo and Mill shows, as discussed above, that a country will surely be better off (have higher real income) if it exports the things that it produces relatively cheaply and imports those that it produces relatively expensively. The general case for free trade is built upon this demonstration. From this arises the case for liberal trade policies, as a keystone of LDC growth policies.

Most LDC's have small domestic markets. Only a half dozen of them, out of a worldwide total of over one hundred, have populations of more than 50 million, which at current Southern GNP levels of $150 per capita would probably be adequate for a wide range of domestic industry.

A small market is by definition an obstacle to growth that encompasses all other economic barriers. Obviously, if the domestic market is small and resources are immobile among occupations, the vent for surplus case cited by Adam Smith takes on added interest. The world market is then the only readily available way to exploit resources. But, as pointed out in Chapter 3, we do not need to assume that resources are immobile in order to affirm that trade can promote the growth of income. In Nurkse's words:

> The case for international specialization is firmly based on considerations of economic efficiency. The world is not rich enough to be able to despise efficiency. The optimum pattern of specialization is governed by the principle of comparative advantage. And yet there is some question whether it alone can give all the guidance needed by countries whose dominant and deliberate aim is economic development (that is increasing real income per capita).[6]

[5] *The Theory of Protection and International Trade,* London, P. S. King, 1931.
[6] "International Trade Theory and Development Policy," in H. S. Ellis, ed., *Economic Development for Latin America,* London, Macmillan, 1961, p. 234.

The modern neo-classical writers have affirmed that the disadvantages of small size reinforce the efficiency motive and therefore give LDC's an added incentive to look toward the world market as a basis for growth. In fact, for the free trade advocate, trade-oriented growth offers a unique combination of advantages: maximum output and consumer satisfaction from the world's resources (thereby offering the possibility of maximum rates of capital formation) combined with important effects as an engine of growth. It provides indispensable knowledge of technique; facilitates transfer of capital; promotes competition, and hence, presumably, productivity; overcomes the disadvantage of small domestic markets; and also provides the capital goods required for increasing output.

The classical economists saw no conflict between the gains from trade and those from growth.[7] Since free trade tended to maximize national output at any moment of time, it would presumably permit the most rapid rate of growth. But it is agreed today that this is not necessarily true. It is possible that the requirements for maximizing national income this year are different from those of maximizing the rate at which national income grows. Furthermore, if prices do not reflect real costs, then free trade will not reflect the structure of comparative advantage, and the free trade arguments lose much of their force. This discrepancy is a basis of infant industry arguments for protection. As noted above, the recent experience of LDC's seems much less congenial to the growth through trade thesis than that of the 19th century. Growth of the export sector has often not carried over to other sectors. Countries that rely on primary commodity exports have tended to remain dual economies, with a relatively efficient, though often slow growing, export sector; and a large subsistence economy little affected by the growth of trade.

Why should trade fail to transmit growth throughout the domestic economy of many LDC's, although it so obviously succeeded for Canada, Sweden, Great Britain, Japan and many other countries? First, and most obvious, many LDC's are profoundly different socially and culturally from nations whose economic accomplishments they seek to emulate. The failure of trade (or other traditional sources of growth) to propel general economic growth is hardly surprising in a country where many social circumstances conspire to maintain the present economic pattern.[8] Naturally, if economic

[7] Cf. Meier, *International Trade and Development,* Chapter 7.

[8] See T. K. Basu, H. A. Ali and J. Talukdar, *The Bengal Peasant from Time to*

institutions—land tenure and credit systems, or organization of product and factor markets—are also resistant to change, it is even harder to speed up economic growth.

Second, much may depend on the nature of the export product, in respect to both demand and supply. Is demand for LDC exports increasing more slowly than supply, so that with constant import prices LDC terms of trade are deteriorating? There is no conclusive answer, because so much depends on the choice of base periods for comparison, and the particular definition of terms of trade adopted. As we saw in Chapter 2, however, LDC trade has grown much more slowly since 1950 than Atlantic Community or Soviet Bloc trade. If the demand for certain LDC exports in the aggregate is both price-inelastic and income-inelastic, and the supply increases faster than demand so that prices tend to fall without compensating increases in sales, then the exporters as a group would be better off restricting output, and some individual producers would be better off in other lines of work, if there were any. This is not the situation for all products; petroleum and certain other minerals are clear exceptions. But the record of commodity trade leaves the inference that, for many nations in search of rapid growth, trade may be a rather unreliable source.

This is not to say that the inability of trade to promote growth in such cases is immutable. The tendency of the rich countries to increase their imports of LDC food and certain raw materials rather little, as their incomes grow, reflects more than the pattern of consumer preferences alone. It also reflects rich countries' restrictions, prior and new, on imports. Almost all Atlantic countries restrict imports of temperate agricultural products, and such competing products as sugar, oilseeds, cotton, and citrus. Restrictions on minerals that compete with domestic production are common. A change in Northern import policies could undoubtedly lend new stimulus to trade as an engine of LDC growth.

On the supply side, as pointed out by a number of writers, the conditions of production of export goods help to determine whether trade will promote expansion throughout the economy. If the export good is one that, like cocoa or coffee, can be produced by small-scale farmers with no need for frequently reorganizing farm technology,

---

Time, Bombay, Asia Publishing House, 1962. This interesting study traces the social life of an Indian village near Calcutta from 1872 to 1958. There have been great changes, but the basic social and economic relations have changed very little, despite the legal imposition of land reforms in 1953. Yet the village is less than 70 miles from Calcutta.

nor for domestic industrial processing facilities, nor for large-scale infrastructure expense such as transportation or power networks, then the export sector can operate relatively independently, without major effects in transforming the structure of the national economy and society. Furthermore, in those tropical countries where agricultural labor was relatively plentiful but capital and skilled labor relatively dear, it was natural to turn to such export lines; it was in a sense dictated by the structure of comparative advantage.

In addition to tropical crops, many LDC's had a comparative advantage in mineral products. Mineral production was based largely on foreign capital, foreign skills, and foreign markets. In extreme cases (typically petroleum) except for some unskilled labor, it was essentially an economic exclave of the industrial countries. Of course, the LDC's benefited substantially from mineral tax and royalty payments, but there is little or nothing in the economic organization of oil production that forces LDC's to introduce extensive technological change throughout the rest of the economy.[9]

As we know from the classical economists, if there is no practical domestic alternative to such forms of export specialization, it is pointless to complain on the grounds that the existing structure diverges from an ideal. However, it is obvious that given the choice, national export development policies would normally want to aim at lines that either: (1) distributed the revenues widely so as to build up a market for consumer goods; or (2) resulted in a substantial reinvestment of capital domestically, outside the exclave economy; or (3) forced the domestic economy to build up new skills and capital plant as a technical requirement for export production.

The first case might be exemplified by cocoa farming in Ghana. The traditional structure of society was not profoundly altered, but a relatively widespread distribution of cocoa export revenues meant that a substantial potential domestic market for manufactures was created. In any event, the government of Ghana chose to tap much of the cocoa earnings for particularly dubious forms of attaining what it termed "economic development," so that the results on domestic market expansion were less than dramatic.

The second case is exemplified by most of the 19th-century development of North America and the British white-settler dominions; and also more currently by the development efforts of such countries

[9] These highly capitalized mineral industries often create a small skilled labor force, in contrast with plantation agriculture; but there may be no particular economic or technological stimulus to spread these skills throughout the economy.

as Taiwan, Israel, or before 1961, Algeria under the French-sponsored Constantine plan.

The third case, where the technical requirements of export products impose an economic transformation, offers perhaps the strongest impulse toward accelerated domestic growth. Thus, the development of Canadian grain trade or of Southern Rhodesia's scattered mineral deposits required a national rail network and the training of skilled labor. This network opened up both consumer markets for manufactures and urban and export markets for farmers. Furthermore, the development of the grain trade led to the establishment of milling and storage facilities; and many of the construction and machinery requirements could be met by local industry, so that self-generating elements were built into the process. Similarly, copper mining in Chile led steadily to the growth of copper refining and rolling; and this in turn led to the spread of acquired skills throughout the economy.

By contrast, the Iranian oil industry was established along the Persian Gulf so that no national transport system was needed to bring the oil to market. The construction materials, equipment, skilled labor, and even food were imported; the product was exported, and the country as a whole benefited financially, but not in economic transformation.

Thus, on both demand and supply sides much of the development effects of LDC export specialization depended on the characteristics of the product. When we observe, with Nurkse, that trade is less an engine of growth for LDC's now than in the past, we are making an observation about the conditions of world demand and of domestic supply, not about the merits of trade in a vacuum. The modern neo-classical view simply affirms that these conditions can often be favorable for growth and that the disadvantages of protection outweigh the gains.

The Protectionists. Much of the strongest doubt about the virtues of trade as an agent of development has come from such writers as Prebisch, Myrdal, and Singer, who claim that there are systematic forces at work in the modern world tending to diminish LDC benefits from trade. This viewpoint is exactly opposed to that of the classical economists and of neo-classical economists, including Keynes.[10] They believed that in the long run terms of trade would swing to

[10] "Reply to Sir William Beveridge," *Economic Journal,* Vol. XXXIII (December 1923), pp. 476–488.

favor food and raw materials producers, under the influence of diminishing returns.

There has been a long and wearisome professional controversy on this point, which has emerged at roughly the following: (1) because the data are fragmentary and the effect of quality change hard to measure, we do not have enough evidence to know what has happened since the 19th century; (2) LDC terms of trade have fallen since the early 1950's, and probably since the late 1920's, while they have risen since the Depression of the 1930's; (3) the impact of the recent declines has been uneven, with Latin America harder hit than Asia and the Middle East.[11]

In any event, most LDC's today are dissatisfied with their rates and levels of economic development. For many of them, the neo-protectionist views of Myrdal, Prebisch and Singer are very attractive and are expressed in current LDC efforts to recast the world trading system.[12]

Myrdal, departing from Folke Hilgerdt's findings that the growth of trade had not closed the income gap between industrial countries and the thickly populated LDC's, goes on to argue that trade tends to widen the income gap between rich and poor countries.[13]

> If left to take its own course, economic development is a process of circular and cumulative causation which tends to award its favors to those who are already well-endowed and even to thwart the efforts of those who happen to live in regions that are lagging behind. . . . If left unregulated, international trade and capital movements would thus often be the media through which the economic progress in the advanced countries would have backsetting effects in the underdeveloped world . . . forces in the markets will in a cumulative way tend to cause ever greater international inequalities between countries as to their level of economic development and average national income per capita.[14]

Myrdal's arguments against trade as an agent of growth are based on low price and income elasticities of demand for primary exports,

[11] See Chapters 2 and 7 of this study.

[12] G. Myrdal, *An International Economy,* Harper, New York, 1956, and *Rich Lands and Poor,* Harper, New York, 1957; Singer, *International Development,* Chapter 13; R. Prebisch, *Towards a New Trade Policy for Development,* UNCTAD Document E/Conf. 46/3, United Nations, February 12, 1964; also "Commercial Policy in the Underdeveloped Countries," *American Economic Review, Papers and Proceedings,* Vol. XLIV (May 1959), pp. 251–273.

[13] *Industrialization and Foreign Trade,* Geneva, League of Nations, 1945.

[14] *Development and Underdevelopment,* Cairo, National Bank of Egypt, 1956, pp. 48–50.

and the weakness of trade's propulsive effect on the economy as a whole. The labor supply in LDC's is plentiful and world markets for primary exports are competitive, so that the benefits of technological progress are passed on to the importing countries. This is, in effect, the terms of trade argument that we have discussed above.

Myrdal believes that LDC's should not try to attract foreign capital because it will flow mostly into export sectors, thereby further unbalancing the dual economy and depriving the exporter of any genuine developmental benefits. He does not say, however, why LDC's would be better off without foreign investment.

Myrdal also attacks trade along the Ricardo-Nurkse lines of its demonstration effect in raising consumption demand, thereby inhibiting savings in poor countries. It may be seriously doubted, however, whether trade is the major source of demonstration effects today, considering the wide availability of Western publications, movies, and radio, to say nothing of tourists. Furthermore, neither Myrdal nor anyone else has demonstrated that the unfavorable economic effects of international emulation outweigh the favorable ones.

In light of these considerations, Myrdal recommends that LDC's follow a protectionist policy that will: (1) permit domestic market growth; (2) lead to higher rates of employment; (3) realize external economies for the country considered as a unit; and (4) redress the domestic price structure that discriminates against industry.[15] This approach extends the infant industry argument to the growing up of the economy as a whole.[16]

Myrdal's formula for LDC growth therefore envisages a situation in which each country will largely reserve to itself the domestic market for industry. This, he says, will stimulate growth, and eventually the nation need no longer fear the cumulative disequalizing forces that now result from North-South trade.

Hans Singer has made the same points as Myrdal concerning (1) the unfavorable effect of foreign investment, creating a dual economy that fails to spread its benefits within the exporting country; (2) the consequences of investment that diverted LDC's into "types of activity offering less scope for technical progress, internal and ex-

[15] Interestingly, it is often claimed that LDC price systems discriminate against agriculture, because industrial tariffs are too high, and domestic foodgrain prices are sometimes fixed at low levels by the government. Burma is a case in point. Cf. Chapter 5 below.

[16] Meier, *International Trade and Development,* p. 125.

ternal economies taken by themselves and withheld from the course of their economic histories a central factor of dynamic radiation which has revolutionized society in the industrial countries." [17] But Singer's fire is reserved principally for the terms of trade effects. The argument is simple. Productivity increases faster in the North than in the South, yet the terms of trade tend to move against the South. The fruits of technical progress accrue in fact largely to the North, because Northern product and labor markets are monopolistic, while those in the South are competitive. The South does not even benefit from sales increases resulting from the price fall, because demand for primary exports is generally inelastic with respect to both price and income. Meanwhile money incomes rise in the North, and the real cost of Northern imports from LDC's falls, thanks to competitive world markets for Southern exports.

There is a certain kinship between this view and the Marxist theories of imperialism discussed in Chapter 3. As Singer says:

> Thus industrial countries have had the best of both worlds, both as consumers of primary commodities and as producers of manufactured articles; the underdeveloped countries have had the worst of both worlds, as consumers of manufactures and as producers of raw materials. There is perhaps a legitimate germ of truth in the charge that foreign investment of the traditional type formed part of a system of "economic imperialism" and of "exploitation." [18]

The terms-of-trade school has been most forcefully represented by Raul Prebisch, the Secretary-General of UNCTAD. His policy views, as expressed in his report to UNCTAD, were summarized in Chapter 2. This chapter examines the theoretical groundwork that he has attempted to construct in three relatively recent expositions.[19]

The terms of trade of "the periphery" (LDC's) tend to decline relative to "the center" (Atlantic Community) for four reasons: (1) the periphery fails to benefit from technological progress, because LDC exports are priced competitively while the center has monopolistic markets (the Singer argument); (2) during business cycles, LDC terms of trade improve on the upswing and decline on the downswing, but presumably decline each time by more than the prior

[17] *International Development,* p. 165.

[18] *Ibid.,* p. 167.

[19] "Commercial Policy in the Underdeveloped Countries," pp. 251–273; "The Economic Development of Latin America," *Economic Bulletin for Latin America* (February 1962); and *Towards a New Trade Policy for Development.*

rise, so that the long-term effect is downward; (3) the periphery has a higher income elasticity of demand for imports than the center, so that to achieve balance between imports and exports, LDC's must reduce domestic wages and prices, accepting a deterioration of their terms of trade; (4) because most people in LDC's produce food as subsistence or commercial farmers, productivity increases in the export sectors simply mean that LDC's will offer larger supplies in the world market at prices that are fixed by the real cost of food, if the export market is competitive—thus the gains from productivity increase are channeled to the foreign consumer.[20]

It is sufficient here to point out that market structure and cyclical effects are not necessary to Prebisch's argument for protection. As long as world demand for industrial imports is rising faster than world demand for primary imports, the terms of trade of primary exporters will tend to deteriorate, other things being equal. The data of Chapter 2 indicate that LDC exports are rising more slowly in quantity than Atlantic Community exports, despite falling relative prices. This tends to support the case for a differential growth in demand.[21]

The significant point to Prebisch is that the mechanisms he describes inexorably reduce LDC export earnings below the levels they would reach if the structure of world trade were different. Furthermore, in his eyes, the remedy—industrialization—cannot be achieved by import substitution alone. Indeed, in view of the small size of the market, it has already gone too far in many countries, raising costs unduly. The North must open up its markets to both Southern commodities and manufactures. For two reasons, the South cannot rely on its own actions to redress the balance. First, agricultural labor is in perennial surplus so that increases in farm productivity are not passed on in the form of higher real wages (or, more precisely, greater buying power for non-farm products). This in turn means that commodity prices will be below the levels they would reach if farm wages were able to rise. The benefit, according to Prebisch, is transmitted to consumers of the commodities and to those who supply

[20] This argument has been widely criticized on technical grounds. The most complete statement is found in M. J. Flanders, "Prebisch on Protectionism," *Economic Journal,* Vol. LXXIV (June 1964), pp. 305–326.

[21] It has been argued that this slow export growth reflects supply shortages of traditional exports in LDC's, but the evidence for the argument is not convincing. A detailed discussion is found in A. Maizels, "Effects of Industrialization on Exports of Primary Producing Countries," *Kyklos,* Vol. 14, No. 1 (1961), pp. 18–46.

manufactured goods. The only effective remedy is population control, which involves, for the South, an uncomfortably remote time horizon.

Second, even if it were possible to raise commodity prices, as proposed at UNCTAD, its primary role in Prebisch's view would apparently be as a source of investment capital for industrialization. Income elasticities of demand for most commodities are too low in view of supply increases to allow commodity specialization to be a source of continued prosperity. But, as we have seen, Prebisch believes that industrialization requires not only investment capital but also opening up Northern markets for manufactured goods to the South. Thus, for Prebisch, protectionism of the traditional variety is not enough. It must be supplemented by the measures described in Chapter 2.

An Evaluation of Neo-Protectionist Arguments. The Prebisch-Singer-Myrdal view is now considered as received doctrine by LDC official representatives and has essentially been formalized in the Final Act of UNCTAD. The principal policy issues of North-South trade revolve around the merits of LDC proposals designed to create a balance that according to the terms of trade argument cannot be established by the free play of market forces.

I will not discuss the merits of the policy proposals in this chapter because they constitute much of the subject of Chapters 6–8. The analysis of this section is primarily directed to the terms-of-trade argument. There is no doubt that LDC terms of trade have declined in the past 15 years, and also over the period 1928–65. Furthermore, from Chapter 2 we know that LDC exports have increased more slowly than those of developed countries over the same period. Thus LDC exports are a declining proportion of world exports. Furthermore the decline in terms of trade often is not sufficiently compensated for by the increase in volume. This doesn't mean that there is an inherent tendency for LDC terms of trade to fall but it does indicate that LDC development efforts are likely to be handicapped by foreign exchange shortages unless present commodity trends are reversed or new sources of foreign exchange are made available.

The analytical case is not particularly strong, but neither is it easy to refute. The principal arguments against the terms-of-trade school are:

(1) In estimating what has happened to terms of trade, everything depends on choice of a base year, and on the choice of a particular definition of terms of trade.

(2) The analysis is not complete. For example, if wages are rigid in the center and flexible in the periphery, it should be possible for LDC's to compete increasingly on a price basis in fields where both North and South produce, or to enter fields where the North was formerly the only producer. Even if the North effects barriers to new exports from the South, increased real wages in the North mean that it is less able to compete with the South in Southern markets.

(3) The analysis tends to treat labor as the only factor of production, so that its conclusions about changing cost relationships apply only to a part of total costs.

(4) The fact that a product or factor market is monopolistic in one country doesn't mean that it is monopolistic in the North as a whole. There is substantial price competition in world export markets among different supplying countries.

(5) Prebisch does not explain why the downward pressure on wages in LDC's which accounts, in his theory, for the terms of trade decline, could not be offset by channeling surplus labor into construction and other industries that need no protection.

(6) He passes by with bare mention the alternative of devaluation for LDC's (although in other writings,[22] he objects to devaluation on the grounds that it would result in a higher level of LDC exports than is desirable from a welfare viewpoint). In the UNCTAD report, he simply says that devaluation or subsidy of exports is inferior to preferences as a method of encouraging LDC manufactures, because

> the costs of promoting exports . . . would have to be borne by the developing countries themselves [so that] neither of the solutions would be as satisfactory . . . as preferential treatment for their exports.[23]

What emerges from the controversy is not clear. Able critics have pointed out the technical defects of the Myrdal-Prebisch analysis,[24] but it is hard to avoid the conclusion that they occasionally try to prove too much. After all, the facts are clear. LDC income is growing

[22] "Commercial Policy In Underdeveloped Countries," pp. 260–261, 269–273.

[23] *Towards a New Trade Policy,* p. 93.

[24] Flanders, "Prebisch on Protectionism"; Meier, *International Trade and Development,* Chapters 3, 7; also Johnson, *Economic Policies,* Chapter 1. Margaret G. De Vries has surveyed the neo-protectionist controversy and provided a comprehensive bibliography of the literature in a recent article, "Trade and Exchange Policy and Economic Development: Two Decades of Evolving Views," *Oxford Economic Papers,* Vol. 18 (March 1966), pp. 19–44.

slowly per capita; and while there are a number of reasons for slow growth, one important one is the foreign exchange constraint. Whether this constraint results primarily from the mechanism hypothesized by Myrdal and Prebisch, or simply from factors that they fail to stress—income elasticities of demand, differences in factor mobility, or over-valued exchange rates—the policy prescriptions probably require something more than a movement to freer trade by the rich countries, desirable as that may be in itself.

Prebisch and Myrdal are undoubtedly right in their insistence that the present structure of international trade is in some respects a serious barrier to rapid economic growth in many LDC's (for example, LDC's would clearly be better off if the Atlantic Community removed barriers to agricultural imports). Where growth is hampered by foreign exchange restrictions, and if devaluation or more aid is ruled out, the logical remedies would seem to include import substitution, and promotion of exports of commodities and manufactured products. For LDC's that do not export oil and a few other minerals in strong demand, trade growth is held back both by inelastic demand and by agricultural protectionism in the Atlantic Community. World demand for manufactures, on the other hand, is buoyant. But tariff structures and quantitative restrictions in industrial countries aggravate the supply difficulties created by inexperience and small scale of production. Prebisch himself points out that import substitution in many countries has long since passed the point of economic rationality, as defined by the opportunity cost of the import-substituting factors in export industries.

It may very well be that the critics are right for the wrong reasons. Their emphasis on the alleged unfairness of the existing system may divert LDC attention from internal reforms, which in themselves might go far in correcting the trade gap. This is all in the realm of speculation, and each observer is his own ultimate authority. Nonetheless, as Chenery and Strout have shown, restrictions on the ability to import were clearly among the limiting factors in the growth potential of a number of underdeveloped countries in recent years.[25] Among the countries whose growth appears to be held back by import restrictions were Brazil, Colombia, and Turkey; while Mexico, Pakistan, India, and Taiwan may also have fallen into this category.

[25] "Foreign Assistance and Economic Development," *American Economic Review,* Vol. LVI (September 1966), pp. 679–733. The results are based on 1957–1962 data.

Recent empirical work seems to be consistent with this aspect of the Prebisch thesis, but the resulting policy implications are by no means clear. Even if his appraisal of the illness were, despite its logical lapses, basically correct, it does not follow that his remedies—domestic industrialization, a worldwide preference system, and disguised income transfers—are likely to cure the disease. These questions will be examined later in the study.

Finally, the simplest logical case for protectionism rests on somewhat different grounds from those advanced by Prebisch and others—namely, that the results of free trade may not reflect the structure of comparative advantage. For example, industrial wages in LDC's may, for institutional reasons, be higher than the real cost of labor, defined in terms of a subsistence budget. In that case, protectionism or subsidy may be the only feasible way to redress the balance. Second, if exchange rates are pegged at levels that diverge from equilibrium, LDC's may find that their propensity to import manufactured products is greater than would prevail under a foreign exchange equilibrium. To the extent that protection is used to offset divergence from true comparative advantage, either in the static sense as discussed here or from long-term evolution of comparative advantage as in infant-industry protection, then the case is on a relatively sound footing. However, the adoption of comparative advantage arguments as a rationale for protectionism logically entails the obligations to show the connection between policies that are adopted and the static or dynamic structure of comparative advantage. Prebisch has frequently stressed that much LDC protectionism is irrational, essentially because it is often inconsistent with long-run comparative advantage. However, he has chosen to base his case for commercial policy reforms primarily on somewhat different grounds, where the footing, as I have tried to show above, may be somewhat more slippery.

Balanced and Unbalanced Growth

While the free-traders and the new protectionists were jousting, the balanced growth controversy apparently held an equally warm spot in the theorists' affections. The chief writers on balanced growth—both those who propose it such as Lewis, Rosenstein-Rodan, and Nurkse, and those who oppose it, such as Hirschman and Streeten—have tended to reinforce the attack on trade as an agent of growth. Economists have come to recognize that this controversy was largely sterile, because growth is inevitably balanced in the sense that demand and supply for products and factors of production must ultimately equalize; while even a balanced growth will stress some sectors more than others in accordance with the structure of comparative advantage, demand, and technical linkages in production.

Balanced Growth. The case for balanced growth builds on Young's description of the development process. The basic point has been expressed by Nurkse: [26] "Say's law is never valid in the sense that the output of any single industry, newly set up with capital equipment, can create its own demand." Thus, in a static economic situation, rapid growth must come from the simultaneous expansion of a number of industries, benefiting both from external economies on the supply side and from the simultaneous expansion of demand.

Furthermore, because the market is small, the case for balanced growth has a second element—the need for high levels of balanced investment in order to attain a reasonably efficient scale in production. It has sometimes been argued that balanced growth is not in itself a prescription for accelerating the rate of growth. But there is no doubt that in the eyes of those who advance the theory, notably Nurkse and Rosenstein-Rodan, the balance will: (1) by making Sav's law operative, promote market expansion, (2) enable more effective use of much more capital than could be invested without a simultaneous expansion of many industries related in respect to supply, demand, or both. In Nurkse's words: "balanced growth is an exercise in economic development with unlimited supplies of capital." [27]

Why is it a better recipe for investment than specializing for the international market? The answer, according to Nurkse, is a question of fact. "The real trouble is that in the mid-twentieth century, with a few notable exceptions, conditions for this type of growth do not seem to be as promising as they were a hundred years ago." [28] His argument points out that income and price elasticity of demand for most LDC exports seem to be declining because of the tendency for unprocessed food to play a small role in rich countries' spending in-

[26] *Problems of Capital Formation in Underdeveloped Countries,* pp. 9, 12.

[27] *Equilibrium and Growth in the World Economy,* Cambridge, Massachusetts, Harvard University Press, 1961, p. 250. See also P. N. Rosenstein-Rodan, "Notes on the Theory of the Big Push," published in *Economic Development for Latin America,* London, Macmillan, 1962.

[28] *Equilibrium and Growth in the World Economy,* p. 244.

creases; while demand for industrial raw materials may be quite elastic because of competition from synthetics.

Thus income increases must come primarily from the domestic market, and the balanced growth pattern simultaneously enlarges the market and assures the supply of goods that consumers want. Thus Nurkse views balanced growth and trade as supplements:

> Once a country has adopted an optimum pattern and optimum degree of specialization [in international trade], how is it to achieve *continued* further growth if external demand conditions do not induce it? . . . There is no guarantee [of trade growth], especially if the export products which the comparative-advantage principle tells a country to produce face an external demand which (a) is generally inelastic with respect to price and (b) what may be more important, shows only a sluggish rate of increase in total volume.[29]

> The case for specialization as such is just as strong as ever, but that the forces making for transmission of growth from advanced to less developed countries may not be as powerful as they were. . . . Nor is this an argument for autarchy. There is plenty of room for home-market expansion without interfering with international trade.[30]

Other writers espousing balanced growth express the position on trade differently, but none deny its value in the economic system. Thus Lewis:

> The conclusion of this analysis is not very startling: it is that in development programmes all sectors of the economy should grow simultaneously, so as to keep a proper balance between industry and agriculture, and between production for home consumption and production for export.[31]

Lewis's interpretation of balance implies both a larger potential role for trade and a lesser emphasis on the simultaneous expansion of domestic manufactures as an alternative to trade: "the maintenance of equilibrium in world trade depends upon a balanced growth of manufactures, of raw materials and of food in the world as a whole." [32] His approach to the issues makes much less of such matters as the big push and external economies than other writers on the sub-

[29] *Ibid.*, p. 253.
[30] *Ibid.*, pp. 253–255.
[31] *The Theory of Economic Growth,* London, George Allen and Unwin, 1955, p. 283.
[32] *Ibid.*, p. 354.

ject. He stresses primarily the need for supply to expand according to income elasticities of demand.

Unbalanced Growth and the Critique of Balanced Growth. As Hirschman has said, the principal point to be advanced against the balanced growth approach of Nurkse and Rosenstein-Rodan is that it fails as a theory of economic development.[33] If it were possible to expand a number of economic sectors at once, so as to take advantage of external economies, and of expanded markets, then the problems of development would be relatively easy. It is precisely because the domestic capital, skills, and organization for the big push are lacking that LDC's remain poor. Balance in growth remains a sort of long-run national objective for poor countries. Rich countries with populations of more than ten million or so generally invest in a large number of domestic industries, even if they are heavily dependent on trade.

In that sense, growth will ultimately be balanced as a consequence of long-run market expansion. And Hirschman follows his critique of balanced growth with the observation, "it is the experience of unbalanced growth in the past that produces, at an advanced stage of economic development, the possibility of balanced growth." [34]

But, development policies must operate through proximate goals toward this possibility. This is the point where unbalanced growth theorists enter the picture. Starting from the point that balanced growth in Nurkse's sense (and *a fortiori* in the big push version) is a sign of a nation that is already developed, they ask in effect "what process is most likely to stimulate growth?" starting from a low level equilibrium where markets are small, productivity low, and the great majority of employment and consumption is agricultural. In such a case, Singer writes, "It is by no means certain that the right strategy for an underdeveloped country is the frontal attack of this sort—the 'wave of capital investments in a number of different industries' that Nurkse writes about. Perhaps guerrilla tactics are more suitable for the circumstances of underdeveloped countries than a frontal attack." [35] Singer points out that the existence of export markets and of import substitution possibilities in themselves mean that only a

[33] Albert Hirschman, *The Strategy of Economic Development,* Yale University Press, 1958, pp. 50–51.

[34] *Ibid.,* p. 93.

[35] *International Development: Growth and Change,* p. 50.

closed economy or the world as a whole face the problem of low level equilibrium deadlock. Other sectors that he proposes as being amenable to "guerrilla tactics" include: increasing agricultural and industrial productivity;[36] buildup of economic infrastructure, notably transportation; and investment in industries complementary to existing industries.

The most complete formulation of unbalanced growth doctrine is Hirschman's. "Development as a chain of disequilibrium" is the title of one section of his exposition. A public investment in a hydroelectric dam, for example, creates pressure for a power distribution system, this in turn for electrical appliances. It may simultaneously make possible the establishment of a caustic soda-chlorine plant heretofore in need of cheap power. This process, built up of complementarities in demand and external economies, is essentially a method of inducing investment decisions with a relatively narrow range of effective choice. On the other hand, some private investment, such as a fertilizer plant, may induce the government to build lower cost power supplies, improve its rural road system, or invest in agricultural extension. The inducement can be effective either through the pressure of private investment on the government decisions (as in the automobile industry's pressure on roadbuilding) or through the pressure of government investment on the private sector (an outstanding example in the United States was the Tennessee Valley Authority).

In like manner, the establishment of a new industry broadens the market for its inputs and may also create a cheaper and more assured supply for its output. Thus, by the effect of such backward and forward linkages, pressures are created within the industrial system for investment in the linked sectors. In a sense, this is simply a statement of the role of inter-industry relations in affecting economic decisions.[37]

In addition to the operation of inducement mechanisms: (1) as among infrastructure and "direct productive" activity and (2) as among linked industries, there is also (3) the inducement provided by the foreign trade sector, either in the form of import substitution or production for export where domestic markets are lacking.

[36] Although this seems to go beyond the province of guerrilla tactics.

[37] Naturally, linkages are only part of the story; they have to be combined with a reasonable economic efficiency. Otherwise, the recipe for economic development would simply be to choose industries with the largest number of sizable positive input-output coefficients.

The unbalanced growth emphasis is reminiscent of Schumpeter's views in which the exploitation of a specific opportunity generates a swarm of investments which may in turn lead to others.[38] Growth, by implication, is an uneven process based on linkages, a point also stressed by Young, who is not ordinarily viewed as a precursor of unbalanced growth theory.

Streeten points out that economic history provides numerous examples of unbalanced growth based on trade, reaping advantages from internal and external economies; and also often inducing a more rapid rate of innovation in the export lines. He apparently agrees with Nurkse, however, that current prospects for this type of growth are not favorable for most LDC's.

Balance and Unbalance in the Scale. The following comments point out some of the problems associated with the balance controversy.[39]

First, both balanced growth and unbalanced growth are vague ideas, and much of the disagreement rests in differences of terminology and assumptions. If, as Rosenstein-Rodan has said, "complementarity makes all industries to some extent 'basic'"[40] there could be no unbalanced growth, except through trade. If, on the other hand, there were few linkages in production and consumption, the choice of balanced and unbalanced strategies would be primarily determined by demand, assuming flexible factor supplies to each industry; or with inflexible factor supplies, by the production function for the various industries.

Second, the time scale affects the definition of balance. A consecutive series of investments in industries related by production or consumption can be called unbalanced in the short run and balanced in the long run. Much of the unbalanced growth argument can be

[38] See for example, *Business Cycles,* New York, McGraw-Hill, 1939, p. 102.

[39] For a more technical approach to these issues, see J. M. Dagnino-Pastore, "Balanced Growth: An Interpretation," *Oxford Economic Papers,* Vol. 15 (July 1963), pp. 164–176; S. K. Nath, "The Theory of Balanced Growth," *Oxford Economic Papers,* Vol. 14 (June 1962), pp. 138–153; Paul Streeten, "Unbalanced Growth: A Reply," *Oxford Economic Papers,* Vol. 15 (March 1963), pp. 66–73; Robert B. Sutcliffe, "Balanced and Unbalanced Growth," *Quarterly Journal of Economics,* Vol. 78 (November 1964), pp. 621–640; Ashok Mathur, "Balanced v. Unbalanced Growth—A Reconciliatory View," *Oxford Economic Papers,* Vol. 18 (July 1966), pp. 137–157.

[40] P. N. Rosenstein-Rodan, "Problems of Industrialization of Eastern and South-eastern Europe," *Economic Journal,* Vol. LIII (June–September 1943), p. 205.

viewed as a strategy for achieving the balance that is manifestly impossible in the short run.

Third, circumstances vary among countries; no LDC, not even a capital-rich one, can follow a "complete" balanced growth policy, because resource supplies are too limited; if all resources were present in large enough quantities the country would be rich, not poor. But the possibilities for simultaneous development of a number of industries may be more favorable in large semi-industrialized countries such as Mexico, Brazil, or Turkey than in many small African countries where the restrictions on both the supply and demand sides are much greater.

Fourth, all underdeveloped countries must have unbalanced investment programs in the sense that certain sectors have to wait, even if they are "basic" by some definition. The real question is what industries (or what agricultural improvements) should receive priority. The particular sequence chosen may constitute balanced growth by Nath's definition (a programming of investment decisions that takes into account the difference between private and social marginal productivity of investments); [41] or unbalanced growth by Streeten's. Properly qualified, most of the disagreement about definition vanishes, and what remains is the operational problem of choosing investment sequences with due regard for external economies. Thus, as in so many discussions, semantics lies at the heart of the differences.

Fifth, both approaches concentrate unduly on investment problems, which perpetuates the tradition of looking on the problem of development as an investment problem. Naturally if we define investment to include "investment" in skills, and even in new motivations, we can preserve the appearances, but the content is lost. Kuwait and Iraq can program investments with unlimited supplies of capital; but it makes little difference whether the chosen sequence is "balanced" or "unbalanced." The operative economic constraints now are of human resources and of the narrowness of the domestic market. Libya until recently had a dominant shortage of capital; today, thanks to oil, it is in Iraq's position. The Netherlands and Switzerland, on the other hand, have an excess of capital and certain skills, and a deficiency of raw materials. They export chocolate, restaurateurs, engineers, and savings; and import wheat, cotton, or cocoa. All five countries are classic examples of unbalanced growth; but the differences in their

[41] S. K. Nath, "The Theory of Balanced Growth," pp. 138–153.

states of development and in the nature of the unbalance indicate the error of stressing the capital investment component unduly.

Inflation and Price Stability

No aspect of development can have been more extensively discussed than the relationship among prices, trade, and growth.[42] Price levels can start to rise from any of a number of stimuli, such as an increase in domestic or import costs or in government spending. Whether they will continue to rise steadily depends in part on the responses of the government and in part on other forces in the economic system. The government can in theory prevent a spiral of inflation by some combination of taxation and control of its spending policies. The same effect can result from other factors such as a fall in import prices, good domestic crops, changes in commercial policies, restriction of money supply, more efficient use of productive capacity, and so on.

The question that arises in connection with attempts to stop inflation in the South is whether there is a conflict between price stability and economic development. The so-called "monetarist" school, while recognizing that the effort to speed up growth brings inflationary pressures, believes that price stability tends to promote development and inflation tends to retard it.[43] In opposition, the "structuralist" school, while recognizing the harmful consequences of inflationary spirals, states that in some Southern counties (notably in South America), economic and political conditions make it impossible to develop at a satisfactory rate without inflation, despite its admittedly harmful effects on the structure of incentives to save and invest.

The arguments on each side may be summarized briefly. Inflation, according to the monetarist outlook, discourages domestic and foreign investment and channels the reduced investment into socially undesirable uses. This rise in domestic prices naturally en-

[42] See, for example, D. C. Hague, ed., *Inflation,* St. Martin's Press, New York, 1962; W. Baer and I. Kerstenetzky, eds., *Inflation and Growth in Latin America,* R. D. Irwin, Homewood, Illinois, 1964. In nearly every issue, the IMF *Staff Papers* and the ECLA *Bulletin* provide articles on the relation between prices and growth, the former invariably denouncing inflation, and the latter explaining its inevitability. The IMF view is represented by G. Dorrance, "The Effect of Inflation on Economic Development," *Staff Papers,* Vol. 8 (March 1963), pp. 1–47. The ECLA view is expressed by Dudley Seers, "A Theory of Inflation and Growth," *Oxford Economic Papers,* Vol. 14 (June 1962), pp. 173–195.

[43] Dorrance, "The Effect of Inflation."

courages imports and discourages exports under a system of fixed exchange rates, leading to balance-of-payments problems, controls, and probably creation of more incentives for capital flight either to avoid the inflation "tax" or from fear of devaluation. Devaluation is part of the indicated remedy but resistance to it is strong on various grounds, discussed below. Unless steps are taken to control inflation, the result is likely to be low rates of investment and savings, slow growth, and chronic balance-of-payments crises. Monetary stability is therefore necessary for growth, although it is not enough in itself.

From the structuralist viewpoint, this is all based on a misconception. It may be perfectly true that LDC monetary, fiscal, and exchange rate policies are often not calculated to restrain inflation. But, the structuralists believe, the nature of the situation makes it impossible to combine effective stabilization and acceptable rates of economic growth in many countries, notably in Latin America.

The structuralist case is based on the belief that domestic resources are immobile (supplies therefore inelastic) and world demand for LDC exports generally weak. At the same time, popular pressure for economic growth is great. In these circumstances, some inflation is almost certain. For example, as income rises, so does demand for manufactures. If imports are increasing slowly, import-substituting industry must develop rapidly. With skilled labor in short supply and urbanization speeded up by industrial growth, urban demand for food and other domestic products will rise. This puts pressure on domestic prices because domestic supplies are inelastic. Thus the demand for imports increases at least as fast as income. But export markets are sluggish, so there is no equivalent increase in foreign exchange availability. This leads to import regulations, but also to an increase in domestic prices of scarce imports. Naturally these inflationary pressures are not desirable. But the choice, for the structuralists, is not between stability and growth. It is between stability with stagnation on one hand and inflation with some growth on the other. From this viewpoint, increases in aid and export receipts are an important element of any long-term solution to inflationary pressures.

Since both parties agree that growth with stability is preferable, the question to be answered is whether this solution is feasible. Obviously, the answer is sometimes yes, sometimes no; discussion of the issues is reserved for Chapter 5. In terms of the trade-development relationship, at least one generalization seems valid: If world commodity prices are declining and volume is sluggish, then some domestic inflation is almost sure to occur at early stages of a development effort. If they are buoyant so that the capacity to import rises rapidly, then inflation will be much easier to control.[44] This is one of the reasons why, in the Latin-American political context, inflation has been a persistent problem. However, the roots of persistent inflation obviously reach deeper than that. Behind the adverse trade statistics there must also be a situation that allows no practical alternative to rising prices, in view of development aspirations, differences of political interest, and the reigning set of social standards, customs, and institutions.

Investment Criteria

Economists have long looked upon capital accumulation and investment as the central factors in economic growth. Today, capital theory and development theory are no longer considered synonymous. There has been great emphasis recently on such factors as the quality and quantity of education and training, population problems, and the effects of the underlying social matrix.

Nevertheless, the formal structure of some development theories still emphasizes maximizing the returns to investment (variously defined) over some time period, and all such theories assume in effect that investment follows maximizing rules. The emphasis on capital comes from two sources. First, capital is both scarce and important to economic development. Wealthy countries have much higher capital per worker than poor ones. Second, for economists, capital-output relations and maximizing rules are easier to handle than most other variables, both for the formal structure of growth models and for statistical testing.

For these reasons, a good deal of thought has been devoted to investment criteria for developing countries. We need not devote much time to it here. In many respects, it is an extension of the balanced growth controversy. In fact, that discussion is about a specific kind of investmen. criterion. Furthermore, the discussion of investment criteria has treated trade and development questions as peripheral. Naturally, it arises in such issues as free trade vs. protection; but

[44] For a similar view see W. A. Lewis' remarks in Baer and Kerstenetzky, eds., *Inflation and Growth in Latin America*, pp. 28–29.

the professional discussion of investment criteria has not focused on the trade relationship.

The theory of investment for growth has evolved to a considerable degree of theoretical refinement, and there is general agreement about the implications of different approaches.[45] It is not clear, however, that the theory is very useful, as we will see below. We lack much of the information that an effective system of investment programming would require, if indeed such systems were politically or administratively feasible.

The basic issue is what is the best rule for investing resources, particularly capital. In purely economic terms, there have been several proposals: (1) minimizing the ratio of capital to output, or of capital to labor, because of the relative scarcity of capital in the South; (2) maximizing the so-called social marginal product, which is the addition to total real product resulting from a given investment (after taking account of the real cost of labor and capital, external economies or diseconomies created by the investment, and so on); (3) maximizing the reinvestment potential of a given investment so as to provide the highest possible investment rates over time, even at the expense of current income gains.

Each criterion leads to different recommendations. Low capital-output ratios mean a labor-intensive form of industrialization and probably a low rate of investment in overhead capital. Maximizing the social marginal product tends to mean relatively more short-run growth in consumption than does the reinvestment criterion, which stresses distant goals. However, it has been pointed out that the latter two approaches give relatively similar or different results depending on the rate of interest used to discount future earnings. If the rate is zero, then the results of the two policies are not far different. If the rate is high, then the divergence will be great. The social marginal productivity criterion will in this case favor investment projects with a relatively quick payoff, while the reinvestment approach will heavily stress transport, power, heavy industry, and other highly capital-intensive industries. The choice is thus seen to depend upon the goals that society sets for itself, as reflected in different valuations of present and future consumption.

[45] The subject has been surveyed by Hollis Chenery, "Comparative Advantage and Development Policy," *American Economic Review*, Vol. 51 (March 1961), pp. 18–51. He demonstrates the relationship of investment criteria to trade in operations research terms.

In terms of the general theory of economic equilibrium, these methods are defective because they do not take account of supply and demand for all products and all means of production. Mathematical programming methods allow these factors to be taken into account, including the appropriate valuation of capital, labor, and foreign exchange. These methods, too, have their limitations, particularly in underdeveloped countries, where the effects of increasing returns, economies of scale, and non-quantifiable factors may be substantial. Furthermore, computational methods currently in use are linear—they assume that a given increase or decrease in production will result in a proportional change in factor use. Where this assumption is invalid, so are the systems of linear equations.

A certain professional bias tends to support the use of productivity or programming criteria for investment, and thus to spread their use among LDC's. But it is hard to believe that purchasers of economists' advice about national investment criteria are receiving a very useful commodity, however satisfying it may be intellectually. A number of countries use shadow pricing systems to estimate the real value of resources and foreign exchange. But even if such accounting prices are used, they apply only to investment that the government can control. They are entirely inappropriate for private decision making, and in the South, governments generally control a smaller proportion of GNP than in the North. There is no assurance that a system that uses shadow prices for a fraction of its economic decisions and market prices for the rest will be better off than an economy that relies entirely on an economically inefficient set of market prices. Furthermore, there are some important practical problems in using shadow prices for factors whose quality is constantly changing, as in the case of steady improvement of labor skills.

More important in practice, under any system of prices used, cost and revenue estimates are normally very inaccurate, even without the attempts to consider external effects. Project costs are always underestimated, revenues normally overestimated, and the degree of error often varies according to the project's favor in the eyes of those who control the funds.

Finally, if the profitability of investment is less important in the long run than its unmeasurable effects on the structure of incentives, then none of the foregoing criteria are relevant because they depend on the ability to assign numbers to the value of benefits.

Naturally, in the absence of information to the contrary, it is safest to assume that productivity or programming criteria will produce more satisfactory results than picking projects out of a hat. But we are still far from the happy situation where we could be sure that the projects rejected by rational criteria are better for economic growth than those accepted. The reasons stem back to lack of factual basis for estimates and to the inability of economic analysis to distinguish and operate upon all of the key factors in growth. If solutions to these problems could be programmed by computer, development economists would be victims of the technological unemployment that, in pursuit of professional aims, they so devoutly seek.

CHAPTER FIVE

An Eclectic View of Trade and Development

INTRODUCTION

The review of contemporary theories in Chapter 4 confirms that there is no accepted and coherent theory of economic development today, except at the restricted level of operations research, where we still lack the knowledge that would allow a correct statement of dynamic functional relations. On the rather limited ground that many contemporary theorists have chosen to explore, the discussion has often foundered on rather sterile issues: balanced vs. unbalanced growth, free trade vs. protection, and stability vs. inflation.[1]

As is clear from the preceding discussion, underdeveloped countries do not in practice face a choice between balanced and unbalanced growth. Undoubtedly, theories of balance and unbalance cast a certain light on aspects of the development process: this is not in question. But they are of little help to a country in quest of an effective development policy.

Second, underdeveloped countries are not in practice faced with a choice between free trade and protection. If they want to industrialize they are going to have to protect most industries, with the exception of those for which transport costs, taste differences, or a favorable domestic resource supply situation provide the equivalent of tariff protection. The only relevant issues are which industries to protect, how much protection to give, and at what cost.

Third, the argument about price stability as debated *ad nauseam* is often conducted on a vastly oversimplified level. The governments of underdeveloped countries have some freedom of choice in deter-

[1] This generalization is partial. For an exception, see E. E. Hagen, *On the Theory of Social Change*, Homewood, Illinois, Dorsey Press, 1962, and bibliography therein.

mining their price policies. But it may be not much use to have freedom of choice when you don't know what you're doing. In the field of price policy, this seems all too often to be the case. As we have seen, there is rather little we can say about the relation between price stability and economic development. Some countries with stable price levels have stagnated economically while others have had rapid growth rates, and the same is true of countries with fairly steady rates of increase in the general price level. The degree of stimulus or deterrence to economic development created by price policy will depend largely on its effects on the structure of economic incentives. These in turn will be closely related to expectations about monetary policies, future price levels, their rates of change, and the expected acceleration of these rates. The structure of each national economy, particularly the way that production responds to price incentives, will in turn influence the nature of those expectations. All too often, the monetarist-structuralist debate is conducted on the basis of *a priori* arguments or on such pointless empirical issues as correlations between rates of real income growth and of price change.

The art of development policy with respect to concrete issues lies in making appropriate use of different theories without being able to rely entirely on any theoretical structure that combines completeness and relevance. From this viewpoint, the operative issues that North and South both face are what choices to make in view of all constraints and not in view of some *a priori* ideal. This means that we have to analyze the presumptive effects of different choices. Chapters 6 through 8 of this study examine specific policy questions. In this chapter, I want to offer a more general approach to the economic policy problems as a sort of framework for what follows.

DEVELOPMENT AND INTERNATIONAL EQUITY

The experience of UNCTAD and the use of polarizing phrases, such as North and South, or rich and poor, used here as elsewhere to discuss the issues, are quite misleading if taken too literally. The expressions are used to cover a tremendous range of economic situations and interests. The unity that the South maintained at UNCTAD does not reflect identical interests, but something less startling—the practical advantages of mutual support. In a forum where the paramount task facing the South was to establish before the world the legitimacy of its efforts to recast the world trading system, the tactic seems unexceptionable. UNCTAD did not negotiate material issues. It was a manifesto, deliberately phrased to offer some promise of benefits to almost any country, but also to be unacceptable to a number of countries that would have to bear the proposed transfer and readjustment costs. In that respect, UNCTAD was an ideological success: it created the platform for a cause.

But that nominal victory has also had its liabilities, to the extent that it represents a retreat from reality. It gave the impression that there might be some single set of trade and aid policies that would benefit all underdeveloped countries equally. The only action that could even approach this effect, by any interpretation of that vague phrase, would be to offer the South as a whole an infinitely large resource transfer. Any other aid or trade policy helps some countries more than others, because no two countries are the same.

The point is obvious, but is no less fundamental. It is these differences between countries that make trade possible, and that also create problems of equity. Thus Prebisch in his report to UNCTAD attempts to construct systems of tariff preferences that will be equitable to all developing countries. Chapter 6 of this study makes it clear that the effort to introduce equity in the sense of equal relative gains to all LDC's and equal relative costs to all Northern countries insures a totally unworkable system.[2]

In terms of the discussion of Chapters 3 and 4, this can be regarded partly as a question of comparative advantage. If, at the same or different states of economic development, countries have different relative resource endowments, any likely set of commercial policy changes will affect different countries' trade and welfare differently. This may be equitable in the sense that all countries may be willing, without coercion, to accept the new policies. But it is sure to be in-

[2] Part of the problem arises from the difficulty of defining equity. Where value systems differ, so do conceptions of equity. So far as donors are concerned, there seems to be some agreement that equity refers to ability to pay or to payments related to benefits received. For recipients of trade or aid largesse, even such vague standards as these are unattainable. Apparently, it has to do with the idea of merit, but this justifies almost any distribution. If a country is constantly on the brink of starvation, despite massive aid receipts, is it more or less meritorious by equity criteria than one that is approaching a relative standard of comfort as a result of regular increases in savings and investment? It all depends on the standard of equity used.

equitable in some sense. Even free trade, as a theoretical optimizing solution from a static viewpoint—if factor and product prices reflect real costs—will not benefit all countries equally,[3] unless it is supplemented by a system of income transfers to equalize the gains. There is no basis for determining the amount and appropriate distribution schedule for those transfers. They depend not only on the distribution of gains from the new policy, but also on the income levels of all nations. It is not even sure that the gains from free trade would increase world income enough to allow those who gain most to compensate those who gain least and those who lose. If one country is hostile to another, there may be no transfer that would make it feel better off, if the new policy benefits its enemy. This is not so far-fetched as it may sound. Suppose the movement to free trade increased U.S. real income by 3 per cent in the short run, and at the same time, China's by 20 per cent. In that event, even a transfer to the United States of all the rest of the world's gains from the increased trade might be insufficient to persuade the United States to accept the new policy. Of course, as a practical matter, it is difficult to predict even the rough magnitude of relative gains or losses. It may be that our very ignorance of the effects is a principal lubricant of commercial policy negotiations. When each party is free to make his own estimate of the consequences, in terms of both efficiency and equity, agreement may be more likely than when the results are known in advance to all.

A free trade situation is likely to fail this kind of equity test. The sorts of policies proposed at UNCTAD are certain to fail it. Of course, in one sense that is the intention. Where the objective is to recast the world trading system in the interests of the underdeveloped countries, then automatically all parties do not receive benefits, let alone equal benefits. The equity issue on the donor's side is a question of burden-sharing, not benefit-sharing.

But in another sense, the preoccupation with equity among LDC's is a blind alley unless equity is the only goal. If countries differ in population, skills, capital plant, natural resources, tastes, incomes, and almost every other economic dimension, it is certain that the attempt to legislate equity among beneficiaries into trade concessions

[3] In terms of some measurable criterion, such as equal per cent of absolute increases in per capita income. More generally, it is a question of acceptable increases in welfare, of a very special kind, where each party thinks that it has gained at least as much as any other party.

will greatly restrict the total amount of economic benefits. It will reduce the maximum benefit any one country can gain to a level set by those countries that are least able to benefit from the concessions. For example, if it were decided to set up commodity price-fixing agreements or tariff preferences for manufactures to equalize each country's per capita trade increase, a Hong Kong would set the standard for agricultural commodity benefits, and a Central African Republic for manufactured preferences. Clearly, no one is explicitly proposing such an exaggerated version, but this is one direction in which UNCTAD trade policy points. The doubter has only to look at the record of discussions in its Committee on Manufactures (May 1965).

Such considerations as these forcefully underline Nurkse's insistence that the world is not rich enough to ignore efficiency. What is true of the world is even more true of the South, because it is poor and most of the nations are small. Enlarging the market with regard for comparative advantage is likely to be essential for unsubsidized growth.

But, of course growth can be subsidized. This in theory allows countries to live at virtually any standard of living they want, if donors are willing. To the extent that such capital transfers are direct, it is sometimes said that aid can be used to remedy the defects in equity that result from a market economy or from discriminatory policies such as tariffs and preferences. Therefore, economists usually prefer aid to restrictive trading practices as a method of helping the poor. But aid is not a solution to all problems of equity. It poses its own equity problems, not only for the reasons implied above (limitations on the amount of aid and the inseparability of economic welfare from considerations of pride and power), but also because the various recipients will use aid differently. Some recipients' income and wealth will therefore grow faster than others, unless aid levels are set so as to assure equal growth rates. But this remedy in equity is itself open to the charge of unfairness. Why should a country that invests with spectacular inefficiency in terms of output, or with equally striking efficiency in terms of corruption, be allowed to set the pace at which other countries can grow (to the extent that aid is a factor)? In other words, equity arguments are circular, at least to the observer who is unruffled by inefficiency. The fact that countries are different and will remain different is fundamental. The effort to remedy inequity and, more important, to eliminate its sources should be a central objective of policy. But it cannot be the sole criterion. So long as the world seeks both growth and equity, conflict is unavoidable.

We cannot expect any set of policies to combine growth and fairness in proportions that will be acceptable to all those who benefit, let alone all those who give aid. This is one reason why economists are often unable to say whether one public policy proposal is better or worse than another. Some value system is always built into the choice.

THE PRINCIPAL POLICY ISSUES

What we can expect of economic analysis, and of the trade and development theories that are our subject here, is that they will illuminate the nature of the choices we face. I will examine some of the broader issues of trade and development policy in this spirit, trying to relate it to the theorists' initiatives discussed in Chapters 3 and 4. Three controversies merit particular attention: trade and aid (discussed in Chapter 2), agriculture and industry, and internal and external reforms. Before going on to the latter two, I will first review the relations of these issues and of development theory in general to formal systems of maximization, discussed briefly in Chapter 4, sometimes used or proposed for development planning.

Programming Models in Development Theory

At the beginning of this chapter, I said there was no accepted and coherent theory of economic development today. Some economists might disagree, on the grounds that mathematical models, notably programming techniques, in theory allow a formal solution of resource use problems, by criteria of consistency and efficiency. We start by specifying some set of output targets, with given availability of inputs (or input supply functions), alternative known techniques of production at constant costs, the prices of imports and exports, and the factor opportunity costs of domestic production compared with production for export. It is then possible to state, as a result of solving the linear equation system incorporating these data: (1) whether the targets can be reached with the available resources; (2)

the most efficient allocation of resources in terms of real factor costs, which emerge simultaneously with the appropriate activity level; (3) the appropriate production techniques and levels of output by each technique; (4) the optimum choice of industries for import substitution; (5) appropriate level of resource use for the export sector; and (6) the real cost and value of foreign exchange.[4]

In this approach, economic development becomes by definition a question of sectoral balance. Each sector must move in pace with the others as determined by the techniques of production and demand conditions, except to the extent that external capital (or involuntary changes in domestic saving or spending) is available to compensate for the imbalances.

Naturally, none but the most eager convert to quantitative methods would claim that the existence of theoretically determinate solutions to programming problems constitutes a theory of economic development. First, economic development patterns may vary depending on the political and social consequences of the productive decisions that society makes. Therefore, the choice of an economic optimum, even if the data were available to fuel the model, could be irrelevant to the actual choices that a nation faces. Second, the data used are likely to be highly inaccurate, because we know little about the conditions of production in LDC's, particularly in the new lines of endeavor that development planning tries to foster.

Third, the phenomenon of increasing returns, as described by Young, is not yet capable of being quantified. Yet it is at the heart of economic development. For the more wide-eyed model builders, it might seem self-evident that the most efficient use of scarce resources will leave society with the largest surplus above consumption needs for use to simulate profit incentives, expenditures on improving skills, social and economic infrastructure, or whatever else society may need to improve its economic performance in the next period. But this is not really self-evident at all. The government may find it impossible to reallocate the income created by the plan so as to achieve its developmental goals. Resistance to surrendering the proceeds of labor or investment may be too great. In economic theories, we sometimes, for convenience, separate the question of efficient production from the spending power it creates. But only a foolish government—or a tyrannical one—can ignore the public demand to retain the fruits of its own labor and investment, and its reluctance to allow large-scale

[4] Cf. H. B. Chenery, "Comparative Advantage and Development Policy."

redistribution. There is no reason why production and pricing levels emerging from a programming model need be inconsistent with the optimum pattern of spending required to move an economy from stagnation; neither is there any particular reason why they should be consistent. For example, it is conceivable that large-scale farming might represent the most efficient use of agricultural resources in India today. But the consequences on the distribution of income and the development of the Indian labor force might be entirely unacceptable, not only for the obvious political reasons but also for longer-term economic goals. If economic development is viewed as a process of creating a socio-economic machine that both fosters and adapts to constant economic change (and to the social changes it induces), then the consistency and efficiency of macro-economic plans may be almost irrelevant to this broader problem.

By extension, Hirschman has gone on to point out that the rate of economic development may be profoundly affected not only by the pattern of industrial evolution in general, but also by specific policy choices about individual industries. The decision to invest in a particular project may increase effective pressures for educational reform, or for road building programs, or for improvements in the marketing and distribution network, or provide some other non-quantifiable stimulus to economic change. In that event, too, the efficiency calculus evolved from model-building exercises may well miss the heart of the matter.

Finally, even with the framework that model-builders choose to adopt, there are intractable technical problems: data on LDC economic activities are lacking in the detail and accuracy required; problems of uncertainty are difficult to handle, because we may be working with distributions that depart from normal probability assumptions; and functional relations among variables may be difficult to specify correctly.

Therefore, programming techniques now offer no general solution to the economic issues that beset developing countries. But they can tell a good deal about the relationships among economic activities, including some guidance as to the feasibility of particular output or income targets. Perhaps their most important contribution as yet is to provide an orderly system for examining the ways in which productive activities are related, and to illustrate the relations among output levels, value of inputs, and opportunity costs. Furthermore, these methods are flexible and can in theory accommodate various kinds of supply and demand situations beyond the customary assumptions of elastic demand and constant costs. Nonetheless, when applied to macroeconomic development problems they create, for all their flexibility, a Procrustean framework for those dimensions of economic development that they cannot encompass.

One virtue of the programming approach is to demonstrate the irrelevance of some of the earlier theoretical discussion. For example, the use of national economic models makes clear that long-run growth must always be balanced among sectors, and even short-run departures from balance must be paid for by changes elsewhere in the system. As noted earlier, it makes possible some reconciliation between development theory and principles of comparative advantage by expressing investment choices in terms of opportunity costs under appropriate pricing systems for domestic resources and foreign exchange. Another case in point is the perennial debate about agriculture versus industry as growing points for development. The steady growth of an economy will normally involve increases in the productivity of all sectors, and the actual choice of investment will depend on the profitability of each investment in light of demand conditions and opportunity costs. The following discussion of agriculture and industry in development programs takes these facts as a point of departure.

Agriculture and Industry

The balanced growth approach implies that development policies should be strongly slanted to industrial investment. Among the opponents of balanced growth, Singer specifically equates industrialization and development. Hirschman's stress on linkages created by inter-industry structure also looks toward an industrializing society.

But economists are not unanimous. Lewis has suggested that rapid growth in many LDC's requires heavy emphasis on increasing farm productivity.[5] Other writers have advised LDC's to develop agriculture, thereby emulating the example of advanced agricultural countries such as Denmark, New Zealand, or Australia.[6]

In a closed economy, farm productivity will have to increase at

[5] "A Review of Economic Development," *American Economic Review, Papers and Proceedings,* Vol. LV (May 1965), pp. 1–17.

[6] For example, Stephen Enke, *Economics for Development,* Prentice-Hall, Englewood Cliffs, New Jersey, 1963, p. 124.

least fast enough to allow the transfer of people off the land. In an open economy, food can be imported, but increases in farm productivity are still an essential part of the process of market expansion and urbanization. Therefore, it is incorrect to pose the case as one of agriculture vs. industry.

To the extent that rapid growth is the desideratum, rising farm productivity is probably not the primary technique. Lewis and others have argued for it on grounds that make a strong *prima facie* case. Most people in LDC's are farmers. Therefore if farm productivity can be increased even a small amount, the total effect on GNP will be greater than if large increases are achieved in the tiny manufacturing sector. Furthermore, the apparent productivity differential in favor of manufacturing may be an illusion, because it fails to include the attendant costs of organization. Finally the increase in farm income enlarges the home market for manufactures.

This sounds eminently reasonable, but I think it is somewhat beside the point, except for very underdeveloped countries. It seems perfectly clear that the primary economic characteristic of development is a switch in the structure of production from rural subsistence farming to urban industry. References to Denmark and New Zealand as agricultural countries are, in this connection, totally misleading. They are agricultural compared with Belgium or the United Kingdom, but they are highly industrialized compared with underdeveloped countries. Every Atlantic Community nation (including Denmark and New Zealand) produces more than twice as much (and in some cases, seven times as much), by value, in manufacturing as in agriculture.[7] No LDC (except Hong Kong and Singapore) produces as much manufacturing output as farm output. Thus, to arrive at the structure of even the least industrialized member of the Atlantic Community, a relatively industrialized LDC would have to more than double its *relative* manufacturing output.

There are nonetheless two weighty arguments presented in favor of more incentives to agriculture. One is the view that price relations

[7] Thus for the year 1961:

		GNP Originating in	
	GNP	*Mfg.*	*Agriculture, etc.*
Australia (million £)	7,284	1,862	814
Denmark (million crowns)	45,591	13,265	6,119

Source: UN, *Yearbook of National Accounts Statistics,* 1964.

in underdeveloped countries are distorted in favor of industry. Protection of infant industry leads to high-priced domestic production. Insistence on keeping the farm price of agricultural products low through price controls, commodity export taxes and food imports (usually on concessional terms through U.S. surplus disposal programs) means that the domestic terms of trade are turned against farmers. If food prices were left free to respond to market forces and if industrial prices were lowered by subsidy or tariff protection, then farmers would have an incentive to raise output.

This argument can be supported by evidence. Countries that use large amounts of commercial fertilizer on specific crops have a low ratio of fertilizer price to crop price. LDC's that use little fertilizer generally have a high ratio of fertilizer price to crop price. Also some countries' industrial protection levels greatly exceed the degree of currency overvaluation, so that the net effect is to raise the price of industrial output above what it would be under free trade with balance-of-payments equilibrium.

Obviously if agricultural growth is being crippled by misguided efforts to force feed industry, a country will be better off if it restores incentives to agricultural output. The problem becomes one of balance in Lewis' sense. Lewis has in fact argued that industry will be unable to expand if agricultural output stagnates. He reasons that one of two effects will follow: either the domestic price of food will rise as a result of increasing non-farm demand, or else rising food imports will create balance-of-payments problems. These effects will hinder industrial growth. While these are ultimately questions of fact in each case, it should be noted that Lewis' argument implies a redressing of the domestic terms of trade in favor of agriculture and thus an offset to the adverse effect of industrial protectionism as discussed above. Thus it is not certain that the net effect of these two tendencies will be harmful to industry.

The second argument against excessive emphasis on industry stems from the relatively high productivity of advanced countries' agriculture. But, as Singer has pointed out,[8] the ratio of per capita income in agriculture to per capita income in other sectors tends to

[8] *International Development: Growth and Change,* p. 43. Singer says that the relationship tends to be $x = \frac{150 - y}{100 - y}$ where x is the ratio of income per capita outside agriculture to that in agriculture, and y is the percentage of the population in agriculture.

increase as the percentage of the population in agriculture declines. High output per farmer in advanced countries is associated with industrialization, for reasons explained below. In fact, the agriculture of advanced countries is itself industrialized.

How does this relate to the point that rapid growth in LDC's requires higher output per farmer? First, in very primitive economies, this doctrine is largely true. Almost everyone depends on subsistence farming, and transition to predominantly cash farming is essential. This will require a relatively large effort in agricultural investment and training. Industrialization cannot proceed in the virtual absence of a money economy. In practice this means that countries like Malawi and Uganda cannot yet grow by reliance on industrial development.[9] Investments and training in agriculture and promotion of extractive industries, where possible, are preconditions of industrial development.

At a higher stage of welfare (South America and much of Asia, North Africa, and the Middle East), the situation is different. In most of these cases, I believe, even when more than half the people are farmers, growth rates will not be maximized by sole or primary reliance on improving traditional farming operations.

First, and by far the most important, traditional agriculture shows massive resistance to change. It is common to attribute this resistance in part to the perverse incentives introduced by large-scale landlordism, peasant sharecropping, price distortions, and inefficient marketing. It can be demonstrated that the typical sharecropping system, in which each party's earnings are not proportional to his share of the productive resources used, is sure to call forth less than an optimum output. Furthermore, if output is marketed through local monopoly buyers, price incentives may not be transmitted to farmers.

Second, the element of risk is of major importance too. Introducing new techniques involves a danger of output reduction, particularly during the first crop seasons. Output reduction, in countries like India or Pakistan, is a euphemism for near-starvation. It is possible to reduce the costs of innovation to farmers, for example, by subsidizing fertilizer or insecticide prices. And such innovations as pesticides involve virtually no risk of output reduction. Nonetheless, most innovations involve certain cash costs, and uncertain effects on output. Therefore, unless the government is in a position to guarantee indi-

[9] Foreign investors may find extractive industries profitable, but for reasons discussed later, this may not lead to significant industrialization throughout the economy.

vidual farmers an acceptable minimum income if they take the risks of innovation (virtually impossible if farmers are a large part of the labor force), they can hardly be blamed for preferring to follow tradition.

Third, there is a sort of paradox about the agricultural sector that makes it very difficult to emerge from stagnation. Some agricultural improvements are easy to obtain, in the sense that large increases in output can follow relatively small capital investments. Typical examples are better seeds, insecticides, improved farming practices, and fertilizer application. But these are hard to introduce because of social resistance to change and because of the distorted incentives created by tenure systems and by the effect of prices paid and received by farmers.[10] On the other hand, new farming areas or massive irrigation projects are popular with farmers because the potential benefit is unmistakable. However, for these investments, the return to society is typically very low, particularly when water is priced at opportunity cost. The effect is that the quick and cheap forms of productivity increase are hard to attain, and the expensive, slow forms gain easy acceptance.

Finally, there is another apparent paradox. Increased productivity in agriculture is invariably associated with a relative decline in farm population. This means a relative increase in urban population. This is fine, if you want to increase the urban labor force for industrialization. But most LDC's are already plagued with excess migration to the cities, which involves high political, social, and economic costs. On the other hand, measures to increase farm productivity have historically either encouraged people to leave farms, or else been brought about by the departure of labor. This constellation of circumstances implies that any massive efforts to increase farm productivity in countries where there is Malthusian pressure will fail because there is too much cheap labor, or, if it succeeds, will aggravate the often critical urban problems of LDC's.

However, the picture is not quite so bleak. This argument ignores the fact that development is possible and that it does take place through an increasing returns sequence, so that either agriculture or industry can be considered the sparkplug, according to the observer's preference.

[10] It has also been pointed out to me that Western knowledge of tropical agricultural conditions is deficient, so that it is far from clear whether these techniques would in fact be so productive under actual conditions as they are in test situations.

Why should industrialization be the key to a more vigorous agriculture? Industrialization breaks into the low-income circle, and initiates changes that affect the entire structure of production.[11] It increases the off-farm demand for food, and cash farming becomes more important when there are more city people to feed. It also reduces the farm supply of labor, thereby tending to force adoption of new techniques, which could previously be avoided. Finally, the development of the cash economy creates a market for industry, which in turn further raises the demand for food. Increased demand for food means higher farm income, and so on. This sequence of increasing returns, associated with cost reductions, tends to call forth improvements throughout the entire system of farm processing and marketing.

Naturally, agricultural improvements will not spring forth automatically once industrialization gets under way. It will require encouragement in the form of investment, technical assistance, and education. But, unless forces external to traditional agriculture are introduced to affect demand and supply relations among products and the labor and capital that produce them, the effect is likely to be unavailing. It therefore seems impractical to suggest in the contemporary world that agricultural improvements offer LDC's an alternative to industrialization, once the economy has passed a relatively primitive level. With limited funds to invest in capital goods and training, the relationship between increases in farm output and in industrial output is to some extent competitive at any moment; but the record of economic development indicates that over time they are normally complementary. Output and investment per man increase in both sectors; and total agricultural output also normally rises, though at a slower rate than in manufacturing.

Since both ideology and history lead LDC's to promote industrial development, it is small wonder that agricultural improvements often receive a far smaller share of public investment than industry and general infrastructure. In countries where food supply is chronically inadequate (India, Pakistan) this is often the subject of critical comment. As we have seen above, this may well be justified. However, to the extent that the industrial investment is import-substituting at reasonable cost, or export-promoting, it may be the best short-run route to increases in food availability. This will depend on the facts of each

[11] Development of export crops has historically played a similar role.

case, because there is a range of development alternatives, reflecting great differences in economic structure and potential.

External and Internal Reforms

Virtually anyone will agree that to grow faster LDC's will benefit from changes both in their own domestic policies and in the policies that other countries adopt toward them. The general view among most Northern economists is that the LDC's plight is largely a consequence of their own domestic problems. The major ones only need be listed. They are a familiar recital: political instability; resistance to change on the part of vested interests; social attitudes that may be inconsistent with economic efficiency, as conceived in the West; Malthusian population pressures; major defects and shortages in education, training, and administration; and a variety of ill-conceived economic policies. These include ideological opposition to foreign or private economic activity; nationalistic desires for autarchy, incompatible with the real resource situation; overvalued exchange rates; excessive tariff protection (which unsystematically offsets overvaluation); insistence on central economic planning in inappropriate circumstances; built-in inflationary policies. The list could be extended indefinitely.

At the same time, the list of external constraints, which at least in theory the North could modify, is impressive. It includes the elements listed in Chapter 4: trade restriction and protectionism (particularly toward commodities and labor-intensive manufactures), monopoly elements, unfavorable demonstration effects, and the like. It also includes such other constraints as: (1) immigration controls, which prevent Southern workers from seeking work in the North; (2) controls over capital export, notably those exercised by many Northern governments over World Bank bond issues and other investments aimed at benefiting LDC's;[12] (3) factors that reduce the real value of aid to the beneficiary, such as requiring that purchases be made in the donor country; (4) possible adverse effects of aid in the form of food surpluses; (5) maneuvering for political advantage through such devices as military or economic aid, thus giving Southern governments the economic ability to carry out more easily any inclinations toward political and military adventures against their neighbors—

[12] See IBRD, *The Horowitz Proposal,* Washington, D.C., June 1965.

these inclinations might be harder to follow in the absence of aid; (6) creation of a sense of impotence based on the failure of independence to create viable economies, and (7) the widening of the already vast gap in living standards.

Some of these criticisms are exaggerated; some are simply statements about conditions that are unpleasant and unavoidable; and some are inconsistent with each other. This is natural enough. Everyone seeks scapegoats for frustration. The North is a convenient one; and one can hardly expect different people to make consistent criticisms. The strongest and most valid of the economic points is the criticism of protectionism, because it substantially restricts exports in which LDC's have comparative advantage.

Obviously, this is not a question of heroes and villains; all parties are to some extent at fault, if higher standards of living are considered the primary goal. It seems equally obvious, to me at least, that most countries will have to depend primarily on their own efforts to develop. The North does not want to take on the task of guaranteeing Southern prosperity. Furthermore, there is a general belief that individuals and nations should rely primarily on their own efforts; outside assistance should be a helping hand, not a cradle. This last is an ethical judgment and is thus valid only if accepted, but it seems to be widely held, and to correspond not only to Northern self-interest but also to Southern resentment of dependence.

In this sense, external versus internal reforms is a phony issue; each will accomplish something. If a country has a favorable resource base and large enough population, external constraints may play a relatively minor role, in theory at least. In a sense, the same is true of a subsistence economy during the first stages of its development. Technical assistance, broadly defined, is likely to be its main external requirement at the early stage. New Guinea today might be an example. On the other hand, if a country derives a large fraction of its income from commodity exports and then loses its market to synthetics or agricultural protectionism abroad, the external constraint is genuine and serious, however desirable the change may be for the rest of the world.

In general the relationship is likely to be reciprocal, although economists have not yet studied the connections between domestic and external reforms in sufficient detail. Domestic reforms make it easier to take effective advantage of increased external opportunities, and those opportunities may facilitate reforms. It is often stated that aid makes it easier for the South to avoid painful reforms. This may be true at times, but this is a problem of aid criteria, not of the aid itself, from the economist's viewpoint. But aid is one instrument, and there are many goals, so the problem is perennial.

Therefore, I prefer to look at the matter not as a question of external versus internal reforms in principle, but rather in terms of the problems actually faced. We have discussed some of these problems already. Let us review them briefly in light of the theories discussed in Chapters 3 and 4.

BARRIERS TO GROWTH AND THEORIES OF DEVELOPMENT

In the light of these observations, we can see that theories about the trade-development relation in general are neither "right" nor "wrong," but simply partial, relevant only to a particular set of circumstances, or to some aspects of all situations.

The role of comparative advantage, stressed by Ricardo and Mill, is seen as being perhaps more relevant as a guide to import substitution than to trade-led growth. If governments are determined to industrialize, comparative cost calculations can indicate which import-substituting industries involve the least real cost as compared with imports, or export alternatives.

Schumpeter's emphasis on innovation, as amplified for LDC's by Hirschman's stress on inducement mechanisms for public or private entrepreneurship, is clearly related to contemporary development problems, although Schumpeter's formulation provides no useful policy guidance for LDC's. Hirschman's policy-oriented approach is more suggestive, primarily because stressing bottlenecks and linkages is one way to economize entrepreneurship. Nonetheless, the question of efficient choice remains undefined by linkages alone.

By this token, balanced growth takes on its prime policy significance in Lewis' formulation. The Nurkse-Rodan view can be seen as a brilliant statement of the development problem and of the vital role of increasing returns in the breakthrough. But Nurkse's definition of balanced growth as an exercise in economic development with unlimited supplies of capital is only partial; in effect, unlimited supplies of skills (and very elastic supplies of labor) are also needed. Thus, balanced growth, in this sense, is of little practical value for policy in

LDC's. Lewis, on the other hand, states the policy issues correctly, in terms of constraints actually faced, and of a definition of balance that essentially recognizes the interdependence of supply and demand in formulating development targets.

The Marxist stress on capital and accumulation is dominant in most academic discussions of development. Some modern formulations, with their emphasis on maximum reinvestment (maximizing surplus value) can be viewed as neo-Marxist descriptions of historical formulas for development.[13] Similarly, the Singer-Prebisch-Myrdal views are, in some aspects, modern translations of Marxist writing on imperialism.

Whether LDC's are well advised to adopt Marxist solutions (which none of the foregoing writers suggest) is not primarily an economic question. I have suggested above that very underdeveloped countries might well lose more than they gain economically from socialist control of the economy. This conclusion is much less certain for more advanced LDC's (for example, Turkey, Argentina). In such countries as these, development (under a predominantly market economy) has proceeded more slowly on the face of it than resource levels and skills would seem to allow. Draconian measures of expropriation, high taxation, and manpower reallocation might well raise growth rates sharply, after an initial shock.

Recent economic analysis has concentrated on the investment problem, particularly on criteria for choosing investment projects, by cost-benefit analysis or by comprehensive programming methods. Unfortunately, although the work is logically correct, it is of rather little help to developing countries. With future costs, prices, and quantities demanded generally unknown, particularly for export products, the concepts of maximizing some cost-benefit calculus lose a good deal of significance. Furthermore, the magnitude of external effects is generally unknown. Therefore, formal economic analysis of investment alternatives makes much less contribution to development choices than surface examination of the cost-benefit formulas might imply. It finds its greatest value in comparing similar project proposals—the merits of two alternative power projects, for example, rather than in choosing between an oil refinery and an irrigation project. The major decisions about the relative importance of the different economic

[13] W. Galenson and H. Leibenstein, "Investment Criteria, Productivity, and Economic Growth," *Quarterly Journal of Economics,* Vol. 69 (August 1955), pp. 343–370.

sectors must, in practice, precede the application of formal investment criteria.

Despite the many thousands of pages devoted to the trade-development relationship since Nurkse's 1953 formulation,[14] his view of the matter remains authoritative in my opinion. LDC's must trade. The world is not rich enough to ignore efficiency; and poor countries in particular need foreign exchange and external capital as conditions of rapid growth. But this is completely apart from the question of whether trade will be a propulsive factor in growth. The answer varies greatly among countries, depending on their size and/or the structure of comparative advantage. In general, though, prospects for LDC trade expansion are not favorable given existing trade policies in both North and South. This generalization excludes producers of primary products in strong demand, and small, thickly settled countries that are pushed to export of labor-intensive manufactures, because of the smallness of the domestic market.[15]

Even where exports grow rapidly, the relation with economic growth in general will vary according to the links between the structure of export production and the structure of the economy in general.

THE TRADE-GROWTH RELATIONSHIP

Despite all of our review and critique, we have not answered the two policy issues raised by UNCTAD. To what extent can trade be a leading sector for development? To what extent can excess demand for available foreign exchange limit the rate of economic growth? This chapter has discussed aspects of both of these questions. I want to review and summarize the state of current knowledge about these two issues, because they are the central questions to be resolved in selecting appropriate trade policy toward LDC's development is a prime objective.

The data of Chapter 2 show that for all poor countries together,

[14] *Problems of Capital Formation.*

[15] To some extent, and for some areas (for example, Mexico, Tahiti, Jamaica, Spain, Puerto Rico, Trinidad) tourism has come to play a role in this century that trade may have played for other countries in the past. But for most LDC's, there is no such ready alternative.

the rate of export growth has been slow in recent years compared with that of rich countries.[16] It seems clear that this reflects in part the slow growth of demand for commodities in the aggregate. Furthermore, over the next decade, LDC exports are likely to grow more slowly than those of the Atlantic Community. Nor, in general, are export price prospects buoyant.

Obviously, there are important exceptions by commodity—petroleum mainly, but also including iron ore, aluminum, fish meal, and several other products. There are also important exceptions by country. Any country that is a low-cost producer of a commodity has an incentive to expand output, unless it is a dominant supplier in the world market, for a product facing very inelastic demand. Thus, despite the very moderate level of world coffee prices, West African countries have found it profitable to increase output, because their long-run production costs are low and their proportion of world output small.

If we agree that for some countries and some commodities it is profitable to make new investments in commodity production for export, particularly if the alternative to export production is low-yield subsistence farming, we are only at the beginning. Presumably any profitable investment[17] in LDC's can promote economic development, except in the unlikely event that the investment is *entirely* for the benefit of outside interests. What is of interest to us are the circumstances under which such an export-biased investment is likely to promote growth throughout the economy. These conditions were discussed in Chapter 4 and are summarized here.

International trade is most likely to act as an engine of growth when the conditions of its production call for induced investment throughout the economy and for at least a moderately wide distribution of income increases. What kinds of LDC exports provide such a sequence? First, there are some of the temperate agricultural crops such as wheat or feed grains. These are typically subject to extensive and mechanized cultivation; they therefore require, when produced for export, a substantial transportation system, storage and milling facilities, and a sales and service network for machinery, equipment, and supplies. In the 20th century, very few LDC's produce these crops for export. The reason normally advanced for this is the

[16] Although most LDC's that have grown rapidly have also had rapid export growth (Taiwan, Thailand, Puerto Rico, Malaya).

[17] Defined to include external economies and diseconomies.

superior efficiency of such large producers as Canada, Australia, and the United States. However, it is not clear in fact how much of the credit should go to superior efficiency and how much to agricultural subsidy in those countries, plus agricultural protection in Europe. We are not likely to learn the answer soon, because agricultural protectionism has become a pillar of industrial countries' economic policy.

Another possible sequence that would promote induced investments and demand is the processing of mineral and agricultural exports—refining petroleum or other minerals, refining of sugar and oil seeds, production of jute cloth, cotton gray goods, canned fruits and vegetables, and so on. This is an obvious kind of forward linkage, which in itself involves backward linkages for inputs into production. As pointed out in Chapter 2, it is precisely in these simple manufactures that LDC exports have increased the fastest over the past decade. However, the growth of such exports is clearly handicapped by the present structure of industrial countries' tariffs, to say nothing of the widespread use of formal and informal quantitative restrictions against low-wage manufactured imports. This is not to say that such a developmental sequence is impossible. Some countries, including Yugoslavia, Israel, Hong Kong, India, and Pakistan, have made significant efforts, with varying success.

Exporting cheap labor, in the form of labor-intensive manufactures, can be successful, if the *real* cost of labor is cheap. Japan, Hong Kong, and India have expanded trade by reliance on this method; but for reasons discussed earlier in this chapter, a number of forces are at work to impede this process today. One important point should be added here. The cost of industrial labor may turn out to be very high, even if its opportunity costs are low.

This is sometimes overlooked in the theoretical literature, although recent empirical work demonstrates it clearly.[18] Industrialization tends to bring very rapid increases in factory wages, thanks to government-supported minimum wage legislation and union efforts. The low shadow price of labor implies, for planners, that LDC's have a comparative advantage in labor-intensive manufactures. But employers pay money wages, not shadow wages. The consequence, in the absence of government subsidy, is that labor-intensive manufactures may be discouraged. Therefore manufacturing employment rises rather slowly, and there is a tendency to invest in

[18] L. G. Reynolds, "Wages and Employment in a Labor Surplus Economy," *American Economic Review*, Vol. LV (March 1965), pp. 19–39.

capital-intensive industries despite the apparent labor surplus. Naturally, the force of these tendencies varies greatly among countries. Real wages are likely to rise fastest in countries where: (1) there are close geographical, political, and cultural ties with industrial countries, including freedom of movement between them; (2) the government attempts to follow enlightened social policies and promote high minimum wages; (3) the trade union movement is strong. Puerto Rico and Jamaica are archetypical examples. One result of this enlightenment is that manufacturing employment rises slower than it otherwise would. In Puerto Rico, for example, a decade of industrial development (1952–62), characterized by unlimited access to capital and to markets, resulted in creation of only 50,000 manufacturing jobs, an increase of 50 per cent in total manufacturing employment. Real wages in manufacturing doubled during the decade under the pressure of wage demands, prompted in part by U.S. trade union efforts to defend their membership's interests.

On the other hand, in such countries as Hong Kong and Taiwan where the forces acting to raise the level of manufacturing wages are on balance weaker, the expansion of labor-intensive industry has proceeded faster. Thus in Taiwan, during the 1952–62 decade, real wages increased only one-third as fast as in Puerto Rico, and relative manufacturing employment rose 50 per cent faster than in Puerto Rico. It should be noted that this rapid wage increase in LDC industry tends to conflict with Singer's theoretical reasoning concerning the causes of terms-of-trade deterioration in LDC's.

If exports of manufactures are a primary objective, such rapid wage increases are likely to act as an impediment. Puerto Rico is exceptional, being in a position to substitute capital for labor and still remain competitive in the U.S. market. But most countries are not so fortunate, and their prospects, in the face of upward wage pressures, are less favorable.

The prospects for major expansion of such growth-promoting exports, whether based on domestic processing of primary goods or on labor-intensive exports, are spotty at best, unless the Atlantic Community accepts major changes in its own commercial policies (see Chapter 6). The obvious alternative in the absence of foreign markets is to build up industry and agriculture for the home market. Some countries have developed successfully this way starting from an agricultural base. In fact, for countries with more than about ten million people this has been the normal development pattern.

The 19th-century growth of France, Germany, the United States, and Japan followed this rule. The United Kingdom was an exception, because she dominated world export trade in manufactures for many decades.

The difficulties of following this path today are well-known. Nevertheless, some such sequence has its appeal for developing countries.

Countries that rely on farm exports are vulnerable to agricultural protectionism abroad (for example, the effect of EEC farm policy on the agricultural exports of New Zealand and Denmark). More important, rich agricultural countries are agricultural only compared with the big, industrial, exporting nations; as we have noted, their domestic economies are highly industrialized compared with those of LDC's.

Import-substituting industry offers a natural start for industrial development. Despite its apparent inconsistency with principles of efficiency, it can logically be based on comparative advantage grounds. A major part of industrial growth comes from import substitution, defined as an increasing share of imports in total consumption. Even the most disadvantaged country can turn to its customs records to find at least a few growing points for industrial development. This pattern of import substitution has characterized LDC growth in all countries ever since the industrial growth of the United States first took hold in the years before the Civil War. When nations have attempted to speed up industrial development under absolutist rule (Germany, the Soviet Union, Japan), import substitution has been elevated virtually to a patriotic principle.

The growing points chosen for import-substitution policy should obviously be based on the country's relative cost situation, as well as on the size of import bill. For example, petroleum and coffee are the largest U.S. imports. An import-substituting policy that looked only at those facts would be at best half-right. Where import substitution takes place at high real cost the net effect on economic growth may be negative.

Whatever the difficulties inherent in industrialization, and in instilling the habits of mind, social attitudes, and technical skills needed to assure it, LDC's are aware that in the long run all countries that have become rich and powerful have done so via a steady relative decline in the farming population; and, up to a point, by an increase in the proportion engaged in manufacturing. It is, on the whole, idle to stress the virtues of static comparative advantage in a free trade situation, in face of the obvious fact that today's rich countries always favored industrial development via protection when they were relatively poor. The desire to industrialize is a basic element of contemporary nationalism. Economists who criticize excessive emphasis on industrialization miss the point. Southern leaders do not seek rising incomes alone; they want rising incomes in an industrializing society. If high-cost industry conflicts with maximizing the growth of income, most LDC governments are willing to pay the price. The imputation of irrationality arises only when the price is very high. But how high is too high? Again, each witness is his own final authority. If a nation prefers, politically, industrial investments with a zero rate of return to agricultural investments that return 10 per cent, is it irrational? Obviously not, if it prefers industry to agriculture at that cost. It simply would rather have more industry and less income.

There are other considerations. A "developed" country is not simply one with a high level of income per head (if it were, Kuwait would be considered the world's most advanced nation). An economically advanced country is one that can perform a wide variety of complex economic functions. As a country develops, it introduces an ever larger variety of industries, financial agencies, and services. While a Switzerland, a Denmark, or a Belgium, because of its small population, makes no effort to produce everything, it is also true that such countries produce an ever wider variety of manufactures. If development essentially consists in building up both the variety of productive sectors and the level of output per worker, then export specialization can be only part of the story; domestic industrialization must play a major role.

If the domestic market is too small for some industries, then it may be necessary to join markets. This is the story of the United States and the unifications of Germany and Italy. However, countries that join markets generally incur losses as well as gains. Therefore, when small LDC's seek to industrialize they face a dilemma once the easy import substitution is out of the way. This is one reason why customs unions among LDC's tend to be stronger in rhetoric than action.

For a number of reasons, therefore, domestic industrialization offers a powerful appeal, reinforced by the feeling that it permits that "dynamic radiation" of economic and social change, in Singer's phrase; a dynamic denied to mere hewers of wood and drawers of water. Beyond a certain point, heeding this appeal may prove costly to the South. Prebisch has succinctly described the disadvantages of excessive reliance on import substitution as a development policy.[19]

Whether or not trade is a leading sector, a second question arises, nevertheless: to what extent can insufficient supply of foreign exchange limit the rate of economic growth, even if import substitution is the basis of development policy?

If all resources were freely flexible among occupations, then a country could produce what it couldn't import, with two qualifications: (1) it couldn't produce things that can't be produced locally, such as minerals or exotic agricultural products; (2) if it were a small country, it couldn't produce, except at prohibitive costs, certain articles that require large-scale minimum outputs (automobiles are a standard example), unless it could also export them. In fact, as the classical economists perceived, resources are not flexible among occupations. There are a variety of reasons for this, but the principal one is that most people in LDC's are farmers, artisans, or unskilled laborers. Therefore, labor mobility is restricted by a skill factor.

Given these limitations on labor, as well as the well-known limitations on savings, the country will need foreign capital goods to build up its domestic productive structure. It will also need foreign financing, because of the savings constraint. Just how much of both it will need depends on a formidably complicated series of issues: what things it now produces and exports; what things it wants to produce; how developed it is now, socially and economically; how fast it wants to grow; how much it now saves, and how it can save more without creating serious political and economic problems; what people, firms, and government want to buy; and what the present and potential availabilities of natural resources are. Obviously there is no short-cut answer.

In light of some such analysis as this, the appropriate policy issues are quite specific: what industries to protect and how much protection; what export lines or import-substituting industries to invest in, and, more generally, how to choose public investments and stimulate private ones; how to invest most effectively in education and training; how to move from plans to action. The counsel to be derived about such issues by discussion of the merits of free trade is slight; and the exposition of the benefits of massive balanced invest-

[19] *Toward a New Trade Policy,* Chap. III.

ment even slighter—a hungry man may recognize that he ultimately requires a balanced diet, but in the short run, he must settle for what he can get.

Precisely because many LDC's are hungry, they are likely to have chronic balance-of-payments problems. They are trying to increase their investment without making compensating reductions in private purchasing power through taxes or private savings. The result, inevitably, is increased demand for imports. This may be accompanied, depending on the structure of domestic demand, by reductions in export supply.

Because most countries are, for a variety of reasons, reluctant to devalue formally, they tend to resort to *de facto* devaluations through such devices as export subsidies, import controls and taxes, multiple exchange rates, and so on. Systems of foreign exchange control and manipulation become central issues of development policy.

It has often been pointed out that even if devaluation is excluded, these payments pressures could be reduced if appropriate measures were taken to increase domestic savings. But given the political, administrative, and incentive problems resulting from the attempt to increase tax rates, and the difficulties of stimulating investment by reducing uncertainty, it is not surprising that LDC's often see little room for dramatic short-run results along these lines.

Consequently, unless exports are increasing rapidly, LDC's will tend to perceive foreign exchange availability as the major constraint on growth or, at least, the major constraint where results may be obtained with a minimum of domestic political costs. This view of the development process is likely to change only slowly in the South. The conditions that would be required for exchange problems to fade away in LDC eyes involve either singly or in combination (1) the adoption of those domestic policies that the South naturally balks at, and (2) Northern willingness to increase capital outflows enough for the required income redistribution to take place in an atmosphere of growth. There are some countries where these conditions have apparently been met during the past two decades: Greece, Puerto Rico, possibly Israel, possibly Taiwan. But the list is small, and in all cases massive capital inflows have been the lubricant for adoption of economic policies that were adapted to development needs.

Therefore, we can continue to expect North-South economic issues to be debated from the LDC viewpoint largely as if the key to riches lay in a transformation of Northern trade and aid policies. This seems, in light of our discussion, both oversimplified and distorted.

At the same time, this attitude is entirely natural. The North is wealthy; the South is poor. The North has long exercised political and economic domination in many LDC's. In this light, the South can view its proposals as just claims for redress rather than as the high-flown mendicancy that it sometimes appears to irritated Northern eyes. Finally, as a general proposition, aid and trade concessions benefit the recipients without engendering as many immediate political problems as domestic reforms might. Therefore ideology and self-interest conspire to fix the South's gaze abroad, and thus also to fix the terms of North-South debate.

PART THREE

The Policy Issues

CHAPTER SIX

Issues in Commercial Policy: Trade in Manufactured Products

THE PRESENT SITUATION

There is no general answer to the question, "What is the relationship among trade, aid, and economic development?" But it seems clear that many poor countries would develop faster if they could command more imports and dispose of more capital. This chapter and the two that follow investigate different avenues of North-South cooperation that might lead to increases in the South's foreign exchange resources and might therefore bring faster progress toward acceptable material standards of life.[1]

The predominant economic element in the South's desire to industrialize as a means of becoming prosperous stems from differences in the income elasticities of demand for manufactures and commodities. World output of manufactures grew at the rate of 4.2 per cent annually from 1937 to 1957 and at 8 per cent annually from 1958 to 1964. Output of commodities, including petroleum, grew less than half as fast. The world economy has changed, therefore, and the South seeks to change with it. Domestic industrialization normally affects world trade in two ways: It increases the demand for manufactured imports in the industrializing countries and it leads eventu-

[1] I have benefited in writing this chapter from the opportunity to read manuscripts by other authors dealing with the same range of subjects. The most evident kinship is with H. Johnson, *Economic Policies Towards Less Developed Countries,* Chapters 3 and 6; Robert Baldwin has written an unpublished paper for the Committee on Economic Development that discusses free trade and preferences; Richard Cooper's volume in the Atlantic Policy Studies for the Council on Foreign Relations, *National Economic Policy in an Integrated World Economy,* touches on some of these points in Chapter 3.

ally to the development of manufactured exports by countries that formerly exported only commodities.[2]

At UNCTAD, as we have seen in Chapter 2, the South produced a formula and a rationale for increased trade and aid, in which industrialization was perhaps the most important element. The formula consisted of six principal elements: (1) higher prices for commodities; (2) greater trade access in Northern markets; (3) payments by the North to developing countries whose export earnings are persistently below some reference level; (4) preferential treatment in Northern markets for Southern manufactured products; (5) creation of preferential regional trading systems in the South; (6) creation of a permanent UNCTAD as the forum for LDC trade and aid demands. This chapter deals primarily with trade access and trade preferences for manufactured products.

Both the Secretary-General's report, *Towards a New Trade Policy for Development,* and the Final Act of UNCTAD stressed that industrialization is the key to economic development and that increases in manufactured exports could act as the catalyst promoting that industrialization. In the words of the Final Act:

> The Conference recognizes the urgent need for the diversification and expansion of the export trade of developing countries in manufactures and semi-manufactures as a means of accelerating their economic development and raising their standards of living. *It considers that individual and joint action by developed and developing countries is necessary to enable the latter to obtain increased participation, commensurate with the needs of their development, in the growth of international trade in manufactured and semi-manufactured products.*[3]

This view that industry is the key is commonly expressed by LDC spokesmen, from motives that I discussed in Chapter 5. The novelty in the UNCTAD approach lies in the assertion that industrial development can be fostered by export of manufactures, *before* a broad industrial base exists. Normally, the export of manufactured products on a large scale follows the long-term buildup of domestic industry.[4]

[2] A. Maizels, *Industrial Growth and World Trade,* Cambridge University Press, 1963, Ch. 1.

[3] *Final Act,* paragraph 62, reprinted UNCTAD, *Proceedings,* Vol. I, p. 13. Emphasis supplied. There was also a Special Principle favoring trade preference for the South in the draft Final Act, but it was not voted on.

[4] The exceptions are of two kinds: (a) materials-oriented industries, of which minerals refining (Chile, Mexico), pressing vegetable oils (Nigeria, Senegal), and refining sugar (Taiwan) or petroleum (Iran) are typical; and (b) industries that

The South is making rapid strides in industrial development. From 1950 to 1962, its manufacturing output increased by nearly 8 per cent a year; at the end of the period volume of industrial production was 120 per cent greater than in 1950. During the same period Northern industrial output grew by 80 per cent. As pointed out in Chapter 4, much of the South's new output has been import-substituting, in the standard pattern described by Chenery and verified by Maizels' detailed study.

Maizels' work also confirms the difficulty of achieving substantial export trade in manufactures, before industrialization takes firm root. Therefore, LDC aims seem to conflict with the experience of this century. In Southern eyes, this serves only to reinforce the case for special promotional measures and concessions. This powerful desire to industrialize quickly stems both from the close relation between industrialization and economic development cited above and from the foreign exchange problem that dominated discussions at UNCTAD. During the period 1955–63, value of world exports of manufactures increased at the rate of 8.1 per cent annually, compared with a rate of 3.1 per cent for commodities. Countries seeking rapid increases in export earnings are therefore naturally enticed by the prospects of trade in manufactured goods. Furthermore, Southern trade in manufactured products (excluding processed foods and refined metals), although still very small, grew at the rapid rate of 7.4 per cent annually for the eight-year period. The contrast with the relative stagnation in commodity trade is not lost in the South.

Table 11 gives a regional summary of LDC exports of manufactured products for the years 1955, 1959, and 1963–64. Asia is by far the most important exporter, accounting for half of the total, and is also increasing its manufactured exports faster than other areas, thanks largely to the Hong Kong trade.

Table 12 compares underdeveloped countries' 1955 and 1963 exports of manufactures, by exporting and importing region and type of product. This computation excludes metals, thereby changing the totals substantially compared with Table 11.[5]

By this more restricted definition of Table 12, which is also more

---

benefit from low-cost labor, notably textiles and certain other light manufactures (Hong Kong, India, Mexico).

[5] Refined metals accounted for 40 per cent of the LDC's manufactured exports in 1955 and 33 per cent in 1963. Exports of other manufactures thus increased faster than those of metals during the period. The 7.4 per cent export growth rate cited above drops to 6.0 per cent when metals are included in the totals.

in keeping with the view of "manufactured" products as envisioned by planners and politicians in the South, Asia's predominance is still more striking, although perhaps not disproportionate in view of its large population. The region accounted for two-thirds of LDC manufactured exports in both years cited. African export growth, impressive in Table 11, turns out to consist mostly of non-ferrous metals from the Congo, Rhodesia, and Guinea. As might be expected, Africa's manufacturing industry accounts for very little of the region's

TABLE 11. Growth of World Exports of Manufactured Goods,[a] by Region, 1955–1964

	$ billions				*Per cent Increase*
Region	*1955*	*1959*	*1963*	*1964*	*1955–1964*
World	45.5	61.1	86.3	98.7	117
Industrial Countries	37.8	49.9	70.2	80.8	114
Eastern Europe	4.4	7.2	10.3	11.5	161
LDC's	3.0	3.2	4.8	5.5	83
Latin America	0.7	0.7	1.0	1.1	57
Middle East	0.1	0.2			
Middle East and Africa (combined)			1.8	1.8	100
Africa	0.8	0.9			
Asia	1.3	1.5	2.4	2.7	108

Source: UNCTAD, *Handbook of International Trade Statistics,* Doc. E/Conf.46/12/Add. 1, February 28, 1964; United Nations, *Monthly Bulletin of Statistics,* various years.
Note: [a] Includes refined metals.

total exports—less than 5 per cent; this compares with 10 per cent of manufactured exports for the South as a whole, and 22 per cent for Asia.

The Atlantic countries take 60 per cent (about $2.2 billion worth in 1964) of LDC manufactured exports. This is a tiny fraction (less than 4 per cent) of the North's manufactured imports. The rest go largely to the South, mostly within Asia. Communist countries play a minor role in the market for LDC manufactures.

Among the Northern countries, the United States is the biggest buyer (about $700 million in 1964) followed by Great Britain, France, and Germany. Japan's imports are disproportionately small, less than 2 per cent of the total, reflecting both the high Japanese tariff level and her comparative advantage in many products that LDC's seek to export.

The principal LDC exporters are Hong Kong, India, Israel, Mexico, Iran, Philippines, Pakistan, Taiwan, Argentina and Brazil. Table 13 shows the value of their exports by major product in 1963. They accounted for 70 per cent of all LDC manufactured exports; the first four countries alone accounted for 57 per cent. The nine countries listed in the table were the only LDC suppliers to export more than $50 million by value of manufactured products in 1964. However, some smaller exporters have shown very rapid growth in this field since 1960, notably South Korea, Malaysia, Venezuela, and Colombia.

Several points emerge from the data of Tables 11, 12, and 13.

1. LDC exports of manufactures are small compared with both total LDC exports (about 10 per cent) and world exports of manufactures (about 4 per cent). On the other hand, the South buys nearly one-fourth of the manufactured products entering world trade.

2. Tables 12 and 13 reveal how specialized this export trade is. The handful of developing countries that export manufactures in quantity have so far concentrated either on light manufactures with a high labor content (carpets, textiles, footwear, clothing) or on processing local raw materials, with a rather small value added by manufacture (metals, plywood, jute products). The degree of this concentration is great by country, region, and product: nearly half of LDC manufactured exports come from two countries; one-third of LDC manufactured exports are textiles; two-thirds of all LDC manufactured exports are from Asia.

3. The export concentration is matched by import concentration. The United States and the United Kingdom account for nearly half of all Northern imports of manufactured products; both countries take more than 10 per cent of their manufactured imports (including metals) from the South.

4. The rapid growth of world trade in manufactured products shows no signs of slowing down; this tends to reinforce the preference of the foreign exchange-starved South for industrialization as the high road to development.

TABLE 12. Underdeveloped Countries' Exports of Manufactured Goods by Commodity Class and Region, 1955 and 1963 ($ billions)

	World		North America		Western Europe		Japan		Oceania		Industrial Countries	
Exports from ↓ *Exports to* →	*1955*	*1963*	*1955*	*1963*	*1955*	*1963*	*1955*	*1963*	*1955*	*1963*	*1955*	*1963*
All LDC's:												
Chemicals	240	375	49	63	66	91	7	11	5	10	125	177
Machinery	120	290	4	19	19	40	—	1	3	5	25	65
Other Manufactures [a]	1,440	2,528	250	705	350	803	7	45	92	106	690	1,714
Total Manufactures	1,800	3,193	303	787	435	934	14	57	100	121	840	1,956
Latin America:												
Chemicals	85	120	37	46	25	34	3	1	—	—	65	81
Machinery	10	37	2	5	2	7	—	—	—	—	4	12
Other Manufactures	140	272	95	150	5	44	—	7	—	1	105	202
Total Manufactures	235	429	134	201	32	85	3	8	—	1	174	295
Middle East: [b]												
Chemicals	8	16	—	—	3	6	—	—	—	1	3	8
Machinery	9	18	—	1	3	17	—	—	—	—	3	18
Other Manufactures	98	221	20	43	33	96	—	2	1	2	54	143
Total Manufactures	115	255	20	44	39	119	—	2	1	3	60	169

Asia:												
Chemicals	100	144	8	11	13	13	3	10	2	5	26	39
Machinery	75	203	1	13	2	17	—	1	—	2	3	33
Other Manufactures	990	1,777	126	474	180	447	7	28	71	94	385	1,056
Total Manufactures	1,165	2,124	135	498	195	477	10	39	73	101	414	1,128
Africa: [c]												
Chemicals	35	66	2	4	18	34	1	—	3	4	24	42
Machinery	25	14	—	—	10	7	—	—	2	—	12	7
Other Manufactures	190	248	5	27	105	144	—	—	15	12	130	183
Total Manufactures	250	328	7	31	133	185	1	—	20	16	166	232

Source: UNCTAD, *Handbook of International Trade Statistics,* Doc. E/Conf.46/12/Add. 1, February 28, 1964; United Nations, *Monthly Bulletin of Statistics.*

Notes: [a] All figures for Other Manufactures (SITC Categories 6 and 8) exclude 67 and 68 (refined non-precious metals) but include 681 (precious metals).

[b] The Middle East is defined exclusive of African Middle East countries and including Iran.

[c] Africa includes continental Africa and associated islands excluding South Africa.

TABLE 13. Leading LDC Exporters of Manufactured Products, 1963

Country	*Product*	*1963 Export Value ($ millions)*
Hong Kong	Total Exports	873
	All manufactures	740
	Pharmaceuticals	19
	Textiles	138
	Electrical appliances	30
	Clothing	244
	Footwear	26
	Toys	37
India	Total Exports	1,610
	All manufactures	689
	Jute products	322
	Other textiles	220
	Leather	55
Israel	Total Exports	350
	All manufactures	224
	Diamonds	116
	Textiles	19
	Clothing	12
	Rubber tires	9
Mexico	Total Exports	984
	All manufactures	231
	Copper, lead, zinc	56
	Silver	47
	Textiles	34
	Iron and steel	25
Philippines [a]	Total Exports	724
	All manufactures	48
	Plywood	16
	Clothing	16

TABLE 13. (*Continued*)

Country	*Product*	*1963 Export Value ($ millions)*
Pakistan	Total Exports	416
	All manufactures	108
	Jute products	64
	Other textiles	23
Taiwan	Total Exports	332
	All manufactures	129
	Textiles	39
	Plywood	17
	Cement	13
	Clothing	10
Argentina	Total Exports	1,365
	All manufactures	82
	Dyes	13
	Iron and steel	13
Brazil	Total Exports	1,406
	All manufactures	47
	Organic chemicals	11

Source: United Nations, *Yearbook of International Trade Statistics.*

Notes: These nine countries exported 26 per cent of all LDC exports in 1963; 70 per cent of LDC exports of manufactured products.

[a] Philippines data are for 1962.

This sounds obvious and innocuous enough. But on consideration, it turns out to imply some intractable problems.[6] The fact that the South is a large importer and a small exporter of manufactured products means that it has a comparative disadvantage, or that money costs do not reflect real costs (as, for example, where industrial

[6] The following discussion lacks full theoretical elaboration. The detailed statement of assumptions and spinning out of qualification would not significantly affect the argument, but would significantly affect its intelligibility for the general reader.

wages are maintained at higher levels than required to call forth a given labor supply).

Almost all underdeveloped countries will have to change their economic structures and, often, their economic policies before they can export these products. The North does tend to erect high tariff barriers against labor-intensive manufactures as demonstrated below. The effect is to discriminate somewhat against LDC's. In terms of today's realities, that discrimination is confined to the semi-industrial countries; and elsewhere, to the rather limited prospects for materials processing and refining.[7]

Therefore, the UNCTAD contention that preferential access (and to a lesser extent, non-preferential reduction of Northern trade barriers) will be the catalyst for industrial development implies one or more of the following beliefs: (1) Northern protection is so high that tariff preferences will allow today's inefficient industry to compete; (2) access to the vast Northern market will encourage new domestic and foreign investment on a scale that will permit preference-aided Southern industries to reduce costs through economies of production by large scale firms; (3) preferences will encourage those more widely diffused economies, arising from the growth of industries in general, that ultimately transform economic and social structures; (4) the preferential system will benefit only the semi-industrial countries directly, but the repercussions will ultimately influence the most backward countries, by increasing world demand for their commodities, by concentrating the flow of foreign aid toward them, or by a gradual shift of labor-intensive industries toward the countries that are today least developed.[8]

Each of these points can also be used to justify the demand for non-preferential reduction of Northern trade barriers, although the advantages to the South would be diluted. Let us start our discussion of policy choices by looking at these issues in terms of reductions of trade barriers and going from there to see how preferential systems might alter the results.

[7] Limited in terms of effects on export earnings because the value added by manufacture is small. For example, in the year 1963, the value per ton of U.S. imports of refined copper and tin was only about 35 per cent greater per ton than that of the ore equivalent.

[8] This last point is probably inconsistent with (1) above; if the South believed that tariffs were very high, then graduated preferences, higher for the least-developed countries, would do the job directly.

POLICY CHOICES AND EFFECTS

Non-discriminatory Reductions of Tariffs and Other Trade Barriers

Since the end of World War II, reduction of barriers to trade—tariffs, quantitative restrictions, exchange controls—has been a significant causal factor in the rapid growth of Northern trade. As yet, it has not shown the same catalytic effects on the South, despite the fact that under the GATT procedures the benefits of reductions have generally been available to all nations. The major reason is that the South exports commodities, raw or processed, for which effective trade liberalization has been much more modest. Another reason, of less immediate importance, is that the North has often failed to reduce its tariff on the labor-intensive manufactures for which the South presumably has a long-run comparative advantage.

In the domain of processed products and manufactured goods, Southern exports have grown more rapidly—at the rate of 5 per cent annually from 1953 to 1963, and at nearly twice that rate in recent years (1958–64). It is not clear how much of this recent advance is attributable to cost reduction or to increases in demand induced by income growth and by tariff reduction abroad and how much to improved statistics; all statistics about underdeveloped countries are legitimate objects of suspicion. If Prebisch is correct in asserting that easy lines of import-substitution have been exhausted in many LDC's,[9] then increases in export supply of these products may be a dominant reason. The argument for dominance of supply factors is reinforced by the fact that Northern incomes have not risen faster since 1958 than they did before, nor have tariff reductions proceeded faster.[10]

The GATT negotiations for general tariff reductions that began in 1963 under the title of the Kennedy Round were aimed partly at counteracting the discrimination against outside suppliers created by the two European trade blocs, particularly EEC; and primarily, in

[9] His contention is supported by empirical and theoretical studies. See for example John H. Power, "Import Substitution as an Industrialization Strategy," paper presented at conference of Society for International Development, March 1966.

[10] Except for extension of preferences to overseas associates of the EEC, who so far still export commodities, not manufactured products.

U.S. eyes at least, to promote British membership in the Common Market as a proximate step toward building a united Europe.

However, some Northern governments also claimed that the Kennedy Round, if it achieved its goal of a 50 per cent reduction in Northern tariffs without requiring reciprocity from the South, would also greatly benefit Southern exports. Thus, in the words of the U.S. delegate to UNCTAD:

> The industrial countries have done much in recent years to reduce these barriers. More can be achieved by deep, across-the-board tariff cuts in the "Kennedy Round"—and we are prepared to have these benefits accorded to the developing countries without asking reciprocity. Such tariff cuts can be of immediate help to the developing countries. But even more important they can provide an environment that will make it possible for them to build productive export industries. It is at this point that UNCTAD and the GATT Conference, which is to follow, so strongly complement each other.[11]

Such viewpoints as this find their rationale in the case for free trade. It is therefore not surprising that the EEC countries, led by France, were less enthusiastic about the effects of free trade. The French proposals, as discussed below, dismissed trade liberalization as of negligible importance, and advocated adoption of preferential systems for LDC's. At UNCTAD the politico-economic interest of the United States, and also of the United Kingdom, lay in promoting freer trade as a method of reducing EEC discrimination against outsiders. The EEC interest was to promote the international propagation of discriminatory systems; and the LDC's, since the systems would have been for their benefit, had every reason to endorse such discriminatory proposals.

The merits of free trade as a vent for surplus, source of new methods, and incentive to economic efficiency have been discussed in earlier chapters, as has the protectionist rejoinder, based on infant industry and infant economy arguments, as well as on skepticism about the North's interest in actually allowing "low wage" manufactures to enter its markets.[12] What are the facts? Will non-discriminatory removal of trade restrictions have a great effect, a small one, or none at all on the growth of Southern trade and income?

[11] UNCTAD, *Proceedings,* Vol. II, p. 396. Statement of George Ball, U.S. delegate.

[12] This skepticism about Northern *bona fides* was elevated to the status of a Southern tenet when the North imposed restraints on imports of cotton textiles and clothing from the South in the name of "market disruption."

First, what would be the result of Northern adoption of free trade: removal of all restrictions on trade in manufactured products? There are two kinds of short-run effects to consider: (1) substitution effects resulting from replacement of domestic products by imports, and (2) income effects resulting from the growth of world income as a consequence of free trade. The income effects, it can be confidently predicted, would be negligible.[13]

The substitution effects would be far greater. It is impossible to estimate anything more than orders of magnitude, because we know so little about cost levels or about price elasticities of demand and supply. Johnson has made a valiant effort to estimate the effects, and emerged with a minimum figure of a 40 per cent increase in LDC manufactured exports, resulting from abolition of Northern duties on manufactures.[14] In 1963, this would have amounted to $800 million if only manufactured articles are included, or to about $1.3 billion if other processed products are included.

Johnson's estimate of a 40 per cent increase is, as he recognizes, very conservative. It assumes that imports from LDC's would increase at the same rate as imports from the world. But both nominal and effective protection of manufactured products that LDC's are likely to export is greater than that on manufactured goods in general.

This point has been made often by other writers, and a brief summary should suffice here.[15] It has long been recognized that effective rates of protection are often higher than the nominal tariff rates im-

[13] A rough calculation illustrates the point. It has been estimated (cf. Johnson, *Economic Policies,* Chapter 3) that free trade would increase Northern trade in manufactures by 40 per cent. In 1963, this represented an increase of $20 billion. If average tariffs were 15 per cent, this means, given standard assumptions about free competition, constant costs, absence of "water" in tariffs, etc., that the resources formerly used to produce protected import substitutes could now produce $23 billion worth of output. Real income increases by $3 billion. This amounts to less than 0.3 per cent of Northern income. On the basis of 1962–64 data, it seems that each $1 billion increase in Northern income is associated with an increase of imports from the South amounting to $40 million. Abolishing tariffs on Northern trade in manufactures would, on these assumptions, have an income effect on Southern exports of $120 million. This low figure is consistent with other estimates of income effect on resource misallocation. See for example, Cooper, *National Economic Policy,* Chapter 9, and H. Leibenstein, "Allocative Efficiency vs. X—O Efficiency," *American Economic Review,* Vol. 56 (June 1966), pp. 392–415.

[14] Johnson, *Economic Policies,* Chapter 3.

[15] Johnson, *Economic Policies,* Chapters 3, 6; see also Sidney Weintraub, "The Foreign Exchange Gap of the Developing Countries," *Essays in International Finance,* No. 48 (September 1965), International Finance Section, Princeton University, pp. 14–15.

ply. If copper ore, for example, bears no import duty, and refined copper is dutiable at 10 per cent, then the effective protection is much higher than the duty implies. If ore accounts for 75 per cent of the costs of refined copper production, then a domestic manufacturer of refined copper who purchases domestic or imported ore benefits from a 10 per cent duty on the full value of output, not just on the 25 per cent of its total value that the manufacturing cost represents. Thus, the height of the tariff on value added is not 10 per cent, but 40 per cent (10 per cent tariff on total value, divided by 25 per cent value added by manufacture). The difference between nominal and effective tariff rates results from the fact that some goods are imported, not for immediate consumption, but as inputs into production. Normally, calculations of effective tariffs show that nominal tariff rates understate the real degree of protection, because tariffs on raw materials are usually higher than those on finished products.[16] This is demonstrated by Table 14, which was computed by comparing the tariff on each finished product with those on the commodities used in its production, weighted according to their relative contribution to value of final product. These effective tariffs were averaged into a national average of effective protection by weighting duties according to the commodity composition of total trade.

Industrial countries' effective protection for all goods combined is roughly double the nominal rate for all products combined; it is generally highest on consumer goods; and is significantly higher in Japan and the United Kingdom than elsewhere in the North.[17]

Effective protection is not only greater than nominal; it is also particularly high on manufactured products of interest to developing countries. Table 15, also prepared by Balassa, shows that for a number of these products, effective tariffs generally range from 25 per cent up.

Johnson contends that the best estimate of effective protection is not simply protection of value added by manufacturing, as shown in Tables 14 and 15, but protection of value added by labor. His argument assumes that capital and technique cross frontiers freely in the long run, so that tariffs ultimately protect wages by setting up an in-

[16] Nominal tariffs may be lower than effective tariffs, when the weighted average of duties on components exceeds that on final product. This happens for example when there is a revenue duty on raw materials and no duty on the finished product.

[17] This seems inconsistent with Britain's position as a large importer of manufactured goods from the South. The explanation lies in two factors: Commonwealth Preference and the importance of imports in a few low-duty categories.

efficiency differential that low-cost labor must surpass in order to compete. Using this approach to the U.S. tariff, the effective rates of protection on products of interest to LDC's are shown to be very high—at least double the rates shown above.[18]

His argument, however, is not convincing for policy purposes. Capital and technology are far from perfectly mobile in practice, even over rather long time periods. If they were, the geographical distribution of world output would be very different from what we see today, and probably less unequal. It is of no avail to point to capital and exchange controls or riskiness or ignorance of investment opportunities as causes of persistent international differences in rates of return on capital. These "imperfections," as well as those arising from the operation of increasing returns, are the data of the problem; they cannot be wished away in considering the impact of protection. Tariffs on manufactured products may in fact raise the returns not only to labor but to other productive agents in the protected industry, compared with what they would receive in that industry without protection,[19] unless domestic markets are highly competitive. If all production is protected and monopoly elements are present, the degree of effective protection will be a determinant of the distribution of non-wage returns by industry.

The game of averaging or listing tariffs, nominal or effective, often leaves writer and reader with the inference that the higher the average tariff, the greater the restrictions on the South's ability to enter the market. This is not so, and it is useful to make the point explicit. The United States, United Kingdom, and Japan have the highest average nominal and effective tariffs in the North, but the first two take relatively more manufactures from the South, and the third relatively fewer, than any other industrial countries. There is no evidence of any association between height of average tariff and discrimination against developing countries. LDC's export only a few manufactured items, so that the general level of tariffs gives no indication of the discrimination against them for those products. Thus, Table 15 gives a better indication than Table 14. Again, a number of European

[18] G. Basevi, "The United States Tariff Structure: Estimates of Effective Rates of Protection of U.S. Industries and Industrial Labor," *Review of Economics and Statistics,* Vol. XLVIII (May 1966), pp. 147–160.

[19] I abstract here from special cases that may arise from the combination of high tariff and elastic domestic demand. Similarly, if there is a tariff on synthetic rubber and none on natural rubber, then the world price of natural rubber is liable to be controlling when it falls below the world price of synthetic rubber plus the tariff.

TABLE 14. Average Effective and Nominal Duty Rates by Commodity Category, 1962

(per cent ad valorem)

Category	United States		United Kingdom		Common Market		Japan	
	Nominal	*Effective*	*Nominal*	*Effective*	*Nominal*	*Effective*	*Nominal*	*Effective*
Intermediate Products I [a]	8.8	17.6	11.1	23.1	7.6	12.0	11.4	23.8
Intermediate Products II [a]	15.2	28.6	12.2	34.3	13.3	28.3	16.6	34.5
Consumer Goods	17.5	25.9	23.8	40.4	17.8	30.9	27.5	50.5
Investment Goods	10.3	13.9	17.0	23.0	11.7	15.0	17.1	22.0
All Commodities	11.6	20.0	15.5	27.8	11.9	18.6	16.2	29.5

Source: Bela Balassa, Tariff Protection in Industrial Countries: An Evaluation," *Journal of Political Economy,* Vol. 73 (December 1965), pp. 573–594.

Note: [a] Intermediate Products I and II refer to successive degrees of processing raw materials. Nominal and effective duties are generally higher the greater the degree of processing.

TABLE 15. Estimated Effective Rates of Protection of Value Added for Manufactured Products of Special Interest to Developing Countries in Four Major Markets, 1962 (per cent)

Item	*United States*	*United Kingdom*	*Common Market*	*Japan*
Textile fabrics	50.6	42.2	44.4	48.8
Hosiery	48.7	49.7	41.3	60.8
Clothing	35.9	40.5	25.1	42.4
Other textile articles	22.7	42.4	38.8	13.0
Shoes	25.3	36.2	33.0	45.1
Wood products, incl. furniture	26.4	25.5	28.6	33.9
Leather	25.7	34.3	18.3	59.0
Leather goods other than shoes	24.5	26.4	24.3	33.6
Rubber goods	16.1	43.9	33.6	23.6
Plastic articles	27.0	30.1	30.0	35.5
Synthetic materials	33.5	17.1	17.6	32.1
Chemical products	19.5	19.8	16.0	28.8
Ingots and other primary steel forms	106.7	98.9	28.9	58.9
Metal manufactures	28.5	35.9	25.6	27.7
Non-electrical machinery	16.1	21.2	12.2	21.4
Electrical machinery	18.1	30.0	21.5	25.3
Bicycles and motorcycles	26.1	39.2	39.7	45.0
Sports goods, toys, jewelry, etc.	41.8	35.6	26.6	31.2

Source: Bela Balassa, "Tariff Protection in Industrial Countries," *Journal of Political Economy,* Vol. 73 (December 1965), pp. 573–594.

countries, with relatively low tariff levels, use quantitative controls and other non-tariff barriers to prevent entry of LDC manufactures.[20] Therefore, it is misleading to concentrate on average tariff levels, nominal or effective, as the criterion of discrimination against the South.

The distinction between nominal and effective protection of value added remains a valid one, and leads to the presumption that there would be substantial substitution effects of benefit to the South arising from free trade in manufactures. More reliable calculations than those cited above would require detailed research into demand and cost conditions; this has not yet been attempted.[21]

In practice the choice is not between free trade and current tariff levels, but between current levels and average reductions far smaller than those originally aimed at in the Kennedy Round. The announced objective was a general 50 per cent tariff reduction (except that the parties agreed that the South would not be expected to offer reciprocal reductions, in deference to the sanctity of its infant industry protectionist views). This goal has been steadily eroded. The EEC, led by France, wants to make smaller cuts in cases where U.S. *ad valorem* rates greatly exceed those of the EEC. The list of products to be exempted from tariff negotiations has grown much larger than anticipated and probably amounts to one-fourth of Northern trade in manufactures (including textiles and many other products of interest to developing countries).[22] By far the most important, the EEC, led by France, shows no particular desire to make sharp cuts in its tariff.

This EEC attitude is somewhat inconsistent with the export-minded, producer-oriented approach that guides most tariff negotiations. The evidence seems to indicate that Europe's exports would increase more than those of the United States as a result of general tariff reduction.[23]

[20] For details on types of restrictive practices used, see UNCTAD, *Proceedings*, Vol. IV, pp. 14–20.

[21] Removal of existing quantitative restrictions on clothing and textile imports would by itself lead to annual increases of several hundred million dollars in Southern export levels.

[22] The products that are exempted from reductions provide the GATT negotiations' biggest source of potential discrimination against the South. If Northern countries are concerned about Southern competition, the easiest thing to do is leave tariffs where they are. The South has no way to retaliate.

[23] Bela Balassa, *Some Considerations on Trade Liberalization in the Atlantic Area*, Université Libre de Bruxelles, 1964, pp. 20 ff.; and M. E. Kreinen, "Effects of an Atlantic Free Trade Area on the American Economy," *Southern Economic Journal*, Vol. 33 (July 1966).

The political considerations are likely to remain dominant, although they will probably not foreclose some general tariff reductions. The EEC is not in great need of an expansion of its extra-Community markets, which are growing rapidly despite existing tariffs. Thus, the eventual extent of tariff reductions will depend on whether political gains are likely to outweigh political losses from the French viewpoint. If France tries to block negotiations, its EEC partners are not powerless. They may wish, for political reasons, to force France to the bargaining table. At this writing, it seems likely that tariff negotiations will eventually proceed but unlikely that the EEC will consent to sharp reductions.

For these reasons, the trade-enlarging scope of GATT negotiations is likely to be far smaller than is implied by estimates based on free trade assumptions.[24] Thus, the South's skepticism toward the benefits of the Kennedy Round is well-founded, though not for the reasons usually advanced.

The judgment that current tariff negotiations are likely to bear little fruit for the South implies nothing about the future. It may be that existing divisions over commercial policy will be dissipated and that the North will eventually become an area of virtual free trade in manufactures, with access open to all. But the South is seeking jam today, not jam tomorrow. Offered an uncertain vision of distant benefits—benefits that it is disposed in any even to discount—Southern enthusiasm is noticeably restrained.

The foregoing discussion referred entirely to static income and substitution effects of free trade. The dynamic consequences were discussed in Chapters 3 and 4: changes in the location of investment leading to development of new skills and of product lines that, with the assurance of export markets, can operate at low unit cost; and the association of this cost-reducing pattern with growth of supply and demand in the pattern of increasing returns. These consequences of free access to Northern markets are more important than static effects, particularly if reciprocal tariff concessions are not required from the South.

It is impossible to estimate the extent of these dynamic effects, except by historical examples; these are always open to the objection that they reflect special circumstances. In recent years Puerto Rico and Hong Kong, by selling manufactures largely into zero-tariff or low-tariff areas, have experienced a vast growth of industrial output which has fed upon itself, bringing rapid improvement in living stand-

[24] Balassa, "Tariff Protection in Industrial Countries."

ards, providing capital and skills for new investments, and improving the relative cost position of the economy.[25] In essence these cases seem to validate the classical economists' case for free trade as an agent of growth.

But both territories benefited from special circumstances: preferential access to U.S. markets and tax advantages for foreign investors in the case of Puerto Rico; and Commonwealth preference, plentiful local capital, and a huge, low-cost, adaptable labor supply in Hong Kong. The dynamic gains from free trade are much less striking in other Southern countries that have benefited from preference—notably France's former colonies and British Commonwealth members. In the French case, industrial exports, except for metals, are nil. In the British Commonwealth, the textile exports of India, Pakistan, and Hong Kong have been the principal beneficiaries of preferences for manufactures. As a general proposition, each case is *sui generis,* so the conclusions must remain agnostic. Some beneficiaries of Commonwealth preference seem to have grown no faster than the South as a whole. Trade liberalization seems to be a necessary condition of industrialization only for small nations and is never a sufficient condition of itself.

The GATT aim of reducing tariffs on manufactured goods without requiring reciprocity from the South, nevertheless, remains a goal worth striving for, by the criterion of Southern self-interest. Any such reductions are overwhelmingly likely to benefit the South rather than hurt it; the only practical qualification arises from the operation of preferential systems, as discussed below. If tariffs are reduced on labor-intensive manufactures, LDC exports of such products are likely to rise dramatically.

But the race is generally to the swift, at least in the short run; and liberalization, to the extent that it does materialize, will obviously most favor countries that are initially prepared to export. This means above all the North; and next, the nine Southern nations listed in Table 13, perhaps roughly in the order of their current exports. For most of the rest of the South, there is little or no short-run capacity to supply the market. The advantages, for their trade and industrial development, of a non-discriminatory system of one-way tariff cuts for manufactures are long-run, except where tariff reductions facilitate simple raw material processing.

[25] See Chapter 4 for qualifications to this effect, resulting from wage increases exceeding productivity growth.

Preferential Systems

The South, in the name of economic justice, seeks preferential treatment, not free trade. The call for preferences is the clarion of UNCTAD's own Great Society and must be understood, as any such rallying cry, less for its content than for the aspirations it embodies. Prebisch's economic theories and policy proposals are the rationalizations for a profound sense of injustice. Therefore, the economics of preferences are only a minor aspect. Nonetheless, we will begin our discussion of the subject with a review of the economic issues.

THE ARGUMENTS FOR AND AGAINST PREFERENCES

There are two kinds of preferential systems for manufactured products in effect today: (1) customs unions and free trade areas, which in principle offer duty-free entry to members only on all products (EEC, EFTA) and (2) preferences for all or some products, offered by rich countries to poor ones on a reciprocal or non-reciprocal basis (EEC preferences to associated overseas states, U.S. free trade with Puerto Rico and preferences to the Philippines; Commonwealth preference offered by the United Kingdom). The two are similar in many respects. In this study, I will deal only with the second, particularly with its worldwide application.[26]

There have been a number of discussions of this subject.[27] The only respectable excuses for reexamination are completeness and novelty either of analysis or opinion. Unfortunately, my analysis here is not based on new computations either of effects of existing preferences or of cost and demand conditions. Both would be essential for an authoritative empirical study.

[26] For a discussion of the prospects for customs unions and free trade areas among LDC's, see a report prepared for UNCTAD, Trade and Development Board, *Trade Expansion and Economic Cooperation Among Developing Countries,* TD/B/68, March 25, 1966.

[27] Johnson, *Economic Policies,* Chapter 6; Baldwin, CED manuscript, Chapter III; Gardner Patterson, "Would Tariff Preferences Help Economic Development?" *Lloyd's Bank Review,* Vol. 76 (April 1965), pp. 18–30; UNCTAD, *Proceedings,* Vol. IV, pp. 26–35.

A preference system in its simplest form allows free entry to the exports of preference-receiving countries in the markets of preference-granting countries, while the exports of countries not receiving preferences continue to be dutiable. The principle proposed, but not voted on, at UNCTAD would have been such a one-way preference. The South would receive preferences in Northern markets, but not grant them to the North in return. An infinite number of variations of one-way discriminatory free trade is possible and we will discuss some of them, after examining the basic theme.

The arguments for a worldwide system of preferences from North to South are all based on the judgment that it is desirable or expedient for the North to promote the industrialization of the South; or, from other motives, at least to give the impression of promoting it. The economic case is based on the belief, reinforced by the effective tariff argument, that preferential treatment will hasten industrialization by offering the LDC's the near equivalent of a protected infant-industry market in the North, as well as the possibility of economies of scale in production, arising from the size of that market. Underlying that belief is the tacit assumption that income-elasticities of demand virtually dictate industrialization as the route to prosperity and trade growth. Given these beliefs, the principal arguments favoring preferences are as follows: (1) the future gains accruing to the South from further trade liberalization are uncertain, both because of doubts surrounding the results of the negotiations and because of the effects of exemption lists, which drop products of interest to the South from the tariff-cutting procedure; (2) even if those gains were forthcoming and large, infant-industry and equity grounds conspire to warrant further concessions to the South; (3) the income transfer involved in making price concessions to the South is small but is more acceptable politically to donor and recipient than the equivalent foreign aid subsidy; (4) many LDC's have gone as far as—and often farther than—they should in import substitution, so that any device to encourage export-promotion is desirable; (5) the South wants preferences, and the North's costs would be negligible, whether or not the alleged gains materialize.

The arguments against preferences are: (1) they tend to promote and perpetuate economic inefficiency—even the valid infant-industry and scale-economy arguments are grounds for subsidy rather than preference; (2) rather than improving North-South relations, preferential systems would exacerbate them for a variety of reasons—they inevitably discriminate in effect against some LDC's and some Atlantic countries, they would create an automatic obstacle toward further efforts to liberalize world trade (because reduction of tariffs also reduces the preference margin), and they would, if successful, create a type of economic dependence on Northern concessions that is inconsistent with the South's struggle for independence; (3) preferential systems are strikingly complicated to administer in any event, and impossible to manage without inequity to some parties; (4) preferences are likely to bring with them the reverse of the effects intended, because the introduction of preferences gives Northern producer interests a chance to legislate restrictive "safeguards," that would be impossible under a non-discriminatory tariff policy (known technically as "most-favored-nation" or MFN system); (5) the gains from preferential systems would be small, because tariffs, even effective tariffs, are generally low now in light of the South's cost disadvantage, and would be still lower after GATT negotiations are completed; (6) preferences are an inferior way to give aid and lead to an inequitable distribution of aid costs.

It must be obvious by now that the differences in assumptions, goals, and estimates of the fact are so great that there can be no final answer. I favor extension of preferences to the South, whether or not on a worldwide basis, providing they are temporary with fixed expiration dates (preferably set by reduction of MFN tariffs to the preferential rate), or, failing that, are limited by quota or other device. My reasons for supporting preferences are based on the beliefs that the North should do more than it now is to help improve Southern living standards, and that preferences will make some contribution in that direction. They would create both administrative problems and incentives to inefficiency but would also provide positive incentives to domestic and foreign investment that could make a big difference to the rate of economic and social development of some countries. The stress on efficiency overlooks material issues: (a) short-run efficiency and long-run growth are not necessarily achieved by the same methods; (b) there may be a conflict between efficiency and equity; (c) preference-induced increases in Northern investment abroad will strengthen the Southern lobby in the North, and may therefore be a risk worth taking, at least for those who generally support Southern claims. In practice, the best way to reconcile the conflicts between the gains and losses from preferences is to tie the adoption of temporary preferences into a general system of progressive reduction of MFN tariff rates, as discussed below.[28]

Preferences and Economic Efficiency

In terms of economists' main preoccupation over the past century —efficient resource allocation in a static setting—it is argued that preferential systems are difficult to justify because they contain built-in incentives to inefficiency. First, they tend to promote investment in industries according to the height of tariff barriers, and not according to comparative advantage, other things being equal. This argument, though, is only part of the story. No reasonable firm or government will make substantial investments in a strikingly inefficient industry whose survival depends on a temporary preference. Furthermore, there is a facile assumption that there is no relationship between the height of the tariff barrier and Southern comparative advantage. Recent studies of effective protection indicate that protection is often highest for labor-intensive industries. LDC's might well find that the list of appropriate industries to investigate from the viewpoint of comparative advantage would include those with the highest effective protection. If preferences are temporary, however, the investor is forced to take heed of comparative advantage, otherwise the reimposition of barriers may prove fatal to the new industry.

Second, it is said that the system encourages people to ship goods around more wastefully than they would if the world were organized according to the principles of economic efficiency. It may pay to produce a product, ship it to a preferential high-tariff market, and then import the same product from a low-cost supplier. Although this possibility may set the theorists' nostrils aquiver with the joy of procreating a paradox, it is trivial in practice. If Ecuador wants to export shower curtains to Canada and import them at untold gain from Belgium, no great harm is done; but the likelihood of such a development is slim. Producers in the South have proven quite effective at reserving domestic markets to themselves and are not likely to

[28] UNCTAD officials have recently stressed the political advantage of the link between MFN reductions and granting of preferences. Cf., address of Raul Prebisch to Society for International Development, New York, March 16, 1966.

lose their grip as a consequence of receiving preferential treatment abroad.[29]

Third, if the preference is effective and Mexico, for example, is the low-cost preferential producer, foreign producers will invest in Mexico, instead of in non-preference countries where the real costs of production are lower. This is obviously a far more important practical consideration than the points discussed so far, but it is not clear whether the net effects are good or bad. From Mexico's viewpoint, it is a net advantage. Other countries lose from a protectionist standpoint (as with any preference that diverts trade or manufacturing investment). Consumers gain or lose according to whether the investment does or does not create efficient industry in Mexico. If preferences are successful, the international location of investment *will* change (for example, Puerto Rico, Hong Kong, EEC), but as a general proposition, conclusions about efficiency are not warranted. The static assumptions about rising supply price are generally not valid in such cases, because the conditions of production do not remain constant.

Fourth, the theory stresses that efficiency will be increased or decreased according to whether the preferences create new trade by replacing higher cost domestic production, or divert trade by replacing non-preferred foreign suppliers. The answers depend on cost conditions, supply elasticities, and the height of the preference, and have been much discussed in the literature.[30] The issues are of considerable analytical interest, and assume policy importance, because they involve the question of damage to third parties not sharing in the preference. It has not yet been possible to reach any agreed conclusions empirically, even in the much-investigated case of the EEC and its relations with other countries. We cannot attempt to discuss these convoluted issues here in any detail. From a welfare viewpoint, the theorists' conclusions have generally not been subject to meaningful empirical tests. Even at the relatively simple level of static theory it is not possible to say whether trade-creation is necessarily beneficial to the world as a whole, nor trade-diversion harmful.

[29] A "rational" government would import the product at the world price even over a domestic protective tariff; this form of rationality would require that the government be insensitive to producer influence.

[30] R. G. Lipsey, "The Theory of Customs Unions," *Economic Journal,* Vol. LXX (September 1960), pp. 496–513; Bela Balassa, *The Theory of Economic Integration,* R. D. Irwin, Homewood, Illinois, 1961, Chapters 2–3.

These welfare *cum* efficiency criteria, however, have been used to analyze the effects of preferences on economic efficiency and do cast a certain flickering light on the static aspects. Let us start with the situations that follow from differences in tariff levels among preference-granting countries. We have seen that preferences offer a certain incentive to choose export products according to the height of the preferences; they also invite the producer to ship to the high-tariff country, where the preferential margin is greatest. Whether this incentive offers a source of inefficiency or inequity raises rather complex issues of welfare that have been discussed elsewhere.[31] Assume, for example, that Canada grants preferences to all LDC's (or alternatively that Canada's effective tariffs are twice the height of those in other preference-giving countries, so that all preference-receiving countries seek out the Canadian market first). Does the preference create inefficiencies or inequities?

If the supplying countries face perfectly elastic demand in Canada (which means that they are small suppliers in the Canadian market), then (1) Canadian producers are unaffected *as producers* because LDC suppliers simply replace others; (2) Canadian consumers are unaffected (*as consumers of that product*) [32] because the market price is unchanged; (3) Canadians as a whole are worse off, because the market price is unchanged, but the government no longer collects the tariff which is, in effect, transferred to the LDC exporter. If he was already selling in the world market, the transfer is pure profit; if he was previously priced out of the world market, part of the transfer is a production subsidy and part of it profit.

If the supplying country faces less than perfectly elastic demand in Canada, then preferences will result in driving down market prices in Canada toward world price levels, with the following results: (1) Canadian producers are worse off unless they have some equally profitable alternative, because their output is replaced by the LDC export; (2) Canadian consumers are better off as consumers of that product because they pay less for the product; (3) Canadians as a whole may be better off, worse off, or the same as before. In this situation, the full tariff is not transferred as profit to the LDC producer, because he has in effect shared the gain from preferences with the Canadian consumer. The actual proportions of the split could range,

[31] J. Vanek, "Discriminatory Liberalization of Imports of Manufactures from the LDC's by Advanced Countries: A Comment" (unpublished).

[32] I abstract here from second-order effects arising from changes in taxation.

depending on demand elasticity, from virtually all of it going to the LDC producer to all of it going to the Canadian consumer.[33] The part of the tariff that is transferred to the LDC producer will be all profit, or part profit and part production subsidy depending on production costs.

The answer to the efficiency question also depends on what happens to other countries. If the effect of the preference is to displace a low-cost supplier, foreign producers are worse off because of the loss of markets, unless they have equally profitable alternatives. Foreign consumers are no worse off, unless the opening of the Canadian market to LDC producers who are already exporting at the world price results in a rise in the world price.[34] Foreigners as a whole may be better off, worse off, or the same as before.[35]

In general, therefore, there is not much we can say about the consequence of preferences on efficiency, except for the obvious point that there is *prima facie* evidence of inefficiency if the preference is a subsidy to production that would otherwise not take place. This is very much like the argument for free trade: anything that substitutes high-cost for low-cost production is inefficient (unless the high-cost producer's alternatives involve a greater loss of output than the low-cost producer's). But if the purpose of the subsidy is to lower costs, then even that presumption fails. Infant industry arguments are much criticized, perhaps correctly, as being a plea for special interests. But no country that faced international competition from industrialized countries has ever become competitive in world markets for manufactures until it developed its own industry behind a protective barrier. The call for free trade in manufactures arises after the country has become competitive.

In these dynamic terms, therefore, preferences may lead to cost reductions and a consequent increase in welfare resulting from the initial decrease. In the same way, they may lead to changes in tastes in the importing country. Most manufactured products are not identi-

[33] This latter result occurs when the Canadian price falls to the world price.

[34] Very unlikely, because LDC's today are too unimportant in world markets for manufactures.

[35] Worse off and the same are obvious; better off perhaps a little less so. Here are two examples: (1) Canada transfers the tariff as profit to India which uses the additional proceeds to buy U.S. manufactures, thereby increasing U.S. output and employment; (2) India exports product X to Canada, driving down the price; Canadian resources shift from producing X to Y (an export product) which was previously unprofitable because of the high price of X.

cal. If India, through preferences, introduces madras cloth into the Canadian market, it may succeed in changing Canadian fashions. The demand for madras will then increase, and in the new situation, Indian producers and Canadian consumers have both gained. Manufacturers, Canadian or foreign, whose output is displaced, or whose output growth is restricted by the change in tastes, lose as before unless they can shift resources readily. In short, and as might be expected, our recourse to theory, unsupported by evidence, tells us only that anything can happen. For three underlying reasons, static efficiency criteria can provide us with no general guidelines: (1) there can be conflict between static efficiency and development; (2) the economic theory of welfare itself is open to challenge according to the value system of the beholder; (3) even if the usual welfare assumptions are accepted, they entail the use of subsidies and other transfers, which governments and individuals will resist. The "second best" device of preferences may be the best choice in practice.

Creation of Political Problems

How can 24 industrial countries negotiate with 100 underdeveloped ones for a preferential trade system and emerge with results that leave all parties content? The question answers itself, and the answer has been fully confirmed at the meetings of the UNCTAD special committee on preferences.

First, there are differences among Northern countries. Some want to maintain political ties with preferred LDC's. Therefore they want to select the countries that they offer preference to. The Brasseur Plan, enunciated by Belgium's Finance Minister and set forth in one section of the French memorandum to UNCTAD,[36] is representative. Some, like Great Britain, want to offer preferences equally to all LDC's, but only if all major Northern countries join them. Some want to offer preferences, but to limit sharply the amounts and kinds of preferential imports, by quotas. This is the policy adopted by Australia in 1965.[37] Some don't want to offer them, and have endorsed "further study" as the optimum tactic. Japan and the United States were representative of this group at UNCTAD.

Second, differences are equally great on the Southern side. Coun-

[36] Reprinted in UNCTAD, *Proceedings,* Vol. VI, pp. 23–25.

[37] Statement by the Rt. Hon. J. McEwen, Deputy Prime Minister, in the Australian House of Representatives, May 19, 1965.

tries that are now producing or exporting substantial amounts of manufactured products would prefer that there be no discrimination among preferred suppliers. Countries that are very underdeveloped want some of the market expressly reserved for them either by a system of quotas according to country of origin, by higher preference margins, or by selective preferences, as in the Brasseur plan. Countries that now receive preferences (from EEC or the British Commonwealth) want compensation for the export losses they might suffer in those markets as a consequence of generalized preferences.

Third, there are differences between North and South. All Southern countries seek some form of preference, while some Northern countries want none.

There are five principal Northern political objections to preferences: (1) they will create a vested interest in maintaining preference margins, thereby preventing worldwide moves to liberalize trade; (2) they discriminate against some LDC's and some Atlantic countries; (3) they will hurt domestic producers; (4) they will increase the South's unwanted sense of dependence on the North; (5) they may hurt rather than help LDC efforts to increase exports, because they will open the door to restrictive legislation in the North.

The first point has some validity—no one wants to surrender material advantages. On the other hand, LDC's desires do not control Northern policy decisions to the same extent that domestic producers' demands do. Therefore, the fear that this type of "infant" protection will become permanent is probably not warranted. Furthermore, there is no assurance that, in the absence of preference, there will in fact be a general reduction of trade barriers.

The second point listed above is certainly true. It is not possible to devise a workable system that will benefit all parties equally. In that sense there will always be inequities that can lead to friction. Among preference-receivers, some countries are more industrialized than others and none of the suggestions for offsetting that advantage is likely to succeed in soon establishing the Central African Republic as an exporter of manufactures. This is not, in itself, an argument against preferences, providing those who gain least from preferences are otherwise compensated. The difficulty is that it may create a need for continually adjusting recipients' claims for equity.

Among preference-granting countries, some will experience more trade diversion than others. Japan is presumably the leading example in the short run. From a political viewpoint, much of the assessment of burdens so created depends on whether the net effect on any preference-granting country's balance of payments is adverse. Another kind of potential inequity in burden stems from differences among Northern countries' tariff levels as discussed above. Other things being equal, the high-tariff countries would transfer more income to the South and undergo more widespread domestic readjustment costs.

The concern for impact on Northern producers is the principal political issue for some Northern governments. Supporters of preferences question this concern by pointing out that the potential readjustments implied by the Kennedy Round as originally conceived were far greater than those that could stem from preferences, yet the difficulties faced in the GATT negotiations do not primarily reflect fear of adjustment problems. It might be argued that preferences would affect weak industries more than MFN reductions, but there is no evidence that this is true. But, as discussed below, free trade may offer advantages for some producers that are, in effect, political compensation for the adjustment problems, while preferences offer no obvious benefit to any important Northern producer interest.

Creation of increased dependence is very difficult to evaluate. It is reminiscent, by undiplomatic analogy, of certain difficulties inherent in child-rearing. Is it a good idea to offer a child the things he asks for if they increase his sense of dependence? Will he not come to be both handicapped by and resentful of that dependence? There is no general answer. It depends on the people involved and on the way that the gift is granted and accepted. There seems to be no empirical evidence to support a belief that these problems are necessarily serious. British relations with Commonwealth countries, and the development of the latter, show no signs of having been adversely affected by preferences. But, where neo-colonial ties are often regarded as a badge of shame, the acceptance of preferences is bound to create domestic political conflict in some LDC's. Such complex and impalpable issues as this rarely offer legitimate grounds for inaction. Experience itself often offers the best guide for dealing with them.

In addition to issues that divide the North and the South, or one from the other, domestic political considerations have made some Northern officials, notably in the United States, reluctant to advance legislation establishing preferences. They fear two kinds of consequences. First, legislatures could use the preferences as a protectionist device, by establishing restrictive quotas, or as a patronage system for foreign countries by assigning larger or smaller country quotas according to criteria that, from the viewpoint of national interest, may appear whimsical.

The problem posed by the use of preferences to promote special interests is no novelty; it exists with many legislative proposals. Sometimes it is solved by the ability of the political leadership to insist that its legislative intent be carried out; at others, leadership is unsuccessful, and the effects of the legislation are transformed by the play of political forces. There are the normal risks of political innovation; they are ultimately a question of the political power and adroitness of the various parties. The decision to go ahead or refrain from trying requires judgment of gains and losses. In the American system, the threat of Presidential veto usually suffices to prevent new legislation from subverting the Administration's intent; however, it does not guarantee that the original intent will somehow emerge pristine from the process. Furthermore, it is easier for a President to threaten a veto than actually to carry it out.

Another concern is expressed by Northern officials seeking to promote Southern development and faced with the prospect of dealing with legislatures. They fear that there will be powerful pressures to win preferences for the Northern country in Southern markets. For example, some American officials fear that preferences would be turned into a mechanism for creating a U.S.–Latin American preferential trade bloc. The adverse results, it is claimed, could include the establishment of several such North-South blocs (for example, Europe-Africa, U.S.-SEATO). These could create and sustain interbloc conflicts of economic interests that would be inconsistent with the political objectives of Atlantic cohesion, and could also create neo-colonial economic relations, in which Northern countries or trading groups receive special preferences in selected Southern countries.

This is perhaps the most difficult political issue that arises in judging the merits of preferences. It underlies all of the differing views of preferences that divide the North, and also accounts for differences that split North from South. The basic question is how world trade should be organized. The United States has considered trade policy as a tool of its efforts to weld Atlantic unity. It has also supported trade liberalization over the past three decades, in the somewhat dogmatic belief that lowering economic barriers between countries would be conducive to world peace. In recent years, there has also been a general—although not universal—feeling that U.S. economic strength was great enough for it to benefit from trade liberalization, even by the protectionist standard, which regards export surplus as a policy goal.

European countries' attachment to free trade has varied with their economic and political situations. Nations that depend heavily on trade (Netherlands, Switzerland) have generally been confident of their ability to compete, and at the same time saw no important political gains from restrictive policies, because they were not great powers. Great Britain, France, and Germany, each for different motives, have tended to regard trade policy partly as an instrument of political aims that are not fully consonant with America's. France, under De Gaulle, has wanted to use trade and aid to spread French political and cultural domination and world influence. Hence, it has viewed EEC, with its 18 African associated states, as a domain to be preserved for its members, where France can consolidate its power base.

Germany also has political aims—to assure Atlantic support against Soviet aggression and for German unity, as well as to convince the world that post-Nazi Germany will play a constructive role in world affairs. At this stage of the game, German aims are not consistent with the development of preferential trading blocs if these weaken American guarantees to Germany. Furthermore, Germany, like America and Japan, considers that its interests are well served by moving toward Northern free trade, because of its apparent comparative advantage in many manufactured products.

The United Kingdom's special problems are also well known: how to reconcile Commonwealth political-economic ties, close political association with the United States, a desire for a voice in the formation of Europe, and persistent problems with balance of payments and slow economic growth.

With these varying perspectives on the role of trade policy, it is not surprising that Northern attitudes toward preferences and most-favored-nation treatment are so different. The preferential systems sought by France and Great Britain each represent an expansion along the lines of their existing policies. For Britain, the extensions of preferences to all LDC's by all industrial countries can be viewed as a worldwide application of Commonwealth preferences, which also compensates Commonwealth LDC's for loss of the favored position in the U.K. market. For France, the system of selective preferences by country and product continues the French tradition of maintaining close political and economic ties in a French sphere of influence.

For the United States, however, preferential systems are a departure, both from recent tradition and from the vision of policy that sustained it. To sustain traditional U.S. policy, the British preference proposal is the most palatable choice; it implies no necessary breach in Atlantic unity. But generalized extension of one-way free trade offers the United States no immediate prospect of material advantage in Congressional eyes. The political advantage takes the form of good will from the South, an asset that Congress is likely to view as particularly evanescent, and certainly not worth endangering the interests of U.S. producers. The probable economic advantage is long-run; it has been demonstrated conclusively that the industrial growth of the South normally results in increased trade with the North.[38] If preferences promote Southern growth, and do not materially reduce that of the North, then they presumably will expand trade and welfare. But this is remote, and the short-run prospects are different. First, the United States is concerned with its balance-of-payments deficit. Therefore, there is a tendency to look suspiciously at anything that might tend to increase imports. As we will see below, there is some presumption that preferences, particularly those that divert trade from existing suppliers, would benefit U.S. payments.

In addition to balance of payments uncertainties, preferences, if they are trade-creating, hurt domestic producers. Therefore, from a protectionist viewpoint, worldwide preferences involve granting favors with no corresponding political or economic advantage.

A U.S.–Latin American trade bloc, however, does contain the promise of both political and economic advantage. In many people's eyes, preferences for Latin America would cement Latin American political dependence on the United States with the bond of material interest. This is seen as a method of combating the growth of hostile political forces and as a way of preventing erosion of the U.S. position as Latin America's principal supplier. It is probable that Congress would be willing to support one-way preference for Latin America, during a lengthy transition period, somewhat in the manner of EEC relations with Greece, Turkey, and African associates.

First of all, this implies that U.S. foreign policy would change. If Latin America is to be a favored supplier, what will African and

[38] Maizels, *Industrial Growth and World Trade,* pp. 148–149.

Asian countries do? They could ask for preferences elsewhere (Europe, Japan), but even if these were granted, there would be resentment and doubt about the strength of U.S. interest in maintaining friendly regimes in those areas. This would be matched by European and Japanese objections to American economic domination in the potentially rich Latin American market.

It has been claimed that the result would be to divide the world into preferential trading blocs with disastrous consequences for Atlantic cooperation, and for the development of an orderly world economy and society under U.S. leadership. This is possible, but it is no less possible that the attempt to create a Western Hemisphere trading bloc would lead either to rapid liberalization of world trade, or to general extension of one-way preferences from North to South. If Latin America receives preferences from the United States, other major trading nations may make similar concessions there, with an eye to long-run advantage.

At the same time, pressure from excluded LDC's for preferential treatment in the United States will be very great. The result could be snowballing of preferential concessions.

The prospect of competitive bidding of this kind may be so abhorrent to the North that substantial MFN tariff reductions on products of interest to the South may take on a new luster. Somewhat ironically, therefore, the free traders' last best hope may arise from the attempt to set up "divisive" preferential systems.

This doesn't tell us how the creation and maintenance of such blocs would affect America's interests, if no general liberalization did result. This is too large a subject to discuss here. The net effects are by no means clear in advance. There is a tendency, both in some U.S. official circles and in the UNCTAD discussion, to view with concern, but it is doubtful if these extremely complex issues have been analyzed fully and dispassionately. My own view is that such groupings would not be permanent, but I don't pretend to know where they are likely to lead. There seem to be no grounds for any *a priori* views about the consequences, or even whether they would be good or bad for the North.

There is some evidence to support the view that a system of regional economic groupings would not endure. If we hypothesize, for example, a system of trade blocs consisting of United States–Canada with Latin America, EFTA with the Commonwealth LDC's, and EEC with Africa, it is possible to make some rough quantitative estimates of the trade effects that might materialize. The estimates are based on the proportions of total trade carried on among members of existing preferential systems. Essentially such computations show that countries excluded from a Western Hemisphere trading bloc stand to lose more than they gain from the establishment of their own preferential systems. The Western Hemisphere is more important in world trade than the other hypothetical trading areas, so that from the viewpoint of each nation, establishing a system of preferential blocs is not an equal balance of loss and gain, even from the restricted viewpoint of protectionist economics.

American ears are perhaps too attuned to a key that emphasizes the harmful effects of trade blocs. This seems odd in view of U.S. endorsement of EEC and the Latin American Free Trade Area. In these cases, the ruling view was that the political gains outweighed both the economic and political losses. Yet the persistent sentiment remains, in part an echo of Cordell Hull's influence, that non-discrimination should be the goal of trade policy. Clearly, trade blocs offer both gains and losses, and not an unrelieved specter of economic loss and political liability. The analyst's job is to assess these gains and losses according to a system of values that does not prejudge the issues.

In economic terms, preferences offer one major long-run advantage for LDC development. They direct attention to export markets and therefore, potentially, away from high-cost import substituting industry. In other words, introduction of preferences might be a step in the general direction of production according to long-run comparative cost. This advantage is largely potential, and not actual, unless it is accompanied by measures that reduce effective protection for the more fanciful forms of infant industry development, and measures that promote more rational price relations among the various forms of labor and capital domestically.[39] It seems likely to me that a number of underdeveloped countries could then make major strides as exporters of industrial products. In some cases promotional exchange rates for manufactured exports, or appropriate devaluation of overvalued currencies, might also be required. Even without these measures, a half-dozen of those that are more advanced industrially (India, Brazil, Mexico) would be sure to benefit.

[39] The existing factor price relationships are of course in part the result of domestic political influences. In many cases, a repricing of productive factors according to opportunity cost is simply not in the cards. In such cases, preferences are nonetheless a step in the right direction.

Administration of Preference Systems

The critique of preferences invariably stresses its inherent administrative complexities. Even its supporters point to the truly awesome possibilities for endless negotiation, quota revision, and trade control that could materialize. No one has yet affirmed that these difficulties make it impossible to introduce workable preferences; there are, after all, existing preferential systems that work.

The complexity of the system naturally depends on its objectives. The attempt to insure that all LDC's share equally in the benefits, without damage to Northern producers' interests, insures an administrative nightmare. More modest goals bring fewer such difficulties. Let us look at the alternatives briefly.[40]

The French Plan. The Brasseur plan, advanced by France, provides for negotiations of separate bilateral agreements in a system of selective, temporary, and decreasing preferences. Each preference-granting country decides in each case to whom it will accord preferences, for what products, with what tariff quotas, with what preference margin, and with what duration.

The application of this system by 20 Northern countries to 70 LDC's for 1000 products would require the equivalent of 1½ million bilateral negotiations. Furthermore, each preference-granting country would not operate in a vacuum. Its decisions about each bilateral preferential offer would be made in light of the decisions made by other Northern countries, so that *de facto* multilateral negotiations would be superimposed on the system. These are virtually certain to be crippling obstacles to a large-scale system. The French government has tacitly recognized the defects and its current proposals for preferences no longer stress the merits of the Brasseur plan.

The French system, however, offers some decided advantages in theory. It assures one or a few preference-receiving countries of exclusive preference. Therefore, domestic or foreign investors in the preference-receiving country are able to rely on a relatively sure export market, once they are able to meet the preference-granting country's domestic price for the product. Worldwide extension of preference offers no such guarantee. A second advantage, for governments,

[40] They have been tabulated and discussed in UNCTAD, "Preferences: Review of Discussions," Report by the Secretary-General of the Conference, United Nations, March 23, 1965 (TD/B/AC-1/1).

of the French system is its flexibility. Internationally, it can be used as a device to help friends or punish the recalcitrant; at home, it can be used to protect domestic industries, or to threaten those who fail to agree to government price, investments, or employment guidelines. Finally, in theory, it is the most equitable system, in terms of equalizing benefits received, because it allows the preferences to be adapted to provide for the circumstances of each country. In practice, of course, the political pressures for foreign and domestic interests would prevent the attainment of such a goal, even if the preference-granting country were inclined to aim at it. LDC's have shown little enthusiasm for the Brasseur plan, because of its complexity and the evident colonialist connotations.

The LDC Plan. The administrative headaches are by no means dispelled if the South's most recent proposals are accepted instead. At UNCTAD meetings in 1965, the LDC's asked for general one-way preference, with larger margins for the least-developed countries than for those that are already semi-industrial. This plea for equity requires the very difficult determination of which preference category each LDC falls into. The LDC proposal also specifies a quota-free preference, with no products exempted. This is a blow in favor of administrative simplicity, but if insisted upon as a condition, it would foreclose the possibility of general preferences. The prospects for Northern acceptance of a system that allows unlimited preferential access to all comers can best be judged by reference to the recent history of textile imports on MFN basis.

Furthermore, the graduation of preference margins is a plea for equity in Southern eyes, although its short-term effectiveness in promoting, for example, African exports of manufactures may be doubted. But it implies an inequity in the North. High-tariff countries in the North would bear a greater adjustment burden than low-tariff countries. Equity in this sense requires equal tariff reductions among preference-granting countries.

But in practice, this kind of "damage-limiting" equality can be achieved only by setting preferential rate import quotas by product and, thereby, creating considerable administrative problems. If, as has been suggested in the name of equity, portions of each product quota were assigned to each LDC, effective administration would become a real challenge.[41] Furthermore, if, as Johnson proposes,

[41] How to distribute country quotas to exporters offers no fewer difficulties than how to set the size of the quotas initially.

exporters' quotas were made negotiable to allow non-exporting LDC's to sell their rights to those than can benefit from the preference, the claim to equity would be increased at the expense of still greater administrative novelty.

One-way Free Trade. The optimum system, to combine ease of administration, Northern political imperatives, and genuine impact on development, requires: (1) quota-free preferences; (2) a list of excepted products—those that now compete effectively in the North; (3) an escape clause that allows tariffs to be reimposed if imports exceed some stated proportion of domestic demand; (4) and, most important politically, establishment of general preferences as a step on the road to a worldwide MFN system.

This system, like most income-redistributing policies, is rife with inequity. It also leaves unanswered such knotty questions as which countries should be elegible for preferences, what the escape clause criteria should be, and whether the preference should be permanent or temporary, worldwide or selective. But it has the sovereign advantage of being workable, and of encouraging the industrial development of those countries that are actually ready to industrialize.

It is generally believed that preferences should be temporary to avoid setting up a permanent vested interest in discrimination. Prebisch has suggested that no LDC be allowed to benefit from preferences for a specific product for more than ten or fifteen years, for example. This device would allow new producers to enter the market over time and submit established LDC producers to the test of world competition. However, this approach introduces substantial complexity because of the large numbers of countries and products. Furthermore, established LDC suppliers will be reluctant to surrender their "temporary" preferential advantages. They may well band together under the banner of "la justice exige que seul le provisoire dure."

The politics of the situation therefore dictate a somewhat different approach. If preferences are to be temporary, they should be established on the principle of according advance reductions to LDC's in a general program of worldwide MFN reductions. For example, if the North accords LDC's a 50 per cent tariff reduction on manufactured products for ten years, the preference would end not by raising the preferential rate back to the pre-existing MFN rate, but by lowering the MFN rate to the preferential rate. This method presents dual advantages. First, it increases the pressure on Northern countries to reduce their trade barriers. Failure to reduce their tariffs simply perpetuates LDC's competitive advantage. Second, and for similar reasons, it reduces the ability of LDC's to perpetuate the preferential margin.

If preferences are integrated into a system of staged MFN reductions in this manner, no major recasting of the existing trade system would be required (although GATT rules would have to be amended). Furthermore, it even offers some prospect of mutual advantage. Countries that seek liberal trade can then look upon preferences as a way station toward that goal. Countries that seek to help LDC's can harness free trade efforts to their wagon.

On the other hand, a system of this kind is likely to meet opposition on several counts: from countries that are not interested in general tariff reductions, from LDC's seeking perpetual preference, and particularly from LDC's that are still at very early stages of development. The latter group might fear that progressive MFN reductions would in fact leave them with no significant preference margin by the time they were ready to export manufactured products.

No system of preference administration can avoid the problems raised by the fact that some people will be hurt more than others and some helped more than others. But the remedy for this does not lie along the lines sought by France and the LDC's. It requires instead adjustment assistance for Northern firms that suffer damage and shifts in the distribution of foreign aid for those LDC's that fail to benefit.

Are Preferences an Inferior Form of Aid?

Most people agree that some kind of workable preferential systems can be introduced. But many argue that it is a bad way to give aid, for any of several reasons: inequity in sharing the burden, inequity in sharing the benefits, doubts about the value of the benefits, ill effects on economic efficiency. The second and fourth points were discussed above. Inequity in benefit sharing is not a vital objection. Effects on efficiency are small; for a system of temporary preferences, it is of little importance.

Burden-sharing. The burden-sharing objection is more effective than the efficiency argument. One-way free trade tends to put the burden of adjustment and income transfer on preference-granting countries, according to their existing tariff levels, and not according to per capita income, which should presumably be the primary criterion.

One-way free trade diverts some countries' trade more than others. Japan is the standard example. Much of the force of this argument depends on unknown factors—the extent of the readjustment required and the economic mobility of the country affected. In any event, some random inequity is certain, but it is unlikely to be major, because trade diverted from the North is likely to be compensated for by increased demand from the South.

Finally, balance-of-payments preoccupations should also be included under this heading. Will a preference-granting country find itself saddled with payments deficits as a result of trade-creating or trade-diverting preferences? The answer depends on the country. The next section of this chapter offers some estimates as to balance-of-payments effects for the United States.

Benefits Worth Little. This last point takes two forms: [42] (1) the South has such great comparative disadvantage that preferences won't help; (2) tariffs are so low that the preference margin is trivial.[43]

Both points are incorrect. First, the theory of effective protection demonstrates that protective margins are much greater than they seem to be. Granting preferences to LDC's will have particularly strong effects in shifting the world location of processing industries toward the source of the raw material. For example, Japan now imports non-ferrous ores and oil seeds from the South and refines them. Under one-way free trade, this processing will take place in the South.

Second, for other kinds of manufactures, the preferences will induce Northern companies to invest in the South, wherever they find it profitable. This investment will reduce Southern costs in those industries, because the investment decision will be taken with reference to profit possibilities. There will therefore be a selection process at work that will assure substantial benefits to some countries.

Productivity increases and economies of scale will encourage the

[42] Statement of Anthony Solomon, Assistant Secretary of State for Economic Affairs, to Joint Economic Committee of Congress, September 10, 1965.

[43] Gardner Patterson, "Would Preferences Help Economic Development?"

modernization of many economic sectors. The size of the effects cannot be estimated, but there is no doubt that they would be significant for a number of countries. This is in addition to the generally favorable effects on balance of payments and the direct income transfer involved in preferential pricing.

This is not to say that preferences will revolutionize the world economy, or offer the solution to Southern trade and development problems. By such standards of aspiration, all policies fail.

Arguments in Favor of Preferences

The principal arguments in favor of preferences are:

They Can Help Promote LDC Output and Exports. This is supported by four points: (a) infant industry analogies; (b) economies of scale; (c) promotion of export-mindedness in the South that will allow it to make better use of the resources it already has; (d) encouragement of foreign investment.

Only two comments seem necessary. First, we have no way of estimating the size of these effects. Second, it is obvious the infant-industry arguments are limited. LDC industry will have to meet the prices of protected industries at home. Thus the effect of the preference is to allow entry only for those firms that can produce at prices *above* the world price and *below* the domestic price in the importing country. This margin may often be narrrow, although broader than the nominal tariff rates imply. If LDC's readjusted their existing structure of protectionism to favor exports relative to import substitution, this seemingly narrow margin might prove uncomfortably wide for Northern producers.

Preferences Better than MFN Reductions. There are a number of economic arguments to support the case for MFN reductions as a possibly superior alternative for LDC's. But if MFN reductions are likely to be little and late, then this alternative is not genuine.

MFN advocates can, however, offer a counter-argument. Should current GATT negotiations fail to achieve deep and general reductions, perhaps the North could agree to reduce tariffs on products of interest to the South. It is hard to conclude now that prospects for such an agreement are good; it is even likely that the effort to negotiate would simply mean a delay in considering preferences, without any significant trade liberalization. Perhaps the more appropriate sequence, if GATT negotiations fail, is to turn to selective MFN reductions only if preferential agreements have been tried and found to be impossible to achieve or administer.

Even if GATT negotiations succeed and are helpful to the South, it is argued that preferences should also be introduced for reasons of equity, as well as to promote industrialization. This argument is partly a question of point of view, partly of fact. It is unnecessary to review the first once more. The second is relevant, because preferential treatment is of no value where existing tariffs are very low. The data presented by Balassa and Basevi indicate that even a 50 per cent MFN tariff cut would still leave margin for effective preference. Obviously, however, it would be less important, both as a form of income transfer and of market expansion, than before such reductions.

Preferences as an Acceptable Form of Aid. It is claimed that the North is unlikely to increase direct aid payments—the trend has been down since 1962. It might be more acceptable politically to transfer income and stimulate growth through the higher prices and increased access implicit in effective preferences.[44] This assertion derives its strength from the recurrent Northern practice of financing its domestic income transfers by tariffs, price supports, and output restriction rather than by taxation for subsidy. It should be recognized that the direct income transfer through higher prices will not be large; the next section presents some estimates. But this serves only to reemphasize that the major role of preferences is as a potential catalyst of growth.

Political Gains Outweigh Costs. How much or how little the South would benefit from preferences is, from one viewpoint, of no great concern. If developing countries want preferential treatment, the North is in a position to give it at no great cost as a gesture of solidarity with Southern aspirations.

The obvious counter-arguments have been made frequently. If there are no gains for the South, then the North would be dissipating domestic political capital in the process, capital that could most effectively be used in pursuit of fruitful policies. If there are no gains, the South will naturally be dissatisfied, so that the good will will be short

[44] In theory of course, the more successful the preference, the less the transfer per dollar of sales. Large LDC exports into preferential markets would drive protected prices down, thereby reducing the preferential windfall.

lived. If, on the other hand, preferences should benefit the South a great deal, then the adjustment costs to the North may also be great.

Preferences as a Stimulus to Outward Looking Policies. Southern development has been too much concerned, it is claimed, with import-substitution, which leads to high-cost production, over-valued exchange rates, discouragement of exports, and a consequent crippling of economic potential. Even if preferences are of little direct value, they will stimulate export promotion, and thus more rational and successful economic policies in the South.

THE EFFECTS OF PREFERENCES

The attack and defense of preferences seems to become more intense as our ignorance of its effects becomes more apparent. Instead of responding by trying to clarify the facts about trade, development, and industrialization, policy makers all too often seem to take ideological refuge in one or another version of whatever theory happens to be congenial.

Unfortunately, we know rather little about the effects of preferences. Sometimes, when other incentives or prerequisites were present, they have apparently had a marked effect on trade (Puerto Rico). In other cases, the results have not been striking.

Commonwealth Preference

Only one preferential system, that of the British Commonwealth, has been studied in detail.[45] The studies review the effects of preferences from the time they were introduced (1932) until 1962. During that period, U.K. imports from the Commonwealth increased relatively by nearly one-third, accounting for 30 per cent of all British imports by value before preferences were introduced and rising to an average of 40 per cent during the period 1960–64. During the early postwar period this increase was even more marked, but both GATT tariff cuts and the easing of the dollar shortage have had their effects. In

[45] Political and Economic Planning, *Commonwealth Preference in the United Kingdom,* London, 1961; R. W. Green, "Commonwealth Preference," *Board of Trade Journal,* June 11, 1965, pp. iv–xix, and December 31, 1965, pp. 1551–58.

the period 1959–65, for example, Commonwealth imports fell from 44 per cent to 36 per cent of the U.K. import total.

The preference is highest for manufactures, averaging about 20 per cent, *ad valorem,* in 1962, compared with an average of 11.8 per cent for all imports enjoying preferences in that year. If non-dutiable imports are included, the figure is much lower, because most foodstuffs and raw materials are duty-free from any source. The average duty on Commonwealth imports has fluctuated considerably over the years, as follows:

Year	*All Commonwealth Imports, Ad Valorem Duty Average (per cent)*
1937	11.0
1948	6.5
1957	5.7
1962	7.2

The decline from 1937 to 1957 primarily reflects decreases in tariff protection, hence smaller effective preference margins. The subsequent rise reflects a relative increase in imports of manufactured products, carrying higher preference margins.

The areas that export manufactured products to the U.K. therefore benefit from higher margins than the 7.2 per cent Commonwealth-wide average.

Manufactured products accounted for 9 per cent of U.K. imports from the Commonwealth in 1957, 14.5 per cent in 1962, and 16 per cent by 1964. The principal beneficiaries in respect to manufactured imports were Hong Kong, India, and Pakistan, benefiting respectively in 1962 from average preference margins of 19, 11, and 14 per cent.

The pattern of U.K. trade was significantly affected by the preferential system. The U.K. took 14 per cent of its total imports of manufactured products from LDC's in 1964, a higher proportion than any other industrial country. Three-fourths of this amount came from preferential suppliers.

Although the effects were significant, they were hardly revolutionary. The principal factors in mitigating preferential effects were: the gradual erosion of preferential margins resulting from MFN tariff reductions; the United Kingdom had a comparative advantage in manufactures and received reciprocal preferences in Commonwealth markets in some cases; Asian members best able by virtue of economic structure to profit from preferences were remote from the United

Kingdom, so that transport costs and unfamiliarity of the market may have loomed large; after independence, these countries generally turned to import-substitution as the easiest form of industrialization.

There is no evidence that Commonwealth countries, or other preference-receiving LDC's, have had a more rapid growth of manufactured exports than non-preferred suppliers. In fact for the period 1960–65, for a group of sixty-five LDC's including all the major exporters, manufactured exports of those not receiving preferences increased by 100 per cent, while those of preference-receiving nations rose by only 67 per cent. Part of this difference reflects a statistical factor. Hong Kong, India, Pakistan, and the Philippines, all receiving preferences, accounted for half of the sixty-five countries' manufactured exports. All preference-receiving LDC's combined accounted for two-thirds of the South's manufactured exports in 1964. Therefore, the more rapid relative growth of exports to the North from non-preferred suppliers largely reflects the fact that they started from a small base, about $320 million in 1960, compared with $914 million in that year for preference-receiving countries. These data for the 1960–64 period illustrate both the gains from preferences and their limitations. The grant of preferences undoubtedly makes some contribution to the dominant role of preference-receiving nations in world markets for LDC manufactures. But the data also illustrate that preferences are not essential to the development of LDC trade in manufactured products, as witness the very rapid growth of exports from Mexico, Israel, Taiwan, and South Korea since 1960.

The results of Commonwealth preferences offer an example of the primacy of preconception over analysis in these matters. The preference system demonstrated modest but helpful effects for the beneficiaries. These presumably would have been greater if the preferential market was larger and less remote, and the exporting nations' independence longer established. The steady growth of U.K. manufactured imports from the preferential area since 1957 supports this latter opinion. Yet much contemporary public discussion ignores this, by stating either that the results would be negligible for the South or difficult for the North.

Balance-of-Payments Effects

A second point at which the scanty observed results differ from the evidence is in the estimate of what preferences would do to balance of payments. Currently, this is an important preoccupation of the U.S. government. It is claimed that the United States cannot give preferences because they would lead to increased imports, thereby worsening the balance of payments. The problem is analytically quite complex, because increases in U.S. imports from LDC's have a series of effects on the balance of payments.

If the new imports from LDC's substitute for goods previously imported from the North, then the balance-of-payments results will depend on the relative extent to which North and South spend additional foreign exchange earnings in the United States. Obviously, if Northern countries use dollar earnings to build up reserves, while LDC's use them to finance imports, then a switch in the source of supply from North to South benefits the U.S. balance of payments. But the full effects depend not only on the initial disposition of the dollars earned by foreigners, but also on subsequent rounds of spending. Assume that the United States spends one dollar on Indian textiles, which replace textiles formerly imported from Italy. India spends one-fourth of this dollar for U.S. products, one-half on British goods, and the remaining fourth on Common Market exports. We then must analyze how Britain and the Common Market respend their foreign exchange earnings. The ultimate balance-of-payments effect must of course reflect a comparison of the differential balance-of-payments effects of all such respending rounds, depending on whether India or Italy is the marginal supplier.

Some research has been carried out along these lines in order to measure the balance-of-payments effects of tied aid compared with untied aid. This research indicates that there are sharp differences among LDC's in their marginal propensities to spend additional dollars, tied or untied, in the United States, but that these inter-country differences narrow when additional rounds of respending are taken into consideration.

Research currently in progress should throw more light on the nature of the variations in respending effects when LDC suppliers replace Northern suppliers in U.S. markets. The comparable analysis for trade-creating imports is simpler, because it involves no substitutions among foreign supply sources. A 1963 study by the Brookings Institution cites the following respending patterns for various underdeveloped regions of the world, in terms of cents returning to the United States per dollar spent in untied aid by the United States:

Latin America	.55
Far East (excluding Japan)	.47
Near East and South Asia	.31
Africa	.15

These feedback coefficients, as they are called, are somewhat questionable for gauging the effects of trade-creating preferences because they are based on average respending ratios, rather than on respending stemming from receipt of additional dollars. Furthermore dollar earnings arising from preferences imply a different pattern of spending by recipients, because preferences affect LDC economies differently from aid.

Finally, both trade-diverting and trade-creating imports may result in income effects in some countries. The effects of income growth on foreign exchange use are uncertain as among supplying countries, in the present state of economic knowledge.

Some light on these various effects is afforded by the following table:

Trade Increases, 1960–1964 [46]

	1960–1964 Per Cent Change
1. *Exports to World* (c.i.f.):	
From the North	37
From the South	24
2. *Exports of the North* (f.o.b.):	
To the North	45
To the South	16
a. *Exports of the United States* (f.o.b.):	
To the North	30
To the South	31
b. *Exports of Other Northern Countries* (f.o.b.):	
To the North	48
To the South	11
To the United States	34

[46] Author's computations from IMF data.

Two points stand out: during this period, LDC's increased their imports from the United States one-third faster than the growth of LDC exports, while their imports from the rest of the North increased only half as fast as LDC exports; although U.S. exports to the North increased at the same rate as to the South, these increases were smaller than either the rate of Northern trade growth or growth of Northern exports to the United States.

These data offer some implication therefore, that diversion of U.S. imports from North to South results in an improvement of the U.S. trade balance. Naturally, these aggregative computations offer only an indication. The data for the 1960–64 period also reflect an accentuated emphasis on tied aid, as introduced under pressure of America's balance-of-payments concerns. For the period under review, this may have been a dominant element in the rapid growth of U.S. exports to LDC's.

A full analysis of the balance-of-payments effects of preferences would require a step-by-step estimate of the following effects: (1) each rich country's loss of exports through diversion; (2) each rich country's gain of imports through trade creation; (3) underdeveloped countries' respending patterns resulting from their increased foreign exchange patterns, compared with the respending patterns of the rich countries who lose foreign exchange through diversion.[47]

Countries that face substantial trade diversion from preferences (such as Japan) are unlikely to recoup fully through these respending effects. But those whose exports are not highly competitive with potential LDC exports may well gain on balance. If, as seems likely, LDC's spend all their additional foreign exchange earnings, the effect for all industrial countries, as a group, is neutral. The question at issue, however, is the country-by-country incidence of that effect. Some industrial countries would benefit, in balance-of-payments terms, while others would lose. The analysis that would help to answer the questions "who?" and "how much?" remains to be performed.

The dynamic effects of LDC industrial growth have been reviewed by Maizels, whose exhaustive study implies that demand for Northern exports is stimulated by Southern economic development, even where the growth also diverts Northern exports or competes in Northern domestic markets. However, no forecast of long-run balance of payments effects on particular countries seems useful, be-

[47] Full consideration would also require calculation of how the resources displaced by imports would be used in the North.

cause too many variables can affect the result, and preferences are not likely to be a major determinant.

Predicting the Trade Effects of General Preferences

Whatever the likely balance of payments effects, or the record of existing preferential systems, they give us no sure guide to the trade effects of the proposed general system. The estimates that have been made so far are not very helpful, because they are based on static analysis, and are defective, even in those terms, because of our ignorance of the relevant supply and demand elasticities. However, they serve some purpose in indicating whether short-run effects are large or small.

One such estimate has been made by Grant L. Reuber.[48] He has made various assumptions about trade effects for LDC's of: (1) reducing MFN tariffs to zero; (2) reducing MFN rates only enough to maintain existing preference margins; (3) maintaining MFN rates for the North and reducing LDC rates to zero. Not surprisingly, he concludes that the South would benefit most from the last alternative. With an average tariff of 12 per cent and a demand elasticity of minus 2, he estimates that LDC exports of manufactured products subject to significant tariffs, but not now subject to quantitative controls, would increase by 25 per cent (or $250 million), and exports of non-competing unmanufactured products by 2.4 per cent (or $350 million), for a total effect, at 1961 trade levels, of $600 million. If quantitative restrictions were removed from competing goods, he estimates an additional $1.1 billion of imports would result under "optimistic" assumptions. Reuber points out that these effects are negligible compared with current levels of trade and aid.

Johnson has said that Reuber's is too low an estimate because it neglects effective protection. He offers an estimate for increases in manufactured exports alone under free trade of $600 million. Preferential trade results would be correspondingly greater. But if a figure of $600 million is used to adjust Reuber's estimates, the short-run trade effect of preferences becomes about $1 billion, even if existing quantitative restrictions are retained.

As an alternative to this approach, I have estimated the effects on a different set of assumptions, and emerged with a result that is not

[48] *Canada's Interest in the Trade Problems of the Less-Developed Countries,* Private Planning Association of Canada, Montreal, 1964, pp. 23–29.

significantly different. My method was to assume that the developed countries would allow a preferential duty-free tariff quota to the South on a product-by-product basis. There were three additional assumptions: (1) Preferences would not be extended products for which the South is now competitive; (2) tariff quotas would not be effective in stimulating imports of manufactured products either when existing tariffs are below 5 per cent *ad valorem,* or when, no matter what the tariff level, technology and scale problems seem insurmountable; (3) preferential quotas would be set at 5 per cent of last year's imports of all products. Using 1962 data for Western Europe, Japan, Canada, and the United States, this exercise produced the following results:

I. Manufactured Products with Average Tariff Below 5 Per Cent

A. *1962 Northern Imports from*		B. *Potential Preferential Imports*
All Sources	*LDC's*	*Under 5 Per Cent Tariff Quota* [a]
$ 4.1 billion	$ 30 million	$175 million

II. Manufactured Products with Average Northern Tariffs Greater than 5 Per Cent [b]

A. *1962 Northern Imports from*		B. *Potential Preferential Imports*
All Sources	*LDC's*	*Under 5 Per Cent Tariff Quota* [a]
$31.8 billion	$277 million	$1.3 billion

[a] If all quotas are used by LDC's. Tariffs weighted by trade.
[b] Excluding products for which LDC's are now major suppliers.

This figure of $1.3 billion assumes that all preferential quotas granted are filled, which is obviously unrealistic; but it errs on the other side by not attempting to estimate the consequent increase in dutiable Northern imports above the tariff quota. Furthermore, the results obviously depend on the size of the quota assumed, and the choice of products that are included in the effective preference range.

At the May 1965 meeting of the UNCTAD special committee on preferences, the South asked for a preferential system that would allow duty-free entry under a global quota of 10 per cent of all Northern imports. Table 16 shows what the effect would be compared with present trade levels (1963) for Northern countries, if each of them took 10 per cent of their manufactured imports from the South, equivalent to $5.1 billion. The total increase in imports under these assumptions would have been $2.5 billion, because 1963 Northern imports from the South, including metals, were worth $3.1 billion. If, on the other hand, we assume that the global duty-free quota would result in a 10 per cent *increase* in imports, then the value of the trade increase would be $5.2 billion, a sum far in excess of any current estimates. In practice, the entire range of aspirations represented by the $2.5 billion "minimum" and the $5.2 billion "maximum" lies above what can reasonably be expected from preferences in the short run.

Table 17 shows the same data, with imports of processed metals subtracted. This naturally reduces imports from the South as a percentage of total imports in this category. The United States and United Kingdom are still the major importers. The United States and Canada show the smallest relative declines in imports, while the Common Market countries and Japan turn out to be much smaller importers of manufactures than the aggregate data of Table 16 implied. Total imports under a 10 per cent quota would amount to $2.6 billion ($4.4 billion under a 10 per cent increase), with Canada, Belgium, France, Netherlands, Italy, Sweden, Denmark, Austria, and Norway playing particularly laggard roles, in terms of present import levels. These countries would therefore have to make the largest increases in order to reach a 10 per cent import quota.

Halting as these initial estimates are, they can be considered solid compared with estimates of the full effects, allowing for all the dynamic considerations discussed earlier in this chapter. The best we can say now is that the evidence supports neither LDC hopes nor Atlantic countries' fears of "market disruption." Obviously, if under a 5 per cent tariff quota, or similar limiting device, the initial (2–5-year) trade effect is of the order of $1–$2 billion, the aggregate damage to Northern producers is negligible.

How much of this trade would be an income transfer resulting from higher prices? The answer obviously depends on the differences between the importer's domestic price, at a given level of effective tariff, and the world price. The domestic price may fall as a consequence of preferences, reducing the amount of transfers. Of course, the exporter's costs may be above the world price, but the transfer is no less genuine; it simply takes the form of a production subsidy.

TABLE 16. Northern Imports of Manufactures, 1963

Country	Total ($ millions)	From LDC's ($ millions)	Share of LDC's (per cent)	Increase in Imports Required for 10 Per Cent Quota ($ millions)
United States	7,801	1,079	13.83	—
Canada	4,143	70	1.68	345
Belgium-Luxembourg	3,076	200	6.48	108
France	4,047	186	4.59	219
Netherlands	3,604	44	1.22	316
Germany	5,497	323	5.88	226
Italy	3,556	124	3.49	315
United Kingdom	4,355	683	15.68	—
Sweden	2,246	57	2.55	167
Switzerland	2,187	65	2.95	154
Denmark	1,338	20	1.49	114
Austria	1,078	13	1.16	95
Norway	1,272	33	2.64	94
Portugal	361	4	1.19	32
Spain	1,034	14	1.33	90
Turkey	486	13	2.73	35
Greece	540	11	2.07	43
Ireland	489	3	0.69	46
Iceland	78	1	0.51	7
Finland	804	4	0.49	76
Australia	1,770	70	9.60	7
New Zealand	719	21	2.93	51
Japan	1,622	145	8.95	17
Total	52,105	3,185	6.11	2,557

Source: Computed from United Nations, *Commodity Trade Statistics,* 1964.
Note: —Indicates not applicable.

TABLE 17. Northern Imports of Manufactures (excluding processed metals),[a] 1963

Country	*Total ($ millions)*	*From LDC's ($ millions)*	*Share of LDC's (per cent)*	*Increase in Imports Required for 10 Per Cent Quota ($ millions)*
United States	6,275	754	12.02	—
Canada	3,865	60	1.55	327
Belgium-Luxembourg	2,623	46	1.75	216
France	3,275	86	2.63	242
Netherlands	3,201	40	1.25	280
Germany	4,347	187	4.30	248
Italy	2,773	36	1.30	241
United Kingdom	3,522	443	12.58	—
Sweden	1,963	29	1.48	167
Switzerland	1,905	57	3.00	134
Denmark	1,172	19	1.62	98
Austria	993	12	1.21	87
Norway	1,147	33	2.88	82
Portugal	306	3	0.98	28
Spain	885	13	1.47	76
Turkey	428	12	2.80	31
Greece	482	7	1.45	41
Ireland	451	3	0.67	42
Iceland	73	1	0.55	6
Finland	699	3	0.43	67
Australia	1,684	65	3.86	103
New Zealand	621	20	3.22	42
Japan	1,405	77	5.48	64
Total	44,095	2,006	4.55	2,622

Source: See Table 16.

Note: [a] Processed metals include SITC categories 67 and 68 excluding 681.
—Indicates not applicable.

Under the assumptions discussed above, the North imported in 1962 about $310 million in manufactured goods that would be entitled to preferences [49] and might increase that total in the short run by about $1 billion at world prices under a preferential system. If the average tariff on preferential trade is 15 per cent of world price, then the annual transfer from North to South would be of the order of $200 million, if Northern demand is perfectly elastic. In practice, the preferential trade is likely to benefit from a weighted average tariff of more than 15 per cent, thus increasing the amount of the transfer. On the other hand, demand is likely to be less than perfectly elastic, which would reduce the amount of the transfer. These offsetting differences may or may not be equalizing.

This estimate, however rough, does serve to make one point that seems incontestable. The transfer or aid element in preferential trade is relatively small. It therefore seems puzzling that the North shows concern about the disguised transfer, and even more so that the South insists that the North's trade concessions take the form of preferences, instead of Southern export subsidies. This insistence can be understood only if we remember that the rallying call for preferences is not only a demand for market access but a political demand for justice. The political appeal is reinforced by the hope that preferences will somehow solve the problem that many LDC's have created by establishing high-cost protected industries that often operate at far less than full capacity. Preferences, in the eyes of some LDC's, offer an escape hatch for premature industrialization and are preferable to export subsidy because the North bears the costs. Again, ideology and conscious pursuit of self-interest combine toward the same end.

Conclusions

For many Southern countries, sharply increased production and exports of processed materials and manufactured goods are probably one condition of rapid economic growth. In some cases, the possibilities are fairly good under a liberal nondiscriminating trading system. Some countries would really not benefit much unless they could get preferred treatment. Others are now too underdeveloped to export manufactures (except refined ores and foodstuffs), even with prefer-

[49] This estimate was based on the assumption that preferences would not be extended to LDC exports that are already fully competitive at existing tariff rates.

ences. They will need considerable time and assistance before they can look even to domestic industrial markets.

In theory, preferences in Northern markets benefit the South more than free trade, because they confer a price advantage over competitors. This advantage could be offset if the grant of preferences were tied to restrictions on entry. In any event, the benefits of preferential systems are likely to be important only to the semi-industrial countries in the short run. These short-run increases in LDC exports might be of the general order of $1 billion annually under a system of one-way free trade, if existing quantitative restrictions are maintained.

In the long run, preferences should help shift world location of processing industries toward the raw material sources, encourage greater domestic and foreign investment in industry, and promote a greater awareness of trade opportunities. Not even the roughest guess of the size of these effects is possible.

The case for preferences is in large part political, because they involve, among other elements, a transfer of resources and adjustment costs to Northern producers. If the North wants to be associated with the South and influence its policies, encouragement of trade ties can have its uses, at modest cost. Conversely, the refusal to grant preferences, unless it is accompanied by some other form of aid, does nothing to reduce North-South tensions. This is an important consideration for the United States, which is still saddled with its somewhat negative UNCTAD record. Unfortunately, its stand on preferences remained unaltered, despite strong pressures from other OECD countries and LDC's at the 1966 meetings of the UNCTAD preferences committee. Ultimately, U.S. policy will be forced to change, but the prolonged delay probably benefits neither North nor South. The system proposed by other OECD countries was objectionable because it was based on tariff quotas, which are all too likely to be used as tokens of preferential treatment with little real effect. Nonetheless, the U.S. refusal to agree to any scheme can hardly be viewed as a constructive alternative.

It is one thing to affirm, as I have, that political and economic advantages could stem from preferences, and quite another to claim either that the benefits would be vast, or the pitfalls negligible. There is no evidence to support the view that the economic transformation of the South awaits only the infant industry effects of preferences.

Nor can the view be dismissed that the use of preferences is likely to be either as an instrument of trade restriction, somewhat in the manner of U.S. sugar legislation, or as a token gesture that will arouse more resentment than support in the South.[50] But new policies normally have their risks, and these are no different. In this case, the political risks seem more modest than the gains.

[50] The system announced by Australia in 1965 is a case in point. It offers annual preferential tariff quotas amounting to $15 million worth of manufactures, of which a considerable part consists of products not now exported by LDC's. Australian 1963 imports of manufactured products amounted to $1.76 billion.

CHAPTER SEVEN

Issues in Commercial Policy: Commodity Trade

PRESENT SITUATION AND PROSPECTS

About 85 per cent of LDC exports are primary commodities—food, tropical beverages, agricultural raw materials, fuels, and mineral ores, some domestically refined for further processing after export. Table 18 shows the trends, by category, in recent years.

No matter what the long-range hopes for LDC manufactured exports may be, most underdeveloped countries today must rely primarily on commodity trade. Prospects for trade in commodities vary greatly, both by product and by country.

World demand for LDC commodities in the aggregate rose slowly during the decade 1952–62. The principal factors were probably slow growth of demand for food in rich countries; substitution of synthetics for natural raw materials (rubber, plastics, synthetic fibers, detergents); a tendency for industrial buyers to use smaller amounts of raw materials per unit of final output; agricultural protectionism in the Atlantic Community; low elasticity of demand for commodities in the aggregate with respect to price changes (although the actual market situation product by product is complex). During the 1950's, these tendencies were reinforced by the decline in prices, following the speculative effects of the Korean War.

There were several factors at work tending to maintain and increase LDC export supplies despite the slow growth of demand. The principal ones were immobility of resources in LDC's, leading to continued production of traditional export crops even when demand was unfavorable; high prices during the Korean crisis bringing expansion of supply for many products, notably minerals and tree crops; new countries, seeking additional foreign exchange sources, turning to expanded commodity production as the easiest way to compete in world markets. In the past 15 years, regions that previously exported little coffee, tea, or petroleum have entered the world market as significant producers.

TABLE 18. LDC Exports by Category, 1956–1964
($ billions)

Year	*Food and Beverages*	*Agricultural Raw Materials and Mineral Ores (not refined)*	*Petroleum and Other Fuels*	*Manufactures (including refined ores)* [a]	*Total*
1956	8.0	7.0	6.5	3.3	24.8
1958	8.2	6.2	7.4	2.8	24.6
1960	8.1	7.6	7.7	3.8	27.4
1962	8.5	7.3	8.9	4.2	28.9
1963	9.4	7.6	9.6	4.8	31.5
1964	10.3	7.7	10.8	5.5	34.4

Source: United Nations, *Monthly Bulletin of Statistics,* March 1962 and March 1966.

Note: [a] In recent years, refined ores have accounted for \$1–\$1.7 billion of the LDC exports under this category. The estimated figures for 1960 through 1964 are, in billions of dollars: 1960—\$1.4; 1961—\$1.4; 1962—\$1.4; 1963—\$1.5; 1964—\$1.7. (Cf. United Nations, *Monthly Bulletin of Statistics,* May 1966.) Rows may not add to totals shown because of rounding.

The net effect of LDC export supply growth outpacing demand growth for their products was a general reduction in commodity export prices during the period. The UN index of LDC export prices declined from 113 in the 1951 boom to 100 in 1952, and drifted down to 84 in 1962. Subsequently, agricultural commodity prices rose and LDC export unit values were about 5 per cent above 1962 levels at the end of 1964. Atlantic Community export prices meanwhile remained relatively stable, so that terms of trade (export price index divided by import price index) of LDC's declined by about 8 per cent over the 1952/53–1962 decade, and by about 5 per cent for the period 1952/53–1964.

Although the quantity of LDC exports rose more slowly than the Atlantic Community's (see Chapter 2), there was a substantial increase in total LDC export quantity and value during the decade following the conflict. LDC commodity export values rose from about \$18 billion equivalent in 1952 to about \$28 billion in 1964.[1] If these figures are corrected for terms-of-trade declines during the interval, purchasing power of LDC commodity exports apparently rose by about \$7 billion equivalent during the 13-year period, or at the compound rate of 2¾ per cent annually. This is much slower than the real growth rate of Atlantic Community exports or of LDC manufactured exports, but it is by no means negligible, compared with LDC export growth over the past 50 years. A continuation of this trend would result in a doubling 1952 commodity export value by 1977.

Trends and Prospects by Commodity

This is not a detailed review of world commodity trends, as other sources are readily available.[2] I want to stress here the elements that are particularly important for North-South economic policy.

For LDC's the most serious trade problems are created by competition from industrial countries' natural or synthetic products, often reinforced by import restrictions and by low price and income elasticities of demand in importing countries. For some products, produced both in LDC's and in the North (rice, oilseeds), LDC domestic demand for export products is rising faster than supply so that there is less left to export. Yet because of increases in Northern production, LDC export prices have not risen.

Table 19 shows how important a role Atlantic Community competition plays in commodities exported by LDC's. It is often stressed that the South depends for its export earnings on commodity trade, whereas the North depends on manufactures. In fact, in 1963 the industrial countries exported about 48 per cent by value of the commodities entering world trade (55 per cent excluding petroleum). Thus, competition between the Atlantic Community and the LDC's is a major factor in world commodity trade. From the LDC point of

[1] UNCTAD, *Handbook of International Trade Statistics* (E/Conf. 46/12 Add. 1), 28 February 1964; *Monthly Bulletin of Statistics,* April 1965.

[2] For example, B. Balassa, *Trade Prospects for Developing Countries,* Homewood, Illinois, R. D. Irwin, 1964; FAO, *Agricultural Commodities: Projections for 1970,* Rome, 1962 (Doc. E/CN 13/48 CCP 63/5); Pincus, *Economic Aid,* Chapter 6; UNCTAD, *Proceedings,* Vol. III; "Primary Commodities," *Encyclopedia Britannica, Book of the Year,* 1967.

view, some of this competition is "unfair," because much of the agricultural production in the North is subsidized or protected. From the Northern viewpoint, agricultural protectionism is a fact of political life, not subject to amendment lightly. For some tropical products, however, there is little or no Northern competition.

TABLE 19. LDC Commodity Exports to the Industrial Countries, 1962, Classified According to Competition They Face

Nature of Competition in Industrial Countries	*Industrial Countries' Imports from LDC's, 1962* [a] *($ millions)*	*Per Cent Distribution of Imports*	
		Including Petroleum	*Excluding Petroleum*
1. No close substitute produced	3,615	18	27
2. Close natural substitute produced	1,093	5	8
3. Close industrial substitute produced	1,804	9	13
4. Same commodity produced	13,722	68	52
Total	20,234	100	100

Source: UNCTAD, "Access to Markets for Primary Commodities in the Industrial Countries: Existing Obstacles and Measures for Trade Expansion," Doc. E/Conf.46/7, February 26, 1964.

Note: [a] Imports c.i.f. except for United States and Canada.

Non-Competing Products. The chief LDC products for which there are no close substitutes are coffee, tea, cocoa, bananas, manganese,[3] and tin, accounting for 95 per cent of non-competing exports. Although there is little prospect of dramatic increases in demand and price, LDC's can look to a fairly steady growth of sales. Tin and coffee are at present marketed under international commodity agreements de-

[3] Manganese is produced in several industrial countries, but South Africa is the only significant "Northern" exporter.

signed to stabilize prices and keep a floor under them. Recent estimates look toward varying increases in Atlantic Community import values by 1975 by product, as indicated in Table 20.

Balassa's 1975 projections for non-competing crops seem optimistic in light of the trend from 1960 to 1963. However, export values of coffee and tin rose sharply in 1964–65, and volume of exports expanded at the same time, so that the recent virtual stagnation of trade in these products may prove to have been temporary.

For the non-competing products as a whole, it must be recognized that world demand prospects are simply not favorable compared with those for manufactures and minerals. Export supplies of these non-competing products normally increase at least as fast as demand. Although East European imports will probably increase faster than those of Atlantic countries (except for tin and manganese, in which Eastern Europe is self-sufficient), their percentage of total imports is so small that the effects on world prices and quantities will remain relatively unimportant for some time. Eastern Europe is a major customer only in the world tea market, and its imports have declined in recent years, contributing thereby to the persistent sluggishness of world tea prices.

Competing Products. The principal products in this category are: (1) rubber, facing competition from Atlantic Community production of synthetics; (2) cotton, jute, and oilseeds, which compete with both synthetics and domestic substitutes or domestic production of the same commodity abroad; (3) rice, sugar, citrus fruits, tobacco, petroleum, copper, lead, zinc, and aluminum, which are also produced in the Atlantic Community.

Table 21 shows 1960 and 1963 Atlantic Community imports of these products from LDC's, with projections to 1970 and 1975. For these competing products, prospects are mixed. Exports of foods and agricultural raw materials will be sluggish; exports of non-ferrous metals and petroleum should be buoyant.

The mediocre markets for competing agricultural exports are the result of several factors:

1. Synthetic rubber and fiber production will make considerable inroads on the market growth of natural products.

2. For oilseeds, rice and sugar, protected domestic production in the Atlantic Community will limit LDC exports; for the first two crops, domestic demand in LDC's is growing rapidly, thereby tending to

TABLE 20. Industrial Countries' Imports of Non-Competing Commodities, 1960, 1963, 1970, and 1975

Commodity	*Industrial Countries' Imports from LDC's as Per Cent of World Imports 1960*	*Industrial Countries' Imports from LDC's ($ millions)*				*Per Cent Increase, 1963 to Midpoint of 1975 Projection*
		1960	*1963*	*1970 (projected)*	*1975 (projected)*	
Coffee	92	1,785	1,777	2,427–2,478	2,778–2,863	59
Tea	75	495	457	522– 526	561– 568	24
Cocoa	94	485	463	578– 592	655– 659	42
Bananas	89	246	290	326– 332	367– 375	28
Spices	55	84	63	99	108	72
Manganese	N.A.	125	105	167– 175	200– 216	98
Tin	N.A.	248	251	324– 334	352– 366	43
Total		3,468	3,406	4,443–4,536	5,021–5,155	49

Source: Col. 3: United Nations, *Commodity Trade Statistics,* Vol. XIII; Cols. 2, 4, 5: Balassa, *Trade Prospects for Developing Countries,* Appendix Tables; Col. 1: computed from UNCTAD, *Agricultural Trade Statistics,* Doc. E/Conf.46/52, February 13, 1964.

limit export supplies. The phenomenally high sugar export earnings of 1963 exaggerate the apparent decline projected for 1975. In comparison with typical years, such as 1960–61, projected LDC export levels to the North should decline by not more than 10 per cent over the next decade.

3. LDC exports of citrus fruits and tobacco have increased steadily in recent years, and should continue to. There is some threat of long-run overproduction for citrus, but demand is responsive to price changes. For tobacco, the chief long-run factors are U.S. price support policies and the effects on demand of the health dangers that arise from smoking cigarettes.

4. LDC mineral export prospects, particularly for petroleum and non-ferrous metals, seem to be much more favorable than for other competing products. LDC's have large and relatively low-cost reserves available for export. Furthermore, world demand for these products increases as fast as world industrial production and, therefore, somewhat faster than world income. Thus in respect to both supply and demand, LDC export prospects are relatively favorable. Estimates of exact price and quantity trends vary greatly, depending on what support policies the Atlantic countries choose to follow, and by producers' supply responses (mineral production and prices are apparently regulated to a degree by informal agreements among producers). However, even if prices weaken, volume increases should be great enough to assure a steady growth of mineral export proceeds over the next decade.

Implications for LDC Trade Growth. A number of factors, operating with different strength for different products, tend to support the conclusion that LDC export proceeds for many commodities will grow rather slowly. Among agricultural products, the chief exceptions are minor crops—fruits and lumber. The prospects for petroleum and minerals are much better. Balassa estimates that 1975 LDC mineral exports will be at least twice as large as those of 1960, and on the basis of 1960–64 results, his projections seem conservative, particularly for petroleum. Unfortunately for the majority of LDC's, there are only a limited number of potential exporters of these products. A high growth rate of Northern non-fuel mineral imports (5 to 6 per cent annually) would result in a \$3–\$4 billion increase by 1975. Although this sum is substantial, it is not large compared with total LDC export earnings because these minerals now account

TABLE 21. Industrial Countries' Imports of Competing Commodities, 1960, 1963, 1970, and 1975

Commodity	*Industrial Countries' Imports from LDC's as Per Cent of World Imports 1960*	*Industrial Countries' Imports from LDC's ($ millions)*				*Per Cent Increase 1963 to Midpoint of 1975 Projection*
		1960	*1963*	*1970 (projected)*	*1975 (projected)*	
1. *Close substitutes produced in Industrial Countries*						
Jute	78	139	137	135–140	143–149	6
Rubber	71	1,072	735	816–867	900–984	28[d]
Vegetable oils and oilseeds	35[a]	857	906	876–916[c]	965–1,015[c]	9

2. *Same product produced in Industrial Countries*						
Rice	8	50	59	36	40	—32
Sugar	58	982	1,337	853–875	898–924	—32
Tobacco	23	236	277	299–306	323–335	18
Cotton	30	727	881	886–922	921–979	7
Citrus fruits	32	178	194	247–256	289–301	52
Copper	N.A.	1,191	959	1,739–1,874	2,116–2,342	127
Lead	N.A.	90	75	125–129	157–176	123
Zinc	N.A.	70	59	126–134	173–192	210
Petroleum and products	41[b]	5,071	6,770	8,066–8,770	9,657–12,168	61

Source: See Table 20. Rice and citrus fruits extrapolated from Balassa data for "wheat and rice" and "oranges."

Notes: [a] Per cent of world imports of fats, oils, and oilseeds.

[b] Per cent of world imports of fuels.

[c] Fats, oils, and oilseeds.

[d] But a 10 per cent *decline* from 1960 levels.

for less than 10 per cent of all their exports. A similar growth rate for agricultural exports would, by contrast, mean a $10–$12 billion rise in exports. The growth rate for minerals imports will very likely be much lower. Balassa has projected an increase of only one-third of that amount by 1975.

Underdeveloped countries themselves offer perhaps the major source of market growth for commodities in the long run. As income and population grow in the LDC's, their demand for food, and possibly for raw materials, will rise faster than in industrial countries. LDC population, even excluding China, is more than twice that of the industrial countries, and is growing faster. Clearly, in long-run perspective, LDC's will ultimately provide the major world market.

In the shorter run, over the next few decades, the South's problem is one of effective demand, in this case reflecting underdevelopment. Today the LDC's buy only one-fifth of the world's food exports,[4] one-tenth of the raw materials traded, and one-sixth of the petroleum and other fuels. The value of intra-LDC commodity imports rose from $4.7 billion in 1959 to $5.4 billion in 1964, or by $700 million. This increase was both relatively and absolutely slower than that of industrial countries' imports from LDC's, which rose by $3.7 billion during the same period.

It would be a mistake to assume that this recent trend can be projected over long periods of time. If this book were focused on long-run prospects, then a major element would be the growth of LDC demand for both its own commodity output and the North's. But my perspective here is shorter, and my principal theme the relations between rich and poor countries. Therefore, this chapter will stress North-South trade and commodity policy.

LDC commodity exports to Communist countries have increased very rapidly in recent years, compared with the growth of LDC exports in general. But this trade too, is only a tiny fraction (less than one-tenth) of LDC commodity exports. Its future growth depends primarily on Soviet and East European choices concerning the relative future roles of increases in consumption and investment; and to some extent on the future of East-West trade. Both of these elements seem unpredictable, and, in any event, are beyond the province of this book.

Before going on from these considerations to examine the possible

[4] About $6 billion worth in 1964, of which $1 billion was U.S. surplus food grants. The comparable figures for LDC imports of raw materials and fuels were $2.4 billion and $3.0 billion.

effects of Atlantic Community policies aimed at expanding and stabilizing LDC commodity export earnings, let us first review the commodity situation by country, with an eye to assessing export prospects.

Trends and Prospects by Country and Region

General and Regional. LDC commodity trade follows the general pattern of trade discussed in Chapter 2. It has grown more slowly than the commodity exports of the North, but with considerable variation by region. Table 22 shows the growth of world commodity trade by exporting region. Table 23 shows the pattern of LDC commodity trade by category (foods and beverages, raw materials, fuels) in 1955 and 1963.

TABLE 22. Growth of World Commodity Exports,[a] by Region, 1955–1963

Region	*1955 ($ billions)*	*1959 ($ billions)*	*1963 ($ billions)*	*Per Cent Increase, 1955–1963*
World	46.1	52.4	65.0	41
Industrial Countries	20.8	23.6	31.2	50
LDC's	20.5	22.4	26.5	29
Latin America	7.2	7.5	8.8	22
Middle East	2.9	3.8	5.0	72
Africa	3.6	3.9	5.1	42
Asia	5.5	5.7	6.0	10

Source: UNCTAD, *Handbook of International Trade Statistics*, Doc. E/Conf.46/12/Add. 1, February 28, 1964; United Nations, *Monthly Bulletin of Statistics*, various years.

Note: [a] Food, raw materials, mineral ores, fuels.

As Table 23 shows, the pattern of LDC commodity trade remained relatively stable among exporting regions, once the effects of petroleum trade are removed. Latin America was the major food and beverage supplier; all areas but the Middle East play an important part in the raw materials trade. Value of LDC petroleum exports increased at an annual rate of 7½ per cent during the period, far out-

TABLE 23. LDC Exports of Commodities by Commodity Class and Region, 1955 and 1963 ($ millions)

Imports From ↓ / *Exports To* →	*World*		*North America*		*Western Europe*		*Japan*		*Oceania*		*Industrial Countries* [c]	
	1955	*1963*	*1955*	*1963*	*1955*	*1963*	*1955*	*1963*	*1955*	*1963*	*1955*	*1963*
Total LDC's:												
Food and beverages	7,690	9,370	2,480	2,490	3,180	3,988	240	380	135	130	6,040	6,978
Raw materials	6,960	7,640	1,440	1,240	3,300	3,262	550	990	145	150	5,430	5,642
Petroleum	5,890	9,520	1,210	1,840	1,880	4,061	150	590	290	365	3,520	6,861
Total	20,540	26,530	5,130	5,570	8,360	11,311	940	1,960	570	645	14,990	19,481
Latin America:												
Food and beverages	3,760	4,210	1,980	1,680	1,180	1,629	54	86	6	8	3,220	3,399
Raw materials	1,540	1,930	500	510	600	802	170	295	11	17	1,280	1,622
Petroleum	1,900	2,620	730	1,090	235	529	—	18	3	12	970	1,649
Total	7,200	8,760	3,210	3,280	2,020	2,960	225	399	20	37	5,470	6,670
Middle East [a]												
Food and beverages	205	330	9	19	99	154	2	3	—	2	110	175
Raw materials	230	220	21	11	150	110	12	15	—	—	180	136
Petroleum	2,490	4,436	210	331	1,290	2,239	110	500	195	270	1,810	3,350
Total	2,930	4,986	240	361	1,540	2,503	125	518	195	272	2,100	3,661

Asia:												
Food and beverages	1,720	2,410	245	385	485	617	185	265	66	76	990	1,342
Raw materials	3,210	3,000	670	400	1,220	915	325	610	94	70	2,310	1,995
Petroleum	550	585	20	31	52	65	38	70	76	72	185	237
Total	5,480	5,995	940	816	1,760	1,597	550	945	235	218	3,490	3,574
Africa [b]												
Food and beverages	1,720	2,058	195	268	1,230	1,355	1	11	45	33	1,470	1,751
Raw materials	1,810	2,010	170	147	1,270	1,335	32	54	20	33	1,490	1,573
Petroleum	35	1,032	—	28	10	920	—	1	—	—	10	950
Total	3,570	5,100	365	443	2,510	3,610	33	66	65	66	2,970	4,274

Source: 1955 data from UNCTAD, *Handbook of International Trade Statistics,* Doc. E/Conf.46/Add.1, February 28, 1964; 1963 data from United Nations, *Monthly Bulletin of Statistics,* March 1965, revised to conform to regions of world as defined in Notes below. The *Monthly Bulletin of Statistics* data for 1963 were revised slightly in March 1966, and therefore do not conform exactly to the above table.

Notes: Totals do not necessarily equal the sum of their parts, because of rounding.

— Indicates negligible or zero.

[a] Middle East excluding African Middle East (Libya, Sudan, U.A.R., Ethiopia).

[b] Africa includes continent and associated islands, excluding South Africa.

[c] North America, Western Europe, Japan, and Oceania.

stripping the growth of other categories. Africa emerged as a major exporter thanks to the development of Algerian, Libyan, and Nigerian reserves.

On the import side, the principal elements have been the very rapid growth of Japanese trade with LDC's, the steady expansion of West European imports, and the relative stability of LDC trade with the United States for all products but petroleum.[5] In 1955, Western Europe and Japan bought 45 per cent of LDC commodity exports; by 1963, the figure had risen to 50 per cent, while the U.S. share of imports had fallen from 25 per cent to 21 per cent over the period.

Prospects for LDC commodity exports, as set forth in most projections, also vary widely by region. Balassa anticipates the following per cent increases in commodity exports to developed areas by region:

Projected Per Cent Growth of Commodity Exports by Value, 1960–1975

Latin America	45–57
West Asia	77–111
Africa	126–144
Far East	36–50
All LDC's	66–83

In the aggregate, this would amount to an annual compound growth rate of 3.5 to 4 per cent. But the projected growth rates by region range from a low of 2.5 to 3 per cent in Latin America to a high of 5.5 to 6.2 per cent in Africa.

There is no definitive way to check on the accuracy of these and similar projections. During the period 1960–64, LDC commodity exports to the Atlantic Community increased at the rate of about 5.5 per cent annually, paced by a 12 per cent rate in the Middle East, reflecting strong world demand for petroleum.

Prospects by Country and Region. Latin America is generally believed to have relatively poor commodity trade prospects, although its exports grew rapidly from 1945 to 1957–58. Sharp increases in

[5] Even in petroleum trade, growth of U.S. imports from the South was much slower than that of other industrial countries, thanks to the U.S. import quota system.

population, persistent inflationary trends in many countries (tending to promote domestic demand for imports and for export products) and export specialization in products with rather low price and income elasticities of demand are the principal factors behind the unfavorable expectations. Table 24 lists the principal commodities exported by each Latin American country. In light of our discussion earlier in this chapter, it appears that only Venezuela, Peru, and Mexico among the larger nations have favorable export prospects over the next decade. Venezuela should hold its position as one of the world's largest oil exporters. Mexico, with a diversified export base of $1 billion annually (1963), 20 per cent of it in manufactured products, could continue its current rapid trade expansion (see Chapter 6).

Among the other major countries, Chile, Argentina, Brazil, and Colombia all face serious problems in expanding exports. For Chile, much will depend on the choices made by major copper producing companies and on the relative prices of substitutes, notably aluminum and plastics. Meat and grains, Argentina's traditional commodity exports, face competition from protected output in the United States and Europe. Brazil, heavily dependent on coffee, and vulnerable to African competition, would benefit from greater export diversification, following Mexico's example. Colombia is even more dependent on coffee, and currently shows no signs of increasing its petroleum exports. Domestic industry has expanded rapidly in recent years, but export possibilities remain largely untapped.

For the Central American countries, direction and composition of trade may be strongly affected by the Central American Common Market. But at present they rely heavily on bananas, coffee, and sugar, and their commodity trade prospects are moderate at best, depending in part on preferential treatment in the U.S. market.

In the Middle East, which produces one-fourth of the world's petroleum, oil is king, and will remain so over the next decade and beyond. Table 25 shows its preponderance. Over the past decade petroleum has risen from 68 per cent of total regional exports to a current level of 75 per cent.

The major oil exporters—Iran, Iraq, Saudi Arabia, Kuwait—should fare well. Israel, with chronic import surpluses, will probably turn increasingly to manufactured products. Among the other countries, Syria, Sudan, and the United Arab Republic rely heavily on exports of cotton; and the other countries primarily on citrus fruit, cereals, and vegetables. In general, these other countries' trade

TABLE 24. Latin American Commodity Exports

Country	Value of All Exports, 1963 ($ millions)	Principal Exports: Commodity	Principal Exports: Per Cent of Total Exports, 1963
Argentina	1,365	Meat	24
		Cereals	21
		Wool	12
		Hides and skins	5
Bolivia	81	Tin	71
Brazil	1,406	Coffee	53
		Cotton	8
		Iron ore	5
Chile	542	Copper ore and metal	66
		Iron ore	11
Colombia	447	Coffee	67
		Petroleum	17
Ecuador	166	Bananas	65
		Cocoa	12
		Coffee	11
Paraguay	40	Meat	26
		Wood	12
		Coffee	8
		Cotton	8
		Tobacco	8
Peru	541	Fish meal	19
		Cotton	17
		Copper ore and metal	16
		Sugar	12
Uruguay	165	Wool	51
		Meat	22
Venezuela	2,629	Petroleum	93
		Iron ore	5

TABLE 24. (*Continued*)

Country	*Value of All Exports, 1963 ($ millions)*	*Principal Exports*	
		Commodity	*Per Cent of Total Exports, 1963*
Costa Rica	95	Coffee	50
		Bananas	25
Dominican Republic	174	Sugar	51
		Coffee	11
		Bauxite	6
		Tobacco	5
El Salvador	154	Coffee	48
		Cotton	24
Guatemala	154	Coffee	51
		Cotton	16
		Bananas	7
Honduras	83	Bananas	41
		Coffee	17
		Wood	10
Nicaragua	100	Cotton	40
		Coffee	18
		Meat and meat animals	8
Panama	60	Bananas	70
		Fish	18
		Sugar	5
Mexico	985	Cotton	20
		Non-ferrous ores and metals	14
		Sugar	7
		Meat and meat animals	7
		Coffee	5

Source: United Nations, *Yearbook of International Trade Statistics, 1963;* and national statistical sources.

prospects are not very favorable unless new export lines can be developed. In recent years (1960–64), there has been a striking increase in Middle Eastern agricultural output and exports, largely reflecting favorable weather. It is generally believed that this trend will not continue, and that fluctuating weather will continue to be a prime determinant of agricultural exports in the dry-farming areas.

TABLE 25. Middle East Commodity Exports

Country	*Value of All Exports, 1963 ($ millions)*	*Principal Exports* *Commodity*	*Per Cent of Total Exports, 1963*
Aden	132	Petroleum	65
Cyprus	61	Fruits and vegetables	38
		Copper	22
Jordan	18	Fruits and vegetables	50
		Fertilizers	27
Iraq	781	Petroleum	94
Iran	933	Petroleum	87
Israel	350	Citrus fruit and vegetables	31
Saudi Arabia	978	Petroleum	97
Sudan	226	Cotton	60
		Oilseeds	20
Syria	189	Cotton	49
		Cereals	17
U.A.R.	522	Cotton	53
		Rice	9
		Petroleum	9
Kuwait	1,110	Petroleum	98
Lebanon	59	Fruits and vegetables	31

Source: United Nations, *Yearbook of International Trade Statistics, 1963.*

Africa is in a relatively good position among commodity exporters. Production costs for tropical beverages, oilseeds, and other crops are relatively low, so that African exporters have succeeded in increasing their shares of world trade in a number of products. In addition, mineral and oil production has increased sharply in recent years. As a consequence, African commodity exports have increased faster than those of any other region, except for Middle East oil. Furthermore, Africa's comparative advantage in a range of primary commodities should persist over the next decade, so that its exports are likely to continue to grow faster than those of other developing areas. Table 26 shows Africa's share of world exports, by quantity, over the period 1948–63, and Table 27 shows principal exports by country.

TABLE 26. Africa's Share of World Exports of Selected Commodities, 1948/1952 and 1963 (per cent)

Commodity	*1948/1952 Avg.*	*1963*
Coffee	14.5	27.4
Tea	3.8	8.1
Cocoa	71.6	80.8
Cotton	8.0	8.0
Sugar	6.6	11.4
Bananas	9.4	11.1
Citrus fruit	21.3	28.0
Tobacco	11.1	15.1
Hardwood	6.8	14.0

Source: Food and Agriculture Organization, *The State of Food and Agriculture, 1964,* Rome, 1964.

There are more than thirty countries on the continent of Africa, and this is not the place for a detailed review of their trade.[6] In general, the coffee exporting countries (Ethiopia, Cameroons, Angola, Kenya, Ivory Coast, Uganda) can expect to take still more of the

[6] See United Nations, *Economic Survey of Africa Since 1950,* New York, 1959; for historical approach, S. D. Newmark, *Foreign Trade and Economic Development in Africa,* Food Research Institute, Stanford University, 1964.

TABLE 27. African Commodity Exports

Country	Value of All Exports, 1963 ($ millions)	Principal Exports: Commodity	Principal Exports: Per Cent of Total Exports, 1963
Tanzania	179	Sisal	34
		Cotton	15
		Coffee	10
Somalia	32	Bananas	44
		Livestock	36
Uganda	153	Coffee	53
		Cotton	28
Rhodesia and Nyasaland	625	Copper	56
		Tobacco	21
Kenya	142	Coffee	25
		Cotton	17
		Sisal	17
		Tea	13
Ghana	274	Cocoa	73
		Lumber	13
Algeria	800	Petroleum	61
		Wine	13
Nigeria	531	Oilseeds and oils	42
		Cocoa	18
		Petroleum	11
		Cotton	6
		Tin	5
Morocco	384	Phosphates	24
		Citrus fruit and vegetables	24
		Non-ferrous ores	8
Congo (Leopoldville)	378	Copper	44
		Vegetable oils	11
Libya	337	Petroleum	99

TABLE 27. (*Continued*)

Country	Value of All Exports, 1963 ($ millions)	Principal Exports: Commodity	Per Cent of Total Exports, 1963
Ethiopia	105	Coffee	50
		Oilseeds	13
		Fruit and vegetables	10
Cameroons	122	Cocoa	32
		Coffee	20
		Aluminum	18
		Cotton	7
Liberia	81	Iron ore	50
		Rubber	38
Senegal	111	Ground nuts and oil	75
Sierra Leone	81	Diamonds	65
		Iron ore	18
		Palm kernels	10
Angola	165	Coffee	40
		Diamonds	16
		Sisal	12
Malagasy	82	Coffee	29
		Sugar	11
		Sisal	9
		Spices	8
Tunisia	125	Vegetable oils	20
		Phosphates	20
		Wine	20
		Cereals	10
		Fruit and vegetables	10
Congo (Brazzaville)	42	Diamonds	46
		Lumber	34
Central African Rep.	22	Lumber	48
		Cotton	39

TABLE 27. (*Continued*)

Country	*Value of All Exports, 1963 ($ millions)*	*Principal Exports*	
		Commodity	*Per Cent of Total Exports, 1963*
Guinea	55	Aluminum	60
		Bananas	10
Chad	23	Cotton	77
Dahomey	13	Oilseeds	78
Gabon	71	Lumber	41
		Manganese	19
		Petroleum	15
		Plywood	9
Ivory Coast	230	Coffee	43
		Lumber	22
		Cocoa	20
Niger	20	Ground nuts	75

Source: United Nations, *Yearbook of International Trade Statistics, 1963.*

market away from South American producers, unless they are restricted by the export quotas of the International Coffee Agreement. African cocoa countries (Ghana, Nigeria, Cameroons) have less favorable prospects because they already dominate world cocoa trade; furthermore, there is some doubt about the future of world cocoa prices.

Africa is a major exporter of oils and oilseeds, although it faces strong competition from the U.S. and Asian exporters. Those that rely on oilseed exports most heavily are Nigeria, Senegal, Niger, Dahomey, Sierra Leone, Ethiopia, and Congo. Their ability to compete with other producers in world markets is restricted by increases in African demand, by the rising rate of production of natural oilseeds and synthetic substitutes in the North, and particularly by rapid expansion of U.S. production and export of soy beans. Most projections indicate that export prospects are mediocre.

For the minerals exporters (Libya, Congo, Guinea, Rhodesia,

Cameroons, Liberia), trends are more favorable. Over the next decade, Africa should increase its exports of iron ore, copper, and aluminum faster than other supplying regions. Balassa has projected that Africa's exports of these products will rise from $100 million in 1960 to over $2 billion by 1975. Lumber exports, now supplied by the former French West and Equatorial African states and Ghana, should also increase quite rapidly. For both lumber and metals, African exports should increase faster than the LDC average. Production costs are relatively low, and domestic demand often smaller than in many Latin American and Asian countries.

In respect to other agricultural raw materials (cotton, sisal, and rubber), African prospects are less promising. Liberia is the only rubber exporter and its trade has increased little in recent years. Moderate increases of cotton exports are in prospect for a number of East and Central African states (Uganda, Kenya, Tanzania, Chad); whereas trade in sisal (of importance to East Africa) is unlikely to increase substantially. For nearly all of these products, however, Africa is generally a low-cost producer, so that its exports may well rise, even for products facing a stagnant world demand.

Asia faces major obstacles to increasing its commodity trade: pressure of domestic demand, and competing natural and synthetic production by importing countries. Table 28 shows the principal crops by country.

The rubber exporters (Malaya, Indonesia, Thailand, Ceylon) have relatively little chance of raising aggregate exports, although some countries may gain at the expense of others. Jute exporters (India, Thailand, Pakistan) also face rather poor demand prospects, because of competition of other materials.

Demand for tea in the North is likely to rise only slowly. Ceylon, and even more so, India, with increasing domestic demand and high costs, will be unable to count on much increase in export earnings. For rice exporters (Thailand, Burma, Cambodia, Vietnam), the principal clients are LDC's, themselves striving for self-sufficiency. Sugar, a major export crop for only three countries—Taiwan, Philippines and Mauritius—has more favorable prospects. For oil-seed exporters (Indonesia, Philippines, India), domestic demand is likely to increase faster than supplies, so that prices are likely to rise, and Africa thus to continue its relative gains.

Asian commodity export prospects are most favorable for minerals (Malayan and Indonesian tin, Indian and Malayan iron ore, Indo-

TABLE 28. Asian Commodity Exports

Country	Value of All Exports, 1963 ($ millions)	Principal Exports: Commodity	Principal Exports: Per Cent of Total Exports, 1963
India	1629	Tea	16
		Jute	14
		Oils and oilseeds	8
		Iron ore	5
Taiwan	332	Sugar	31
		Fruit and vegetables	14
		Rice	6
South Vietnam	77	Rice	47
		Rubber	45
Malaya	884	Rubber	51
		Tin	24
		Iron ore	7
Indonesia	682	Petroleum	39
		Rubber	35
		Oils and oilseeds	6
		Tin	5
Burma	271	Rice	63
		Lumber	15
Pakistan	417	Jute	52
		Cotton	16
		Fish	5
Cambodia	89	Rice	53
		Rubber	26
Ceylon	363	Tea	67
		Rubber	15
		Coconut oil	6
Philippines	727	Sugar	22
		Copra	22
		Lumber	22

TABLE 28. (*Continued*)

Country	*Value of All Exports, 1963 ($ millions)*	*Principal Exports*	
		Commodity	*Per Cent of Total Exports, 1963*
Korea	87	Fish	10
		Iron ore	7
		Silk	6
Mauritius	90	Sugar	98
Thailand	466	Rice	37
		Rubber	20
		Corn	9
		Tin	8
Afghanistan	69	Caracul	25
		Cotton	19
		Dried fruits	15

Source: United Nations, *Yearbook of International Trade Statistics, 1963.*

nesian petroleum). Malaya appears to be in a stronger position for tin than Indonesia. Iron ore exports will depend on government export policies, particularly in India. At least the export opportunities for these commodities are relatively favorable, thus providing an offset to the unfavorable situation faced by these countries' other exports. It seems clear that most Asian countries, particularly the heavily populated ones, such as India, Pakistan, Taiwan, Philippines, will have to turn more and more to manufactured exports to meet their import requirements, unless proven or new mineral resources can be exploited. Presumably, this was one objective of the Indian devaluation of June 1966.

Some Generalizations

In discussing the commodity trade situation of some seventy countries, there is a great deal of variation, perhaps too much to allow any all-inclusive statement. However, a few points seem clear:

1. Many Latin American and Asian countries will be able to rely less and less on commodity trade for financing import growth.

2. The Middle East and Africa are better off, thanks largely to petroleum in the former region and favorable supply conditions for a number of products in the latter.

3. Two conditions will tend to favor the growth of any country's commodity export trade:

Low-cost productive potential, even if the particular commodity faces sluggish world demand (as in the postwar expansion of African tea and sisal exports).

Specialization in products with good demand prospects (as in Peruvian fishmeal trade, African copper exports, Middle East oil, or Malayan tin).

4. For most countries, this last condition does not apply. Those that are semi-industrial (India, Brazil, Argentina, Mexico, Taiwan) can hope to shift increasingly from commodities to manufactured exports, although this is no easy task. Those whose industry is not yet established have even fewer trade alternatives. For them, unless tourism or other service industries can be developed, the foreign-exchange limitation is likely to loom as a major obstacle to desired rates of growth.

ATLANTIC COUNTRIES' POLICIES: MARKET ACCESS

The discussion above assumes tacitly that neither the North nor the South will take action to change existing commodity policies. If these policies could be changed, either by Northern moves toward free trade in commodities or by deliberate rigging of commodity prices, then LDC export prospects would be more favorable. This section discusses what the Atlantic nations could do to increase LDC commodity earnings by more liberal trade policies ("improving market access" in the standard jargon), and estimates some of the costs to the North. The next section discusses the effects of the second line of action, price-fixing.

World commodity trade is subject to a wide range of restrictions imposed in the Atlantic Community. Most of them reduce LDC export earnings below the free market potential. A few, however, often as a by-product of other Northern policy objectives, have the effect of raising Southern earnings above free market levels.

The principal Northern restrictions on commodity trade are:

1. Protective duties and, to a lesser extent, customs duties aimed at collecting revenue.
2. Quantitative limitations on imports.
3. Excise taxes or other internal taxes with revenue objectives.
4. Preferential trade systems largely aimed at benefiting particular countries at the expense of other exporters.

LDC's and the Communist countries impose similar restrictions; their impact in restraining trade is probably smaller now than those of the Atlantic Community. However, their long-run effects in restraining trade are probably substantial because these are the countries whose demand for commodities has the greatest capacity for increase. Thus, per capita food consumption (calories) in LDC's is about one-third less than in the North; for proteins, the figure is about one-half. For agricultural raw materials and minerals, present-day North-South consumption differences are far greater than for food; increases in South-South trade and South-East trade are potentially of great importance in the growth of LDC raw materials exports. In other words, income elasticity of demand for commodities is much higher in poor countries, and is likely to remain so until their per capita consumption approaches current Atlantic Community levels.

For the short run, however, the Atlantic Community is the principal target of demands for free access to markets. It is the biggest buyer. It is more vulnerable to political pressure than the Soviet Bloc and furthermore, from the LDC viewpoint, a more emotionally satisfying target for demands.

What would Northern trade liberalization in favor of LDC's consist of? The general line has been set out in the recent GATT Action Program—a presumably unintentional irony in nomenclature—of May 1963, and in the new GATT articles on trade and development (February 1965). The Action Program provided that: (1) no new tariff or non-tariff barriers should be established by the GATT members on products of interest to LDC's; (2) quantitative restrictions on imports from LDC's should be removed by May 1964; (3) tropical products should be allowed to enter the North duty-free effective January 1964; (4) the North should remove customs duties on primary products of interest to LDC's; (5) the North should reduce its duties on processed and semi-processed materials imported from LDC's by at least 50 per cent below present levels before May 1966; (6) internal charges and revenue duties on products primarily exported by LDC's should be removed before January 1966.

The 1965 GATT chapter (Articles 36–38) on trade and development commits the members to:

> accord high priority to the reduction and elimination of barriers to products currently or potentially of particular export interest to less-developed contracting parties, including customs duties and other restrictions which differentiate unreasonably between such products in their primary and in their processed forms. (Article 37.)

Article 37 also reiterates the Action Program's strictures against establishment of new tariff barriers. Article 36 sets forth a number of goals of development policy: rapid growth of exports and a larger share of world trade for LDC's; better market access and higher prices for their exports; and diversification of their export economies so that they will be less dependent on primary commodities.

Needless to say, neither the Action Program nor the trade and development articles of GATT have resulted in any significant changes in the present pattern of trade restrictions. The dominant factors are the North's fiscal interest in maintaining revenue sources (for example, German taxes on coffee); and, more important, its protective interest in preventing loss to domestic producers (for example, U.S. import controls on sugar and petroleum, or Italian duties on bananas). Therefore, the GATT commitments are likely to remain nothing more than a ritual acknowledgment of the "justice" of LDC claims.[7]

The idea of liberalizing world commodity trade for the benefit of LDC's is superficially appealing as a remedy, because it involves none of the complicated systems of control inherent in most forms of commodity price-fixing. Unfortunately, the practical possibilities are slight; the measures that could be adopted would have little effect on trade; those that would spur trade are not likely to be adopted.

[7] There have been a few moves toward greater access for LDC commodities: (a) The European countries have removed duties on tea and tropical hardwoods; (b) Japan has liberalized restrictions on banana imports, with a consequent 200 per cent increase in import levels—before 1963, duties were so high that Japanese consumption per capita was well below 1939 levels; (c) In 1965, the United States removed its import controls on lead and zinc in response to supply shortages, although it continued to subsidize small domestic producers. (It has been estimated that this action will result in a $45 million increase in U.S. imports annually.)

For non-competing commodities, removal of existing Northern duties and internal taxes would have only a modest effect. Taxes on coffee, tea, cocoa, tin, and spices are a nuisance to LDC's but they do not greatly affect consumption of these commodities because demand is so inelastic. Tinbergen has estimated that removal of duties and fiscal charges on coffee, tea, and bananas in 1959 would have increased Atlantic Community imports of those products by $64 million, about 2½ per cent of the value of world trade in these commodities. A similar estimate by GATT, for 1961, worked out to about $100–130 million for coffee, cocoa, and bananas, worldwide. An FAO projection made in 1962, adding cocoa and citrus fruits to the list of crops, emerged with a trade effect of $180 million for Europe (the United States doesn't tax imports of these products), or about 4 per cent of the projected 1970 value of world trade in these crops.

Whatever the correct figure, it is clear that removal of charges, although moderately useful, is not a panacea for producers of tropical products. However, Latin American producers have a special interest in removal of tariffs and fiscal charges, because EEC tariffs on coffee, cocoa, and bananas will apply to them, not to the EEC's associated African states. The duties for non-members on cocoa (5.4 per cent) and coffee (9.6 per cent) are not high, but they discriminate against Latin America, particularly in light of Africa's apparent long-run supply advantage in these crops. The EEC duty on bananas (20 per cent) is clearly discriminatory (despite duty-free quotas in the important German market) and may well be sufficient to overcome consumer preferences for the variety mainly exported from Latin America. The often-voiced statement that Latin American exports will benefit from the EEC's rapid economic growth is cold comfort. These benefits will be freely available to everyone, but the discrimination in tropical crops primarily hurts Latin America. Asia's principal tropical exports—tea, rubber, and hardwoods—enter the EEC duty free (as do oilseeds, which are much more important to Africa and Asia than to Latin America).

In short, removal of restrictions on tropical products, particularly those that discriminate against certain suppliers, is probably desirable on several counts, despite the losses that EEC and British Commonwealth associates might suffer. But the really significant Northern restrictions are against products that are produced in both North and South.

This is the second aspect of market access; the North is unlikely to make any genuine concessions for these products. National governments apparently feel politically unable either to devaluate their currencies or to reduce agricultural protectionism except under great pressure; and if the North will not contemplate the latter, nor the South the former, large increases in commodity trade are ruled out, except via the slow and undramatic process of income-produced increases in import demand.

The major commodities in LDC export trade (1959–61 average) are:

Coffee	$1.9 billion annually
Cocoa	$520 million
Tea	$550 million
Natural rubber	$1.4 billion
Petroleum	$8.0 billion
Sugar	$1.2 billion
Fats and oils	$1.1 billion
Cotton	$1.1 billion
Non-ferrous metals (tin, copper, lead, zinc)	$1.5 billion
Total	$17,270 million

These exports amounted to nearly two-thirds of all LDC merchandise exports during the 1959–61 period. The first four products are tropical crops, amounting to about one-fourth of the listed commodities by value. The effects of improved market access for these products were discussed above. The remaining products compete with Northern production.

It has been estimated that one-third of all LDC commodity exports to the Atlantic Community is subject to protective tariffs and quantitative controls.[8] Some of this, however, is not relevant to the questions that concern us here. For example, the United States now imposes controls on petroleum imports; LDC suppliers now provide the U.S. market with about $1.5 billion of crude oil and refined products annually. This figure would soon double if controls were removed; [9] but foreign exchange is hardly a stumbling block to the

[8] The figure is probably nearer to one-half if we subtract tropical crops. UNCTAD, *Proceedings,* Vol. III, p. 22.

[9] Cf. estimates by Lichtblau, cited in Johnson, *Economic Policies,* Chapter 3.

growth of petroleum-exporting nations. Sugar is more relevant to development problems. It is produced under protection everywhere in the North. In the absence of controls, there would be almost no production in Europe, and very little in the United States. Johnson has estimated that free trade in sugar would have increased the value of LDC exports by $900 million in 1959.

The situation for non-ferrous metals, oilseeds, and cotton is more complex, because LDC's would not be the sole exporting beneficiaries of free trade. Production in some Northern countries is relatively low cost. Thus, removal of controls on fats and oils would benefit the United States and New Zealand while reducing protected production of vegetable oils and animal fats in Western Europe. Similarly for nonferrous metals, Canada, Australia, and South Africa, as well as the LDC's, would benefit at the expense of producers in the United States and Western Europe. World cotton prices are in effect supported by the U.S. domestic control program. The problem for this crop is not primarily one of market access—U.S. protective policies probably benefit LDC's in the aggregate—but of competition from synthetics.

The Atlantic Community shows few signs of reducing its effective protection for those competing commodities for which the LDC's could increase their exports substantially as a consequence of trade liberalization (sugar, and to a lesser extent, copper, lead, zinc, and fats and oils). Table 29 shows the change in imports as a per cent of consumption for the United States, EEC, and Japan from 1948–52 to 1958–61.

The United Nations secretariat and the Secretary General of UNCTAD have proposed a general Northern liberalization program, based on global commodity import targets to be set by each Atlantic Community nation. This recommendation is based on the assumption that market expansion for LDC commodity exports is unlikely to arise either from a commodity-by-commodity approach or from uniform cuts in Northern trade barriers.[10]

The UNCTAD approach to commodity trade liberalization seems unrealistic. The Atlantic Community has no serious intention of helping LDC farmers and miners at the expense of its own. The North is perfectly willing to endorse LDC demands for access with words by resolution after resolution in GATT, UNCTAD, and the other UN economic forums, but it is not disposed to move on any significant

[10] UNCTAD, *Proceedings,* Vol. III, p. 5.

scale from words to actions that hurt domestic producers. This is why the UNCTAD rejects a commodity-by-commodity approach. The realities become far too clear for comfort. The global target system beclouds the issues enough so that some appearance of progress could be achieved. Clearly, most Northern countries could set global commodity import targets only if the targets were modest enough to be met by the normal growth of trade as Northern incomes rise—in other words, only if the targets were meaningless. The North can en-

TABLE 29. Imports as Per Cent of Consumption of Commodities, United States, EEC, Japan (1948/1952 compared with 1958/1961)

	United States		*EEC*		*Japan*	
Commodity	*1948/ 1952*	*1958/ 1961*	*1948/ 1952*	*1958/ 1961*	*1948/ 1952*	*1958/ 1961*
Sugar	45	50	23	6	96	89
Coconut oil	14	28	15	8	2	0
Ground nut oil	−6	−1	−8	0	38	30
Crude petroleum	7	13	94	91	88	98
Refined petroleum	2	8	−13	−12	4	21
Cotton seed	0	0	81	56	93	100
Rubber	66	29	100	84	100	92
Refined copper	9	−15	26	45	−24	16
Lead	41	27	−2	20	7	2
Zinc	7	11	−19	−1	2	6

Source: UNCTAD, *Proceedings,* Vol. III, pp. 57–58.

courage a faster rate of imports of competing goods only by making genuine concessions in tariffs and quotas. As has been repeatedly demonstrated, the current trend in commodity policy is, if anything, in the opposite direction. Thus the global target policy has at least the negative virtue of preventing declines in Northern commodity imports.

The only significant exceptions for individual commodities are: (1) when Northern producers also own the Southern production facilities (for example, petroleum, copper, lead, zinc, and aluminum); (2) when Northern demand is growing faster than its own supply (meat, oilcake, fishmeal, citrus fruits); or (3) when the products are non-competing. In all of these cases the welfare of domestic producers is not visibly affected; at most, their rate of income growth is affected, although this too may prevent liberalization (for example, U.S. meat producers' objection to competing imports and Italian fruit growers' insistence on high duties against bananas and other competing fruits).

In the free trade literature, this reluctance is often discussed as if it were akin to villainy. The rich countries are so rich, the poor so poor; both would benefit from freer trade. Only a narrow-minded protectionism, it is implied, interferes with the fruitful pursuit of mutual benefit. Thus, in praising the unanimity of views among the LDC delegations at UNCTAD, the Colombian delegate said, "the agreements reached owe their origin not to cold realism or selfish calculation, but to a sense of justice and an ideal of social democracy transcending frontiers and revitalizing the whole field of international economic policy." [11]

Without denying the value to LDC's of a united front on issues of international economic policy, it may be doubted whether there is much distinction between "social justice" and "selfish calculation" in the event; they both amount to a demand for concessions by Northern producers to Southern ones. Whatever the claims of disinterested motives made by North and South, the fact remains that UNCTAD has yet to move from words to deeds in the sphere where producers' material interests clash.

Industrial countries want to protect their farmers' incomes by a combination of price supports and import restriction. Farmers are generally the lowest-paid group in the North. The income and price elasticities of demand for their products are low; therefore, in a free market, their incomes are likely to rise more slowly than the national average, even in the absence of foreign competition. Considerations of social justice and political interest on the domestic scene thus tend to outweigh the universal conception of justice quoted above. It is sometimes asserted by free traders that the remedy lies with urbanization, which reduces farmers' political power. However, this effect is partly offset by the fact that agricultural protectionism tends to gain strength as the economic position of the industry is threatened. This, after all, was a major consideration underlying the protectionist agricultural policy of the EEC, which not only discriminates in favor of some LDC's tropical products at the expense of others, but also

[11] UNCTAD, *Proceedings,* Vol. II, p. 483.

against all foreign producers of temperate agricultural products, North and South.

In all likelihood, barring successful Southern pressure at UNCTAD and in other forums, expansion of LDC exports of competing products to the Atlantic Community will come largely from the growth of Northern income and demand, and not from dramatic moves toward free trade in commodities.

ATLANTIC COUNTRIES' POLICIES: PRICE-FIXING

Background

The vision of free trade in these products is largely chimerical so long as conflicts of producer interest persists. But what about the prospects for higher earnings through greater regulation? Northern agriculture now operates with substantial controls over output, prices, marketing conditions, and imports, usually designed to put a floor under farm prices and incomes. Prices of minerals are often regulated *de facto* by tariffs, private agreements among producers, quantitative restrictions on imports, and, on occasion, government output controls (state petroleum production quotas in the United States are the chief example).

These control systems are explicitly designed to change the distribution of national income in favor of commodity producers. They usually operate by raising prices, through output and marketing controls, sometimes combined with government purchases for stockpile or export dumping. If domestic supplies are less than domestic consumption, as with grains and poultry in the EEC, then output controls may not be needed and producers can be guaranteed some price objective by government regulation of imports or by government-established prices for producers.

The defects of such systems are well known: they stimulate surplus production, lower consumer welfare, require complex apparatus for control (and normally create serious problems of control over supply), encourage production by inefficient producers, and tend to institutionalize historical production patterns without appropriate regard for changes in cost and demand conditions. Generally, price and output controls are an inefficient way to redistribute income, compared with direct subsidies, because for a given outlay they lead to less efficient production and a lesser satisfaction of consumer preferences than subsidies do.

Nonetheless, governments continue to base their aid to domestic and foreign commodity producers primarily on price-fixing systems for two reasons. First, such systems preserve for the producer the valued illusion that it is market prices, rather than direct welfare payments, that are maintaining his income. Second, the costs to the government budget of systems based on production and import quotas are less than those of a direct subsidy system if demand for the product is inelastic, for any given level of target prices; although the total cost of subsidies to government and consumers combined is smaller per unit of product consumed. As a corollary to these motives, it is harder for consumers to isolate their out-of-pocket losses under a price support system because there is usually no easy way to measure the aggregate effect of the differences between support prices and the lower equilibrium prices.

The next section of this chapter and Chapter 8, treating compensatory finance, analyze a form of subsidy on the international scene. This section, however, concentrates on price-fixing arrangements, because they are, by analogy to domestic policies, more acceptable to national governments.[12]

The goals of such agreements are, singly or in combination:

1. to raise (or prevent declines in) prices, thereby increasing producers' earnings, or, if benefits are taxed, increasing the foreign exchange revenues of government;

2. to diminish fluctuations in prices and earnings;

3. generally of lesser importance, to guarantee market access for specified quantities, as a method of counteracting protectionism in importing countries.

These agreements have been applied to tea, sugar, coffee, tin, and wheat but are now operative only for the last three products. In addition, private understandings among producers apparently regulate prices and quantities in world petroleum and copper trade, to some degree.

What could price-fixing agreements accomplish if extended to other products and aimed primarily at raising prices? I have previously estimated that such agreements, if applied to five tropical crops—coffee, cocoa, tea, bananas and sugar—could have increased

[12] Boris C. Swerling, "Current Issues in Commodity Policy," *Essays in International Finance*, No. 38, Princeton, Princeton University Press, 1962; Pincus, *Economic Aid*, Chapter 6; UNCTAD, *Proceedings*, Vol. III, pp. 113–167.

LDC revenues by $600 million annually in 1961, and by about $900 million a year by the end of the present decade, compared with the results under free market conditions.[13] I excluded other tropical crops—jute, rubber, palm oil, copra, ground nuts, rice, spices—for a variety of sufficient reasons: competition from substitute products (jute, rubber, vegetable oils); complexity of regulation (vegetable oils, spices); nature of demand (rice).

Furthermore, I excluded competing products (non-ferrous metals, cotton, tobacco, meat, citrus fruits, and so on), on the grounds that importing countries would have no incentive to make disguised income transfers to Northern exporters; and petroleum on the grounds that world prices are already fixed informally, to the benefit of LDC's. The implications of price-fixing arrangements for individual commodities are discussed in more detail below.

Price-fixing Proposals at UNCTAD

General Price-fixing. First, let us explore the implications of more comprehensive regulation of commodity trade, covering most or all of the world's traded primary products. Such a regulation could include both temperate and tropical crops, whether or not competing with natural and synthetic substitutes. This has been proposed at times by various writers, and has in effect been espoused as an objective of French government policy.[14]

[13] "What Policy for Commodities?", *Foreign Affairs,* January 1964. Harry Johnson has pointed out (*Journal of Political Economy,* February 1966) that each of my estimates was in effect an average of two different price elasticity figures. If each elasticity figure is used separately as a basis for estimating gains, the 1961 range is $441–$896 million, and the 1971 range is $592–$1256 million, depending whether higher or lower demand elasticities are used.

In the earlier work, I also advanced the proposition that such regulation would be ineffective for products having elastic demand. Johnson states that this formulation, by concentrating on foreign exchange requirements, overlooks a relevant point. Output restriction frees resources for potential production in other sectors. Therefore, even if demand for the product is elastic, restriction may be warranted up to a certain point *if* there is a profitable alternative use for the labor and capital made available by production control. This apparently reasonable approach ignores the uncertainties concerning the actual alternative uses to which these factors might be put. For a number of tropical crop producers, the short-run value of alternatives may be close to zero. Given the present state of our knowledge of opportunity costs in the South, it is both safer and more realistic to stick to foreign exchange guideposts as a proximate measure of the gains from restriction.

[14] M. J. 't Hooft-Welvaars, "The Organization of International Markets for Primary Commodities," UNCTAD, *Proceedings,* Vol. III, pp. 458–521.

The French government proposal submitted to UNCTAD calls for world-wide organization of primary commodity markets.[15] It is based on the proposition that trade is a better way to transfer income than aid: "In general, world trade should take place in such a manner that the transfers of income which it produces are from the richer countries to the poorer countries."

The French scheme for commodities has two principal elements:

1. Industrial countries should set high prices for temperate-zone products that they import (grains, meat, and so on). Exporting countries should use the additional earnings, in excess of world market prices, that they thus receive to finance concessional exports to LDC's of their surplus production.

2. Instead of concentrating on trade liberalization for LDC products, the North should follow a policy of paying higher prices for Southern commodities financed by domestic import levies on the products. Arguing by analogy from domestic commodity policies that transfer income to primary producers, the French memorandum argues for a similar policy by the North in favor of the South. "The fundamental principle of such an organization would be to replace the present process resulting from the free play of supply and demand by systems of internationally agreed prices fixed at levels which will be reasonably remunerative for the producing countries."

The first proposal essentially calls for those Northern countries that import competing crops to subsidize the Food for Peace programs of the Atlantic Community countries that export them; and for a system of levies that would also subsidize the LDC's that export these products. The memorandum suggests that such a system could be operated through a device like that used by EEC with respect to grain imports. It essentially sets a domestic price target for grain production, and imports at that price by charging an equalizing import levy on foreign grain. If all countries traded at EEC domestic prices (or some other set of agreed support prices), then no import levy would be needed, and surplus products could be sold at concessional prices or given away in LDC markets.

The principal importers of temperate zone crops are shown in Table 30. Under the French plan, they would share the costs of surplus exports to an extent measured by the difference between support

[15] "Memorandum Concerning Certain Items on the Agenda of the United Nations Conference on Trade and Development," submitted to UNCTAD by the French Government, reprinted UNCTAD, *Proceedings*, Vol. VI, pp. 18–27.

TABLE 30. Principal Importers of Competing Commodities, 1963 ($ millions)

Commodity	*United Kingdom*	*West Germany*	*United States*	*Japan*	*Italy*	*France*
Meat and meat animals	905.6	333.6	608.7	36.9	406.9	177.8
Dairy products and eggs	523.2	240.3	40.4	19.1	129.1	36.1
Fruits and vegetables	297.6	867.6	342.6	93.1	79.8	492.6
Cereals	605.4	387.5	42.8	472.0	311.3	118.1
Fats and oils	260.8	338.6	139.0	308.6	240.2	260.3
Tobacco	279.0	166.1	102.5	36.6	45.7	50.6
Hides and skins	164.7	147.1	179.7	60.8	91.6	126.6
Wood and pulp	800.0	469.7	731.0	482.3	388.2	274.7
Feedstuffs	174.8	179.5	57.1	58.0	54.4	91.8
Textile fibers	715.0	444.6	380.6	879.6	462.3	496.1
Total	4,726.1	3,574.6	2,624.4	2,497.0	2,209.5	2,124.7

Source: Food and Agriculture Organization, *Trade Yearbook, 1964.*

price and equilibrium price times quantity sold, each multiplied by quantity consumed. Consumers in importing countries would also lose through reduced consumption resulting from higher prices. The effect of such a system for competing crops can be calculated from the example of grains, for which EEC target prices have been established. See Table 31.

We assume for this purpose either a short-run situation in which the importing country's supply does not have time to respond to price changes, or a commitment by importers to maintain the 1963 level of imports. If price elasticity of demand were —0.3, and 1963 imports were made at the target prices, the North's import costs would have increased as follows:

Crop	*1963 Actual Import Value (\$ billion)*	*Value at Target Prices (\$ billion)*
Wheat	1.061	1.341
Barley	0.235	0.291
Corn	1.006	1.280
Rye	0.048	0.061
Total	2.350	2.973

The total increase in import values would have been $623 million, or 26.5 per cent, at the assumed elasticity. This would have financed, under the French proposal, free provision to the South of about ten million metric tons equivalent of grains valued at 1963 world export prices, or slightly less than half the value of actual LDC imports of these grains in 1963.

In practice of course, there is no expectation now of introducing the French proposals for temperate and competing products. There is no good reason for EEC to object if the rest of the world chooses to trade at its target prices. The Common Market would lose customs revenue that would otherwise be exacted by the variable levy system. This element is of decreasing importance because one objective of ECC agricultural policy is to increase the ratio of domestic production to imports. Other importers, with lower domestic food prices, have a considerable stake in keeping prices of food imports down. Thus, for example, the major importers, Great Britain and Japan, would have paid nearly $500 million more for their imports of cereals in 1963—which would have significantly affected both their balance of payments and their consumer price levels. Furthermore, most of the income transfer would in effect go to finance disposal of U.S. and Canadian surpluses—a form of involuntary burden sharing. If the importing countries want to increase their foreign aid, they can do so directly with greater political advantages at home and abroad.[16]

The second strand of the French proposal is aimed more directly at tropical crops. In effect, the North would impose a system of import or consumption taxes for tropical crops, whose proceeds would be turned over to exporters. This is almost equivalent to the proposals

TABLE 31. Industrial Countries' [a] Grain Imports and EEC Target Prices

Commodity	*EEC Target Price ($/metric ton)*	*Industrial Countries' Import Price, 1963 ($/metric ton)*	*Industrial Countries' Import Quantity, 1963 (million metric tons)*
	(1)	(2)	(3)
Wheat	107.25	72.94	14.55
Barley	91.64	64.76	3.63
Corn	90.98	60.93	16.51
Rye	94.04	64.29	0.75

Source: Col. 1: EEC Commission, Division of Agricultural Information, *Newsletter on the Common Agricultural Policy*, No. 27, Brussels, January 1965 (mimeographed); Cols. 2–3: computed from Food and Agriculture Organization, *Trade Yearbook, 1964*.

Note: [a] Includes Western Europe and Japan only.

that I have discussed elsewhere, with one significant difference. Because the French scheme provides for price-fixing through levies imposed by importing countries instead of by export quota arrangements, world prices of the products are not affected much. They might be somewhat reduced, if Northern consumption declines as a consequence of higher consumer prices. Thus LDC's can import at low prices, the North pays the full income transfer, and Southern earnings are further increased by the existence of a two-price market.

[16] On the other hand, Northern grain exporters might see a distinct advantage in combining to fix the prices of their exports to the EEC at levels no lower than EEC internal prices.

However, as pointed out above, there are only a few tropical products that can effectively be adapted to such a system. It is unlikely, all factors considered, that price-fixing for tropical crops, whether operated by export quotas, export taxes, or refundable import levies, could result in a transfer of more than $1 billion or so annually at current demand levels. Governments of importing countries are unlikely to make the effort of negotiating and legislating commodity agreements for minor crops, or to involve themselves in the complexities of regulation for international trade in products threatened by the competition of close substitutes. Furthermore, unless the products are important in the political-economic affairs of a number of countries, it is difficult to gain widespread support for regulation.

The major tropical products that could be considered for regulation, given these restrictions—in addition to coffee, cocoa, tea, sugar, and possibly bananas—are tin (already subject of international controls), oilseeds, and spices. Rubber, jute, and sisal face close competition. Regulation for cotton, tobacco, citrus crops, non-ferrous metals, and all temperate-zone farm products would have to be done through some such system as the French proposal to prevent the big Northern exporters from making windfall gains. They therefore should probably be ruled out on the grounds that importing Northern countries are unlikely to agree to subsidize other rich countries' surplus disposal.

In short, a system of general price increase for LDC commodities is ruled out unless accomplished indirectly through long-term "compensatory finance," as discussed in Chapter 8, aimed at assuring LDC's a certain level of foreign-exchange inflow, regardless of the commodity structure of trade; or through creation of a commodity-reserve currency, in which an international authority purchases a variety of commodities as a real asset for backing currencies.[17]

Fixing Prices of Individual Commodities. Although general price-fixing is probably impracticable, fixing the prices of individual products is in some cases entirely feasible, as I pointed out above. The UNCTAD resolution on international commodity agreements recognizes the need for selective judgments about price-fixing. After stating that "remunerative, equitable and stable prices for primary commodities is the goal," it goes on:

[17] A. G. Hart, N. Kaldor, and J. Tinbergen, *The Case for an International Commodity Reserve Currency*, reprinted UNCTAD, *Proceedings*, Vol. III, pp. 522–541.

International commodity arrangements should be usually on a commodity-by-commodity basis and, as far as each commodity is concerned, should take due account of the interests of exporting and importing countries, of the characteristics of the product concerned and of the trade in, and the market arrangements for, that product.[18]

What can we say about the merits and limitations of the commodity-by-commodity approach to price-fixing? Our best source of information is the record of past commodity negotiations and agreements.

International action on specific products dates back to the regulation schemes for tin (1931) and rubber (1934), and the Sugar Agreement of 1937; and has also been applied with price-fixing or stabilization objectives to tea (1933–39), wheat (since 1949), tin (since 1953), coffee (since 1962), and olive oil (since 1958). The current status of each can be discussed briefly.

The record of these agreements has not been striking, either with respect to price increases or price stability; yet it is less dismal than many commentators have implied. As might be expected, the major obstacle to raising prices is pressure of supply, stimulated by improved price prospects. However, the tea, sugar, and tin agreements, when operative, apparently succeeded in reducing price fluctuations, and to some extent in maintaining prices. The wheat agreement, until the early 1950's, *reduced* prices and price fluctuations, thereby helping consumers more than producers. The effects of the recent coffee agreement are still unknown; results will depend on the size of the quotas, and the extent to which exporters honor them.

Coffee, the most important agricultural product in world trade, has been marketed under the provisions of the International Coffee Agreement since 1963. Administration of the agreement has been complicated by several factors. The major producers, Brazil and Colombia, have fought for tight quota control. Smaller Latin American producers, with little or no facilities for storage or marketing control, have argued for larger quotas as a vent for overproduction. They have been joined by African producers, who have increased their share of the market steadily over the past two decades. Although the announced price objective is to maintain the 1962 price level as a floor (22 cents for African coffees, 34 cents for the standard Brazilian grade, and 48 cents for Colombian coffee), the opera-

[18] *Final Act,* Annex A, Vol. II, p. 1, reprinted UNCTAD, *Proceedings,* Vol. II, p. 27.

tion of the agreements seems to aim in fact at the somewhat higher year-end prices of 1964 (30 cents, 45 cents, and 48 cents, respectively). The 1964 price rise reflected a poor crop in Brazil, not the operations of the agreement. With annual supply currently returning to normal levels, it remains to be seen whether the agreement can survive the inherent conflicts between large and small producers, between those whose production is stable or growing, and between producers of different but competing grades. There is evidence that quota controls are widely circumvented by countries that are unable to hold stocks.

In September 1966, the Coffee Council, representing both importing and exporting members of the Agreement, took four steps to deal with some of the most persistent obstacles to the twin goals of high prices and economic development:

1. Instead of treating all types of coffee identically (thereby fixing the export shares of various submarkets for coffee in terms of the 1962 world consumption pattern), export quotas for each of the four principal types of coffee will be determined separately. This will presumably allow African exporters to continue their rapid expansion of sales for the instant-coffee market.

2. Special temporary quota increases were granted to a number of countries, on condition that they devote 20 per cent of the incremental proceeds to agricultural diversification.

3. An export tax of $1 per bag of coffee was proposed by the Council. The proceeds, estimated at $45 million for the 1967 crop year, would be spent under Council supervision, to promote agricultural diversification.

4. As a new approach to the perennial problem of export quota evasion by small producers, the Council established a system that in effect gives the Council power to verify each country's reported exports.

It is too soon to say whether these devices will in fact promote diversification out of surplus coffee production, and into lines that are socially more remunerative. Whether or not they are successful, the Coffee Council's initiatives represent the first effort to use international commodity policy as a deliberate element of economic development policy, subject to international control. In this respect its potential significance extends far beyond the world coffee market, and, indeed, beyond the confines of commodity policy.

The Tin Agreement provides for a buffer stock to stabilize prices, supplemented by export controls when prices fall sharply. After some initial problems, necessitating buffer stock buying and export restriction in the late 1950's, prices have generally risen since 1959. This trend primarily reflects a favorable supply-demand relationship. The buffer stock has purchased tin only at rare intervals since 1960.

The Sugar Agreement lapsed in 1962, reflecting disagreement over quotas. It is generally believed that the Agreement will be renewed despite the failure of recent negotiations, following a sharp fall in prices from record highs of 1963–64. The control system before 1962 applied only to the free market in sugar (it excludes the special premium price arrangements created by national legislation under which the United States and United Kingdom import sugar), accounting for about one-third of world trade. Export quotas were applied as necessary to maintain prices in the range of 3.25–4.25 cents. The systems worked reasonably well to maintain minimum prices, thanks to Cuba's willingness to maintain its stocks in exchange for a large quota in the profitable U.S. market. After the United States closed its doors to Cuban sugar, the agreement fell apart. But the spur of low prices will presumably lead sooner or later to a similar agreement, despite the obvious political barriers.

The Tea Agreement was operative from 1933 to 1939 and succeeded in stabilizing prices relative to those of other tropical products during the period. In recent years, producing countries have occasionally proposed that a new agreement be established, but there has been relatively little sustained interest in international control on producer or consumer side. The Olive Oil Agreement is not concerned with price control, but primarily with production and marketing policy in the Mediterranean countries.

The other international commodity agreement, the Wheat Agreement, is of primary interest to Northern producers. It has no effective price control mechanism, because importers are no longer required to support the market by agreeing to buy stated quantities at a minimum price. Furthermore, world prices have been too low during recent years to require the exporters to honor their analogous commitment to sell stated quantities at ceiling prices.

Of the products of interest to LDC's and not now subject to agreement, the most likely candidate for control measures is cocoa. Prices reached post-war lows in 1965 after an intermittent decline from 1957–58 levels. Negotiations for an agreement were unsuccessful in 1963, foundering over the question of minimum prices. In 1964 the major exporters agreed to control sales in order to maintain earnings, but their accord soon collapsed amid allegations of unauthorized exports. The principal producers (Ghana, Nigeria, Ivory Coast, Cameroon, Brazil) are seeking some agreement on the part of the North to put a floor under prices, in the manner of the coffee and sugar agreements. It has also been suggested that the cocoa problem be approached through price compensation, under which importing countries would pay exporting governments a sum representing the difference between market prices and an agreed target price multiplied by an agreed export quantity. This would allow the market to clear without the necessity for export restriction or expensive storage, which may be difficult for the new African nations to administer. Currently the principal barrier to agreement is the producers' demand for creation of a Northern-financed buffer stock of cocoa. This barrier may be more apparent than real. Negotiations for a cocoa agreement have been proceeding for a decade, and invariably fail because of disagreement between exporters and importers over price policy.

Among the other products listed above, there seems to be no effective force at work now for international price-fixing. Whether or not new demands emerge depends in part on the future of the compensatory financing proposals discussed in Chapter 8. Certainly, some form of control is feasible for a number of products, although the complications are often severe. An example is the case of vegetable oils, some of which are produced in almost every country and which are also partial substitutes for each other. It is certain that we have not heard the last of both general and specific price-fixing proposals, particularly if the North continues to adopt similar systems of management for its domestic agriculture.

So viewed, by the test of feasibility rather than efficiency or convenience, price-fixing within its limited sphere may offer LDC's a supplement to other forms of aid. Economists are offended by such devious methods in pursuit of simple goals. If the rich want to help the poor, it is no great task to give alms, but we persist in complex and often self-defeating stratagems to avoid the imputation of charity. This seems strange to our sense of order; yet most people, in fact if not in theory, prefer to receive charity in disguise. Nations that protect their manufactures with a tariff, their farmers with price supports, their workers with immigration quotas, and their old people with "social insurance" schemes need feel neither wonder nor consternation at the sight of foreigners who also prefer to receive their charity under the pillow.

It has been suggested that concerted Northern action in this field would tend to equalize aid and adjustment burdens, and thus promote agreement. This is a doubtful proposition, however, because some countries (for example, Great Britain, Germany, Japan) import relatively large amounts of commodities, whereas others import relatively little or are net exporters (the United States, Australia, New Zealand, Denmark). Of course, with respect to liberalization, both exporters and importers gain, and the major problem is readjustment of domestic production. But where the goal is higher prices and earnings for exporters, there is a real transfer of income internationally, and the burden will not be equally distributed among the various importers in proportion to their national incomes. As a simple illustration, LDC's exported $11.8 billion worth of foods and raw materials to the North in 1962; but less than one-third of the total went to the United States and Canada, which account for half of Northern income valued at official exchange rates (or at a bit more than 40 per cent if differences in purchasing power are taken into account).

Thus any general increase in the prices of Southern commodities would put a disproportionate burden on Europe—one that would be even heavier, if the French proposals were adopted. Strangely enough in view of this arithmetic, the United States, which provides more than half of the North's foreign aid, has on occasion appeared as a leading opponent of international price-fixing schemes.

It is possible to estimate roughly the effects of price-fixing agreements on each Northern country, both now and over the next decade, on the basis of projected effects of changes in population, prices and incomes. To do this with at least some pretension to realism, I have assumed a range of price elasticities to provide reasonable upper and lower limits for the estimates, and have limited the analysis to four products: coffee, tea, cocoa, and sugar. Table 32 shows what the effects of such a price-fixing scheme would have been on Atlantic countries' imports in 1963, on the assumption that prices would be set to maximize profits. Table 33 projects the effects forward to 1970 and 1975 under the same assumption and in light of probable changes in consumption by product.

As a system of taxation, such agreements have an uneven incidence. As shown in the "high elasticity" columns of Table 32, they would have very little effect on countries that are already paying premium prices for commodities. French coffee imports and U.S. sugar imports are cases in point. Gross import costs are also unaffected where demand for imports is believed to be relatively elastic, as for Japanese tea imports or French imports of sugar. For the four products considered here, elastic demand usually reflects either a high ratio of domestic production to domestic consumption, or else a rather small domestic per capita demand, relative to other Northern countries.

Table 32 also shows in the "low elasticity" column the effects of commodity agreements when each importer's demand elasticity is assumed to be the same for a given product. The profit-maximizing levels were in almost all cases set to increase revenue by 23 per cent for coffee, cocoa, and sugar, and by 30 per cent for tea. Under this uniform elasticity assumption, Atlantic countries' imports of commodities would have cost \$4.7 billion in 1962, an increase of \$900 million over actual 1962 costs. The United States would have paid 44 per cent of the increase. The comparable U.S. share of Northern economic aid in 1962 was 64 per cent (see Table 37). Thus such schemes offer burden-sharing advantages for the United States. The United Kingdom, on the other hand, would have paid 18½ per cent of the incremental costs of price-fixing for these commodities in 1962, whereas its share of combined Northern aid in that year was only 4.4 per cent.

When we take account of the fact that demand elasticities actually vary among countries ("high elasticity" column of Table 32), then the burden-sharing distribution is more unbalanced. The U.S. share declines to 39 per cent and the U.K. contribution rises to 21 per cent of the North's incremental costs.

For projections to 1970 and 1975, the shares shift in diverse ways, reflecting differences in growth of income and population. U.S., German, Japanese, U.K., and French shares, illustratively from Table 33, would be as follows:

	Per Cent of North's Incremental Cost			
	1970		*1975*	
	High Elasticity	*Low Elasticity*	*High Elasticity*	*Low Elasticity*
United States	35	40	25	36
United Kingdom	11	12	9	10
France	7	8	8	9
Japan	9	6	10	8
Germany	8	10	9	11

Computed as per cent changes of increment over actual 1962 costs (Col. 1 of Table 32).

TABLE 32. Industrial Countries' Import Costs for Selected Commodities, 1962, Compared with Costs Under Profit-Maximizing Commodity Agreements.

Country and Commodity	Actual Import Cost 1962 ($ millions)	Estimated Cost Under Commodity Agreement (High Elasticity) ($ millions)	(Low Elasticity) ($ millions)	Per Cent Increase Over 1962 (High Elasticity)	(Low Elasticity)
United States					
Coffee	997	1,136	1,226	14	23
Tea	60	64	79	6	30
Cocoa	131	144	161	9	23
Sugar	509	513	623	1	23
Total	1,697	1,857	2,089		
France					
Coffee	144	153	177	6	23
Tea	3.1	3.3	4.1	4	30
Cocoa	32	35	40	8	23
Sugar	72	78	88	8	23
Total	251	269	309		
Germany					
Coffee	209	215	257	3	23
Tea	12.6	12.7	16	1	30
Cocoa	69	72	84	5	23
Sugar	12	15	15	23	23
Total	303	315	372		
Italy					
Coffee	67	78	82	17	23
Tea	2.6	2.6	3.4	0	30
Cocoa	19	20	23	4	23
Sugar	2.0	2.4	2.4	23	23
Total	91	103	111		

Japan					
Coffee	10	11.6	12.3	16	23
Tea	2.5	2.5	3.2	0	30
Cocoa	11.6	12.2	14.2	6	23
Sugar	113	137	138	22	23
Total	137	164	167		
Canada					
Coffee	44	49	54	11	23
Tea	21	22	27	4	30
Cocoa	7.5	8.2	9.2	9	23
Sugar	55	67	69	23	27
Total	128	146	159		
United Kingdom					
Coffee	39	45	48	15	23
Tea	323	356	421	10	30
Cocoa	47	58	66	7	23
Sugar	159	195	200	23	26
Total	568	654	735		
All Industrial Countries					
Coffee	1,815	2,033	2,232	12	23
Tea	516	558	672	8	30
Cocoa	434	464	531	7	23
Sugar	1,032	1,146	1,264	11	23
Total	3,797	4,201	4,699		

Source: 1962 data from Food and Agriculture Organization, *Trade Yearbook, 1963*, Rome, 1964.

Note: Low elasticities: coffee, cocoa, and sugar, −0.4; tea, −0.35

High elasticities: varies by country. Range for coffee, −0.56 to −0.79; cocoa, −0.54 to −1.04; sugar, −.32 to −.85; tea, −.52 to −2.88. Computations for tea exclude Norway and Sweden.

TABLE 33. Industrial Countries' Estimated Import Costs, for Selected Commodities, under Profit-Maximizing Commodity Agreements, 1970 and 1975

Country and Commodity	1970				1975			
	Import Cost		Per Cent Increase Over Actual 1962 Cost		Import Cost		Per Cent Increase Over Actual 1962 Cost	
	High Elasticity ($ millions)	Low Elasticity ($ millions)	High Elasticity	Low Elasticity	High Elasticity ($ millions)	Low Elasticity ($ millions)	High Elasticity	Low Elasticity
United States								
Coffee	1,351	1,513	36	48	1,525	1,667	53	67
Tea	77	95	28	58	87	109	45	80
Cocoa	193	220	47	68	236	271	79	107
Sugar	589	716	16	40	648	788	27	55
Total	2,210	2,544			2,496	2,835		
France								
Coffee	213	256	48	77	259	315	79	119
Tea	4	5	18	56	4	6	29	76
Cocoa	49	58	52	79	61	73	90	126
Sugar	90	111	25	54	100	138	39	80
Total	356	430			424	532		
Germany								
Coffee	303	379	45	82	375	496	85	138
Tea	14	18	14	44	14	19	15	54
Cocoa	89	107	30	56	103	126	50	83
Sugar	18	18	49	49	20	20	70	70
Total	424	522			512	661		
Italy								
Coffee	131	138	97	107	170	180	155	170
Tea	3	4	13	54	3	5	25	73
Cocoa	31	40	64	108	41	53	116	180
Sugar	4	4	79	79	5	5	127	127
Total	169	186			219	243		

Japan								
Coffee	17	18	156	168	33	38	240	271
Tea	3	4	22	64	4	5	39	92
Cocoa	18	22	53	86	23	30	96	141
Sugar	232	235	105	108	315	319	179	183
Total	270	279			375	392		
Canada								
Coffee	75	86	70	92	98	111	118	150
Tea	26	34	26	60	30	38	43	84
Cocoa	11	13	50	73	14	16	85	115
Sugar	77	80	42	46	85	88	55	60
Total	189	213			227	253		
United Kingdom								
Coffee	66	71	48	80	80	87	105	122
Tea	350	459	8	42	366	485	13	50
Cocoa	70	81	28	49	78	91	43	67
Sugar	203	209	28	32	209	215	32	35
Total	689	820			733	878		
All Industrial Countries								
Coffee	2,614	2,914	45	61	3,087	3,475	71	90
Tea	591	763	15	48	638	831	24	61
Cocoa	616	726	42	67	743	888	71	105
Sugar	1,385	1,532	34	49	1,581	1,752	53	70
Total	5,206	5,935			6,049	6,946		

Source: Author's computations based on 1962 data from Food and Agriculture Organization, *Trade Yearbook, 1963.* Elasticities, author's estimates, see Table 32. Income and population growth coefficients from Bela Balassa, *Trade Prospects for Developing Countries.*

These estimates are illustrative and might vary considerably if the actual elasticities diverged from the estimated values shown in Table 32. In any event, it seems likely that the commodity agreements would prove to be a highly arbitrary form of taxation. From the viewpoint of the two major donors, the United States and France, it offers the important advantage of redressing the relative shares of Northern aid costs. In general, countries that by equity standards are paying less than their fair share of Northern foreign aid would be paying heavier shares of the incremental costs of commodity agreements.

ATLANTIC COUNTRIES' POLICIES: STABILIZATION

Most of the discussion of commodity policy is couched in terms of either market access or stabilization. If the North were seriously interested in unrestricted market access there would be significant benefits for the South, particularly for producers of sugar and petroleum and, to a moderate extent, for producers of oilseeds and other tropical products.

But reducing fluctuations in commodity export receipts seems to offer much less important benefits, despite the attention it has received. The literature usually emphasizes the harmful effect of falling prices in terms of lower incomes, uncertain expectations for producers, and adverse balance-of-payments effects. All these results can and do occur, and are painful. But the fundamental, if unstated, objection is not to fluctuations. If it were, governments could offset the effect of demand changes by taxing receipts where prices were high and paying out the proceeds when prices fell. The demand for "stabilization" is in effect a demand for higher prices, or at least no reduction in existing prices.[19] At this point it is important to be clear, because much of the discussion of commodity policy is confused on these issues.

If someone has the choice between receiving a certain sum of money over the next decade or so, either in equal annual payments or in uncertain annual sums amounting to the same total by the end of

[19] Of course, it may also benefit the seller by reducing buyers' incentive to shift to synthetic substitutes as a hedge against uncertainty. But the Southern argument doesn't stress this point.

the period, he might prefer equal annual sums, assuming that all receipts go for consumption, and not for investment or interest-bearing savings. But he would be unlikely to if he had to pay a high premium for the assurance. Some individuals ("risk-avoiders") would be willing to pay substantial amounts for insurance of stable earnings because of fear that no one would lend to them or because of lack of confidence in their own capacity to save against periods of low income. But governments, unless very weak, need have few such fears.[20] Therefore, they are not usually interested in paying for stabilization. Furthermore, because the future is unknown, there may be some tendency to believe that there will be fewer price declines in the future than in the past. Evidence of several empirical studies [21] is that: (1) LDC's are no more subject to fluctuations in export earning than other countries; (2) fluctuations do not seem to affect growth rates; (3) neither importing nor exporting governments have shown any willingness to insure against risk of price fluctuations.[22]

Second, the fact that individuals and governments are unwilling, perhaps for good reasons, to insure against fluctuations (and also unable to distinguish between prospective trends and prospective fluctuations) is not the end of the story. It still remains likely that if people knew more about the future they could plan better and use resources to better advantage. Although differences in fluctuations have not been associated with differences in growth rates, this is not conclusive evidence. The standard example is tree crops. High prices bring on a wave of plantings, followed several years later by sharp increases in supply and low prices. Long-term price assurances combined with buffer stocks would probably help prevent the cycle of shortage and overproduction, thereby benefiting both buyers and sellers of commodities.

For this reason, greater price stability, as distinguished from higher prices, is probably worth some effort to achieve.[23] The Inter-

[20] Of course, they may seek to avoid fluctuations in order to offset the temptation to spend to the hilt in good years, and then suffer in years of low export earnings. But this form of stabilization, even on the international scale, requires no injection of Northern funds.

[21] Alasdair MacBean, *Export Instability, Growth and Policy,* Cambridge, Massachusetts, Harvard University Press (forthcoming); J. D. Coppock, *International Economic Instability,* New York, McGraw-Hill, 1962; M. Michaely, *Concentration in International Trade,* Amsterdam, North Holland, 1962.

[22] UNCTAD, *Proceedings,* Vol. III, p. 142.

[23] The same objective of facilitating rational planning has been used as a basis for proposing so-called "forward pricing" for agriculture in the United States. The argu-

national Wheat Agreement, providing the guaranteed floor and ceiling sales prices and quantities, was aimed at this goal. The Sugar Agreement had a similar intent (combined with price maintenance goals) through its quota export provisions and national arrangements for holding stocks. International buffer stocks, such as the Tin Agreement, are another device; again, their operations do not in practice distinguish clearly between stability and price maintenance.

If, on the other hand, the ultimate objective of stabilization is to assure a stable or steadily increasing flow of foreign exchange receipts (something that price stability is not sufficient to accomplish in the face of demand and supply shifts), then there is no particular need to tie stabilization efforts to commodity marketing or storage controls. It is much simpler to allow commodity markets to operate freely, and compensate through direct inter-governmental payments. This can be done either on a price compensation basis, as suggested by the United Nations secretariat in various studies and more recently by Meade;[24] or else by general balance of payments compensation, in which countries whose foreign exchange earnings fall below some trend line receive loans from a central fund, to be repaid when earnings go above the trend, or within a fixed period of years.[25]

The Meade-United Nations proposal provides for bilateral or multilateral guarantees in which the exporting countries are guaranteed a fixed minimum export revenue by importers, no matter what the price of the product, so long as the exporter sells at least an agreed amount in the world market. The exporter guarantees not to charge more than an agreed maximum price for the same agreed amount, even if world prices surpass that level. All transactions take place at world prices. Compensation takes place in a separate transaction whenever prices are outside the agreed range. This system offers better protection for shifts in demand than for supply shifts. When supply decreases, world price rises and exporters pay compensation; but if an individual exporter's supply is sharply reduced, he is

---

ment is that if prices are known before investment decisions are made, resources will be used more efficiently. In a sense, of course, U.S. support prices play the same role; the objection is that in contrast to forward prices, they do not serve to promote efficiency, because they are primarily used to transfer income.

[24] Meade's proposal is reprinted in UNCTAD, *Proceedings,* Vol. III, pp. 451–457. The UN report is published in the Secretariat document, "Development Insurance Fund for Single Commodities" (E/CN.13/95), 1962.

[25] Cf. Organization of American States, *Final Report of Experts in the Stabilization of Export Receipts,* Washington, D.C., November 1961; United Nations, *International Compensations for Fluctuations in Commodity Trade,* New York, October 1961.

forced to pay compensation at a time when his earnings are low. When supply increases, so does compensation, because trade volume goes up and market price falls. The result for the exporter is higher than normal earnings.

In short, the system overcompensates for supply increases, if complete compensation is paid, and undercompensates for poor crops in individual exporting countries (those whose output changes have little effect on world price). If aggregate demand is elastic, the system would be completely destabilizing for supply shifts. Nonetheless, it has certain obvious advantages over the export restriction schemes discussed in the previous section of this chapter, and need not be regarded as a perfect substitute for them.[26]

The second type of compensation scheme, general balance of payments compensation, has two aspects: stabilizing fluctuations in export receipts; and, reserved for discussion in Chapter 8, transferring funds from rich to poor countries. The two functions are not always clearly distinguishable in the various compensatory finance schemes that have been advanced. However, three of the schemes are aimed primarily at stabilization. Since March 1963, the IMF has followed a policy of lending up to 25 per cent of its IMF quota to exporters of primary products when export proceeds fall below a recent average, if the IMF is satisfied that the decline is short-term in nature and beyond the exporter's control. This credit extension, an addition to members' existing borrowing authority, could amount to a maximum of $800 million for all LDC's combined, although in practice loans outstanding under this authority at any one time would be far less than this figure. The IMF has recently proposed that its compensatory lending authority be approximately doubled.

The OAS scheme, never adopted, was rather similar to the IMF facility. It provided for a revolving fund, financed largely by the North, which would make short-term loans as partial compensation to countries whose export proceeds fell below a recent moving average.

The United Nations experts' report, *International Compensation for Fluctuations in Commodity Trade,* combined stabilization with income transfer. All countries would contribute annually to a fund, with contributions determined by level of national income or exports. Countries whose export earnings fell more than 5 per cent below the average of the last three years would receive partial compensation,

[26] Meade, *Proceedings,* Vol. III, p. 455.

which would either not be repaid at all, or, in an alternative version, be repaid if the borrower's export proceeds thereafter rose back above the level of the three base years. Under the grant scheme, there would have been (in 1953–59) an average annual transfer from rich to poor countries of $482 million if full compensation were paid.

The stabilizing role of these schemes has been criticized on various grounds. The chief objection of the South at UNCTAD was the inadequate amount of the IMF facility (although one underlying if unstated objection was probably that the system did not provide for income transfer).

An IMF staff report has demonstrated that automatic schemes requiring short-term repayment are inadequate as a method of stabilizing export earnings.[27] The authors tested statistically a number of levels of compensation, repayment schemes, and definitions of shortfall to see what their effects would have been on foreign exchange availabilities, compared with a stable norm. They found that automatic compensation schemes of the OAS-IMF type made rather little progress toward the norm, and some were even destabilizing, because loan repayment is mandatory. It is therefore small wonder that this sort of "stabilization" is more of a discussion point than a goal of policy.

Another proposed form of stabilization, different from those discussed above, is inherent in the proposals for creating an international commodity reserve standard. It combines three elements—stabilization, increases in world monetary liquidity, and potentially at least, raising the relative prices of commodities. The idea of commodity backing for currency is venerable.[28] In its most recent form, advanced at UNCTAD,[29] the proposal is specifically linked to increasing the flow of resources to the South.

The plan calls for the IMF to establish a currency ("bancor") backed partly by gold and partly by a "commodity bundle," fixed

[27] M. Fleming, R. Rhomberg, and L. Boissonault, "Export Norms and Their Role in Compensatory Financing," *IMF Staff Papers* (March 1963), pp. 97–149.

[28] W. S. Jevons, *Money and the Mechanism of Exchange,* London, 1875. During the depression of the 1930's, such proposals abounded. See Benjamin Graham, *Storage and Stability,* New York, McGraw-Hill, 1937. These schemes are reviewed critically by Milton Friedman, "Commodity Reserve Currency," *Journal of Political Economy,* Vol. LIX (June 1951), pp. 203–232. For a general survey of the various monetary reform schemes, see Fritz Machlup, "Plans for the Reform of the International Monetary System," *Special Papers in International Economics,* No. 3, Princeton University Press, 1962.

[29] Hart, Kaldor, and Tinbergen, *The Case for an International Commodity Reserve Currency.*

proportions of standardized, easily storable commodities that enter international trade through competitive markets. This in practice means grains, tropical beverage crops, oils, fibers, rubber, and metals. The price of the commodity bundle would be fixed in terms of gold.

Member countries would turn part of their gold holdings into the IMF in exchange for bancor and would agree to leave additional gold on deposit with IMF, as a reserve against calls on gold. The IMF would buy commodities with bancor, using its authority as reserve manager to stabilize commodity prices, buying commodities when prices are low and selling them when prices are high. Once the scheme is fully operative, the price of the bundle becomes fixed in terms of bancor. If any constituent commodity's price thereafter rises excessively, the IMF can exclude it from the bundle, and sell off its stocks.

Members could buy bancor from the IMF for gold or commodities, and sell bancor for commodities or for commodities and gold. The price of the commodity bundle would be fixed in terms of gold, but members' currencies could fluctuate relative to each other and to bancor.

The proposed system would add to world liquidity by augmenting the backing for, and thus the amount of, internationally acceptable means of payment. It would tend to stabilize the money level of commodity prices (although not the prices of individual commodities), and would also raise them above the levels they would otherwise attain, depending on the extent to which the members allowed the IMF to increase the size of the commodity reserve over time.

This system would also increase the South's command over imports. About three-fifths of the value of commodities proposed in the Hart-Kaldor-Tinbergen scheme are exported by LDC's. If we accept the authors' assumptions (initial level of commodity stocks set at \$20.5 billion, of which \$14.7 billion would be supplied by governments from existing stocks and \$5.7 billion would be purchased by the IMF in the open market), then LDC's would initially benefit from \$3.5 billion in open market purchases.

In addition to these effects, the authors state that the scheme would improve LDC terms of trade and economic development by stimulating increased demand for commodities. They claim that it will at once sustain commodity prices, LDC demand for imported manufactures, and, through income effects, Northern demand for LDC products.

The defects of commodity reserve currency systems have been detailed elsewhere.[30] This book is not primarily concerned with currency reform proposals. They are primarily issues of intra-Northern policy, although they affect LDC's in respect to such issues as aid-tying. In brief, the objections are: (1) the system can include only storable commodities; (2) stabilizing their money prices may in effect destabilize other prices as costs of production and demand change over time; (3) even for commodities in the bundle, prices of particular products might be destabilized by the system, since the open market operations are for the bundle as a whole; (4) storage and stock management costs are likely to be high; (5) the economic stabilization effects are not important for the world as a whole, because commodities account for only a small proportion of world output and are characterized by price-inelastic demand and supply responses.[31]

It is possible to design a more efficient system, in terms of both liquidity and developmental goals, simply by proposing an expanded IMF, offering credit on liberal terms. The commodity reserve currency offers only one advantage over an expanded central bank. It tends automatically, but to a limited extent, to stabilize prices of all commodities, by providing stimuli for contraction or expansion as the prices rise or fall, relative to the commodity bundle. But the problem, of course, is not to design ideal systems. It is to arrive at workable improvements over the present one, which is generally admitted to be deficient in terms of liquidity, development, and stability objectives.

The current impetus and attraction of such plans lie in the effort they make to solve two major problems at once: the shortage of international reserves and the economic development of underdeveloped countries. To oppose programs that offer such benefits is akin to voting for restriction and oppression. These two stigma have not deterred the majority of economists, and I add my vote to theirs, essentially on political grounds. It is a particularly cumbersome device for achieving its goals, but this would be irrelevant were it feasible to enact in the absence of other alternatives. However, commodity reserve currency seems even less likely to be adopted than more efficient solutions, because it is too radical a departure from existing monetary practice, without extra compensating benefits for Northern self-

[30] See Friedman, "Commodity Reserve Currency"; and Herbert Grubel, "The Case Against a Commodity Reserve Currency," *Oxford Economic Papers,* Vol. 17 (March 1965), pp. 130–135.

[31] This point is stressed by Johnson, *Economic Policies,* Chapter 7, who uses a simple model of expenditure and monetary behavior to demonstrate the relatively modest stabilizing effect of a commodity reserve.

interest. If and when the superior alternative of an expanded world central bank is rejected, commodity reserve proposals may take on a new luster. Meanwhile, it fails to offer the promise of sufficient mutual benefit, in terms of the North's cost-benefit calculus. To the extent that Northern commodity exporters benefit, the scheme is open to the same objection as the French proposals to UNCTAD concerning temperate-zone crops—why should rich commodity-importing countries subsidize rich commodity-exporting countries?

If the goal is to combine liquidity and developmental aspirations, then some device such as the Stamp Plan [32] sounds more likely to earn acceptance because it is a smaller departure from existing forms. It proposes that the IMF issue credit certificates, to be lent to the International Development Association. IDA would make loans to LDC's with the proceeds, and Northern member countries would agree to accept the certificates in settlement of international obligations up to a fixed amount, unless there were domestic inflationary pressures. In that event they could notify IDA that borrowers should not spend their loan proceeds in the notifying country for the time. This plan would obviously carry the greatest promise of mutual benefit in a time of general excess capacity in Northern industry. In boom times, some Northern countries naturally want more international reserves but are much less interested in a credit-created export market.

Whatever its disadvantages, the Stamp Plan avoids the complex administrative problems and high storage costs created by commodity reserve currency proposals, with no significant loss in terms of liquidity or development goals. The Stamp Plan offers no automatic stabilizing effect, but it seems doubtful, in light of the above discussion of stabilization, that stabilizing effects are worth any substantial price to North or South.

CONCLUSIONS

International action in the sphere of commodity policy has been concerned with three kinds of measures: (1) trade liberalization; (2) transfer of income from commodity importers to exporters; (3) stabilization of commodity prices and export earnings.

[32] Sir Maxwell Stamp, "The Stamp Plan—1962 Version," reprinted in Herbert Grubel, ed., *World Monetary Reform,* Stanford University Press, 1963.

In theory improved market access is the most efficient way to increase LDC export earnings, because it increases the flow of trade and raises the earnings of exporters, with no corresponding income transfer from rich to poor countries. A liberal trade policy benefits both exporting and importing countries by raising the real incomes of both, but it may create adjustment problems for high cost producers or revenue problems for governments who benefit from customs duties and fiscal changes.[33] Because agriculture in the North is a relatively declining industry, which resists such adjustments, there is little likelihood that barriers to imports of competing crops will be reduced. Some progress might be made, with relatively limited effects on trade, for such non-competing products as tea, coffee, cocoa, and tropical hardwoods.[34] Thus, although LDC exports to the North might well increase by anywhere from \$3 to \$5 billion annually as a result of free trade in commodities,[35] the immediate prospects for change are slim in the short run; for the time, agricultural protectionism seems to be on the increase.

If the prospects are modest for increasing world income through freer trade in commodities, they are perhaps slightly greater for transferring income from rich to poor countries by commodity price-fixing. The persistent international interest in "stabilization" of commodity prices is largely an effort to make importers pay more than they would in a free market. Discussion of such agreements is usually confined to non-competing exports (coffee, tea, cocoa, sugar, bananas, spices, tin) and for these products could be used to transfer an average of perhaps \$1 billion annually from North to South over the decade 1965–75. If extended to competing products, as proposed by the French government, price-fixing could result in a far larger transfer. For example, if price-fixing could increase the South's \$17–\$18 billion annual revenue from commodity exports to the North by 20 per cent, the total annual transfer would be of the order of \$3.5 billion initially. However, a generalized price-fixing policy not only invites substitution of synthetics,[36] but also encourages import-

[33] We abstract here from the possibility that some countries' real income could be lowered by adverse movement in terms of trade stemming from tariff removal.

[34] In fact, the North, through the GATT, has suspended its duties on tea and tropical hardwoods. This seems to have been the major result of the GATT action program in its first three years.

[35] The principal beneficiaries would presumably be producers of petroleum, sugar, cotton, tobacco, lead, zinc, and aluminum; although in the long run, the effects would be widespread.

[36] If all commodity prices are appropriately fixed, substitution of one natural product for another would not be a major problem.

substituting domestic production in the North. The common agricultural policy of the EEC is aimed in part at this latter goal. Therefore the long-run effects of price-fixing for competing products may be harmful to LDC's, unless import quantities are also guaranteed. Furthermore, there is no good reason for importers of competing products to accept the principle of such transfers to other rich countries unless it is simply incidental to a policy of reaching domestic self-sufficiency, *à la* EEC.

The commodity approach to capital transfers suffers from many disadvantages in terms of administrative difficulties, economic inefficiency, promotion of substitute production, and encouragement of overproduction. Its advantages are: (1) it disguises the income transfer, thus apparently easing the recipient's conscience and relieving the donor of the burden of aid administration, a seemingly inescapable adjunct of official aid transfers; (2) it seems, within limits, to be more acceptable to importing countries than free trade in commodities, perhaps because the system is analogous to domestic commodity support programs. For these reasons, it seems likely that international discussion of policies for tropical exports will continue to revolve around price-fixing schemes. However, the increasing interest in long-term compensatory finance, arising from the United Nations experts' report and the UNCTAD resolution on the subject, may presage a gradual turning away from a single commodity approach.

The issue of price and earnings stabilization has become thoroughly confused with that of income transfer. Price stability and earnings stability are not the same for the individual exporter even if aggregate demand remains constant. If Colombian coffee output rises or falls 20 per cent, constant world prices destabilize earnings. Stable earnings are sometimes asserted to be the goal, but it is not worth much to either importer or exporter simply to reduce short-term fluctuations around a trend by borrowing now and paying back later. The South wants to have greater price certainty but is not willing to reduce its freedom of action substantially in exchange for those benefits. It seeks much more strenuously to avoid low prices for products in inelastic demand, but that is not a question of stability.

If the objective were price stability, it would be possible to do something toward this goal by better price forecasting, use of buffer stocks, export controls, or price compensation schemes. The case for price stability is stronger than that for earnings stability because the prices of many commodities fluctuate so widely that they offer a poor set of signals for investment planning. They may also lead buyers to seek substitutes with more stable price levels. Providing that the system chosen to stabilize prices is a reasonably good forecaster of the market, it should help promote more rational investment. The extent to which this is desirable—and therefore also the price worth paying for it—depends on relevant opportunity costs. The amount of these costs is not an appropriate subject for aggregative analysis; and the detailed research that could offer some guidelines remains, as yet, largely prospective. The inference from existing work is that price stability isn't worth much as a guide to investment in terms of effects on GNP growth. However, we are still far from a definitive judgment on this subject.

The dominant conclusion that emerges from investigating all these aspects of international commodity trends and policies is that the South as a whole must look primarily to Northern prosperity as a source of export growth, and not to the UNCTAD policies. Should the effects of these policies be substantial, they are unlikely to be adopted; measures that are likely to be adopted are also likely to be unimportant as sources of increased capital or trade. Policies to increase or stabilize commodity earnings cannot proceed much faster than Northern willingness to act on the broader problem of LDC growth. This forecast offers scant encouragement to those who seek to promote Southern prosperity. But the issue here is prediction, not preference; and I find only faint grounds for Southern optimism about the course of international commodity policy in the decade ahead.

CHAPTER EIGHT

The Atlantic Countries and the South's Demand for Capital

INTRODUCTION

The touchy issues in North-South economic relations all revolve around the same point: why should the North make any more concessions, real or fancied, to the South? When concessional capital transfers are involved, the point is particularly stark. No one wants to give his money away unless he is getting some advantage, however defined.

A major objective of Southern strategy is to increase the capital flow without offering significant concessions in return. For example, the Final Act of UNCTAD nominally stressed trade policy, but its resolutions also laid heavy emphasis on a number of ways of increasing the real flow of aid, including favorable loan terms, increasing the nominal flow of aid, compensatory finance, creation of a United Nations capital fund, and of regional development funds for the South. Their tenor can best be grasped by reading the Final Act. Unfortunately, its relevant sections are couched in the usual abhorrent prose of international conferences, containing a blend of reasoned discussion [1] and leaden-footed fantasy.[2]

[1] As in UNCTAD, *Proceedings,* Vol. I (Annex A. IV. 1), pp. 42–43.

[2] *Ibid.,* pp. 44–46. The operational definition of fantasy at UNCTAD is any proposal that was simultaneously rejected by United States, France, and the U.S.S.R. This is completely apart from any assessment of the merits of such proposals, although no impartial observer can deny that passing this test at least requires ingenuity. As a matter of archaeological interest, only five of the eighty-three resolutions qualified: Northern support of Southern terms of trade; maximum aid at once with no strings, on favorable terms; transformation of the UN Special Fund into a large-scale aid agency; a new international fund to finance the capital costs of regional integration; and Northern subsidy of development loans to the South.

Most of the resolutions pay lip service to the self-help principle but maintain an insistent demand for more aid. Thus:

Each economically advanced country should endeavor to supply (aid) . . . to the developing countries approaching as near as possible to 1 per cent of its national income. . . .[3]

Appraisal procedures for assessing requests for loans . . . should be simplified to the greatest possible extent, and the present arrangements, which tend to be dilatory . . . should be improved with a view to simplification and expedition. . . .[4]

In other words, more aid faster. Although, from the South's viewpoint, it is a legitimate tactic to maintain pressure on the North for concessions of all kinds, there is a certain ambiguity in the request for more aid; UNCTAD thus becomes the vehicle for equity demands, couched in the "trade-not-aid" language of self-help.

This is more than a hair-splitting point. It relates essentially to the trade and aid issues discussed in Chapter 2. It is usually possible for a claimant with a legitimate case to appeal up to a point to people's sense of charity, or even to receive alms on the basis of appeals to justice or of nuisance value. But, sooner or later, the donor stops raising the ante. From there on, the only way to increase the transfer is by appeal to donor self-interest. Self-help makes such appeal. It gives the donor some hope that the transfer will one day cease.[5] But if perennially behind the self-help façade the donor perceives, rightly or wrongly, yet another demand for transfers [6] he is likely to turn stubborn. This is what makes all the major UNCTAD issues touchy. It is fair to ask why the North should care whether its trade concessions are in part disguised forms of aid. The sums are so small, and the South's needs so great, that the form of the transfer may seem irrelevant. However, many donors prefer for ideological reasons, rationalized on grounds of efficiency, to conduct trade on an arm's-length basis. Their preferences are an appropriate subject for controversy. They nonetheless remain, until altered, a fact.

[3] *Ibid.*, p. 44.

[4] *Ibid.*, p. 46.

[5] Although it is legitimate to ask why the North need hope for an end to the burden. If aid continues at its present real level of $4.5 billion a year, the burden will gradually approach zero as a per cent of GNP.

[6] Where the demand is for free trade, the perception is wrong. The demand then is simply for the North to allow itself to be made better off economically, at some political cost.

This chapter deals with the direct capital transfer question in various aspects: (1) aid requirements; (2) aid levels; (3) forms of aid, including proposals for new forms of aid; (4) sources of aid. It concludes with a brief discussion of the role of private investment in North-South relations.

AID REQUIREMENTS

There is no general and objective way to determine the appropriate amount of aid that should be transferred from rich to poor countries. There have been in recent years a number of estimates of LDC aid "requirements." [7] The method of estimating is to start with some historical or target rate of GNP growth for LDC's. Then, one (or a combination) of two methods is adopted. In one case, the foreign exchange problem is tacitly assumed away and aid requirements are arrived at by estimating the annual investment needed to attain the target growth rate. This figure is then compared with projected annual domestic savings; if projected savings are smaller than required investment, the difference, the so-called savings gap, is taken to represent the foreign aid requirement. The second method is based on estimated foreign exchange requirements. If import projections exceed export projections, the difference is the foreign exchange gap.

Table 34 shows the different estimates that have been made of foreign-exchange and capital requirements. Generally they follow a certain pattern. Estimates based on the savings gap cluster around $6–7 billion annually for the year 1970.[8] Because of the nature of the models used for projection, estimates based on the savings gap tend to result in aid requirements that decline over time. Estimates based on the foreign exchange gap are generally higher ($12–$20 billion) and increase over time, because they assume that import demand will steadily grow faster than foreign exchange earnings.

It seems hardly necessary to point out that when estimates of

[7] P. N. Rosenstein-Rodan, "International Aid for Underdeveloped Countries," *Review of Economics and Statistics,* No. 43 (May 1961), pp. 107–138; Bela Balassa, *Trade Prospects for Developing Countries;* General Agreement on Tariffs and Trade, *International Trade 1961,* Geneva, 1962; United Nations, *World Economic Survey 1962,* New York, 1963.

[8] Rosenstein-Rodan, "International Aid"; J. Tinbergen, *Shaping the World Economy,* New York, Twentieth Century Fund, 1962; Paul Hoffman, *One Hundred Countries, One and One Quarter Billion People,* Washington, D.C., 1960.

TABLE 34. Estimates of the Trade and Savings Gaps (annual basis)

ESTIMATES BASED ON LDC FOREIGN EXCHANGE REQUIREMENTS

Source	*Period Covered*	*Growth Target (per cent)*	*Import Requirements*	*Export Earnings*	*Trade Gap*	*Service Gap*	*Foreign Exchange Gap*
			(*$ billions*)				
GATT	1956/60–1975	5	28–32	17	11	—	—
UN	1959–1970	5	41	29	12	8	20
FAO	1959–1970	5	42	31	10	8	18
Balassa 1.	1960–1970	4.5	38	33	5	6	11
Balassa 2.	1960–1975	4.7	49	42	7	7	14
Chenery/Strout 1.[a]	1962–1970	5.2	58	45	13		13
Chenery/Strout 2.	1962–1975	5.2	76	57	19		19

ESTIMATES OF SAVINGS GAP

Source	*Period Covered*	*Per Capita Growth Target (per cent)*	*Capital-Output Ratio*	*Capital Requirement (annual) ($ billions)*
Millikan/Rostow	1953	2.0	3.0	6.5
Hoffman	1960–69	2.0	3.0	7.0
Tinbergen	1959	2.0	3.0	7.5
Rosenstein-Rodan	1962–66	1.8	2.8	6.4
	1967–71	2.2	2.8	6.4
	1971–76	2.5	2.8	5.0

Source: Goran Ohlin, *Foreign Aid Policies Reconsidered,* Paris, OECD, 1965, pp. 92, 95.

Note: — Not estimated.

[a] Chenery/Strout summary prepared by author, from their study, "Foreign Assistance and Economic Development," pp. II–21 and Table A-5, basis simple average of 1962–1975 projections. Their method combines both savings and exchange gaps. My figures are an average of their high and low export plan performance for 50 countries, multiplied by a factor of 1.3 to account for excluded countries, for the years 1970 and 1975.

essentially the same problem produce one set of answers that tends to zero and another set that tends to infinity, there is something wrong. Attempts have been made to rectify this situation by using models that combine savings and foreign-exchange estimates by country, with the larger of the two acting as operative constraint.[9] However, this method also remains open to criticism despite its evident advantages.[10]

The defects of all these methods are obvious to those who make projections and those who use them. First, the estimates lean heavily on assumptions about the ratio of changes in capital stock to changes in output, the ratio of changes in income to changes in savings, changes in imports and exports, and the like. But estimates of these values are rough, and their values are subject to unpredictable variations in time and space. Therefore, we cannot feel much confidence in predictions based on such shaky foundations.

Second, these variables are far from the primary determinants of growth. It is risky to use them as substitutes for variables that are more difficult to quantify, because these hidden values are likely to affect the estimating equations in completely unpredictable ways. For example, a devaluation or a political change may affect all the propensities and ratios systematically. A level of exports that was inadequate to sustain a target growth rate last year suddenly becomes more than adequate in the new situation.

Third, the very concept of a foreign exchange gap or a savings gap is in a sense misleading. The two gaps are interdependent and definitionally equal after the event. If people want to invest more than they can save, the only way that investment plans can be met is by a new inflow of resources. If the payments surplus is smaller than the savings gap, then investment, and presumably growth, must decline below the intended level until investment minus savings equals imports minus exports, which is also equal to national expenditures minus income. There is complete interdependence. Each rate and pattern of investment has its own implications for both balance of payments and the income-expenditure relationship. Thus, all such

[9] H. Chenery and A. Strout, "Foreign Assistance and Economic Development." See also J. Fei and D. S. Paauw, "Foreign Assistance and Self-Help," *Review of Economics and Statistics,* Vol. 47 (August 1965), pp. 251–267.

[10] It shares with Rosenstein-Rodan's method a certain built-in, downward bias stemming from the properties of the equations used to derive the estimates. Cf. Pincus, *Economic Aid,* pp. 36–38.

estimates, as shown in Table 34, are necessarily inaccurate to some degree.

Finally, in technical terms, there is an obvious reason for the progressive discrepancy between estimates based on the savings gap and those based on the foreign exchange gap. The latter implicitly assumes a continuous inflationary pressure. If there is no domestic inflation, then there will be no long-run discrepancy between the two gaps. In that sense, estimates of the trade gap, to the extent that they diverge from those of the savings gap, are simply wrong.

However, the equality of the two gaps is likely to be bought at the price of economic contraction. If there is an import surplus without inflation, some domestic producers are losing money and will have to cut back if the surplus persists. Therefore, by another way of looking at the matter, projections of the trade gap that diverge from the savings gap simply present a realistic view. In the absence of foreign aid, specified growth targets may be impossible to achieve without inflation.

Despite the talent and ingenuity that have been devoted to these projection techniques, all we can say with confidence is that more aid is probably better for LDC growth than less aid, with any given set of political situations assumed constant.

How much more aid, then, if the estimates of Table 34 are not reliable indicators of needs? On rather impressionistic grounds, I have suggested an annual average increase of $5 billion grant equivalent which amounts to about $8 billion of nominal aid, in the forms that aid is currently advanced. The World Bank has suggested an increase of $3–4 billion a year above present levels for the period 1965–70.[11]

But these estimates are neither better nor worse than those shown in the table. The ultimate criterion is how much the donor will give. This is a question of aid levels, not of aid requirements.

The underlying issue is ethical, not technical. There is no way to estimate the appropriate aid total except in light of agreed standards. But the agreement about aid levels implies an agreement about goals and methods of reaching them.

Why should aid requirements be linked *de facto* to some "optimum" growth rate based on the LDC potential for increasing domestic output? There is no obvious reason for the rich countries to

[11] IBRD Study on *Supplementary Financial Measures,* December 1965, p. ii; Pincus, *Economic Aid,* Chs. 2, 7.

limit their aid to the amounts that can directly promote productive investment. Within the Atlantic countries, poor people receive aid of two kinds: one aims directly at making them more productive, through training programs, educational subsidy, or programs of capital expenditure for backward regions; the other consists of direct consumption subsidies for people who are considered to fall below acceptable consumption standards.

By analogy, rich countries have generally attempted to limit their foreign aid to subsidy of directly productive ventures or supposedly prerequisite social and economic infrastructure. They try to avoid direct consumption subsidy except under emergency circumstances, or when a donor finds it convenient to dump surpluses.[12] Yet consumption subsidies from rich to poor are no less meritorious *per se* than investment subsidies. Furthermore, as we saw in Chapter 3, there is some relation between changes in consumption standards and productive potential, although economic theorists have never settled to the general satisfaction just how the two are related.

Once we admit the possibility of consumption subsidy, the idea of a "required" aid total loses all significance. But even if we do not, the idea of a required total is vague for another reason. The economists who have projected aid requirements have succeeded in arriving at their results by the device of assuming some target rate of growth. If no explicit target is set, the same result is achieved by introducing the idea of "absorptive capacity" or a "skill limit," setting a maximum beyond which increases in investment would not bring increases in output. To a degree, this makes sense. No underdeveloped country in modern times has increased its income or investment at a rate of more than about 10 per cent annually over a sustained period. The effort to maintain higher rates runs into all kinds of bottlenecks, some of which, like capital and technical assistance, can be broken with foreign aid. Others are more stubborn; general improvement of the level of education and training, and changes in underlying social attitudes toward economic activity itself, are to some extent beyond the reach of foreign aid, or of any short-term policies.

With existing technology, there is a limit to the rate at which domestic income can grow; however, we are very far from knowing what that limit is. Excluding countries that have struck oil, the non-

[12] Of course, since resources are to some extent transferable, the nominal financing of a steel mill may in effect be a consumption subsidy; but normally such a result would be in spite of the donor's objectives, not because of them.

Communist countries whose incomes have grown fastest since 1950 are Japan, Taiwan, and Israel. These countries could have grown even faster at times if they had not faced capital and foreign exchange restrictions.[13] Even at the growth rates that they have maintained, new investments were still highly profitable. This fact leads to a presumption that more investment would have been possible, had capital been available, even though rates of return might have dropped. In other words, we have no idea of what an LDC's absorptive capacity really is, because rich countries have never brought their resources fully to bear. For example, the level of technical assistance can systematically affect the entire schedule that relates quantity of investment to its yield. If the North increases its provision of technicians, teachers, advisers, training grants, and the like to the South, it simultaneously raises the return to productive investment there at least up to a point. Absorptive capacity is flexible, subject to alteration by policy choice. Therefore, even if we accept the proposition that aid should be devoted to productive investment, the absorptive capacity guideline is elusive.

Ultimately, the aid requirement is entirely flexible. It all depends on donors' and recipients' aspirations. The attempt to define absorptive capacity is in effect an effort to lend the cast of scientism to what is really an ethical judgment.[14] Underdeveloped countries can absorb all the aid that the North is willing to give now or later. The attempt to define aid levels in terms of productivity effects is simply one way of dealing with an ethical issue. But there are an infinite number of such methods, and to each there corresponds a different "absorptive capacity." Nigeria probably has a population of about fifty million. If the North wants to double Nigerian per capita income, it can be done, at an initial price of something in the neighborhood of $5 billion annually. To double the income of all LDC's would presumably cost about $200 billion a year at first. These sums are obviously completely beyond anything the North has in mind. But it is *not* a matter

[13] This is not to deny that such restrictions may also have acted to promote, rather than retard, the growth of domestic output. But there were undoubtedly times when increased foreign aid would have permitted still more production.

[14] The genuineness of the capital shortage has been questioned by those who believe that managerial and technical skills are the operative bottleneck. See, for example, Sayre P. Schatz, "The Capital Shortage Illusion: Government Lending in Nigeria," *Oxford Economic Papers*, Vol. 17 (July 1965), pp. 309–316. However, if the concept of investment is broadened to include anything that increases productivity, the shortage obviously exists in Nigeria as elsewhere.

of absorptive capacity. It is simply a desire not to spend too much money on aid, which is reinforced and rationalized by an ideological preference for investment over current consumption—the desire to help those who help themselves.

All econometric or impressionistic estimates of trade and savings gaps are in effect techniques of quantifying discontent according to a certain set of standards. They put the seal of rationality upon Southern aspirations. Because it is a safe bet that many LDC's could grow faster if they could get more aid, the inaccuracy of such measures does no great harm. In the eyes of those who support increases in foreign aid, some gap is better than none.

This does not mean that it is impossible to define an appropriate aid total. There is always some total that is appropriate to a particular set of standards or targets. But it is important to remember that agreement on those standards is a precondition of agreement as to aid levels. In practice, the decision about how much aid to give may well shape the standards. As in any budgetary decision, resource limitations shape the goals. The donor governments in effect decide to buy themselves $X billion worth of a blend of development, military advantage, and conscience balm. The size of the payment helps determine both donors' and recipients' effective aspirations—I am not speaking here of the world's fantasy life, important as it ultimately must be in shaping events.

From the perspective of the mid-1960's, such substantial aid increases as the gapmen project appear unlikely over the next decade. They bear no apparent correlation to the perceived political and economic interest of the rich countries. Charitable motives are apparently well satisfied by the present level of aid. Substantial changes are always possible, but if they do come, they might just as easily take the form of aid reductions, not increases.

The United Nations General Assembly, in launching its "Development Decade" (1961–70), set forth an aid flow target of one per cent of developed countries' GNP. This would have amounted to about $11 billion equivalent in 1961, rising to about $18 billion by 1970, and $20 billion by 1975—equal to UNCTAD estimates of the South's foreign exchange gap in that year. This happy coincidence takes on added political luster because the figure of one per cent of Northern GNP represents the stated aspirations of both North and South. The same one per cent target was restated in UNCTAD's Final Act, leading to the presumption that the politically agreed level of aspiration remains unchanged.

But the political agreement is restricted to speeches in international forums. In practice, each donor country has different aspirations and different targets, as the computations of aid levels shown in Table 38 below will testify.

ENDS AND MEANS: THE BURDEN-SHARING ISSUE[15]

Each member of the Atlantic Community has different interests in LDC's. Is there then any basis for sharing the costs of aid in some equitable way? There are four elements involved: (1) the appropriate aid total; (2) the appropriate definition of aid; (3) the appropriate contributions schedule; and (4) the appropriate forms and sources of aid.

We have just discussed the complications involved in defining an appropriate aid total. This section reviews the remaining elements.

Before discussing these elements, let us first review why the burden-sharing issue arises. It is clear that each Atlantic Community country gains certain benefits from the aid efforts of the others.[16] These benefits include military and security advantages to the extent that they persist; economic gains, though these may often be indirect, expressing themselves in a general expansion of world trade; benefits of a humanitarian order, impalpable as these may be; and political benefits to the extent that aid promotes peace and stability in the world, or solidarity of views between North and South. It is extraordinarily difficult, and in some cases impossible, to assign quantitative values to these benefits.[17]

This means, among other things, that burden-sharing formulas cannot be based on the familiar principle of public finance that calls for equal sacrifices from similarly situated persons who receive equal benefits. Although there are certain spheres of international public finance to which this benefit principle has been applied, it is clearly unsuitable for foreign aid where it is impossible even to say whether benefits are roughly equal. Does Italy gain more or less than Ger-

[15] This section is based in part on my *Economic Aid and International Cost-Sharing,* Ch. 3.

[16] It may also incur certain losses; I assume that benefits normally outweigh losses.

[17] Charles Wolf, Jr. has attempted to measure conceptually certain aspects of these gains. See his article, "Some Aspects of the 'Value' of Less Developed Countries to the United States," *World Politics,* Vol. 15 (July 1963), pp. 623–635.

many from British foreign aid? Does the Netherlands gain more or less than Norway from U.S. military assistance programs? How much more or less? These questions clearly serve only to stress the general point.

When, for ideological or practical reasons, it proves impossible to apply the benefit principle in taxation, the usual alternative is to base the levies on ability to pay. Most of the discussion of burden-sharing, in respect to official capital, has started from this principle; as we shall see below, it offers its own complexities.

But before we consider this issue, there are some prior questions. First, is it correct to look upon aid as a problem of public finance in the sense of assigning a contributions schedule for expenditures at all? There are some kinds of public expenditures, such as construction of toll bridges, that can be financed by user fees. There are other kinds, as we have pointed out in discussing the benefit principle, that it is impossible or impracticable to exclude the public from enjoying freely. City streets, military defense, or the satisfaction afforded by viewing a public monument might be cases in point. Foreign aid falls into this category. One member of the Atlantic Community can generally not prevent others from benefiting from its aid expenditures. This normally leads governments to think about restoring or creating equity through taxation. What is sometimes overlooked in the discussion, however, is that the United States, or Germany, or any other donor, gives aid because it expects a return, tangible or intangible, on its money, and not from a desire to make citizens of other rich countries happier.

There are rather fine lines dividing social views about spending for which taxes should be levied; spending that benefits society as a whole, but that should be financed by voluntary contributions; or spending that should be left entirely to individual choices. Into which of these categories should foreign aid fall? There is a consensus that it does not fall into the first category. The United Nations taxes its members for the organization's budget but not for large-scale aid. There is apparently a general feeling among Atlantic Community countries that it falls into the second, something like voluntary contributions for local charities. Like local charities, there is some element of social, although not legal, compulsion. The often unvoiced sentiments of one's friends and associates tend to spur the lagging philanthropist. Similarly, resolutions in the United Nations putting that body on record to favor annual contributions of one per cent of rich countries' GNP for the welfare of LDC's probably exert some similar pressure. The annual aid reviews of the Development Assistance Committee (DAC) of the OECD also operate in this direction. Furthermore, within the OECD-NATO framework, there is a sentiment, particularly among the major donors, that economic aid and mutual defense expenditures are to some degree substitutes. Thus, countries that lag in one can compensate by "over-subscription" in the other.

But in another sense foreign aid is also considered to be a matter of private choice, the word "private" referring to the government of each country as the unit of choice. In this context, of course, a burden should logically not arise. For instance, it is usually assumed that a private individual (or a government) will not voluntarily spend money unless the things that he buys are worth more to him than the money he spends for them. Otherwise he could keep the money. The donor nations expect certain advantages to accrue to them from foreign aid. They may be disappointed with the results, but that is another matter. No one is immune from making mistakes in his spending decisions. In the absence of deliberate fraud the "purchaser" of foreign aid is not bearing a burden. He expects a return for his money.

On the other hand, it is obviously true that one consumer's spending decisions can affect the welfare of other consumers. For example, if I hire a landscape architect to beautify my front yard, my neighbors benefit at no cost to them. If you, my neighbor, take steps to prevent polluting your well, my water supply is likely to be safer at no cost to me. Nevertheless, I normally don't ask you to help pay my landscape architect's fee and you don't ask me to buy chlorine for you. Wherever there are such uncaptured benefits at large, the result is that less is spent for the activity than would be spent if all beneficiaries were required to pay a share to enjoy the benefits.[18] Therefore, the amount spent on such public goods is normally below optimum.

When the general sentiment arises that too many people are getting a free ride, then the community begins the sequence that leads to compulsion, often via an intermediate stage of organized voluntary

[18] This can be demonstrated formally. The basic point is quite simple. I am willing to pay an amount \$X to see my yard beautified; my neighbors would be willing to pay \$Y to see my yard beautified, but they don't have to. If there were some way to collect \$Y, then \$X plus \$Y could be spent; or if a decision were made to spend only \$X, then the expenditure would be more equitably shared among beneficiaries, so that we might say that the community as a whole is better off.

contribution systems. On the international scene, foreign aid now stands at an early stage of this route. A later stage might be represented by something like the United Nations annual contribution system, which specified the amount of each country's contributions and imposes, theoretically at least, some sanction for non-payment. The international community has not yet evolved to the point where a body of law, with sanctions applying equally to all, can be enforced. Because international taxation is in such an embryonic stage, burden-sharing issues remain singularly resistant to formal methods of resolution. Each nation tends to feel that a formal resolution of the problem in one sphere will set a precedent for unwanted solutions in others.[19]

Aid Definition and Costs

The Definition of Aid. The appropriate definition of aid and its measurement has been discussed at length elsewhere, and I will not go into much detail here.[20] The Development Assistance Committee of OECD in effect defines aid as consisting of grants, loans of whatever terms or duration, contributions in kind, reparations payments, and consolidation credits (loans that allow a debtor to refinance his debt under more favorable conditions). Under the more inclusive heading of "flow of financial resources," it includes private direct investment, purchase of World Bank bonds, and government-guaranteed private export credits. On the other hand, it excludes trade under preferential arrangements; tariff rebates under preferential systems; and payment of prices above market levels for imports (such as U.S. sugar quota imports or French import prices for African tropical products).

This definition doesn't make much sense, because it lumps together incommensurate transactions. Normally, we would think of aid as a transaction that would not be entered into if only the direct economic rewards were considered. Thus, a grant would usually be considered as aid; the exception would be if it were really a disguised

[19] See T. C. Schelling, "International Cost-Sharing Arrangements," *Essays in International Finance,* No. 24, Department of Economics, Princeton, Princeton University, 1955. For a remarkably suggestive discussion of the issues that determine group behavior in cost-sharing, see Mancur Olson, Jr., *The Logic of Collective Action,* Harvard University Press, 1965.

[20] Pincus, *Economic Aid,* Chaps. 3, 5; Ohlin, *Foreign Aid Policies Reconsidered,* Paris, OECD, 1966, Chap. 5.

transaction, such as a form of air-base rental. From the donor's viewpoint, a foreign loan is not aid if its terms and conditions approximate those of the domestic capital market. Of course, the recipient may still look on it as aid because his alternative borrowing rates are higher. The aid element in a loan can therefore be computed, for donors, as the difference between the face value of the loan and the present value of future interest and amortization discounted at the lender's alternative lending rate.

As is intuitively obvious, the lower the interest rate and the longer the term of the loan, the greater the aid element for the donor. If the loan is made under stiffer terms than prevail in the domestic market, then its aid value is negative from the viewpoint of donor's cost.

For aid recipients, the definition is changed in three respects. First, the appropriate discount rate to use is that prevailing in the country receiving the aid. Second, to the extent that foreign exchange is at a premium in the receiving country, the value of aid is higher than it would be if payments were in equilibrium. A "shadow" exchange rate, expressing the equilibrium value of foreign currency, must be used. Third, financial aid tied to procurement in the donor country is worth less to the recipient than it would be if the funds could be used for procurement worldwide. The value of aid to the recipient in this form should be discounted by an amount equal to the differences between prices paid for the goods and services and their world prices.

These definitions concentrate on the real cost of aid to the donor and the real benefit to the recipient. They are essentially an attempt to express formally and to quantify some obvious points about real levels of aid.[21]

Value of Loans. A loan costs the donor less and is worth less to the recipient than a grant. In fact, if the foreign loan is made at the same interest rates as the lender would receive domestically, it costs him nothing, although it may still be of net value to the recipient if his domestic interest rate is higher than the rate of the loan, or if the real value of foreign exchange is higher than the official exchange rate

[21] The formal expression of these issues has been set forth by Richard Cooper, *A Note on Foreign Assistance and the Capital Requirements for Development,* Santa Monica, The RAND Corporation, RM-4291-PR, February 1965; and by Wilson Schmidt, "The Economics of Charity," *Journal of Political Economy,* Vol. 72 (August 1964), pp. 387–393.

indicates. Table 35 shows the grant-equivalent of loans made at different terms and interest rates discounted at 5, 6, and 7 per cent, which covers the range of most lender governments' alternative return on the funds. For example, a 20 year loan at 3 per cent interest, with 5 year grace period on principal repayment, includes a subsidy element of 25.5 per cent of the face value, if discounted at 6 per cent. If the loan repayment is stretched to 30 years, the grant equivalent rises to 30.5 per cent. At an interest rate of 2 per cent, the comparable grant equivalents are 34 per cent and 40.6 per cent respectively. The 10 per cent column in Table 35 might correspond to recipient's discount rate, and is uniformly higher in grant equivalent.[22]

Value of Contributions in Kind. The principal element in this form of aid is the U.S. contribution of surplus farm products under the provisions of Public Law 480. These contributions are now valued by the United States partly at world market prices and partly at higher levels, reflecting CCC purchase and storage costs. In one sense they might be valued at zero from the donor's viewpoint, because they are the result of domestic price support programs, and foreign aid provides a dumping ground. However, in terms of economic logic, they should be valued at the price they can command on the world market, which for large marketings is less than the current world price.

Tied Aid. It is sometimes claimed that tied aid (requiring the recipient to use aid for purchases in the donor country) reduces the donor's cost below the nominal value of aid. This is most likely to be true when the donor has excess productive capacity, or when he is able to sell the tied good at a price above his resource cost of production. Often, however, it is likely that tied aid from full-employment economies costs the donor just as much as untied aid would. Thus, from the viewpoint of donor's cost, a fully employed economy is, in the absence of balance-of-payments problems, making no greater sacrifice if aid is tied than if it is untied.

In any event, the recipients' real benefits are likely to be reduced when aid is tied, as pointed out in the above definition of aid. It has been estimated that in 1965, tying reduced the value of all aid received by Pakistan by 12 per cent; this amounted to 20 per cent of

[22] Ohlin, *Foreign Aid Policies Reconsidered,* gives formulas and rules of thumb for estimating grant equivalents.

the nominal value of the tied aid itself. This means that recipients may frequently repay *more* than the discounted value to them of tied loans. Whether or not they do depends on loan terms, recipients' discount rate, the degree of foreign exchange restriction, and the overpayment in tying. Overpayment by LDC's is most likely to occur when the procurement is tied to a particular project. A recent sample of twenty projects showed that bids from tied sources have been around 50 per cent more expensive than the lowest competitive worldwide bids on the same projects. For the recipient, therefore, the extra costs of tying are a form of negative aid.

The usual justification for tied aid is that it is necessary in order to protect donor balance of payments. This argument is valid or not depending on the extent to which recipients are willing or able to switch their import expenditures as a result of tied aid. It has been argued that such switching is widespread, so that tying does not affect the total of recipient's imports from the donor, but only the composition of the total. So far there is no conclusive evidence, although the practice of tying aid to projects probably makes import switching harder than it would otherwise be. The most important motive for tying is often the donor's desire to penetrate the recipient's market, in order to create long-run trade ties. This primarily reflects mercantilist national goals rather than short-run balance-of-payments problems.

Other Forms of Aid. As for the other forms of aid included in the OECD definition, reparations payments presumably should be excluded under a donor's cost definition. They are simply a form of debt repayment. Consolidation credits do contain some aid element if the new terms are better than the old, but the grant element is typically a small percentage of face value. Of course, from the viewpoint of the recipient, a lender that continues to increase his annual lending rapidly enough to cover interest and amortization obligations is making a net contribution, no matter what the terms and conditions of the loan. Obviously, under these circumstances, at some point the donor's annual gross transfer tends to become infinitely large in response to the steady buildup of payments due, if debt service requirements grow faster than capacity to service loans. But this apparent pressure of debt repayment may in effect be nothing more than a tacitly agreed device to convert nominal loans into grants.

What about items not included in the OECD aid definitions? First, there is private investment, which is done in the expectation of

TABLE 35. Grant Element in Loans: Lender's Discount Rate (per cent)

Rate of Interest and Maturity Period	5 Per Cent			6 Per Cent			7 Per Cent			10 Per Cent		
	No Grace Period	5 Years' Grace	10 Years' Grace	G=0	G=5	G=10	G=0	G=5	G=10	G=0	G=5	G=10
2 per cent interest												
10 years	12.9	21.2		16.7	24.0		20.0	28.9		29.5	41.8	
20 years	22.1	27.1	31.3	27.8	34.0	39.0	32.8	40.1	45.7	39.8	48.0	53.7
30 years	28.9	34.0	37.0	35.7	40.6	45.4	41.5	47.5	52.4	54.7	62.3	67.3
40 years	34.2	38.0	41.2	41.5	46.2	49.4	47.5	52.7	56.6	60.5	61.6	73.0
3 per cent interest												
10 years	8.6	14.1		12.5	18.0		16.0	23.2		25.8	36.6	
20 years	14.7	18.1	20.9	20.8	25.5	29.2	21.3	32.2	36.6	31.3	38.1	43.1
30 years	19.3	22.6	24.6	26.8	30.5	34.9	33.2	38.1	42.0	47.8	54.5	58.9
40 years	22.8	25.4	27.4	31.1	34.6	37.0	38.0	42.2	45.4	52.9	58.2	63.8
4 per cent interest												
10 years	4.3	7.1		8.1	12.0		12.0	17.4		22.1	31.4	
20 years	7.4	9.0	10.4	13.9	17.0	19.4	19.8	24.2	27.5	34.1	41.1	46.0
30 years	9.6	11.3	12.3	17.8	20.3	22.8	24.9	28.6	31.5	41.0	46.7	50.5
40 years	11.4	12.7	13.7	20.7	23.0	24.6	28.6	31.7	34.1	45.3	50.0	54.6

5 per cent interest												
10 years	0	0	0	4.2	6.0		8.0	11.5		18.4	26.1	
20 years	0	0	0	6.9	8.5	9.7	13.1	16.2	18.3	28.4	34.2	38.4
30 years	0	0	0	8.9	10.2	11.3	16.6	19.0	20.9	34.2	38.9	42.0
40 years	0	0	0	10.4	11.5	12.1	19.0	21.0	22.6	37.7	41.6	45.5
6 per cent interest												
10 years	a	a	a	0	0	0	4.0	5.8		14.7	20.9	
20 years	a	a	a	0	0	0	6.6	8.1	9.2	22.7	27.4	30.7
30 years	a	a	a	0	0	0	8.4	9.6	10.6	27.4	31.1	33.6
40 years	a	a	a	0	0	0	9.6	10.6	11.4	30.1	33.3	36.4
7 per cent interest												
10 years	a	a	a	a	a	a	0	0	0	11.1	15.7	
20 years	a	a	a	a	a	a	0	0	0	17.1	21.6	23.0
30 years	a	a	a	a	a	a	0	0	0	20.5	23.3	25.2
40 years	a	a	a	a	a	a	0	0	0	22.6	25.0	27.3

Source: Adapted from Appendix to Goran Ohlin, *Foreign Aid Policies Reconsidered*, Paris, OECD, 1965.
Note: [a] Indicates negative aid value.

profit and is not a cost to the donor. Second, there is trade, which is also not a net cost to the rich countries. Third, there are preferential tariff reductions favoring LDC's, as discussed in Chapter 6. It could be argued that these contain an aid element that should be included, to the extent that preferences divert trade away from lower-cost suppliers.[23] However, offsetting this is the system, generally followed by Atlantic Community countries, of increasing the tariff rate as the degree of processing of raw materials imported from LDC's increases; this is a sort of negative aid.

The preferential trade-diverting tariff is simply one aspect of the practice of paying higher prices than necessary for imports. The United States has long done this for imports under its sugar quota.[24] France has a policy of paying generally higher "just prices" instead of market prices for tropical products imported from its former colonies; Italy does the same for Somali banana producers. These devices are forms of economic aid; all of them could theoretically be valued at the difference between market prices and the rigged price.[25]

Generally speaking, the complexities are so great in measuring the positive aid element in preferential systems, government-financed investment guarantees, commodity price-fixing schemes, and the like, as well as the negative elements in the policies discussed above, that it is better as a practical matter to separate the categories entirely, rather than try to measure them all as "aid" in the same balance. Grants and loans can be measured together, and are reviewed together in the DAC annual aid reviews. Reductions of trade barriers normally involve little or no long-run costs to those granting the concessions; private investment is obviously a matter of private gain.[26] Nonetheless, as the free-trade-protection argument and the concern with capital outflows indicate, most countries are reluctant to reduce barriers or, often, to promote private investment in LDC's because of the short-term costs. The Atlantic countries have correctly endorsed the division between nominal aid, as discussed in DAC, and aid that

[23] The extensive literature on the theory of customs unions discusses this subject in some detail. See R. G. Lipsey, "The Theory of Customs Unions—A General Survey."

[24] U.S. import quotas for oil, lead, and zinc have the same effect; but there is a dominant element of private price-fixing in these cases.

[25] If sales of the product fluctuated relatively more than product prices, then a rigged high price might be negative aid, in the same fashion as high-interest loans, except that it would be negative for the recipient and positive for the donor.

[26] Although the costs to governments of foreign investment guarantees are a form of aid.

may or may not (depending on the case) be embodied in trade and investment policies, by reviewing the latter issues primarily in the GATT framework. This book follows the same distinction by reviewing the aid element of trade policies as part of the general discussion of commercial policies in Chapters 6 and 7.

In addition to the theoretical complexities involved in estimating the aid component of trade and investment policies,[27] there is an important practical reason for excluding trade and investment from the burden-sharing calculus. The attempt to make the word "aid" embrace everything that rich countries do in their economic relations with poor ones inevitably leads to dodging the aid issue. The refinements of computing the subsidy elements, real or, more typically, fancied, embodied in commercial policies are all too often a mask for inaction on the aid front.

The Current Level of Aid. Using the above definition of aid, I have computed in some detail the real cost of aid, from the donors' viewpoint, for the years 1961 and 1962.[28] In those two years, the North's official aid commitments as defined by DAC were respectively $7.7 billion and $7.8 billion. The real costs of aid, by the present value method[29] with each country's loans discounted to grant equivalent at its domestic interest rate, were respectively $4.6 and $4.8 billion, or about 60 per cent of the nominal cost. From the recipients' viewpoint, the real flow of aid was somewhat higher, because the real marginal rate of return to capital was presumably greater than in donor countries. However, this is partly offset by the extra cost of aid tying to recipients.

Between 1962 and 1965, total DAC aid commitments and actual aid flows have stayed the same as in 1961–62 (at about $7.6 billion in commitments and $6.0 billion in flow of funds). Therefore, with the growth of Northern GNP, and no significant change in aid terms,[30] developed countries' aid has dropped to the neighborhood

[27] For an effort at one aspect of such measurement, see John Pincus, "What Policy for Commodities?" *Foreign Affairs,* January 1964; also Charles Wolf, "Some Aspects of the 'Value' of Underdeveloped Countries."

[28] Pincus, *Economic Aid,* Chapter 5.

[29] With U.S. farm surpluses valued at world prices.

[30] Average interest rates were reduced by about one-tenth over the period, and average loan maturities increased by 3 or 4 years, but this increase in real costs has been compensated for by a reduction in grants, from 60 per cent of aid in 1962 to 50 per cent in 1965.

of 0.45 per cent of combined GNP, compared with 0.50 per cent in 1962. Table 36 shows for recent years both commitments of aid, and actual flows (disbursements) net of amortization received, according to DAC. It also compares the DAC commitment with real cost on a present value basis.

TABLE 36. Nominal and Real Aid Commitments and Flows, DAC Members, 1960–1965 ($ billions)

Year	*Aid Commitment*	*Aid Flow*	*Real Cost of Commitment*
1960	6.3	5.0	—
1961	7.7	6.1	4.6
1962	7.8	6.1	4.8
1963	6.9 [a]	6.1	4.2 [b]
1964	8.9 [a]	5.9	4.9 [b]
1965	7.6	6.3	4.6 [b]

Source: Cols. 1 and 2: OECD data; Col. 3: author's computations.

Notes: [a] The average commitment level in 1963–1964 was $7.9 billion. The gyrations of nominal and real commitments between 1963 and 1964 reflect statistical distortions caused by the time discrepancy between calendar years and U.S. fiscal years.

[b] Rough estimate by author.

— Indicates unknown.

The real cost figures for the years 1963–65 should be considered as rough estimates; they were arrived at by taking the weighted average of the terms and conditions offered by DAC members in those years, and then applying a discount rate of 6 per cent.[31]

The DAC bilateral aid figures omit two elements in Northern aid.[32] One, the aid offered by Northern countries that are not members of DAC is negligible. The second, aid by multilateral agencies —principally, the World Bank (including IDA, its "soft-loan" affiliate) and regional organizations (EEC, Inter-American Development

[31] The 1963 estimate in Table 36 agrees with that made by Ohlin, *Foreign Aid Policies Reconsidered,* p. 8, and with that computed by I. M. D. Little and J. M. Clifford in *International Aid,* London, George Allen and Unwin, 1965, p. 77.

[32] It also excludes estimated Soviet bloc and Chinese aid, of about $1 billion annually.

Bank)—is quite important. Total multilateral lending commitments in 1964 were about $1.5 billion, and have been increasing at about 10 per cent annually since 1960.[33]

The annual commitment of Northern official aid from all sources is thus about $8.8 billion nominally. The net flow of funds is smaller, about $6.7 billion, because of amortization payments, delays in negotiation and disbursements of committed funds, as well as the occasional evaporation of commitments. The real cost of commitments, including multilateral aid, is slightly more than $5 billion.[34]

These figures show a large discrepancy from a real cost target of one per cent of GNP. Average commitments in 1961–64 were about 0.8 per cent of combined GNP. Net disbursement of funds amounted to about 0.6 per cent, and real value of aid, as defined above, was less than 0.5 per cent of Northern GNP.

To meet the U.N. target, the *nominal* flow from bilateral and multilateral sources would therefore have had to increase by more than $2 billion in 1965, but in real cost terms the flow would have to double. This means a $5 billion rise in grant equivalent (more than $8 billion if extended in the current Northern mixture of grants, loans, and surplus farm products). By 1975, application of the one per cent criterion on a real cost basis would raise the annual bill by another $6 billion, to at least $16 billion grant equivalent, or about $25 billion in current nominal values.

The Distribution of Aid. The two principal questions relating to aid distribution are cost sharing and benefit sharing. How should the rich countries share the costs, and how should the proceeds be divided among the LDC's?

Burden-sharing has been an even more popular topic than debt service. The only sensible standard to use in deciding how much to "tax" each donor is income. I have discussed elsewhere the many issues that this raises.[35] Despite a number of complications, the conclusion remains that GNP in some common unit of account (preferably as measured by relative real purchasing power, rather than official exchange rates) is the best measure of ability to pay. Ability

[33] About one-fourth of this sum is in effect double counting in the current year if added to the DAC totals.

[34] $4.5 billion is the real cost of bilateral aid and donations to multilateral agencies, shown in Table 36.

[35] Pincus, *Economic Aid,* Chs. 3, 5.

to pay is in turn the best practical criterion for allocating costs of many international activities, where benefits to any one donor are difficult to measure.

In general, the present distribution of aid is not strikingly unfair by the criterion of flat rate taxation. In relative terms for the year 1962 Table 37 compares the nominal flow of aid resources, the real cost of commitments, and the income of the principal DAC donor countries, at exchange rate equivalents.

By the standards of a flat rate tax, the United States, France, and Belgium are paying more than their share of the real costs of aid. All other major donors are paying too little. By progressive tax standards, only France and Belgium are overpaying. The United States is about right, as are low-income Japan and Portugal. Among the major countries, the United Kingdom, Germany, and Italy are underpaying. A similar computation for 1963 shows no important changes from these results.[36]

The 1962 data (Col. 3) can be used to show what each country would have to pay to increase its real contribution to one per cent of GNP. The aggregate total would have to be doubled, as noted in the last section. Under a system of flat rate taxation, the largest increases in aid would come from Germany, the United Kingdom, Canada, and Italy, among major countries. The largest total increase would come from the United States, which would have had to add $2.5 billion to the real flow of its aid, about half of the total DAC increase under the one per cent standard.

On the recipients' side, the equity question is more difficult. Even if we accept the self-help criterion, it offers little guide to action, because the economist's definition of efficient investment (maximizing the marginal social return) is not operationally useful in underdeveloped countries. The divergence between market price and real costs is often substantial. The unknown linkages between investment in one sector and growth of another sector are potentially great. The possibilities of changes in cost conditions within an industry, resulting from economic expansion, is a recurrent theme of economic history. The difficulties inherent in a self-help criterion are therefore substantial. But, as we have seen, there is no particular reason to accept such a standard. We are forced in effect to reject the search for any single objective criterion for aid distribution. In any event, such a standard,

[36] Ohlin, *Foreign Aid Policies Reconsidered,* p. 87.

if found, would be of little practical import. As we have seen, donors' motives are multiple, and they vary. So long as this is true, standards will be *sui generis* for each donor. In each country, donor or recipient, a constant process of domestic and international bargaining will continue to shape the distribution of giving and getting.

TABLE 37. Relative Shares of Nominal and Real Costs of Aid Compared with Donors' GNP, 1962 (per cent)

Country	*GNP as Per Cent of DAC GNP*	*Nominal Aid as Per Cent of DAC Aid*	*Real Aid as Per Cent of Each Country's GNP*	*Real Aid as Per Cent of DAC Aid*
	(1)	(2)	(3)	(4)
Canada	3.9	0.9	0.16	1.3
France	7.2	13.2	1.32	19.0
Germany	8.8	6.4	0.27	4.9
Italy	4.0	1.8	0.07	0.6
Japan	5.5	3.8	0.24	2.7
Netherlands	1.4	0.8	0.27	0.8
Portugal	0.3	0.8	0.22	0.1
United Kingdom	8.3	7.3	0.27	4.4
United States	58.0	63.5	0.55	64.0
Belgium	1.4	1.3	0.70	2.0
Denmark	0.7	0.1	0.13	0.2
Norway	0.5	0.1	0.21	0.2
	100.0	100.0	0.50 [a]	100.0

Source: Pincus, *Economic Aid,* Ch. 5.

Notes: Columns may not add to totals, because of rounding.
[a] Weighted average.

Table 38 shows the geographic distribution of aid by region in recent years, total and per capita.

There are a dozen countries that receive more than $100 million in aid annually: Turkey, Yugoslavia, Algeria, Egypt, Israel, Brazil, Chile, Colombia, India, Pakistan, South Korea, and South Vietnam, and until recently, Indonesia and Taiwan. These countries combined received 60 per cent of all Northern aid in 1963. Furthermore, four countries (India, Pakistan, Algeria, and Turkey) received one-third of all aid.

The characteristics of the present aid distribution are obvious and need not be dwelt on. The primary criterion is the political importance of the country from the donors' viewpoint. Thus nations under direct Communist pressure (Vietnam, Korea, Laos) receive large amounts, in total and per capita. Israel, Jordan, and Egypt are politically important in the Middle East's perennial struggle. Algeria is France's peculiar treasure, where petroleum plays the role of hostage, should treaty commitments fail to bind. Turkey is a fledgling member of the Northern club, and also a geographical outpost against Soviet

TABLE 38. Flow of Aid from North to South, 1960–1963 ($ billions)

Region	*1960*	*1961*	*1962*	*1963*
Africa	1.5	1.6	1.8	1.6
Latin America	0.3	0.9	0.9	1.1
Middle East	0.3	0.4	0.3	0.3
Asia	2.0	1.8	2.0	2.5

Source: OECD, *Flow of Financial Resources to Less-developed Countries 1956–1963,* Paris, OECD, 1964.

Note: Includes aid from both bilateral and multilateral sources.

pressure. Brazil and Chile face the most insistent, if not the most perplexing, economic pressures; and Brazil is also considered a particularly important source of anti-Communist energies in the hemisphere. The reasons for supporting India and Pakistan combine all kinds of considerations that are both too well-known and too complex to discuss here, including their mutual hostility, and the preference of the North for their present governmental forms compared with most alternatives. Indonesia qualifies on the basis of size, present troublemaking potential, and future importance in Southeast Asia.

The geographic distribution of funds also reflects differences among Northern countries' interests and commitments. African countries get most of their aid from their former rulers, France, the United Kingdom, and Belgium. Latin America is in the U.S. sphere of influence and receives two-thirds of its aid from America. Asia also receives most of its relatively large aid flow from the United States (80 per cent in 1963) although Britain, Japan, and Germany, each for its own reasons, also offer substantial amounts in the region.

This recital slights the issue of development potential. It is secondary, but not always negligible. It accounts at least in part for the relatively small aid totals that go to sub-Saharan Africa and other very backward regions. Other things being equal, some donors, notably the United States and the World Bank, would prefer to transfer capital to countries that could use it effectively. As a general proposition, European governments have been less concerned with this issue, for reasons discussed in Chapter 1.

The Forms of Aid

We turn now from the level of aid, its costs and distribution, to a review of the forms of aid. This section concentrates primarily on: (1) the UNCTAD proposals for compensatory finance and for Northern interest subsidies on international lending; (2) the future of food aid. Before discussing them, we should review briefly the existing forms of aid and their implications. The issues are not difficult to analyze, despite the inordinate amount of space and time that has been devoted to such debating topics as loans vs. grants.

According to the DAC usage, as we have seen, there are five principal forms of official financial aid: (1) grants, (2) loans (repayable in borrowers' or lenders' currency), (3) contributions in kind (which are also either loans or grants), (4) official or officially guaranteed suppliers credits (the archetypical tied loan), and (5) reparations payments. All forms of aid reduce in effect to two categories—grants and loans [37]—although the above classification also has its uses.

"Loans vs. Grants." To ask whether loans are preferable to grants is nonsense. It depends what the purpose is. You can ride or milk both cows and mares; your choice of either animal would depend on which activity was most important to you at the time. With any fixed sum to dispose of, if the purpose is to maximize the capital

[37] In fact, for the purist, they are all loans, in which case a grant is defined as a loan at zero interest and infinite repayment terms; or else, all grants, using the present value system defined above, in which the maximum grant equivalent equals 100 per cent.

transfer, you make grants or loans with a high grant equivalent.[38] If the purpose is to minimize the real transfer, you make loans at commercial rates, and short amortization periods.

Once the decision is made, a large variety of arguments serves to rationalize it. So we sometimes hear that loans should be made for profit-making projects, and grants for those that bring no direct pecuniary return. Sometimes the argument is that loans are preferable, because they instill financial discipline upon the recipient. Because the loan must be repaid, it is less likely to be wasted.

This is all essentially in the realm of ethical observations, unsupported by evidence and of no value for those who seek informed guidance. The fact is that we know nothing about whether loans are "better" or "worse" than grants from recipients' viewpoint, beyond the obvious point that donors are better off the more they get repaid, and debtors are better off the less they have to repay.[39]

More important than this controversy are two issues that relate to the form of aid: debt service and the problems created by offering surplus farm products as aid. A third issue, aid tying, has been discussed earlier in this chapter.

Debt Service. The debt service problem arises because borrowers are supposed to repay debts. As the flow of lending increases, so does the amount of the interest and principal repayments. It is another side of the real cost coin. Heads is the difference between nominal and real costs of aid. Tails is debt service.

The debt service problem has been much discussed, probably too much.[40] There is really very little to be said. An increase in debt service creates no special problems if the investment is productive in the recipient country or if aid increases faster than debt service, or

[38] See Cooper, *A Note on Foreign Assistance,* for rules that maximize recipients' benefit per unit of real cost to the donor.

[39] To that can be added a few logical rules about the ways in which a donor can offer a specified level of benefits to a recipient, at least cost to himself. If returns to capital at home are higher than those abroad, it costs the donor less per dollar of benefit produced to offer grants; if not, it costs him less to offer loans. These rules offer no judgment about the psychological or ethical merits of various forms of aid. Cf. Cooper, *A Note on Foreign Assistance;* and Schmidt, "The Economics of Charity."

[40] The best complete reference is Dragoslav Avramovic and others, *Economic Growth and External Debt,* Baltimore, Johns Hopkins Press, 1964. See also Agency for International Development, *A Study on Loan Terms, Debt Burden and Development,* Washington, D.C., 1965; IBRD, *Annual Report,* 1964–1965, pp. 57–59; and DAC, *Development Assistance Efforts and Policies 1965 Review,* Paris, OECD, 1965.

(what amounts to the same thing) if donors allow recipients to stretch out repayments, convert loans to grants retroactively, and so on. If none of these conditions prevails, the borrower may be in trouble, particularly if the rate of return on investment and the marginal savings rates are low. The rapid increase in LDC's debt service since the end of World War II has led to a good deal of incautious speculation. The President of the World Bank warns us that lending terms must be eased in order to avoid future disaster.[41] The managing director of the IMF echoes him at the 1966 meetings of the IBRD-IMF governors: "The external position of many . . . remains precarious. The burden of servicing their accumulated foreign indebtedness has grown heavier. . . . [This situation is] of the gravest concern." These efforts to increase the transfer to the South via IDA are laudable for those who share the view that the present flow of aid is too small, but it is hardly necessary to rattle the hollow gourd of bankruptcy. The facts lead to no such conclusion. Underdeveloped countries' public debt service is rising by about $300 million annually (1958–64). Their exports are rising by about eight times that amount, their incomes about twenty-five times faster, and their savings seven times faster.

Although this preoccupation with debt service in general is inappropriate, there are two genuine problems. First, if LDC export earnings fall because of adverse demand conditions or a too-buoyant supply, the consequent foreign exchange problems will be aggravated by the need to service a high fixed debt. This, of course, was a major problem of the depression of the 1930's. A similar cataclysm is unlikely, but lesser disturbances could create hardship.

Second, and more important, the emphasis on aggregates masks the fact that only a few countries—Argentina, Brazil, India, Turkey, Chile, Colombia—combine high debt service and modest economic growth. These are the problem countries, and the remedies for mounting debt service there are obvious: Until their income and savings start to grow faster, they should receive more grant equivalent aid and be allowed to stretch out their present debt, or have it forgiven.

Debt service charges have been rising faster than GNP, at the rate of nearly 20 per cent a year in 1956–63, so it is natural that the trend should attract attention. However, it is a mistake to put the emphasis on service requirements *per se*. They are simply reflections

[41] Address to IBRD-IMF Governors, Washington, D.C., September 27, 1965.

of problems that were discussed at length in Chapters 4 and 5. If debt service were a good index of those problems—if we could develop analytical models that would relate economic and political variables to crisis levels of debt service—then these data would be useful.[42] But the ability of countries to service debt (and to negotiate for debt forgiveness or refinancing) varies widely, as does the real cost of debt service. The fact that public debt service in 1964 accounted for 10–12 per cent of export earnings, compared with 4 or 5 per cent a decade earlier, tells us nothing very useful.

In the present stage of our knowledge, therefore, debt service figures are simply another way of looking at facts that are obvious anyway. We don't need debt service computations to understand that the South would be better off if it were wealthier, or received more aid on more generous terms. But it is hardly reasonable to characterize this as a debt service problem. The only good excuse for stressing the subject is that it may be an effective way to dramatize the problem. To that extent, it is of course desirable, as are most serious forms of adult education. In this sense, debt service is more a problem for donors than for recipients. The issue simply calls attention to a difficulty that donors have created and could easily eliminate.

Farm Surplus Donations. Food aid has a major political advantage compared with other forms of resource transfer; this will continue to outweigh the serious liabilities it creates. It disposes of surpluses by gift instead of by destruction. It is a particularly congenial form of philanthropy, because the donor disposes of something that is at once a nuisance to him and of considerable value to the recipient. As an offset to these advantages, food aid creates two kinds of economic problems: trade diversion, by substituting free food for commercial imports; and discouragement of domestic agricultural production in the South, by keeping prices down and by reducing incentives to invest in agriculture. These results in turn can be carried throughout the economic system, affecting income and welfare in all sectors. Those who are concerned by the lag in modernizing Southern agriculture point out correctly that the combination of industrial protection and acceptance of food aid tends to turn the domestic terms of trade

[42] Cf. Avramovic, *External Debt* for some attempts in the economic sphere, particularly a formulation by Hayes, Wyss and Husain setting forth the marginal rates of return on investment and marginal propensities to save required to permit the economy to grow fast enough to service debt increases in perpetuity.

against agriculture, thereby perpetuating agricultural stagnation. (Cf. Chapter 5.)

These possibilities are widely recognized. One of the UNCTAD general principles refers simultaneously to the value of surplus commodity aid and to the importance of preventing trade diversion and also preventing harm to the recipient's agriculture. The Food and Agriculture Organization has drawn up such a set of principles, accepted by 50 members, aimed at assuring that surplus disposal does not interfere with commercial trade. The system is based on agreement by recipients that the aid will be in addition to normal commercial imports. A recent FAO report on the subject admits that these efforts to prevent trade diversion have not fully met "the expectations of competing commercial exporters." [43]

To assure that such large volumes of exports do not divert trade or depress prices is impossible in practice. There is no way of dumping more than $1 billion worth of free food on the world market each year without affecting trade and prices. P. L. 480 wheat and flour marketings alone amount to as much as one-fourth of world trade annually. World trade in all temperate crops (1959–61) averaged $8 billion annually, so that P.L. 480 exports were about 12 per cent of total trade in all these products. It is clear that some P. L. 480 exports substitute for Southern exports, particularly cotton [44] and oilseeds; and some for Northern exports, mainly grains. However, we have as yet no good basis for estimating how much these surpluses substitute for commercial exports, rather than supplement them. The principal direct losers, in terms of diversion and reduction of world price, are presumably Australia, Canada, the major oilseed exporters of Africa and Asia, and Southeast Asian rice exporters.

It seems safe to say that, whatever these costs amount to, it will be a long time before they come to outweigh the constellation of political advantages. They represent at least a partial coincidence of Northern and Southern self-interest, something conspicuously lacking in most of the UNCTAD proposals. Furthermore, that coincidence is likely to grow. The Common Market countries are apparently embarked on a course leading to self-sufficiency and even surplus in crops that they

[43] "Food Aid and Other Forms of Utilization of Agricultural Surpluses. A Review of Programs, Principles and Consultations," UNCTAD, *Proceedings,* Vol. VI, p. 404.

[44] Cotton exporters have no legitimate grounds for complaint. U.S. price supports and output controls provide other exporters with a *de facto* floor price. If cotton output were decontrolled in the United States, the world price would fall.

now export. This will put increasing pressure on their Northern suppliers (and on the EEC also) to dispose of surpluses. At the same time, the growth of Southern population which, in some countries, is pressing on food supply, will help to keep the demand for free food strong. Despite the obvious price disincentives, free food caters strongly to a competing Southern governmental incentive: the desire to keep food prices low and still have plenty of food for the cities. This is a sort of offset to the high costs of infant industries.

This seems to me to be an unbeatable combination politically at least for the donors (food-surplus Northern countries) and recipients (food-deficit Southern countries). The injured parties—commercial exporters in North and South and domestic producers in the South—have no effective weapons against this assault. Furthermore, the food deficit commercial importers (Europe, Japan) probably benefit a little. Food aid drives down world prices because it is a partial substitute for commercial trade.

It seems likely that food aid will grow, although there are some conflicting factors.[45] In the United States, the McGovern bill was introduced in 1965 to supplement P. L. 480 by successive increments of $500 million, rising to $3.5 billion annually at the end of six years. Under this proposal, the Secretary of Agriculture would set domestic acreage allotments with regard to estimated world nutritional needs above commercial requirements. This food program might eventually supplant P. L. 480 so that world requirements rather than historical production patterns would become in theory the sole basis for U.S. food aid.

This sort of approach—which, in the McGovern bill, is on too large a scale to win the Administration's backing—is strongly supported by the U.S. Farm Bureau Federation, the major farm pressure group. The Bureau envisages a world food program as a method of ultimately ending government controls over output, and it even hopes to reduce the subsidy element by making part of the aid repayable in long-term dollar loans.

The main conflicting factor for donors is political. Farmers are only one pressure group in the North. To allow them to expand output on the scale envisaged by the McGovern bill or the Farm Bureau

[45] U.S. food surpluses have decreased somewhat in recent years under the combined effects of P.L. 480 acreage allotments and of payments to farmers for not growing food.

might create a vested interest in feeding the world, one that the United States might be unwilling or unable to undertake.

The net result, therefore, is likely to be some expansion of food aid, without aiming at the more ambitious targets. To reconcile this smaller increase with humanitarian and development goals requires two allied policies: (1) massive support of programs to increase Southern farm output; (2) population control programs.

A third element is not required politically but would be economically useful as a method of encouraging productivity increase, given the economic and institutional pressures that conspire to keep Southern food prices low. This would consist of subsidizing the costs of farmers' means of production, particularly those that increase productivity: fertilizer, insecticides, new crop varieties, and the like.

These three elements have been combined in President Johnson's "Food for Freedom" proposals, submitted to Congress in 1966. These proposals were only partially adopted by Congress when it extended P.L. 480 legislation in October 1966. However it seems likely that they will recur. The proposals were advanced as part of a more general reformulation of the foreign aid planning and authorization processes. The reference to population control, stressed in other recent U.S. pronouncements on aid policy, is muted in the Food for Freedom proposals. The principal element in the new food aid proposal is the recognition that surplus food will be a permanent element in U.S. foreign aid. Each recipient country would receive agricultural products in amounts determined by a five-year projection of its aid requirements. The proposal includes a significant step backwards, in deference to Congress. Food aid would be primarily in the form of dollar loans, thereby exacerbating the debt-service issue.

This proposal would build foreign aid requirements into the structure of the U.S. domestic farm program. To offset the adverse effects that this might have on Southern agriculture, the President also proposed that aid be used as a device to promote productivity of agriculture and industry in less-developed countries. Essentially this proposal is a sort of double rigging of markets. If it can be translated into a system that actually does promote more rapid growth of farm output in the South, then it may be worth the costs, including the damage to other commercial exporters. Food aid is obviously an inferior way of transferring capital. However, if for the time it is the only politically feasible way to increase aid, the remedy is not to abolish the system, but to create systematic offsets to the disadvantages it may produce. If the techniques actually adopted under the Food for Freedom banner to promote LDC farm production prove effective, then food aid may turn out in time to be a self-liquidating enterprise. If not, the long-run costs could outweigh the benefits.

If, as seems possible, LDC food supplies fail to increase as fast as demand, then "Food for Freedom" in some form may become a permanent element of Northern farm policy. It could ultimately lead to higher food prices, and even, if pressures are great enough, for a switch from aid to trade: the exchange of rich countries' food for poor countries' manufactured products. In terms of interest-group politics, however, this prospect seems remote indeed. In the United States it would have to await the day when the Farm Bureau can outweigh both the National Association of Manufacturers and the AFL-CIO. Current generations are unlikely to participate.

New Forms of Aid

Compensatory Finance.[46] In Chapter 7, we saw that fluctuations in export earnings are not themselves of great moment to developing countries (although excessive price fluctuations may in the long run reduce export markets). Such devices as the IMF short-term lending facility for countries whose exports earnings fall as a result of factors beyond their control are adequate because the problem is minor.

The real difficulty lies not with short-term fluctuations around an export earnings trend but with the persistent balance-of-payments problems that plague underdeveloped countries when they try to speed up their economic growth. The two issues cannot always be separated in practice, because a rise or fall in earnings or prices may be temporary or persistent, and there is no way to be sure until after the fact. However, it seems clear that the umbrella expression "compensatory finance" lends the mantle of a just claim to the underlying demand—more foreign aid.

Proposals for maintaining Southern exchange receipts at an agreed and "fair" level have been circulating since the early 1950's.

[46] This subject is discussed in detail by Gertrud Lovasy, "Survey and Appraisal of Proposed Schemes of Compensatory Financing," *IMF Staff Papers*, Vol. XII (July 1965), pp. 189–223; her approach is different from that adopted here, and offers in particular a good summary of the literature of the technical problems involved in choice of base year, use of index numbers, and so on.

They have included: (1) schemes for payments from rich to poor countries when the latters' terms of trade decline below some agreed level;[47] (2) payments aimed at assuring stability of export prices; (3) payments for persistent shortfalls in export receipts, either through a sort of international social insurance fund,[48] or through IDA loans.[49]

The proposals for compensating a country that experiences deteriorating terms of trade usually involve some form of grant aid, automatic or discretionary, if an LDC's terms of trade fall by more than a fixed percentage from some reference point. The payment would be some fraction of the difference between purchasing power of sales at the current terms of trade and their value at the reference point. In some versions, the source of the funds is countries whose terms of trade has improved; in others, it is rich countries in general.

The terms-of-trade approach to compensatory finance has the advantage of being subject to automatic measurement, so that some of the controversy involved in discretionary decision making about how much aid to give to whom can be avoided. The disadvantages are well-known: (1) terms-of-trade is not necessarily a good index of welfare, or of a country's balance-of-payments situation; (2) the reference point chosen may soon become outdated by changes in economic structure; (3) if the gainers compensate the losers, the result could be transfers among LDC's, instead of from North to South; (4) if the rich compensate the poor, with the objective of easing foreign exchange and capital shortages, why go through the indirect and often inaccurate indicator offered by the terms of trade?

The second method of compensatory finance, price stabilization, was discussed in Chapter 7. It is inherent in effective commodity price-fixing schemes, and may either stabilize or destabilize earnings in the long run, depending on demand and supply conditions.[50]

The third technique of compensatory finance (often called supplementary finance) compares actual export receipts and those that

[47] United Nations, *Commodity Trade and Economic Development,* New York, 1963, Appendix D; Prebisch, *A New Trade Policy.*

[48] United Nations, *International Compensation for Fluctuations in Commodity Trade,* New York, 1961.

[49] UNCTAD, *Proceedings,* Vol. I (Annex A.IV.18), pp. 52–53; resolution proposed by the U.K. delegation and approved by the Conference.

[50] More generally, effective price-fixing agreements particularly with buffer stocks reduce the need for compensatory finance. By the same token, compensatory finance reduces the need for commodity agreements. This applies to both price compensation and earnings compensation schemes.

would be expected under "normal" circumstances, and would attempt to guarantee a certain level of foreign exchange avenues, offering aid to supplement inadequate export levels, when necessary. The UNCTAD Final Act reached virtual unanimity in supporting a proposal of this kind, advanced by the U.K. delegation. In enacting the resolution entitled "Supplementary Financial Measures," the conference requested the World Bank to study and report on a scheme aimed at dealing with

> . . . problems arising from adverse movements in export proceeds (defined in the resolution as "shortfalls from reasonable expectations") which prove to be of a nature or duration which cannot adequately be dealt with by short-term balance-of-payments support. Its purpose should be to provide longer term assistance to developing countries which would help them to avoid disruption of their development program.[51]

The World Bank report[52] calls for aid designed to compensate for such shortfalls in export earnings. In the words of the report, the purpose of the scheme is:

> To help assure that the achievement of these [growth] objectives will not be frustrated because foreign exchange earnings from exports do not materialize in the amounts envisaged at the time the investment and aid decisions were made.[53]

The report calls for the following system:

(1) LDC's will review their development programs and their payments prospects with the administering agency.

(2) The agency and the country will agree on a "policy package" designed to meet realistic plan targets that would commit the country to economic policies designed to achieve the targets.

(3) If the country held to the policies and were still faced with a shortfall in export proceeds over the plan period (4–6 years), due to factors beyond its control, then the agency would advance aid on flexible terms. Financing would be on the basis of net shortfalls during the plan period, after prior year earnings in excess of anticipations were deducted.

The anticipated aid level as estimated on the basis of past experi-

[51] UNCTAD, *Proceedings,* Vol. I, p. 52.

[52] *Study on Supplementary Financial Measures,* Washington, D.C., December 6, 1965 (mimeographed).

[53] *Ibid.,* p. iii.

ence would be $300–$400 million annually. This system of compensation would be financed by contributions from "all participants" (an internationalese term meaning rich countries), with benefits going only to the South. The transfers would be administered by IDA or a similar agency, and would be distributed on the basis of export shortfalls below "reasonable expectations," and in light of the needs engendered by national development programs.

Schemes of this kind offer flexibility to the donors. If they want to give small amounts, they have only to set "reasonable expectations" low. If they want to be munificent, the expectations have only to be inflated. In the IDA-IBRD version, "reasonable expectations" appear to be defined as a blend of objective forecast and calculated aspirations. That is, the target would not be based simply on extrapolation of trends, or even of a more sophisticated balancing of supply and demand forecasts. It would combine the latter with the assumption that the approved candidate for compensatory financing could meet at least some of its aspirations for export growth. The result would be to increase each candidate's chance of receiving compensatory repayments.

Judging the merits of such a scheme is a complex enterprise. From the donor's viewpoint, it offers the advantage of setting up performance criteria for aid that (at least in theory) could be applied to all forms of aid. The compensatory funds would act as a lever to assure that performance criteria are met on all scores. The disadvantage of compensatory aid is that it also sets up an obligation to provide more aid on concessional terms, unless the obligation can be offset by reducing other forms of aid. In the IBRD version, the funds would be supplementary finance, in addition to existing aid; but the Bank's aspiration doesn't bind member governments.

For the recipient, the situation is reversed. He loses freedom of action by making performance commitments, and gains from the increase in aid. If, as the World Bank report anticipates, the aid is an increase over previous levels, then the benefit is clear. No LDC is made worse off, and those whose exports lag are better off. In fact, this is simply another way of stating the objective of the scheme, in its proponents' eyes.

If, on the other hand, this form of compensatory finance simply switches aid among recipients without increasing its volume, then countries whose exports prosper are worse off and those whose exports lag are better off than they would be otherwise. It seems obvious that the unanimous LDC support for compensatory finance was based on the tacit, but questionable, assumption that it would be an automatic supplement to existing aid.

Compensatory finance may or may not offer net benefits to the South as a whole, but it obviously does provide incentives to import-substituting industry in the South. When minimum foreign exchange revenues are in effect guaranteed, the guarantee means that a country is penalized (loses capital transfers) if it increases exports above the compensatory finance support level. Therefore, the country is likely to be better off if it uses resources to substitute for imports instead of producing export goods. When import-substituting industry is as profitable as exports, the country is obviously better off. But even when it is less profitable than exports, the recipient may be better off by subsidizing import-substituting industry in preference to exports. The subsidy allows it to retain aid that would not be available if export revenues were higher. Naturally, it is possible to incorporate devices that diminish these incentives for export avoidance. The one usually proposed is partial compensation, for example, to give the country suffering a shortfall only half of the gap between actual receipts and expectations. However, no method appears foolproof; there is an inherent contradiction between simultaneous efforts to compensate for export shortfalls and to prevent countries that experience them from benefiting.

Compensatory finance also offers another incentive, regardless of whether there are aggregate benefits to the South—the incentive to cheat. If payments are based on failure of exports to meet specific targets, then the easiest way to gain benefits is by manipulating trade statistics. To a certain extent this effort can be contained by making sure that the total of recorded imports from country X is equal to X's export record. However, this is far from a perfect check in practice for a variety of reasons—imperfections in data, lags in time periods covered, problems created by unwillingness or inability of some importers to furnish the required detail, and so on.

One way of getting around some of the perverse incentives offered by compensatory finance was proposed by the Indian delegation at UNCTAD. Instead of paying a country directly on the basis of export shortfalls, it would require all Northern importers to commit themselves to a minimum level of imports from all LDC's combined. The importer would pay to a central fund an amount determined by its shortfall. The money would be paid out to LDC's experiencing export shortfalls. This system gives the North an incentive to import rather than pay cash to the fund, and is therefore consistent with the "trade not aid" approach inherent in encouragement of LDC exports. However, the scheme appears to suffer from one signal deficiency. If the import targets are low enough, or the importers zealous enough in meeting their targets, no money will be paid into the fund and there will be no compensation available for the unfortunate LDC that fails to share in the general trade bonanza. In the absence of additional sources of largesse, the prospective recipient is likely to find himself in a "no trade, no aid" position. Even if money is paid into the fund, the fact that it would be distributed according to export shortfalls reintroduces negative incentives.

The best argument for compensatory finance as a technique of aid seems to be that referred to in Chapter 7. It provides the benefits aimed at by commodity price-fixing schemes without introducing the complex control apparatus that these schemes require. However, there is no objective reason why simpler forms of foreign aid could not be used for the same purpose. The decisive issues remain as stated above: do North and South stand to gain more from an automatic aid system (for countries that meet certain initial standards) than they do from the present one? For the North, the answer depends on changes in the leverage it could exert as a result. For the South, it depends on the balance between constraints imposed and additional resources gained (or increased certainty of receipts from year to year). Clearly for some Southern countries, the bargain described by the IBRD could be a bad one. In order to get access to a modest, but uncertain, aid increment the recipient has to allow international review of its domestic policies. This may be a pretty high price to pay for uncertain benefits. On the other hand, it may provide Southern government international support or pressure for measures it would like to take anyway, but feels hesitant about in the face of domestic opposition. In that event, of course, the "interference" by the outside agency is a welcome safety valve.

Interest Subsidies. Another UNCTAD resolution called in effect for Northern subsidy of World Bank (or IDA) lending rates. The IBRD would borrow at normal terms from private investors; the loans would be supported by member government guarantees. The proceeds would be relent by IDA at concessional terms (30 years, one per cent), and the North would subsidize the difference by contributing to an "interest equalization" fund.[54] This scheme, originally proposed by D. Horowitz, head of Israel's delegation to UNCTAD, was also studied and reported on by the World Bank.[55]

The Bank report expressed doubts about carrying out the proposal on the large scale originally proposed at UNCTAD (annual borrowings and relendings of $2 billion a year) or even on the more restricted scale (of $600 million annually) later proposed by Horowitz. The report found that the private capital markets of Europe and America were not likely to make willing purchases of an additional $600 million of Bank bonds annually at going interest rates.[56] The estimate was that, in the absence of payments constraints, the U.S. market might take $200–$300 million annually, if the bonds were appropriately guaranteed, whereas Europe would take far less. However, there *are* payments constraints, and some European countries whose payments are in surplus are unwilling to allow increased Bank borrowing for other reasons. The creation of an interest equalization fund for thirty year loans also requires substantial long-term commitment of funds.[57] Therefore, the report was very dubious about Horowitz' proposal. In light of all this, the report suggested that the donors might be better off if they used other techniques (higher IDA subscriptions, soft loans to IDA) to the same end.

This appraisal may well be realistic, but it is difficult to accept solely on the basis of the report. A major advantage of IBRD, in many donors' eyes, is that its loans are not financed from government budgets. A disadvantage of IDA is that its lending terms are too soft to be self-financed. Yet, IDA terms are increasingly attractive to donors, because the debt service issue is fast becoming politically difficult. It seems likely that this combination of leverage from appropriated funds and avoidance of anticipated political embarrassments may be more enticing than the World Bank report allows.[58] Of

[54] UNCTAD, *Proceedings*, Vol. I (Annex X.III.11), p. 48.

[55] IBRD, *The Horowitz Proposal.*

[56] This would represent a 100 per cent increase above the normal borrowing level anticipated by the Bank.

[57] Borrowing $600 million a year for five years would require Northern contributions to the fund for 34 years rising to a maximum of $120 million a year, and totalling $2,386 million over the period. If lending continued at that rate for 20 years, the peak would be $411 million a year.

[58] Under the Horowitz proposal, the $3,000 million borrowed and relent over 4 years would cost governments $2.4 billion in cash flow over 34 years. If the same amount were borrowed by governments at market rates, say 5 per cent, the cash flow cost would be $13 billion over 34 years.

course, this begs the question of restrictions created by payments problems and by the desire of governments and capitalists in many countries to reserve the domestic capital market for domestic borrowers. Since the Bank researchers apparently talked mostly to finance ministries and money men, it is perhaps not surprising that they reached rather negative conclusions. The politics of money, however, is not the exclusive province of the financial community, so that we may not have heard the end of interest subsidy proposals.

Some Speculations. We have reviewed the existing forms of aid and those as yet unadopted that are currently being considered by international bodies. This of course does not exhaust the list. The most persistent proposals for new forms of aid are associated with monetary reform. They involve increasing the amount of world monetary reserves by one device or another, including printing a new money or creating a commodity backing for currencies—and turning part of the increase over to underdeveloped countries. Two such reforms were discussed in Chapter 7 of this study. These and other proposals have been rather fully analyzed elsewhere.[59] A persistent issue in all such schemes is the divorce between the creation of the increased reserves, which costs nothing, and spending them, which costs the supplying country resources, particularly under full-employment assumptions.[60] In any event, despite its popularity with a number of distinguished theorists, support for this form of aid has never taken enough hold to be enacted.

In this section, I want to advance proposals for other forms of aid, on a speculative basis. None of these are fully worked out, and at least one—tax credits—is, from a policy viewpoint, ethereal.

Tax Credits. Foreign aid is generally a nuisance to donor governments. As pointed out in Chapter 1, there has been considerable political dissatisfaction with aid in the United States and France. It seems clear that most other nations' aid efforts are strongly affected by what the United States and (to a lesser degree) France choose to do.

In both countries, the objections are similar—"What do we get

[59] Johnson, *Economic Policies,* Chapter VII, reviews recent proposals. H. Grubel (ed.), *World Monetary Reform,* discusses a variety of them also.

[60] Whether or not there is full employment, there is a transfer to the buyer, but the full ramifications are beyond our province here.

out of it?" and "Why couldn't we keep it at home?" One way to find out how much political support aid has is to make it voluntary but costless. Each government can set up a non-profit corporation to administer foreign aid, financed wholly from private contributions. All contributions would be credited against income taxes up to the full amount of the taxpayer's liability. Thus, a $1,000 contribution, given to the Foreign Aid Foundation, would reduce the tax liability by the same amount. If the tax liability were equal to or less than that amount, then there would be no tax due.

This device would have the effect of more or less definitively answering the question of the appropriate level of aid, from the donor's side.[61] The amounts given would represent what people want to give for foreign aid. It also offers an interesting experiment in public finance. If the government pledges to abstain from foreign aid appropriations, and reduce its budget by that amount, then we would have some idea of whether people really believe what they tell the public opinion polls—that the present level of aid is about right. It would also take aid out of the realm of domestic controversy.[62]

A simpler scheme with the same effect would be to hold a referendum, in which people in donor countries were asked to indicate their ranking of various specified alternative levels of aid. The aid level receiving the highest weighted preference ranking would be adopted by the donor country. Both systems, while gravid with merit, are far removed from most countries' political traditions, at least in foreign policy. Furthermore, if adopted, they would offer developing countries some incentive to plow back the proceeds into campaigns to influence future voting in donor countries. This activity would introduce a neat economic calculus regarding marginal costs and benefits of public relations efforts.

Financing Export Subsidies. We saw in Chapter 6 that export subsidies are a more logical way of financing LDC manufactured exports than preferences. It has been suggested that the local currency of P. L. 480 sales could be earmarked for industrial subsidies. This

[61] But not completely, because people would have no incentive to donate more than their tax liability. Also the amount given by people wishing to spite their own government might increase the total. Those who refrain from a desire to spite foreigners are not an offset, because they are expressing their true feelings about aid, while the first group isn't—exactly.

[62] If we exclude the effects caused by the determined efforts of other worthy causes to obtain the same tax credit privileges.

has several disadvantages. Once the commodities are sold, the resource transfer is done. There isn't any way to eat the same food twice, normally. Therefore, P. L. 480 proceeds are not needed. Any government that wants to print money can do so anyway. Second, the system would link the ability to subsidize to P. L. 480 receipts. In other words, only food-deficit LDC's could subsidize. On the other hand, once we forget the tie-in to food aid, whether for home consumption or export, subsidy has its own merits and is theoretically superior to protection because it doesn't use restriction as an income vehicle.

Turnover Taxes. It has often been suggested that the costs of multilateral programs be supported by taxes on international economic activity, such as international travel,[63] petroleum products, international waterways,[64] or the value of international trade.[65] These proposals have a certain appeal, because they involve international payment for the use of internationally "owned" facilities—the sea and the air. More important, the value of all these activities is high and fast-growing, so that low rates of taxation would have a high payoff. World trade, for example, is increasing at the rate of about 8 per cent a year. A one per cent tax on the value of world imports in 1964 would have yielded $1.7 billion. By 1975, the sum would double if trade growth rates stayed the same. The Coffee Council tax on exports, proposed in 1966, is an embryonic application of the principle of trade taxation for economic development use.

Trade Targets. One of the UNCTAD resolutions called for industrial countries to set import targets for trade with underdeveloped countries. This is reminiscent of the European trade liberalization targets of the 1950's, by which Marshall Plan recipients progressively removed quantitative restrictions on trade. It seems unlikely that the North could operate a system of import targets with equal success. How can a fixed level of imports be guaranteed without a state-trading system? The only sure way is to set import targets low enough

[63] T. A. Sumberg, "Financing International Institutions," *Social Research* (September 1946), pp. 276–306.

[64] Boris C. Swerling, "Current Issues of Commodity Policy," *Essays in International Finance,* No. 38, Department of Economics, Princeton, Princeton University Press, 1962.

[65] I owe this suggestion to Professor Frank of The Johns Hopkins University, who should not be held responsible for the uses to which I subject his notions.

to assure that they will be met by the normal course of business. But in that case, the target is a token. The Indian proposal discussed earlier is no solution of the dilemma.

The trouble with all these devices, except the impractical suggestion of voluntary aid, is that they offer no appeal to Northern self-interest. Food aid or an equivalent for dumping the surplus manufactures of countries with excess industrial capacity are the only obvious techniques.[66] Unfortunately, this runs into two stumbling blocks: (1) it interferes with commercial trade; (2) Northern excess capacity is frequently not in lines that allow LDC's to increase their imports easily; the South has its own industries to protect.

The Sources of Aid

Ever since postwar foreign aid began, there has been a question of whether it should be a national task or a multilateral one. The question has never been resolved. The proof-of-the-pudding principle indicates a movement away from strict, or "beggar my neighbor," bilateral aid and toward coordinate bilateralism, regional multilateralism, and United Nations agencies.

The first large-scale postwar efforts were almost entirely U.S.-financed: UNRRA, the U.S. bilateral loan to Great Britain, and the Marshall Plan. The first and third were administered through international organizations. UNRRA appeared initially to be a convenient device for promoting the fledgling world organization. Unfortunately, from the U.S. viewpoint, decisions were based on the one-country, one-vote principle, so it was soon rejected as inadequate [67] The Organization for European Economic Cooperation passed on to Europe the touchy task of allocating a fixed Marshall aid total, and also furnished a basis for the U.S. goal of creating a unified West that could effectively resist Soviet pressures.

The World Bank, part of the United Nations system, and nominally multilateral (both because of its voting system and because its loan authority has multinational backing), was *de facto* a device for channeling U.S. funds to the war-damaged countries. Only in the

[66] In a sense, this is what foreign aid now amounts to. The North finances export of its own surpluses. When there are no surpluses, there is a tendency for aid to become untied.

[67] Cf. Robert E. Asher, "Multilateral Versus Bilateral Aid: An Old Controversy Revisited," *International Organization*, Vol. XVI (December 1962), pp. 697–719.

1950's did it start to evolve into a lending agency for the South, and large-scale Bank borrowing in Europe is a more recent phenomenon. As the Bank has become increasingly a multilateral agency, it has spawned offshoots: the soft-loan affiliate International Development Association (IDA), and the private industry promotional agency International Finance Corporation.

The United Nations itself has not developed successfully as a large-scale lender, despite the steady expansion of its technical assistance work and the surveys and studies of the United Nations Special Fund. However, the South lost the battle to make the United Nations a large-scale aid agency in the mid-1950's. Since then, in the United Nations and at UNCTAD, poor countries have nevertheless repeatedly sponsored and voted resolutions aimed at creating a U.N. capital fund. The North, led by the United States, invariably refuses, unimpressed by the one-nation, one-vote principle as a means of distributing funds supplied by the minority.

The evidence demonstrates a steady recent trend toward multilateralism. Between 1960 and 1964, multilateral agency loan and grant disbursements to LDC's rose from $500 million annually to more than $1 billion.[68] In 1964, multilateral disbursements accounted for about 18 per cent of the Northern aid flow, compared with about 10 per cent in the mid-1950's.[69]

Probably of more importance in practice than the steady trend to use of international agencies is the increasing use of new forms of international cooperation in the bilateral aid. The most notable example is the Development Assistance Committee of the OECD. It serves a number of purposes. The DAC annual aid reviews offer a form to examine a member's performance by tacit burden-sharing criteria. It also acts (with the IBRD) as an organizing device for international aid consortia, which are devices for coordinating large-scale bilateral aid to individual developing countries. The consortium technique has been applied to India, Pakistan, Turkey, and Colombia, among others. It offers a potentially useful method of programming aid by country, very similar in effect to the intent of the World Bank supplementary finance proposal, on a coordinated bilateral basis.

From the U.S. viewpoint, DAC has been only a modest success in the effort to push Europe into carrying some of the Northern aid

[68] Includes World Bank agencies, Inter-American Development Bank, U.N. Technical Assistance, EEC Development Fund.

[69] After allowing for double-counting in the current year.

total. However, it has been useful as an arena for steady pressure to relax lending terms; both the United Kingdom and Germany have succumbed. Meanwhile, ironically, U.S. lending terms have become stiffer, thanks to Congressional refusal to allow AID to lend on IDA terms.

These efforts at coordinating bilateral aid have been supplemented by regional forms of multilateral aid on both donor and recipient sides. The Inter-American Development Bank (IDB) is the vehicle for official financial aid under the Alliance for Progress. It is primarily a device for channeling U.S. funds, but it has the advantage in recipients' eyes of being subject to a degree of genuine multilateral control over allocation of funds. IBD loans under multilateral control average about $200 million annually.

The EEC Development Fund is the only multilateral agency that gives capital grants. These go primarily to Africa, with commitment levels now averaging about $150 million annually. In a sense, the EEC fund is a Europe-Africa analog of the IDB. To extend the analogy, the IDB combines aspects of both the World Bank and the IDA. Part of the IDB funds are essentially grants of American aid administered by IDB, under the appealing title of the Social Progress Trust Fund. The EEC fund, on the other hand, gives out its aid straight, without the creation of banking and trust fund superstructures. However EEC has created a European Investment Bank which makes most of its investments in Europe with less-developed regions of the EEC as frequent beneficiaries.

The political appeal of regional development aid funds is apparently strong. UNCTAD approved two resolutions on regional development funds.[70] The United States has successfully negotiated the creation of an Asian Development Bank (ADB). This organization, with an initial capital of $1 billion, will be open both to countries in the region as donors and recipients, and to those outside the region as donors only.[71] The ten-nation board of directors will have seven regional representatives and three extra-regional ones. The initial capital is to be used for lending on self-liquidating terms, much in the manner of the World Bank. It is hoped that the Bank will receive trust funds to administer on concessional terms in the manner of IDA and the Social Progress Trust Fund. The ADB has also been envisioned by both the United States and Japan as a channel for increas-

[70] UNCTAD, *Proceedings,* Vol. I (Annexes A.IV.9 and A.IV.10), p. 48.
[71] The region is defined as Asia eastward from Iran to Japan.

ing Japanese aid levels and political commitment to the development of Southeast Asia.

Africa, too, has sought additional trappings of regionalism and attained them in part through an African Development Bank, with headquarters in Abidjan, and aspirations expressed, at least verbally, throughout the continent.

There is something inconsistent about regional development banks organized on the basis of self-liquidating loans. The World Bank has repeatedly stated that its supply of funds for self-liquidating projects in the South exceeds the effective demand. On purely economic grounds, therefore, there is some mystery involved in the creation of new organizations aimed at the same purpose. The motives are obviously political, fortified by the recipient's aspiration that they will encourage two tendencies: (1) increased flow of funds to the region in question; (2) creation of a magnet to attract funds to be channeled through these banks on concessional terms.

In addition, the voting arrangements for the regional banks give stronger weight to the South than does the World Bank voting system. The donors' interests are still well protected, but the voting system is nonetheless more congenial to the LDC members.

The proliferation of international aid efforts also reflects certain motives on the donors' part, beyond a desire to satisfy Southern aspirations for control of aid funds. First, there is the belief, fostered by the successful record of the World Bank, that international aid-giving may be more efficient than bilateral aid; specifically, more directed for developmental goals and less subject to political pressures. This feeling is reinforced by the demonstrated difficulties of using aid as a political weapon. Generally the political and institutional weight of large-scale bilateral commitments (for example, U.S. aid to India; French aid to Africa) is so great that the donors' freedom to maneuver is limited. If bilateral aid combines political and administrative disadvantages with constant reduction of freedom to maneuver, it is no wonder that the quest for multilateral alternatives is increasing.

On the other hand, despite the flurry of multilateral devices, certain donors and recipients have strong incentives to insist on predominantly bilateral assistance. Some donors feel that they do get substantial political advantage from bilateral aid, despite the difficulties. The United States has used aid as a lever in such countries as Brazil, Turkey, Colombia, Indonesia, occasionally with considerable political effectiveness. Second, some recipients, such as India, Pakistan, and the former French African states, are major beneficiaries of the present bilateral system. They have little interest in a switch to multilateralism.

The forms of multilateral aid and coordinated bilateral aid and their effects on different parties' interests are now so various that simple generalizations have lost whatever value they may once have had. Most LDC's seek more multilateral aid, if it means no net aid loss, providing there is more Southern control over allocation. Similarly, the North generally would prefer multilateral aid, even with diminished control, if it meant no increase in total aid, and if the political gains of the switch outweighed the losses.

Considering the importance that all major donors and recipients place on flexibility for themselves, the trend to multilateral activity will probably continue to be expressed largely through the various hybrid aid sources discussed earlier. The World Bank system, while still in a growth phase, cannot accommodate the parties' search for room to maneuver.[72]

The source of finance for concessional aid is always the same. Whether the paymaster is a government, a regional institution, a United Nations agency, or an international consortium, the grant element is always a transfer of resources whose real cost is paid for by individuals in the North. There may well be tactical advantages in obscuring the point, but the significance is clear. The North controls the decision as to aid sources. Its control is modified by Southern pressure, and by intra-Northern differences. But the present and future distribution of aid sources should be a relatively accurate reflection of Northern interests in the matter. Multilateralism will become the wave of the future only if these interests are served.

THE ROLE OF FOREIGN PRIVATE INVESTMENT

If coincidence of material interest were the only criterion for capital flows, then private investment in underdeveloped countries would be

[72] It can, on the other hand, accommodate other objectives. For the North, there are non-budgetary financing, avoidance of responsibility for investment choices, and an "objective" system of allocation. For the South, the principal advantage, aside from the loans themselves, is the appearance of non-interference by the North.

the primary technique for transferring capital from rich to poor countries. The foreign investor seeking profit, and the host government seeking more rapid growth of income and opportunities to raise the existing levels of technical and managerial skills, would bask in the warmth of their mutual gains. But, as we know, Northern private investment in LDC's has been far smaller than official capital flows in recent years. Private direct investment by industrial countries in underdeveloped areas has varied from $2 billion to $3 billion annually over the past decade, about one-half as much as the flow of official capital. This total is offset by large and generally unrecorded flows of private capital from developing countries to the more serene presence of industrial countries. It has been claimed that these revenue flows may exceed those that move from North to South.[73] There is little evidence of any significant increase in the North's investment, which seems to be heavily influenced by variations in petroleum companies' spending patterns.[74]

If both parties stand to gain from private investment, why isn't there more of it? The chief reasons, from the investor's viewpoint, were cited in Chapter 2: first, rates of return in underdeveloped areas do not compare favorably with those prevailing in industrial countries; second, ignorance of opportunity and uncertainty about political and market conditions in underdeveloped countries act as significant discouragements.

From the recipient's viewpoint, there are several disadvantages. The principal one is ideological opposition to foreign economic power. Another element is the high foreign exchange costs per unit of investment of the return flow of profit and interest compared with the repayment schedules on public lending.

The result of these mutual doubts is mildly comical. There is a sort of two-sided problem of split personality to overcome. The South has both ideological objections to foreign private investment and a genuine material interest in encouraging it. In grudging recognition, nominal Southern concessions proliferate (tax advantages, laws for protection of foreign investment), but are often not carried out to help foreign investors greatly.

[73] Little and Clifford, *International Aid,* pp. 219–221.

[74] DAC figures for 1965 show that Northern private investment increased to $3.5 billion, the highest annual total since 1957. It is too soon to say whether this represents a new trend, a compensating fluctuation from the unusually low 1963 level, or simply changes in statistical coverage.

The North, on the other hand, has an ideological preference for private investment, but no particular motive to invest heavily in the South. Prospective yields are generally not high enough to overcome the combined effects of risk and unfamiliarity. Therefore, Northern governments, notably the United States, in an uneasy attempt to promote their ideological preferences, have offered private investment guarantees, seeking thereby to share the risks of investment in the South. These guarantees take the form of insurance against specified risks (war, inconvertibility, and so on); or of debt issuance supported by guarantee (World Bank bonds); or of joint public-private participations (International Finance Corporation investment policies).

These efforts have not succeeded in mobilizing large amounts of Northern capital for investment in the South. The most detailed study yet made of the various risk-sharing schemes concludes:

> Clearly, they have not become "catalysts" drawing private funds directly into economic development; the term becomes meaningless when it is applied to a mechanism which requires two or three or four public dollars to move one private one. And, in any case, the magnitude of their capital-mobilizing operations is simply not great enough to cope with the problem of development assistance.[75]

Despite the conflict of ideologies and the discrepancy between aspiration and action, private investment retains substantial appeal. It implies an eye for the main chance, a search for profit that may often be a more effective force for growth than government-to-government transfers. Furthermore, direct investment can bring with it major fringe benefits in the form of technical assistance at all levels of management and operation. Finally, there may be political gains. For the donor country, private investment may mean a reduced transfer of government funds, and less involvement with the recipient in the complexities of aid project administration. For the recipient, there may be fewer political strings attached to private investment than to Northern foreign aid.

Therefore, proposals for increasing the investment flow have proliferated since the end of World War II. The principal official proposals have been: extension of investment guarantees on a bilateral or multilateral basis to cover a large variety of risks; extension by Northern governments of investment tax credits to firms that make

[75] Marina von Neumann Whitman, *Government Risk-sharing in Foreign Investment*, Princeton, Princeton University Press, 1965, p. 347.

direct investments in LDC's; increased use of joint ventures combining Northern and Southern capital, to gain the advantages of Northern finance and technology while reducing the onus of imperialism. Each of these proposals has its defects. Very broad guarantees may undermine an investor's economic incentives. Tax credits may simply give a free ride to firms that would invest anyway without providing substantial increases in the capital flow. Joint ventures may be distasteful to both parties because of the control problems that can arise.

If there is a serious interest in promoting private investment flows, none of these objections seems conclusive. In fact, if the transfer of technology is deemed to be particularly important, then there is a good case for having foreign aid finance the investment by paying private firms to construct and operate plants in the South; train the management, sales, and work forces; and progressively turn over the facilities to local management.

None of these devices will prove revolutionary, however. The basic problems are still the gulf between Northern and Southern ideology, and the relatively modest rates of discounted return that await Northern investors.

CONCLUSIONS: THE STRATEGY OF AID

Somehow, in the welter of gapmanship, of Southern pressure and of strident voices calling for more aid in the name of almost anything, we may forget some of the simple points about aid.

Aid may be small in terms of the North's ability to pay, but it is big to many Southern nations. For such countries as Turkey, Brazil, Chile, India, and some of the French-speaking African states, capital flows from the North are vital elements of the existing politico-economic structure. Foreign capital inflows to LDC's from all sources were probably about $10 billion in nominal value in 1964. This amounts in aggregates to about 5 per cent of Southern GNP, or by a more valid analogy, to about one-third of the annual value of Southern gross capital formation in that year. For some countries (for example, Israel, Bolivia, Chile, Liberia, Tunisia, Algeria, Korea), the capital inflows were larger than domestic savings.

Second, this means that no matter how one believes aid should be handled, it necessarily implies a substantial possibility for Northern influence over Southern behavior. Naturally, the room for maneuver is greatly reduced by a number of factors, principally: competition among donors (both North-North and East-West); the political inertia of existing commitments; the political dangers of the obvious attempt to use aid as a lever, even if there were no alternative aid sources for the recipient; ignorance about the relationship between specific policies and donors' long-term goals (Cf. Chapter 1).

If we look on the aid process in economic terms, the effort to exert influence should be viewed as a joint effort by donor and recipient to meet agreed goals. It should be possible to reward performance by increasing aid and to penalize inefficiency by reducing it.

In view of the limiting factors described above, such economic targets can be only the justification for marginal aid changes—variations of perhaps the order of 25 per cent maximum above or below existing aid levels. The presence of conflicting goals makes blanket threats and promises ("if they don't devalue, we'll cut off the aid") entirely incredible, except if there is a prior political motive for large changes. In that case, recipients' development policies are largely irrelevant.

But marginal changes in aid can be important. Suppose, for example, that we are convinced that India's economic development requires more fertilizer output and lower fertilizer price to food price ratios. If India is squeezed for both food and foreign exchange, she is better off allowing foreigners to provide fertilizer factories, particularly if the alternative is less aid. Naturally governments don't like to reverse policies under pressure, but there is usually a price at which it makes sense to concede.

The donor must make the price credible; hence the uselessness of excessive threats. Each Northern aid negotiator should include in his brief a sheet of paper, bearing one sentence: Will we really do it? If the answer is no, there is still no harm in hinting retaliation or bonus. But it must not be presented as an ultimatum; because an ultimatum implies a possible challenge. When the donor, inevitably, backs down, he loses credibility in future negotiations.[76]

Aid strategy is a rather fine instrument in respect of economic goals, one that has perhaps been used improperly. The reason is simple, but reflects no great credit on donors' perceptiveness. Because political considerations are paramount, proponents of the all-or-noth-

[76] Of course, if the donor or recipient fosters, deliberately or otherwise, a reputation for great irrationality, he lessens the chances of being challenged.

ing approach to aid policy invariably lose. Even the suggestion for smaller changes tends to be discussed in donor governments as a predominantly political issue. The opportunities for economic influence are lost, often in the name of political goals that would not be genuinely affected by small changes in aid.

Aid strategy has another face. To use influence effectively, you also have to know what you are doing—in this case, the economic effects of policy changes. Unfortunately, there is not much evidence that the use of influence and the knowledge of how to use it are effectively combined. This is the standard complaint of the structuralist economists against IMF policies. Whatever its merits in that case, the effectiveness of donor-induced policy shifts is far from universally endorsed, in North or South. This uncertainty is no surprise. People in LDC's clearly respond to economic incentives, but the structural economic relations, and those that link politics and economics, are not the same as in the North. Hence Northern advice is worth less abroad than at home. Furthermore, the costs of following bad advice are greater in the South because it is poorer.

This leads to an important corollary for aid strategy. If a donor wants to induce someone to change his policies, he should be prepared to underwrite the costs. This is clearly an appropriate policy for economic motives where a subsidy is desirable anyway. But it is equally appropriate in cases where there are no specifically economic grounds for subsidizing change. It is essentially a form of incentive pay for uncertainty. As an illustration, suppose the donor wants Peru to use new hatrack-producing techniques in order to stimulate greater efficiency in the Peruvian hatrack industry and more purchase of donor's hatrack-turning lathes. Peru may be reluctant to do so because it believes the new method will raise costs, not lower them. The donor should be prepared to underwrite at least part of the risk. This kind of consideration is particularly important for agricultural changes where the producer may fear that change will bring irreparable loss, and for tinkering with foreign exchange rates and controls, where the LDC is likely to view in advance any change as a change for the worse, destined to bankrupt it internationally.[77]

The hatrack example leads us to our final point. The search for coincidence of interest should be the guiding principle. Prebisch claims that the transfer of aid is costless to the North in a certain

[77] Thus IMF-induced devaluations often include an aid commitment from donors who support the change.

sense, because the South spends all its reserves in the North anyway. This is fine as a sort of second-best solution for unemployment, but with Europe and North America both producing at close to full capacity, the argument doesn't stand up—the North is paying the real cost of aid.[78]

It is hard to find much coincidence of material interest in concessional aid. Food aid is one example; support of genuine self-help measures another (but this is a more complex story than models fueled by savings and import propensities imply). A third is as yet largely prospective, and likely to become important only if Northern defense requirements fall. If aid funds can be presented as a major customer for Northern industrial capacity, as military budgets are today, it will naturally tend to build up and sustain its own lobby. A strong Northern producer interest is the South's best friend in court. However, current trends are all in the opposite direction. The North has generally full employment, rising defense budgets, and declining proportions of combined GNP devoted to aid.

The conclusions, provisionally, seem straightforward. There is not much short-run prospect for large increases in nominal aid levels, unless there should be major reductions in donors' military budgets, because in Northern eyes the current price seems right for the diverse collection of benefits received.[79] This reinforces the argument cited above for using effectively whatever influence can be wisely brought to bear for economic advantage. Development resources will be tight on both sides, for different reasons. It is important to use them as catalytic agents, particularly if the reaction favors all parties. If the search for mutual benefits from aid fails, then it is appropriate to seek other approaches, where mutual benefits are clearer. However, for donors, aid possesses the advantage of flexibility, for which there is no ready substitute. Therefore, there is no prospect that aid will be abandoned, despite the sentiments of frustration it induces in North and South alike.

[78] Unless all aid is in the form of surplus commodities, which would be produced anyway.

[79] There is plenty of room however for increases in the real transfer. The scare value of debt service figures plays a useful role here, for aid partisans.

CHAPTER NINE

Policy for the Rich Nations

Most people seem to agree that people in poor countries should be better off. The Northern consensus is "progressive" in appearance and coincides thereby with Southern aims.

But aspirations are cheap. Everyone longs for the almost perfect state. What price in terms of acceptance of change is he willing to pay to reach it? If there is nothing to lose, people may be willing to support radical changes. As the risks of loss increase relative to anticipated benefits, the subjective willingness to "pay" for changes declines. Therefore, people generally don't share identical visions of felicity. Even if they do, the same actors play different roles in your aspirations and mine. At best, we must remain both allies and opponents in the pursuit of material goals. The market place cannot impersonally regulate each man's desire for wealth and power to everyone's satisfaction.

We have seen that the North has relatively little to gain in the short run from Southern prosperity. The political and security motives, which in this case are the dominant ones for granting concessions, are too uncertain to merit larger investments, except under the spur of direct military threat. The political goal, a friendly South, or at least a neutral one, is worth a good deal, but its relation to economic concessions that the South demands is not clearly demonstrable.

As for the other Northern motives: (1) economic aims are clearly subsidiary, not justifying substantial concessions; (2) humanitarian goals are presumably now met by the present level of aid; (3) the desire of some Northern countries to cut a good figure in the eyes of other rich countries (notably the United States) and in those of the LDC's is of diminishing importance because American generosity itself shows evidence of flagging, and the United States thereby becomes a lightning rod for Southern ire toward the North.

This is what North-South economic controversy is about. The Atlantic countries want to see Asia, Africa, and South America bask in material comforts, but they are not willing to pay a high price for the prospect. Therefore, they propose, as is fair enough, that internal reforms set the pace. The South also seeks its own prosperity, more intensely. It suggests, in the remembrance of ancient injustice, economic and racial, that the North pay today's sacrifice, and thereby expiate centuries of exploitation and scorn.

The North therefore has already decided, not deliberately, but by the play of events, what degree of "cooperation" serves its political interests and its sense of justice, in light of other goals. From this point on, barring dramatic political changes, the South cannot look to increases in Northern largesse. The growth of its well-being must come more and more from its own resources (whether used for domestic production or for export), or from exploitation of Northern self-interest.

In this light, UNCTAD is a halfway house on a detour. A halfway house, because it correctly perceives that the unqualified demand for more aid is not fruitful in current conditions; a detour, because the trade concessions are often perceived by the North as either a demand for disguised aid, or a demand for economic adjustment through trade, that the North is not willing to make. Therefore, UNCTAD fails to hit the mark squarely.

It must be admitted that the mark is elusive. What can simultaneously benefit North and South? If the issues are strictly "economic," the answer is trade and investment. But we have seen that these are not usually enough in themselves to assure the growth rates for LDC's that North and South both aspire to. If they were, there would be no significant international aspects to the development problem.

The other avenues of mutual gain are noneconomic. We have seen that the North's present level of concessions is the pragmatic measure of those benefits in Northern eyes.

The South, if it wants to focus on more aid or sharp increases in trade, must find other avenues than these. The most promising line, of course, in the absence of major sources of mutual benefit, is to play on fears. This means playing Northern powers off against each other.

The classic method is to utilize the East-West power struggle. India has proven particularly adept at this tactic. But there are a number of constraints. For the method to work best, East and West should each believe that its welfare will be affected if Country X shifts allegiance and that a shift in allegiance is a consequence of granting or withholding its aid to Country X. But these conditions are only rarely met in practice. The Atlantic countries are likely to believe that changes in the level of concessions will have no significant effects on allegiance, either because of what Country X is likely to do or else because of what the Russians or Chinese are likely to do. Country X is likely to face indifference in response to its suit, or else token concessions. Genuine increases in Eastern or Western efforts may depend on concessions in return—tokens of sincerity from X. The cleverer and the bolder the latter's diplomacy, the larger his potential gain. But as the great powers tend to reach a stabilized global level of concessions, the Southern task becomes harder. Boldness may be rewarded only by loss of support from both sides. Furthermore, the stabilization of effective concessions means that Southern countries are competing with each other for the parcelling out of a fixed sum. It then becomes uncertain whether it is wiser to appear more or less erratic or more or less reliable, because the decision becomes closely conditioned on others' behavior.

As the profitability of cold war bi-polar badminton declines, the South can look for a partial substitute in the breakup of the tight East-West blocks into looser federations of interest. Thus, it becomes possible to play off Russia against China, or the United States against the Common Market. This is currently the most popular exercise, manifesting itself largely in competitive demands for preferential or liberal trade concessions. Like the East-West competition, it will undoubtedly lead to certain gains for the South, although, predictably, less than the South would like. We should expect the South, as a matter of strategy, to persist along these lines.

Ultimately, any substantial increase in concessions must come from changing perceptions of the issues, probably as catalyzed by new trends in political relations; or, in the long run, by the vast prospective growth of Northern income. By the year 2000, Northern per capita product should increase by a minimum of 100 per cent and possibly by as much as twice that amount in favorable circumstances. At such high levels of income, it would be relatively easy for the North to make much greater concessions than it now does, at a smaller relative sacrifice. Furthermore, by that time, continued Northern growth will almost necessarily increase Southern prosperity, through effects on demand for commodities and, ultimately for manufactured products. But this is cold comfort for the South today in its search to raise itself by others' bootstraps. It is almost irrevocably faced for the time being with the need to look to itself for succour. This can be beneficial if it focuses attention and action on some of the domestic barriers to prosperity.

Stimulating economic development is largely a question of elevating society's valuation of economic activity and its valuation of the desire to accumulate capital and knowledge for productive use. In this sense, barriers to development are ultimately domestic in origin, and not basically economic in nature. At the more immediate level of domestic economic policy, there are a number of obvious steps that could be taken, if political conditions allow. The list is a familiar one: realistic exchange rates, elimination of excessive protectionism, encouragement of greater agricultural productivity, promotion of reasonably stable price levels, appropriate educational policies, provision of a relatively unfettered business climate for private industry and for the economic motive in public enterprise. It is far from certain that any of these measures will produce dramatic effects in the absence of a political and social situation where people are willing to pay a relatively high price, in terms of traditional values, for the benefits of economic progress.

Although the economic development of any nation necessarily implies a reordering of internal values and policies, the economic issues are not purely domestic ones. I believe that whatever the defects of LDC's economic policies, further aid and trade concessions are also necessary for many underdeveloped countries. The foreign exchange gap is real enough when defined as a distance that separates aspiration from reality.

The persistence of foreign exchange deficits, the inability to shift resources, the failure to make a rapid and effective development of indigenous sources of skills and capital all point in the same direction. These problems obviously reflect domestic barriers to growth, but it takes a particularly doltish form of attachment to "self-help" doctrines to claim that the remedies are therefore exclusively domestic.

In my opinion the underlying issue is ethical. Economic relations between North and South are, from the Northern viewpoint, satisfactory enough right now. It is on the ethical plane that the present situation is scandalous. One-third of the world lives in comfort and two-thirds in misery. Yet no day spares us the edification of lectures by the prosperous North on the South's grievous economic sins. It is all inescapably reminiscent of economists' nineteenth century diatribes against the idle and spendthrift poor in the emerging industrial states of that era. Unfortunately this century has not yet found on the international scene its Labour Party or its Bismarck to offer from left or right the politically effective retort to such self-serving homilies.

At the same time as the North offers the South free course work on the economics of perfect competition, its own economic policies continue to show a built-in bias against Southern exports, while foreign aid levels stagnate or decline. The North tries to rationalize its failings in a variety of ways. We hear for example that the South isn't taking advantage of existing trade opportunities, that it is now getting all the aid that it can effectively absorb, that the World Bank has more funds to lend than projects to lend to, and so on.

From the ethical viewpoint, this is a preposterous sham. First, as we saw in Chapters 6 and 7, trade restrictions *do* harm the South, whether or not there are unexploited current opportunities. Second, the proposition that current aid levels meet absorptive capacity requirements is at best, by stretching the point to its limit, an admission of Northern failure to cope with the development problem. In fact, it is something much uglier—a refusal to accept responsibility for others, because the South is weak and the North is strong. To make this ripe fish palatable to Northern consciences, policy makers sweeten it with foreign aid and spice it with self-help exhortations.

The standard retort to accusations of indifference is to point out that political realities foreclose a more generous policy. But, as an ethical matter, this is beside the point. It is precisely those realities that constitute the moral defect.

I am not prepared to exhort in the interests of a latter-day moral rearmament aimed at relieving world poverty. Public attitudes toward such matters change with glacial slowness, except under the spur of perceived material interest. Therefore sudden Northern apprehension of the ethical failings of material gluttony offers little hope to the South. But I think it is important for the rich countries to be aware that they are in effect choosing to help keep the South poor. This may be totally irrelevant to political or economic interests, although it encourages all-too-evident nationalist and racial resentments. These cannot benefit the North in the long run.

This is a digression from our basic theme of North-South economic relations, although in a sense it underlies them. Let us return to the issues of economic policy, and to a series of policy recommendations based on the proposition that only an awareness of mutual gains offers any short run basis for increasing North-South economic cooperation.

This chapter offers a summary of what I have said and tries to tie together those elements that are related and to separate those that are not. It is based on the unverifiable assumption that it is in the rich countries' best interests, defined at all levels of concern, to promote quicker economic development in the South. Underlying that is another assumption: that virtually no program of political action verifiably betters everyone's lot; if universal gain were the criterion, political choices would be restricted indeed.

FOREIGN AID: COSTS AND BENEFITS

Foreign aid is cheap for donors. The real cost of official Northern aid is $4.5 billion annually. Its cost (and its value to recipients) is further reduced by aid-tying. Furthermore, from a certain viewpoint, food surplus disposal is not a cost of aid, but rather a cost of domestic farm programs. With these modifications, the cost of the aid bill may be not much more than $3–$3.5 billion.

This aid becomes cheaper every year, because Northern income is rising, whereas aid expenditures have not changed much since 1962. This helps to explain why aid is continued. It costs the North an ever-declining percentage of combined GNP (probably about 0.4 per cent in 1964), and the uncertainties of abandoning it are not worth the risks, particularly in view of the substantial political costs of going back on commitments.

But if we assume that it serves Northern interests to promote development elsewhere, then the cheapness of aid also serves to explain its frequent failures as a catalyst. The success stories of foreign aid are largely in countries where per capita transfers have been vast compared with worldwide averages: Taiwan, Israel, Greece, Yugoslavia, Spain. The point seems clear. To promote economic growth, increase economic aid wherever it can be used productively.[1] This is not to suggest that Laos or Chad can effect instant industrial revolutions as a result of massive capital transfers. In Allyn Young's phrase, the human material is resistant to change. The more primitive the social and economic organization, the greater the relative role of technical assistance, and of investment in education and training, and, naturally, the longer the time horizon for attaining a modern industrial state.

But where, as in much of Latin America and Asia, problems of capital and organization loom large, productive increases in economic aid are possible. It is obvious that the North has barely tapped its constructive energies to increase Southern welfare. "Absorptive capacities" are a barrier in these countries only because foreign aid is a relatively low priority for the North compared with domestic concerns. The vast reservoir of Northern technical skills could be used to construct any kind of industrial facility, to train any kind of skilled worker, to operate and maintain facilities or market new output. It is largely a question of will and organization. At present, the North lacks the will, and both Northern aid agencies and Southern economies are deficient in organization. The modern industrial corporation is the great promoter of material culture. Partly because the will to promote Southern welfare is deficient, the energies of Northern industry have not been put to work, except as contractors and suppliers. Yet it is obviously they who should build factories, organize marketing systems, train labor forces, and turn a going concern over to majority local ownership, if that is a goal.

This is an essential role of Northern corporations in the North. In the South, generally speaking, the risks and the difficulties of doing business outweigh the gains, except for extractive industry. Thus Northern corporate investment in non-extractive industry remains low. In order to expand their operations, they may need various forms of subsidy. It is possible to use aid as a subsidy device of mutual benefit to Northern firms and Southern development aims. One possible method of operation is discussed below.

A second source of mutual benefit is agricultural surplus disposal,

[1] Aid does not have to be used productively, of course, only in the sense of productive plant and equipment. Technical assistance is obviously a case in point, as is consumption subsidy in certain conditions. In a certain sense, much of the foreign aid offered today is indirectly a form of consumption subsidy. It allows LDC's to finance nationalist economic policies that otherwise might be beyond their reach.

as discussed in Chapter 8. It harms the interests of city people in the North, and farmers in the South, but there are ways of circumventing their objections. There is always some combination of subsidy, price support, and production quota that can be reasonably satisfactory to both farmer and consumer in the rich countries. For example, the price of food sold to domestic consumers in the North can be reduced, and farmers can be compensated by the increased production quotas for the food aid program.

Farmers in the South can be encouraged to increase productivity by a number of devices, despite the price-depressing effects of food aid. For example, the proceeds of food aid sales can be devoted to agricultural investment, subsidy of agricultural import prices, and training. Obviously, all such arrangements are essentially optical illusions, from a purely logical viewpoint. Farm investments can be subsidized without food aid, and Northern consumers can pay less for food without simultaneous increases of food aid. But it is precisely such bargaining techniques that allow political compromises to be forged.

A third line of mutual advantage arises from forms of aid that promise both acceptable growth rates and a reduction in aid below what it would otherwise be. The best examples of such direct aid techniques are investments in national birth control programs in overpopulated countries, and in certain forms of education, particularly skilled labor training. Massive investment in education at all levels is probably economically unwarranted, and provides neither North nor South with immediate advantage. For example, a vast supply of primary school graduates would cost West Africa a great deal, without adding enough to productivity or political stability to warrant the expense.[2] However, one objection to overeducation in LDC's —its costliness—could be overcome with large enough foreign subsidies. As the supply of graduates increases, their price would quickly fall. This presents the obvious difficulty. People don't like to earn less money than they are accustomed to, and it is not clear that, politically, the gains of the new educated class compensate for the losses of the old. Nonetheless, development requires vast increases in human capital, in that some of this painful adjustment is inevitable. Obviously, the best way to arrange it, if we want to avoid too much political turmoil, is to respond first to the most urgent political and economic needs. The economic requirement seems to be primarily for

[2] W. Arthur Lewis, "Education and Economic Development," *International Social Science Journal,* Vol. 14 (1962), pp. 685–699.

secondary and adult education.[3] The political requirement is probably strongest for primary education. Therefore, politics and economics lead in different directions, so that the cost of meeting both goals is probably beyond the capacity of most underdeveloped countries, in light of other goals. This fact simply restresses the advantages to be gained from external subsidies to education, appropriately designed.

The case for supporting birth control programs is apparently overwhelming, on economic grounds. It has been argued that the productivity of investment in birth control in LDC's is of the order of one hundred times as great as investments in production.[4] In the United States, a government-sponsored citizens' committee has called for annual U.S. expenditures of $100 million for birth control programs in LDC's.[5] It can be argued legitimately that the "returns" to investment in birth control are not always superior to those in production (if they were, we could achieve both universal prosperity and a Shaker's nirvana by sterilizing all males everywhere). Nevertheless, for such countries as India, Pakistan, Turkey, Ceylon, the issue is not in doubt, nor are the potential savings to North and South alike. Consequently we can expect that, for different reasons, Northern aid will concentrate increasingly on raising farm output, lowering human fertility, and educating the survivors.

Another avenue of aid increase, as discussed in Chapter 8, can stem from the discrepancy between nominal and real costs of aid. As we have seen, this is the source of debt service problems. The North may find that it serves its own interests best, as well as those of the South, by converting its loans to grants or near-grants.

It may seem somewhat surprising to assert that both sides could gain from conversion of loans to grants; but the argument is simple. The South's gains would be material, while those of the North would be political. The North may find it more advantageous to give away its money by philanthropy rather than to lose it by default.

It would be wrong to assume from this discussion of the search for congruence that existing aid programs somehow offer no advantages for the North. If that were so, there would be no aid. The present level is the North's right price for the diverse collection of benefits discussed in Chapter 1.

[3] *Ibid.*, pp. 689–694.

[4] Stephen Enke, "The Economic Aspects of Slowing Population Growth," *Economic Journal*, Vol. LXXXVI (March 1966), pp. 44–56.

[5] White House Conference on International Cooperation. *National Citizen's Commission Report of the Committee on Population*, Washington, D.C., November 1965.

The donors' persistent dissatisfaction with aid, most strongly expressed in the two principal donor countries, the United States and France, should be heavily discounted, as a guide to the future. It is largely a safety-valve for the irritation that naturally arises from the rather loose connection between aid expenditures and political results. Since no one has yet suggested a cheaper and more acceptable alternative (and since the major powers demonstrate no inclination to let the rest of the world alone), it is safe to assume that waves of anti-aid sentiment are in the same category as opposition to the national debt. It is an emotional rallying cry that makes aid increases difficult to legislate in those countries, without succeeding in reducing existing levels.

I have previously pointed out that, in a sense, donors' real costs approach zero when there is substantial excess capacity and unemployment—although, except for farm surpluses, that fact has had relatively little effect on aid levels.[6] When full employment prevails in the North, then the resource cost of aid is real enough. More aid means, in the short run at least, less of some other expenditure, public or private. This may act as an additional force to discourage aid, although it is partly offset by the more rapid growth of capacity and output (and therefore of disposable resources) associated with full employment.

Full employment often brings with it, as we have seen, inflationary pressures and balance of payments problems. Export surpluses may decline,[7] and demand for imports will increase. Therefore aid —even tied aid—may become a target for attack. When this happens, commercial policy reforms may take on considerable appeal, compared with official capital transfers.

PRIVATE INVESTMENT POLICY

Until recent years, of course, the dominant source of capital transfers was not foreign aid, but private investment, in the form of both bond purchases and direct investment.

[6] *Economic Aid,* Chapter 3. One of the major reasons for this, in the United States at least, is the practice of establishing a government budget ceiling as an artificial, but very effective, constraint on total national expenditure.

[7] Although as we saw in Chapter 2, this was clearly not what happened in Europe and Japan during the period after the Korean War.

Since the end of World War II, foreign private investment in LDC's has accounted for a minor and decreasing percentage of total North-South capital transfers. In recent years it seems to have stabilized at a level of about $2.5 billion annually. Most of this flow is in the form of direct investment, although a large fraction is in the form of suppliers' credits. The direct investment is largely in mineral extraction and materials processing. This pattern is a radical change from that of the 19th century, when bond purchases accounted for ⅔ to ¾ of all foreign investment. Today, purchase of World Bank bonds is the only significant element of private portfolio investment in the South. The failure of the South to attract larger amounts of private capital has certainly contributed to holding down rates of economic growth, as well as to the unwanted dependence on foreign aid.

The foreign private investment problem in North-South relations can perhaps best be characterized as a case of dual schizophrenia. The South has ideological objections to foreign direct investment, but a material need for it, as one catalyst of growth. The North has an ideological preference for private investment as an agent of growth, but no great material need to invest in developing countries. The result is predictable. The North preaches the virtues of private investment, but does most of its foreign investing in industrial countries—venturing elsewhere primarily in search of minerals. The South plays a balancing game, simultaneously trying to attract foreign investors by model legislation and frightening them away by a formidable combination of controls and expressions of hostility, the latter usually coinciding with election campaigns or other periods of domestic political disarray.

Although there are genuine economic and political problems associated with foreign investment in poor countries (resentment of foreign control, foreign exchange costs of repatriated profits or debt service, and the like), no one seriously questions that foreign investment can promote LDC growth, if the political hurdles can be crossed on the Southern side and the economic-cum-risk problems can be overcome in the North.

Let us look first at the Southern problem. It is probable that in most underdeveloped countries the only way to break through the barriers of suspicion and unfamiliarity is to exorcise the specter of foreign control. This in effect means transforming the foreign entrepreneur into a co-owner, manager, or agent. There are a number of devices for accomplishing this: local participation requirements, management contracts, agreements to turn over control to local partners after a specified time. The proliferation of guarantees, tax exemptions, and so on, to foreign investors is only a partial substitute at best because neither side trusts the situation of foreign economic control in new countries. In a sense, the guarantees and other inducements, whether offered by North or South, may simply serve to enhance the investor's feeling that the situation is basically unsafe. Such feelings are not necessarily permanent. When the profit prospects are good and supply sources considered essential, as in investment in raw materials sources by integrated international companies, then the inducements aren't needed. Or if the inducements are sufficient, and the political prospects favorable (Puerto Rico, Hong Kong), investor inertia can be overcome. As a general proposition, however, the greatest difficulty, in Southern eyes, is ideological and can be overcome only by promoting new forms of international cooperation in the private sector.

Before discussing these, we must view the issues through Northern eyes. Rates of return for foreign investment in most developing countries are usually not very high compared with alternative uses of capital.[8] When this fact is coupled with risk considerations, investment in LDC's is hardly enticing. Each side then tends to think that he is playing a cat-and-mouse game. But there are, to borrow a luminous phrase, two cats and no mice. The South believes that the North will obey imperialist theory and be anxious to plunge in following the lure of profits. The Northern investor doesn't see much profit forthcoming, and awaits further concessions in the belief that the South will "need" foreign investment. In these circumstances, if each party is patient enough, the world can grow considerably older before there is much progress.

What kinds of new initiatives could be taken to increase the flow? Two, already under consideration, are Northern in inspiration. First, the U.S. Congress has been asked to approve a program of tax credits for those who are willing to make certain kinds of investment in the South. The larger the percentage of investment credited against income taxes, the greater the effect. Second, the OECD has sponsored a proposal for multilateral investment guarantees that would protect investors against non-commercial risks. Both measures are probably desirable. Tax credits will encourage investments even when profit

[8] Kamarck, "The Financial Experience of Lenders and Investors."

rates are low; multilateral guarantee programs will presumably reduce the risk discount that investors must apply in view of political uncertainties.

Neither initiative is aimed at the problem of control. Many devices have been suggested,[9] but none has been translated into action on any substantial scale. The South is the real loser, because the transfer of know-how, if appropriately organized, is probably even more valuable than the increase in capital.

Therefore, one line of approach may be to let foreign aid (or increased sale of IBRD obligations under interest subsidy) provide the capital while Northern corporations furnish the skills. Construction of aid-financed industrial facilities is typically open for national or international bidding in the North. This practice should be extended to include management of the facilities for a specified period, training of labor and staff, build-up of sales, maintenance, and other marketing services. By the end of the period, the contractor would progressively have turned over control to local private or public ownership. The contractor's reward would be in the form of management fees and a share of profits.

The advantage of such a scheme is that it can harness both the energies and national interests of Northern industry without running into the nearly insuperable barrier of Southern nationalism. It can begin on a small scale and be progressively extended at a rate that would reflect not only its contribution to Southern industrial development, but also the extent of its political appeal in the North.

Whether this device or others are unsuccessful, a willingness on both sides to experiment with new initiatives will be a major condition of increasing the level of private capital flows. If the will is not in evidence, then both North and South will only enmesh themselves deeper in the aid dilemmas that we have already reviewed at length.

COMMERCIAL POLICY

Increased capital flows will in general raise LDC demand for imports. Therefore, policies to stimulate capital transfers should be accompa-

[9] See P. N. Rosenstein-Rodan, "A New Philosophy of International Investment for the Second Half of the Twentieth Century," paper presented to IEA Round Table, Washington, D.C., July 1965.

nied by measures to stimulate trade. In theory, the "solution" to the search for mutual gain from trade lies in liberal trade policies. But as we saw in Chapters 5 and 6, the world is less simple than the theory, and it is often easier for the North to give away capital than to increase its own welfare through trade concessions. This is most likely to be true when business is bad. The return to protectionism that characterized the decade of the Great Depression is the most eloquent testimony.

On the other hand, when business is prosperous and prices are rising, the situation may be quite different, for two distinct reasons. First, MFN tariff reductions or preferential concessions increase the supply of goods available, thus tending to hold prices down.[10] For a Northern country facing unwanted price pressures, a move to increase trade offers the dual advantage of combating inflation and building up political capital in the South.

The second advantage of commercial policy concessions reflects balance-of-payments factors, and is not equally beneficial to all countries. We have seen that preferences will initially affect North-South trade in three ways, from the viewpoint of any one Northern country. First, it will reduce exports. Second, it will switch the source of imports from Northern suppliers to Southern suppliers. These two effects are forms of trade diversion. Third, it will increase total imports, thereby creating trade.

The combined result of these effects, up to this point in the argument, is to increase the foreign exchange available to the South as a whole, and to reduce each Northern country's exchange reserves, as well as those of the North as a whole. But there is a second set of effects to be considered that *may* offset some countries' payments losses, although it cannot offset those of the North as a whole. The South has more international purchasing power, which it may use to buy from the North thus possibly improving some countries' payments compared with the situation before preferences.

I argued in Chapter 6, from fragmentary evidence, that the United States might gain on balance, in payments terms, from a move to preferences. Its manufactured exports are largely not competitive with those of the South, while the South's propensity to import from the United States out of increased earnings is higher than that of Eu-

[10] In the early 1960's, the French government used tariff reductions as a conscious anti-inflationary device. It operated through two effects: supply increase and a warning to producers to show restraint in price policies.

rope. Therefore, unless the effect of preferences on import creation is markedly greater in the United States than elsewhere in the North, then America's balance of payments would benefit from a system of generalized Northern preferences. However, more analysis of the data than has yet been done would be needed to test this hypothesis.

It does indicate, however, a potential community of interest between the United States and the developing countries that has been largely overlooked by American policy makers. It seems irrational for America to be the vanguard of opposition to preferences when it has perhaps less to lose from a preferential system than any other major industrial power. U.S. policy seems peculiarly inadequate politically when we consider that Europe and Japan have used the United States as a lightning rod in refusing Southern demands. It is easy to understand that America would be willing to pay the price if the political and economic gains warrant it. But the roots of policy appear to be watered by mystical springs when a nation goes out of its way to oppose changes that may bring it benefits while it allows those who may suffer losses to parade as frustrated philanthropists.

I argued in Chapter 6 that mutual benefit would emerge from both free trade and preferences, although a move toward either lessens Southern benefits from the other. The case for general MFN reductions is stronger politically than the case for preferences. It benefits the North more, it fits in with recent Northern practice, and may well offer substantial benefits to the South, if the right products are included in the bargain. It seems obvious that the South, at least those countries that have industrial capacity, would benefit more from a liberal system of preferences.

But either alternative should, from the viewpoint of a full-employment North, be preferable to inaction, because both help to combat inflation. The creation of the EEC, and of the pool of migrant labor it encourages, plays such a role in Western Europe. The U.S. interest clearly lies in finding a similar external source for additional supply, providing its payments problems are not aggravated as a result. On these grounds, the United States is in a strong position in GATT negotiations. If its partners are unwilling to agree to MFN concessions, the United States has only to beat the drums for the alternative of generalized preferences for underdeveloped countries.

In these matters, the United States has tended to let its own interests, and those of the South, be subordinated to the goal of building a North Atlantic Community. The goal is appealing, but is unlikely to be realized by present policies. There is not much use in building institutions when there is not enough will to unite. There is no harm in the efforts unless the price is too high. But the United States now finds itself in the position of a bridegroom left too long waiting at the altar. To remain faithful for a while offers suitable testimony of devotion. After a time, it becomes embarrassing, costly, and somewhat obsessive. Even if the suitor is wealthy, there is not much point in building empty houses to capture the lingering perfume of a lady who at least knows what she doesn't want.

For the United States, the position is particularly ridiculous, because it is wealthy, its "losses" from concessions to the South or from less Atlantic cooperation negligible, and its freedom of action, in ideology and politics, correspondingly great. If Europe is unwilling either to move toward Atlantic unity or to make genuine concessions to LDC demands, then Europe should take the heat. The United States gains nothing from the dual privilege of being rebuffed by Europe and attacked by the South, in pursuit of goals that, for the time, have been sidetracked by events.

From the viewpoint of U.S. self-interest, the clearest source of mutual benefit in establishing a preferential system would arise from linking temporary preferences to further MFN reductions. The United States is among the group of industrial countries that considers it important to press for liberal world trade policies. Extension of temporary preferences can be used as a device to that end. The North could, for example, offer a 50 per cent tariff preference for LDC manufactured products with the understanding that over a period of years the North would progressively lower its MFN rates toward the preferential level. This technique has several advantages over other proposed preferential systems. Because it is temporary, it avoids the habitual enshrining of infant industry protection. Because it discriminates against Northern suppliers, it gives developed countries an incentive to reduce tariffs in order to be able to compete more effectively with LDC's in foreign markets. Furthermore, the process of reducing MFN tariff levels will tend over the years to eliminate existing trade blocs. From the viewpoint of those who oppose the divisive political and economic consequences of these blocs, this may well be the strongest argument for tying preferential concessions into the general framework of commercial policy negotiation. Of course, this point is equally obvious to the EEC or other trading blocs, and may be, from their viewpoint, a good reason to resist any link between preferences and worldwide tariff reductions. But the proposal would have considerable appeal for LDC's, thereby increasing the political costs of opposition. In accordance with the time-honored principle of letting the cook take the heat, it may make good political sense for the United States to lead the movement for temporary preferences, and let those who oppose the proposal provide their own air conditioning.

The domestic politics of trade concessions are always difficult. But it seems likely that the present conjuncture is relatively favorable. Inflationary pressures, impatience with the results of GATT negotiations, and the probable balance-of-payments advantages of preferential concessions may prove to be the catalysts for a synthesis that only yesterday seemed improbable. The political appeal of preferences in the United States is, potentially at least, in transition from a strong negative to a point where the balance of advantages may appear to outweigh those of any feasible alternative.

But there is not much point to initiating new policies at the price of considerable domestic pulling and hauling unless the benefits are there. First, how would they affect the South? The answer is not very informative. One thing alone is sure. If the North lowers its tariffs on Southern exports, the South will benefit. The benefits are likely to be greatest when existing tariff structures discriminate against Southern exports, as they now do in three situations. First, the current practice of escalating tariffs according to the degree of value added by manufacture clearly discriminates against raw materials producers.[11]

Second, GATT negotiations, following so-called "principal supplier" rules, tend to exclude low-wage industries from consideration. Third, agricultural protectionism in the North discriminates against Southern exports—the principal examples are sugar, rice, peanut oil, tobacco. In the long run, of course, the South may turn out to have comparative advantage in other competing products.

Although we cannot estimate accurately the short- or long-run value of MFN or preferential concessions to the South, it is safe to say that the gains could be substantial, increasing over time. From the Southern viewpoint, broad-based genuine preferential treatment is economically preferable, although it incorporates political risks that might be avoided by MFN systems.

For the North, as we have seen, preferences are a "second best"

[11] Paradoxically, the discrimination is likely to be greater when the North, in the name of equity, reduces revenue tariffs on raw materials. The result is to increase effective protection of manufactures. The solution, however, is not to raise raw materials tariffs, but to lower those on manufactured products.

alternative whose economic and political luster varies with the situation of each country. It is enhanced economically by domestic prosperity, or by favorable balance-of-payments effects. It is enhanced politically by the prospects of reducing Southern dependence on aid or by shifting the onus of obstructionism to other countries (although the gains from playing "Dodgem" with preferences are likely to be soon exhausted). Its greatest appeal is probably as a device for encouraging multilateral tariff reductions.

The bridge between policy on manufactures and commodity policy lies in reducing the tariffs on processed raw materials. It has been cogently argued that the benefits of this concession to the South would not be large, because the South is now free to subsidize its processors. The fact that there has been no stampede to construct processing facilities in the South for export markets is evidence enough, according to this argument. I find it only partly valid. There are obviously cases where, because of marketing problems, transport costs, or problems of scale, local processing for export is not practical. But the presumption remains that as Northern duties fall, the location of processing facilities will shift Southward.

COMMODITY POLICY

As I pointed out in Chapter 7, though the future may lie with industry, it is still remote for most poor countries. Commodities are the wave of the present, and, by and large, there are slim grounds for enthusiasm over the prospects. As we saw, the situation varies enormously by country and product. The general atmosphere of gloom so assiduously purveyed at UNCTAD simply does not hold up. Nevertheless, for many commodities and many countries, no export boom is in prospect. Rapid Northern growth does help—just how much is a matter of unresolved controversy. But despite the bright spots, the trends of the past fifteen years serve to fuel the South's carefully nurtured conviction that its part in the world economy is both menial and unremunerative.

When we examine what could be done by economic policy to improve commodity exporters' positions, it soon becomes clear that there are no dramatic solutions. To allow free entry in Northern markets to LDC competing exports would in the short run add something over $1 billion annually to export earnings, largely from sugar. To fix the prices of tropical crops might add about the same amount, at the cost of considerable administrative complexity.

The third line of approach, stabilization, has been so much confused in public and professional discussion that it may be worthwhile to restate the conclusions. First, there is no evidence that growth of GNP is accelerated by smoothing out fluctuations in the trend of export earnings. The weight of the evidence is that earnings fluctuations don't affect investment or growth rates, a sort of indirect vindication of Schumpeter's views about the nature of growth.

Although there is evidence that *price* fluctuations do not affect the volume of investment either, it seems likely that in some cases they reduce the efficiency with which capital is used. The standard example is tree crops with cycles of overplanting stemming from high prices.

In general, stabilization in either sense is not worth much to the South, except to the extent that periods of high prices or great fluctuation for one commodity lead consumers to shift to synthetics or other natural products. Vegetable oil substitutes for cocoa butter are a case in point.

This conclusion—that stabilization of earnings is not worth much to LDC's—is strangely at variance with the amount of energy that has been devoted to the issue. The reasons seem simple enough. First, it doesn't cost the North much to promote stabilization. Buffer stocks or the compensatory finance facility of the IMF are, in theory, revolving funds that impose no net capital transfer. For the South, of course, the demand for stabilization is really a demand that export earnings be "stabilized" at levels that reflect peak prices and steadily expanding quantities. It is a demand, in effect, for more aid.

The World Bank has responded to this demand, proposing a scheme to increase the North-South transfer by perhaps $400 million annually, by underwriting the export shortfalls of nations whose economic policies meet agreed criteria. The Bank has not explained why aid recipients would care to subject their domestic policies to external control in exchange for sums that are trivial compared with current aid levels, nor how such a system could prevent the recipient from overstating his prospective export receipts. Despite its defects, the scheme represents an increment in the capital transfer, and is therefore desirable in principle. Like commodity agreements, the subsidy element of preferences, or any other indirect method of rationalizing capital transfers, it is a complicated method of redistributing world income. The significant test is whether there are easier alternatives for reaching the same goal; today, there may not be.

It seems safe to assume that officials of the World Bank recognize that this so-called "supplementary finance" scheme turns out to be essentially old aid in new robes. It is therefore the more surprising that they have rejected the Horowitz proposal, which would provide much more aid leverage from appropriated funds. The answer probably lies in a combination of two considerations, both, in my estimation, subject to some question: (1) respect for the opinions of the financial community, which naturally frowns on the Horowitz scheme as new, unorthodox, and potentially disturbing to the existing state of world financial disarray; (2) a desire to exercise more control over LDC policy, in the belief that this will promote economic development.

By and large, measures aimed at "solving" the commodity problem, whether by liberalization, price-fixing, or disguised transfers in the name of stabilization, will have only a limited effect. This is not a reason for opposing them. A series of modest steps may be the best tactic for improving the South's trade and aid receipts. The valid objections are questions of feasibility. It is most unlikely, in the present political circumstances, that the North will reduce barriers to Southern competing crops on any significant scale. Price-fixing is complicated and probably worth the effort only for a few crops at most. Furthermore, in burden-sharing terms, it bears least heavily on the United States, which may be uncongenial to European governments.

The long-term solution of commodity problems lies in very different directions—industrial development in the South and growth of world demand for commodities. The commodity approach to the issues is but a limited response. It may be necessary in the short run, and should be evaluated solely in those terms. It should not be judged by the standard of resolving the underlying grievances, because it treats symptoms, not causes.

THE ROLE OF INSTITUTIONS

It is hard to say whether trade and development problems have proliferated as rapidly as the national and international institutions aimed at dealing with the issues. At times, the institutions take on the shape of yet another problem—the sorcerer's apprentice revisited.

Every major donor has several government agencies active in aid and investment promotion. On the international scene, aid is furnished by three World Bank agencies, the IMF, the United Nations and each of its specialized agencies, the regional lending institutions, the EEC fund, and the OECD membership through its DAC aid consortia.

Trade and aid policies are discussed by official international groups, constantly, and almost everywhere—GATT, OECD, UNCTAD, UN Economic and Social Council (and its regional economic commissions for Africa, Asia, and Latin America), FAO (its international commodity councils and study groups), DAC, World Bank-IMF meetings; every year the list grows. Most of these organizations have elaborate committee and subcommittee structures, working parties, task forces, expert groups, and so on. The payments deficits of the smaller LDC's would be materially eased if their officials could be converted to a policy of staying home and forsaking the present competitive effort to rack up ever-more impressive records for conference-trotting. No less than 1500 delegates attended the six-week 1964 UNCTAD meetings in Geneva, thereby enhancing Switzerland's income and capital accumulation. This particular side-effect, which transfers income from the South to a prosperous corner of the North, is not usually considered as a net improvement in world welfare, unless Swiss votes are heavily weighted in the balance.

The proliferation of international forums, irritating as it may be to the spirit that seeks economy in organization, is not *per se* bad. The era of the perpetual conference justifies itself if it achieves more progress than simpler methods would, in benefiting Southern welfare, at reasonable resource cost to the North.

There is no way to compare the results of the present international system with those that are non-existent. It is well known that purveyors of political, social, or religious remedies for mankind are on unassailable ground. The present situation is always defective to the perfectionist, the revolutionary, the reformer, the disenchanted. It is worthwhile to remember that existing institutions survive because they have a role to play; otherwise they wither away, are transformed, or are overthrown. To say that "X has outlived its usefulness" means only that you are convinced. The test is whether the rest of us are.

In the case we are dealing with, the role of institutions is often somewhat different from the stated functions. The World Bank, IMF,

GATT, and the OECD are primarily aimed at promoting Northern interests. The United Nations bodies and UNCTAD are agents of Southern claims, whereas the regional development banks are emerging as hybrids whose greatest fruitfulness may rise precisely from the possibilities they create for uniting interests.

Let us look first at the Northern-dominated institutions. The IBRD and IMF are financed by the rich countries, and in their foreign aid functions they play toward the South the role of banker or estate steward for the North. Although the South is pleased to receive the largesse, it resents its inability to control the operations. For public consumption, Southern rhetoric ignores the fact that banks controlled by debtors have certain inherent defects in investors' eyes. Furthermore, the World Bank agencies create a useful forum for intra-Northern pressures on laggard donors, particularly in establishing IDA contribution levels.

The defect of the World Bank system is that until recently, at least, it has been perhaps too much impressed by a vision of itself as a banker to the world. A self-liquidating aid program has considerable political merit and perhaps more economic virtues than the South would publicly concede. But it takes no particular insight to see that the goals of behaving like a commercial credit bank and of promoting the development of backward countries are likely to be incompatible at times. This is one reason why the IDA was established. It is still something of a mystery, however, why the Bank trots its applicants through a complicated project review system for loan applications when the ability to repay is only dimly related to the merits of any particular project, and the choice of projects to finance is even more tenuously related to changes in national spending. Presumably this practice reflects the tastes of donors and administrators, not ordinarily a fruitful subject for argument.

Recently, through its sponsorship of larger donations to IDA, its endorsement of supplementary finance, and its contention that more Northern official capital should flow Southward, the Bank appears to have modified its somewhat austere attitude toward aid. This is all to the good, because there is a widespread belief that the Bank deserves high marks for efficiency in the ranking of donors. To some extent this may simply reflect respect for the Bank's trappings of bankerly objectivism. But in one respect, at least, the advantage is clearcut. Bank loans are untied, so that the recipient gets a dollar's worth of goods for each dollar he borrows.

Whether individual Atlantic countries should support expansion of Bank activities depends on their situations. For the United States, it has burden-sharing advantages. Its IDA contributions are relatively smaller than its present bilateral aid share. For some European countries, it offers balance-of-payments advantages, because most IBRD-IDA funds come from the United States, but a significant part of it is spent elsewhere. There are also certain advantages in many donors' eyes to taking some part of the aid total out of the direct political arena.

For the South, in view of existing alternatives, the trend to multilateral aid institutions has varying effects. Countries that fare well under bilateral aid programs (India, Pakistan, Israel, Egypt) have an interest in the present system. But they have no necessary objection to *additional* resources being channeled to the IBRD, if increases in bilateral aid are not feasible. The somewhat more fussy review procedures exacted by IBRD may also be a disadvantage in recipients' eyes. But in general, the South knows that its stated goal of a large-scale UN donor agency is not in the cards right now. In those circumstances, IBRD-IDA offers some obvious advantages, which have been enhanced by recent changes of emphasis in policy. Ultimately, of course, the North pays one way or another, out of different pockets. But the Bank offers certain advantages as a borrower in capital markets, as a relatively "non-political" lender, and as a distinguished lobby for aid increases. Despite its defects, the World Bank should have considerable luster in light of our criteria.

The IMF is not basically an aid organization, although its compensatory finance system has led it nonetheless in that direction. From the LDC viewpoint, it specializes in bailouts from foreign exchange bankruptcy. It is therefore a proper object of loathing, because it enforces an uncongenial discipline on national budgets, credit policies, and foreign exchange dealings. I do not intend to enter here into the perpetual debate about the merits of the IMF.[12] It is sufficient to say that the IMF was not conceived of as an agency to promote development, but to facilitate a workable system of international payments. It is therefore hardly surprising that countries that regularly violate the tacit rules of that particular system without any cushion of reserves to subsidize their policies are disenchanted by the results. Furthermore their appetites are whetted by proposals that

[12] The subject has been expertly treated by Cooper, *National Economic Policy*, Chapter II.

combine reform of the monetary system with gifts of international purchasing power to developing countries. The IMF therefore plays the somewhat dispiriting, but socially useful, role of dart board for LDC frustrations.

The other two major Northern-dominated institutions, GATT and OECD, are not endowed with their own financial resources. The GATT, dealing with commercial policies, is the institutional agent of the effort to return to a "normal" Northern trading system after the autarchic anarchy that restricted trade in the two decades that followed the 1929 crash.

Despite the vociferous criticism of GATT at UNCTAD, it is obvious that the move to more liberal trade has been of some benefit to the South. Furthermore, the recent GATT commitment to forgo reciprocal tariff cutting concessions from LDC's offers, from the balance-of-payments viewpoint at least, a rather valuable concession. Also, the GATT membership is open to all. If the South is dissatisfied with its rules or the progress of particular negotiations in terms of its own interests, the door is open. This applies with particular force to the Kennedy Round negotiations. The South has apparently made little effort to win special consideration for products of particular interest to developing countries. The potential for successful use of pressure tactics was demonstrated by the acceptance in 1965 of new GATT articles on trade and development (see Chapter 7 above). The South has perhaps not fully recognized the potential magnitude of the advantages it could gain from major tariff-cutting efforts to which it need offer no reciprocity. For that matter, neither has the North. Progressive MFN reduction of duties to the South may be less dramatic than preferences, but its long-run effects would be impressive.

The OECD is in a different category, because it is a club open to Atlantic Community members only. In some respects, it functions as an instrument for burying policy issues under clouds of paperwork, in the League of Nations and UN traditions. From the Southern viewpoint, DAC is the principal object of interest. In recent years, the United States and other members have used it as a forum for pressure to increase nominal aid levels and to ease repayment terms. To the extent that these pressures are maintained and new initiatives (investment guarantees, preferences, and the like) prosecuted, it coincides with Southern interests. On the other hand, to the extent that it is an arena where OECD members can disagree on action or agree on inaction, there may be advantages to the North, but no benefit to the South.

Basically, the problem of OECD is that it has not fulfilled the U.S. objective of creating an economic directorate for the West, propagating liberal trade and aid initiatives. The fault, if there is one, lies with events; on balance, the OECD may well have succeeded in reducing separatist influence by providing a regular forum.

The fact that it has already been successfully used as a device to promote aid increases and to foster new forms of aid coordination shows that the potentials for encouraging development are there. It is an open question whether they can be realized.

The United Nations' economic functions were also originally conceived as an agent of Northern interests, but the vast increase in membership has progressively turned that body into a voice for Southern aspirations. The creation of UNCTAD, over predominant Northern objections, is testimony enough of Southern voting control.

Both the UN agencies and UNCTAD therefore perform one very valuable function. They give the South a propaganda forum to exercise constant pressure for concessions, cloaked in a multilateral mantle. They also promote a sense of unity that may make it easier to drive successful bargains with the North. But this benefit, like any other, has its costs. Beyond a certain point, it makes no sense to convene committees, pass resolutions, and vote for the millennium. To achieve the necessary mutual gains, the resolutions must descend from the stratosphere of some of the UNCTAD proposals down to the level of serious bargaining. If the end result is simply to make the North look upon the United Nations as nothing but a propaganda forum, Southern benefits may prove to have been too hard-won.

To use its new majorities to its own best interest, the South will have to resort to statesmanship—a clear-eyed view for the realities of power, and a sense for using them effectively in the steady pursuit of distant goals. This may not come soon. There are too many diversions, and the leverage available to wrest concessions is limited. If, discouraged, the South turns increasingly to internal reform or, in some cases, revolution, it may best serve its own aims in the international sphere. Nonetheless, realistic and unremitting pressures on the North are decidedly in the Southern interest; the United Nations could be used as an effective tool. If the United States can use the organization to promote its world political interests, the way is ultimately open to others in the economic sphere.

NORTH AND SOUTH REVISITED

The antiquarian chancing on this volume a hundred years from now may find his quest for that note of antique poignancy fully satisfied. The world, if great wars can be avoided and population growth moderated, is clearly destined to remember poverty as only a remote souvenir. All the strictures that we parade today about the preconditions for development, the role of trade or aid as catalysts, the bondage created by dependence in commodity production, and so forth will take on significance, if any, in the growing prospects for interplanetary commerce.

The earth is in transition from mass poverty to mass abundance, and the travail is hard. Today's conflicts in North and South alike are much the same as those that racked the North when it laid the basis for its present material wealth, partly from the privation of the many. Just as that era created a bitterness and a legacy of conflict that we all pay tribute to even today, so will the present one. The South will become prosperous, because it wants to and the material means are at hand. But bitterness and conflict may be unavoidable. It is perhaps asking too much of the North to recognize that the interests of the world will probably be best served by generous trade and aid policies toward the South. For that matter, it may be too much to expect the South to respond favorably to more generous policies if offered. A determined resentment is often the cement that binds successful social movements.

The passage of time will bring the South greater confidence in its own ability to shape its material destiny and, therefore, indirectly make it easier to promote international economic policies that benefit all parties. There is every reason to believe that Southern per capita incomes could rise tenfold each century, if birth control methods become widespread, as they inevitably will. Technological advances may make much faster growth rates possible. Taking the lower figure, this would mean per capita incomes of at least $1500 in the South, a century from now.

This is distant comfort for today's poverty and discontent, but it must be remembered that instant prosperity can come only from vast consumption subsidies, which will not soon be forthcoming unless new technological revolutions make contemporary economic beliefs anachronistic. The process will take time, and that inevitable delay will engender and promote resentments. It should be the job of Northern statesmanship to help reduce the time and minimize the resentments.

It seems fair to say that governments of Atlantic countries and their Soviet counterparts are still far from the goal. The reasons are understandable, and I have discussed them at length throughout this book. It is the awareness of this gap in Northern performance that has led Barbara Ward, Gunnar Myrdal, and other writers to plead eloquently for a rededication of Northern energies in the interests of world prosperity. I endorse their motives, but I cannot share what seems to me to be an illusion—a belief that nations are capable of conscious rededication of behavior, except under the spur of clearly perceived self-interest. For that reason I have stressed, in this volume, the gains that might stem from coincidences of immediate interest.

But these potential gains, even if translated into policy, will not have major short-run economic effects, except for a few countries that are particularly well-situated. For more than that, the major potential donors must still await either radical changes in international power relations; or more powerful and far-sighted political leadership than has generally emerged. Earlier in this study, I drew the analogy to Bismarck on the domestic scene. Interestingly enough, it is General de Gaulle on the international stage, who, over domestic objections, has made France the leading donor of foreign aid. It is not necessary to subscribe to his somewhat imperial motives to observe the point. If the will and the vision are there, from whatever motive, the barriers crumble readily enough. Relatively, French aid may well contribute less to LDC growth than to political aims. But France is not the only nation with political aims, and some may eventually find domestic or international political advantages to a generous aid policy, although the prospect is not immediate for most donors. A negotiated conclusion to the hostilities in Vietnam might prove to be a catalyst for increasing the scale of U.S. support for the economic development of Asia.

However, this lies beyond our province here. I lay no claim to writing a history of the future. It will be enough if we can reach out a little further today and tomorrow, in the right directions.

Finally, each underdeveloped country is a special case, and each will develop differently. Whether Northern policies are enlightened or not, some of today's poor nations will inevitably prosper, while others, by comparison, will seem to stagnate. In our century-long perspective there are countries that will far surpass a tenfold growth of per capita income, and others that will not even be close. This in turn will raise new questions of international equity and perpetuate old ones. Arbitration of these discords will be the task of another era. The success of contemporary generations in attacking poverty will be measured by how much or how little its descendants need be concerned with the issues I have analyzed here.

Index

Index

PUBLICATIONS

FOREIGN AFFAIRS (quarterly), edited by Hamilton Fish Armstrong.

THE UNITED STATES IN WORLD AFFAIRS (annual). Volumes for 1931, 1932 and 1933, by Walter Lippmann and William O. Scroggs; for 1934–1935, 1936, 1937, 1938, 1939 and 1940, by Whitney H. Shepardson and William O. Scroggs; for 1945–1947, 1947–1948 and 1948–1949, by John C. Campbell; for 1949, 1950, 1951, 1952, 1953, and 1954, by Richard P. Stebbins; for 1955, by Hollis W. Barber; for 1956, 1957, 1958, 1959, 1960, 1961, 1962 and 1963, by Richard P. Stebbins; for 1964, by Jules Davids; for 1965 by Richard P. Stebbins.

DOCUMENTS ON AMERICAN FOREIGN RELATIONS (annual). Volume for 1952 edited by Clarence W. Baier and Richard P. Stebbins; for 1953 and 1954 edited by Peter V. Curl; for 1955, 1956, 1957, 1958, and 1959 edited by Paul E. Zinner; for 1960, 1961, 1962 and 1963 edited by Richard P. Stebbins; for 1964 by Jules Davids; for 1965 by Richard P. Stebbins.

POLITICAL HANDBOOK AND ATLAS OF THE WORLD (annual), edited by Walter H. Mallory.

TRADE, AID AND DEVELOPMENT: The Rich and Poor Nations, by John Pincus (1967).

BETWEEN TWO WORLDS: Policy, Press and Public Opinion on Asian-American Relations, by John Hohenberg (1967).

THE CONFLICTED RELATIONSHIP: The West and the Transformation of Asia, Africa and Latin America, by Theodore Geiger (1966).

THE ATLANTIC IDEA AND ITS EUROPEAN RIVALS, by H. van B. Cleveland (1966).

EUROPEAN UNIFICATION IN THE SIXTIES: From the Veto to the Crisis, by Miriam Camps (1966).

THE UNITED STATES AND CHINA IN WORLD AFFAIRS, by Robert Blum, edited by A. Doak Barnett (1966).

THE FUTURE OF THE OVERSEAS CHINESE IN SOUTHEAST ASIA, by Lea A. Williams (1966).

THE CONSCIENCE OF THE RICH NATIONS: The Development Assistance Committee and the Common Aid Effort, by Seymour J. Rubin (1966).

ATLANTIC AGRICULTURAL UNITY: Is It Possible?, by John O. Coppock (1966).

TEST BAN AND DISARMAMENT: The Path of Negotiation, by Arthur H. Dean (1966).

COMMUNIST CHINA'S ECONOMIC GROWTH AND FOREIGN TRADE, by Alexander Eckstein (1966).
POLICIES TOWARD CHINA: Views from Six Continents, edited by A. M. Halpern (1966).
THE AMERICAN PEOPLE AND CHINA, by A. T. Steele (1966).
INTERNATIONAL POLITICAL COMMUNICATION, by W. Phillips Davison (1965).
MONETARY REFORM FOR THE WORLD ECONOMY, by Robert V. Roosa (1965).
AFRICAN BATTLELINE: American Policy Choices in Southern Africa, by Waldemar A. Nielsen (1965).
NATO IN TRANSITION: The Future of the Atlantic Alliance, by Timothy W. Stanley (1965).
ALTERNATIVE TO PARTITION: For a Broader Conception of America's Role in Europe, by Zbigniew Brzezinski (1965).
THE TROUBLED PARTNERSHIP: A Re-Appraisal of the Atlantic Alliance, by Henry A. Kissinger (1965).
REMNANTS OF EMPIRE: The United Nations and the End of Colonialism, by David W. Wainhouse (1965).
THE EUROPEAN COMMUNITY AND AMERICAN TRADE: A Study in Atlantic Economics and Policy, by Randall Hinshaw (1964).
THE FOURTH DIMENSION OF FOREIGN POLICY: Educational and Cultural Affairs, by Phillip H. Coombs (1964).
AMERICAN AGENCIES INTERESTED IN INTERNATIONAL AFFAIRS (Fifth Edition), compiled by Donald Wasson (1964).
JAPAN AND THE UNITED STATES IN WORLD TRADE, by Warren S. Hunsberger (1964).
FOREIGN AFFAIRS BIBLIOGRAPHY, 1952–1962, by Henry L. Roberts (1964).
THE DOLLAR IN WORLD AFFAIRS: An Essay in International Financial Policy, by Henry G. Aubrey (1964).
ON DEALING WITH THE COMMUNIST WORLD, by George F. Kennan (1964).
FOREIGN AID AND FOREIGN POLICY, by Edward S. Mason (1964).
THE SCIENTIFIC REVOLUTION AND WORLD POLITICS, by Caryl P. Haskins (1964).
AFRICA: A Foreign Affairs Reader, edited by Philip W. Quigg (1964).
THE PHILIPPINES AND THE UNITED STATES: Problems of Partnership, by George E. Taylor (1964).
SOUTHEAST ASIA IN UNITED STATES POLICY, by Russell H. Fifield (1963).
UNESCO: ASSESSMENT AND PROMISE, by George N. Shuster (1963).
THE PEACEFUL ATOM IN FOREIGN POLICY, by Arnold Kramish (1963).
THE ARABS AND THE WORLD: Nasser's Arab Nationalist Policy, by Charles D. Cremeans (1963).
TOWARD AN ATLANTIC COMMUNITY, by Christian A. Herter (1963).

THE SOVIET UNION, 1922–1962: A Foreign Affairs Reader, edited by Philip E. Mosley (1963).

THE POLITICS OF FOREIGN AID: American Experience in Southeast Asia, by John D. Montgomery (1962).

SPEARHEADS OF DEMOCRACY: Labor in the Developing Countries, by George C. Lodge (1962).

LATIN AMERICA: Diplomacy and Reality, by Adolf A. Berle (1962).

THE ORGANIZATION OF AMERICAN STATES AND THE HEMISPHERE CRISIS, by John C. Dreier (1962).

THE UNITED NATIONS: Structure for Peace, by Ernest A. Gross (1962).

THE LONG POLAR WATCH: Canada and the Defense of North America, by Melvin Conant (1962).

ARMS AND POLITICS IN LATIN AMERICA (Revised Edition), by Edwin Lieuwen (1961).

THE FUTURE OF UNDERDEVELOPED COUNTRIES: Political Implications of Economic Development (Revised Edition), by Eugene Staley (1961).

SPAIN AND DEFENSE OF THE WEST: Ally and Liability, by Arthur P. Whitaker (1961).

SOCIAL CHANGE IN LATIN AMERICA TODAY: Its Implications for United States Policy, by Richard N. Adams, John P. Gillin, Allan R. Holmberg, Oscar Lewis, Richard W. Patch, and Charles W. Wagley (1961).

FOREIGN POLICY: THE NEXT PHASE: The 1960s (Revised Edition), by Thomas K. Finletter (1960).

DEFENSE OF THE MIDDLE EAST: Problems of American Policy (Revised Edition), by John C. Campbell (1960).

COMMUNIST CHINA AND ASIA: Challenge to American Policy, by A. Doak Barnett (1960).

FRANCE, TROUBLED ALLY: De Gaulle's Heritage and Prospects, by Edgar S. Furniss, Jr. (1960).

THE SCHUMAN PLAN: A Study in Economic Cooperation, 1950–1959, by William Diebold, Jr. (1959).

SOVIET ECONOMIC AID: The New Aid and Trade Policy in Underdeveloped Countries, by Joseph S. Berliner (1958).

NATO AND THE FUTURE OF EUROPE, by Ben T. Moore (1958).

INDIA AND AMERICA: A Study of Their Relations, by Phillips Talbot and S. L. Poplai (1958).

NUCLEAR WEAPONS AND FOREIGN POLICY, by Henry A. Kissinger (1957).

MOSCOW-PEKING AXIS: Strength and Strains, by Howard L. Boorman, Alexander Eckstein, Philip E. Mosley, and Benjamin Schwartz (1957).

RUSSIA AND AMERICA: Dangers and Prospects, by Henry L. Roberts (1956).